Keyboarding & Word Processing Essentials

Microsoft® Word 2016

Lessons 1–55

20e

Susie H. VanHuss
Ph.D., Distinguished Professor Emeritus,
University of South Carolina

Connie M. Forde
Ph.D., Mississippi State University

Donna L. Woo
Cypress College, California

Vicki R. Robertson
Southwest Tennessee Community College

COLLEGE KEYBOARDING

Australia • Brazil • Mexico • Singapore • United Kingdom • United States

***College Keyboarding: Keyboarding and Word Processing Essentials, Lessons 1–55,* Twentieth Edition**

Susie H. VanHuss, Connie M. Forde, Donna L. Woo, Vicki R. Robertson

SVP, GM Skills & Global Product Management: Dawn Gerrain

Product Director: Kathleen McMahon

Product Team Manager: Elinor W. Gregory

Product Manager: Amanda Lyons

Senior Director, Development: Marah Bellegarde

Product Development Manager: Leigh Hefferon

Senior Content Developer: Anne Orgren

Product Assistant: Cara Suriyamongkol

Vice President, Marketing Services: Jennifer Ann Baker

Marketing Director: Michele McTighe

Senior Production Director: Wendy Troeger

Production Director: Patty Stephan

Senior Content Project Manager: Stacey Lamodi

Art Director: Diana Graham

Cover image(s): en-owai/Shutterstock.com

Library of Congress Control Number: 2016935648

ISBN: 978-1-337-10302-2

Cengage
20 Channel Street
Boston, MA 02210
USA

Cengage is a leading provider of customized learning solutions with employees residing in nearly 40 different countries and sales in more than 125 countries around the world. Find your local representative at: **www.cengage.com.**

Cengage products are represented in Canada by Nelson Education, Ltd.

To learn more about Cengage platforms and services, register or access your online learning solution, or purchase materials for your course, visit **www.cengage.com.**

Printed in the United States of America
Print Number: 03 Print Year: 2018

Contents

The Power of Word 2016...Starts Here!

LEARN . . . DISCOVER

Touch Keyboarding

Word 2016 Essentials

Document Design

Communication Skills

Co-Authoring in Real Time

Windows 10 Basics

Discover the power of *College Keyboarding, 20th edition* print and digital solutions for *Microsoft Word 2016*.

College Keyboarding, 20e, L1–55 combines easy-to-use tools with a proven track record of ensuring classroom and workplace success.

Keyboarding in Skills Assessment Manager (SAM) provides the tools to master document skills for use in school, career, and personal situations.

NEW to This Edition

- Coverage of *Windows 10*
- Coverage of *Word 2016*
- New section on *Getting Started with Word and Windows 10*
- Correlation with the web-based ***Skills Assessment Manager (SAM)*** to build, apply, and assess skills
- Deletion of KPDO references and updated instructions in the print book so that the book is not dependent on KPDO
- Updated *Know Your Computer* section reflecting changes in computer hardware and software
- Updated drill lines to conform to the key presentation sequence
- New standard plans in the Skill Builders for using timed writings, building speed, and improving accuracy; updated instructions in drills and timed writings to enable students to apply these plans
- Drills and applications are modified to accommodate the change from SkyDrive to OneDrive
- Default theme changed for all projects
- Lesson 27 focuses on Text Formats
- Module 7 reflects the elimination of Clip Art in Office 2016 as well as the change in Online Pictures
- Projects were modified for a more global focus
- Communication Pretests and Post-Tests moved to instructor resources
- Module 9 has been completely rewritten to provide instruction and applications on new *Windows 10* and *Word 2016* features including Save to Cloud, Share, and co-authoring in real time

Meet SAM (Skills Assessment Manager)

SAM's online learning environments enable students to learn *Microsoft Office* and computer concepts essential to academic and career success. Students observe and practice, then apply their skills in the live application. Auto-graded assignments save time and energy.

For the 20th edition of *College Keyboarding*, SAM replaces KPDO as an optional digital companion to the print text. With SAM, the keying drills, timed writings, skill buildings, and other activities can be completed and submitted online. If your course is using SAM, visit http://sam.cengage.com to find out more about how to use SAM with this textbook.

Ready, Set, Key!

The keys to success include carefully designed lessons and reliable, dependable, easy-to-use technology tools.

An abundance of crafted exercises keep lessons fun and help build a strong foundation.

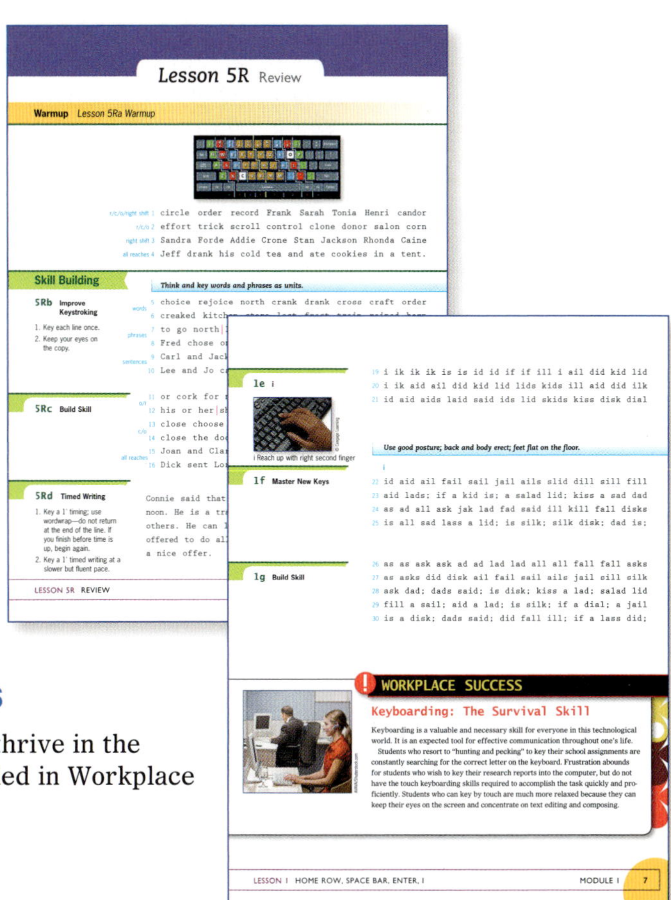
Lesson 5R Review

Warmup *Lesson 5Ra Warmup*

r/c/o/right shift 1 circle order record Frank Sarah Tonia Henri candor
r/c/o 2 effort trick scroll control clone donor salon corn
right shift 3 Sandra Forde Addie Crone Stan Jackson Rhonda Caine
all reaches 4 Jeff drank his cold tea and ate cookies in a tent.

Skill Building

Think and key words and phrases as units.

5Rb Improve Keystroking

1. Key each line once.
2. Keep your eyes on the copy.

words 5 choice rejoice north crank drank cross craft order

5Rc Build Skill

5Rd Timed Writing

1. Key a 1' timing; use wordwrap—do not return at the end of the line. If you finish before time is up, begin again.
2. Key a 1' timed writing at a slower but fluent pace.

LESSON 5R REVIEW

1e i

i Reach up with right second finger

19 i ik ik ik is is id id if if ill i ail did kid lid
20 i ik aid ail did kid lid lids kids ill aid did ilk
21 id aid aids laid said ids lid skids kiss disk dial

Use good posture; back and body erect; feet flat on the floor.

1f Master New Keys

22 id aid ail fail sail jail ails slid dill sill fill
23 aid lads; if a kid is; a salad lid; kiss a sad dad
24 as ad all ask jak lad fad said ill kill fall disks
25 is all sad lass a lid; is silk; silk disk; dad is;

1g Build Skill

26 as as ask ask ad ad lad lad all all fall fall asks
27 as asks did disk ail fail sail ails jail sill silk
28 ask dad; dads said; is disk; kiss a lad; salad lid
29 fill a sail; aid a lad; is silk; if a dial; a jail
30 is a disk; dads said; did fall ill; if a lass did;

WORKPLACE SUCCESS

Keyboarding: The Survival Skill

Keyboarding is a valuable and necessary skill for everyone in this technological world. It is an expected tool for effective communication throughout one's life.

Students who resort to "hunting and pecking" to key their school assignments are constantly searching for the correct letter on the keyboard. Frustration abounds for students who wish to key their research reports into the computer, but do not have the touch keyboarding skills required to accomplish the task quickly and proficiently. Students who can key by touch are much more relaxed because they can keep their eyes on the screen and concentrate on text editing and composing.

LESSON 1 HOME ROW, SPACE BAR, ENTER, I MODULE 1 7

Skill Building Drills and Timed Writings

Build confidence and success through keying exercises and timed writings.

Workplace Success

Learn how to survive and thrive in the workplace with tips provided in Workplace Success boxes.

Skill Builders

Strengthen your techniques and accuracy as well as build speed through extra practice with Skill Builders located at the ends of selected modules.

Skill Builder 1

Skill Building *Emphasis on Improving Techniques*

For each drill, key each line once at a comfortable rate. Tap ENTER at the end of each line. Single-space the drill. Concentrate and key accurately. Repeat if desired.

DRILL 1

Goal: reinforce key locations

Key each line once at a comfortable, constant rate.

TECHNIQUE TIP

Keep
- your eyes on source copy
- your fingers curved, upright
- your wrists low but not touching
- your elbows hanging loosely
- your feet flat on the floor

Drill 1a

A We saw that Alan had an alabaster vase in Alabama.
B My rubber boat bobbed about in the bubbling brook.
C Ceci gave cups of cold cocoa to Rebecca and Rocco.
D Don's dad added a second deck to his old building.
E Even as Ellen edited her document, she ate dinner.
F Our firm in Buffalo has a staff of forty or fifty.
G Ginger is giving Greg the eggs she got from Helga.
H Hugh has eighty high, harsh lights he might flash.

Drill 1b

I Irik's lack of initiative is irritating his coach.
J Judge J. J. Jore rejected Jeane and Jack's jargon.
K As a lark, Kirk kicked back a rock at Kim's kayak.
L Lucille is silly; she still likes lemon lollipops.
M Milt Mumm hammered a homer in the Miami home game.
N Ken Linn has gone hunting; Stan can begin canning.
O Jon Soto rode off to Otsego in an old Morgan auto.
P Philip helped pay the prize as my puppy hopped up.
Q Quiet Raquel quit quoting at an exquisite marquee.

Drill 1c

R As Mrs. Kerr's motor roared, her red horse reared.
S Sissie lives in Mississippi; Lissa lives in Tulsa.
T Nat told Betty not to tattle on her little sister.
U Ula has a unique but prudish idea on unused units.
V Eva visited every vivid event for twelve evenings.
W We watched as wayworn wasps swarmed by the willow.
X Tex Cox waxed the next box for Xenia and Rex Knox.
Y Ty says you may stay with Fay for only sixty days.
Z Hazel is puzzled about the azure haze; Zack dozes.

SKILL BUILDER 1 MODULE 1 1-35

Communication Activities

Build skills in proofreading, composition, and more through practicing communication activities.

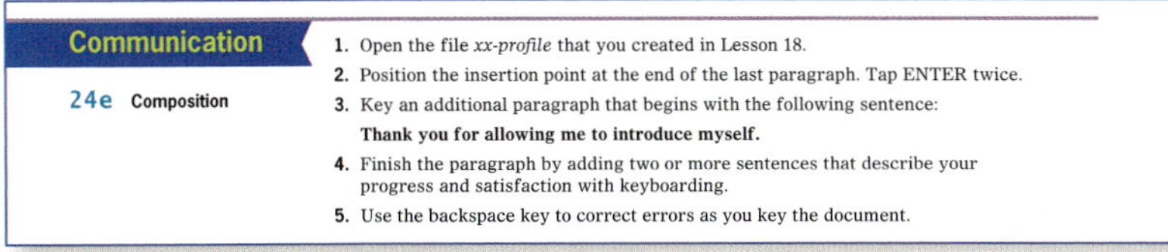
Communication

24e Composition

1. Open the file *xx-profile* that you created in Lesson 18.
2. Position the insertion point at the end of the last paragraph. Tap ENTER twice.
3. Key an additional paragraph that begins with the following sentence:
   Thank you for allowing me to introduce myself.
4. Finish the paragraph by adding two or more sentences that describe your progress and satisfaction with keyboarding.
5. Use the backspace key to correct errors as you key the document.

Accelerate Learning—Follow the Path of Word 2016

Follow Microsoft's path **(Tab/Group/Command)** to learn the main steps of each new command. Once the path is before you, the steps to successfully learning new concepts are easy.

Each new command is immediately applied within a short drill and then reinforced in **Apply It.**

Data files provide immediate opportunities to practice the new command quickly.

Learn and Reinforce with New Commands, Drills, and Apply It

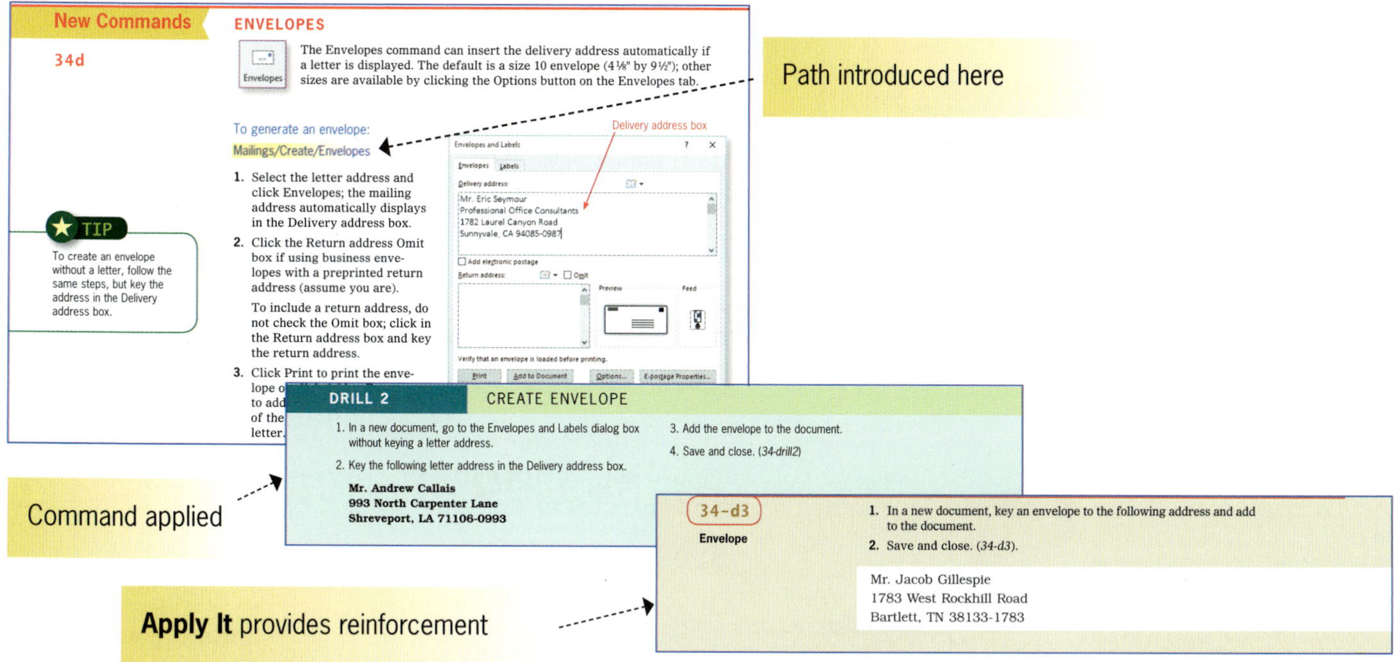

New Commands
ENVELOPES
34d
The Envelopes command can insert the delivery address automatically if a letter is displayed. The default is a size 10 envelope (4⅛" by 9½"); other sizes are available by clicking the Options button on the Envelopes tab.
Path introduced here
To generate an envelope:
Mailings/Create/Envelopes
Delivery address box
1. Select the letter address and click Envelopes; the mailing address automatically displays in the Delivery address box.
2. Click the Return address Omit box if using business envelopes with a preprinted return address (assume you are).
To include a return address, do not check the Omit box; click in the Return address box and key the return address.
3. Click Print to print the envelope
TIP
To create an envelope without a letter, follow the same steps, but key the address in the Delivery address box.
Mr. Eric Seymour
Professional Office Consultants
1782 Laurel Canyon Road
Sunnyvale, CA 94085-0987
DRILL 2
CREATE ENVELOPE
1. In a new document, go to the Envelopes and Labels dialog box without keying a letter address.
2. Key the following letter address in the Delivery address box.
Mr. Andrew Callais
993 North Carpenter Lane
Shreveport, LA 71106-0993
3. Add the envelope to the document.
4. Save and close. (34-drill2)
Command applied
34-d3
Envelope
1. In a new document, key an envelope to the following address and add to the document.
2. Save and close. (34-d3).
Mr. Jacob Gillespie
1783 West Rockhill Road
Bartlett, TN 38133-1783
Apply It provides reinforcement

Ensure Success with QuickChecks, Discover, and Tips

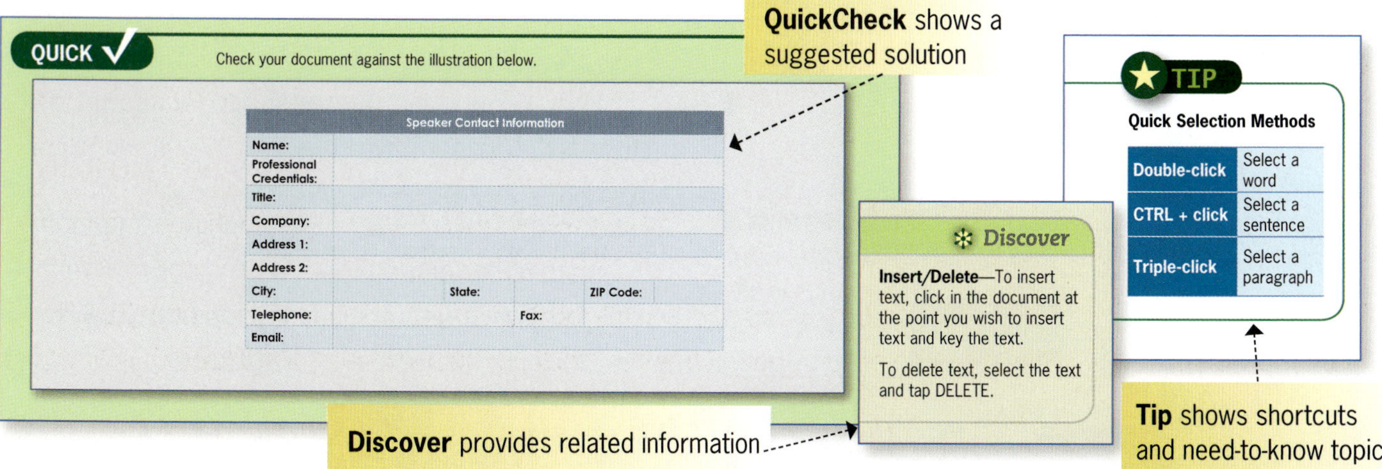

Powerful Tools . . . Working for You

College Keyboarding 20e provides the tools students need to develop expertise in keyboarding, document formatting, and essential word processing skills using *Microsoft Word 2016*.

ISBN 9781337103251

ISBN 9781337103022

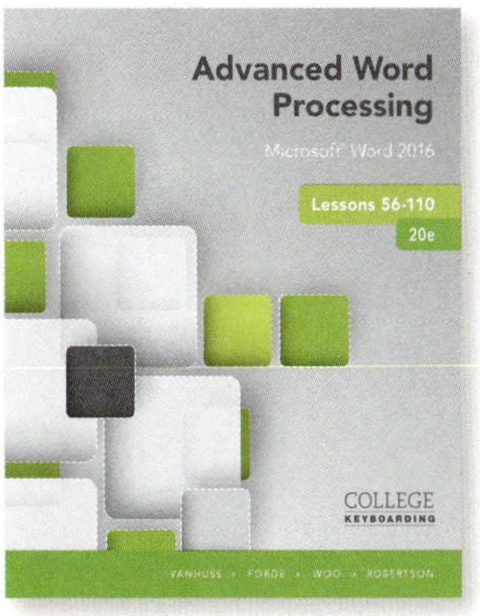

ISBN 9781337103268

ISBN 9781337103275

Supplemental Resources

Instructor Companion Site

A robust instructor companion website provides the materials you need to teach this course, including an instructor's manual; tests; solutions files; syllabus; Communication Skills pretests, post-tests, and references; and more. To access the instructor companion site, sign in to http://login.cengage.com and add this text to your instructor dashboard.

Student Companion Site

The data files needed to complete this text's activities are found on the free student companion website for this text. To access the student companion site, visit http://login.cengage.com and search for this text.

Keyboarding in Skills Assessment Manager (SAM)

For the 20th edition of *College Keyboarding*, SAM replaces KPDO as an optional digital companion to the print text. With SAM, the keying drills, timed writings, skill buildings, and other activities can be completed and submitted online. Most Drills, Apply-Its, and end-of-module projects have been converted into computer-graded SAM tasks and projects.

Instructors may teach the course using the print book only, the print book plus SAM, or SAM only. If your course is using SAM, visit http://sam.cengage.com to find out more about how to use SAM with this textbook.

To purchase SAM with a print textbook, speak to your Cengage Learning Consultant.

Commands by Module

Lesson	Commands
Module 3 Word 2016 Essentials	
26	Launch Word
	Blank Document
	New Folder
	Save, Save As
	Close
	Open
	New
	Print
	Exit
27	Fonts
	Mini Toolbar
28	Alignment
	Show Hide
	Line and Paragraph Spacing
	Quick Access Toolbar
29	Bullets and Numbering
	Navigation (Scroll bars, Slider, View)
	Spelling and Grammar
	Thesaurus
	Word Count
30	Page Orientation
	Clipboard: Cut, Copy, Paste
	Format Painter
	Center Page
Module 4 Memos and Letters	
32	Date and Time
	Vertical Page Position
	Remove Space After Paragraph
	Envelopes
	Left Tab

Lesson	Commands
Module 5 Tables	
38	Insert Table
39	Table Tools—Layout
40	Table Tools—Design
Module 6 Reports	
43	Themes
	Styles
	Footnotes
44	Margins
	Find and Replace
	Add Space Before Paragraph
45	Page Number
	Line and Page Breaks
	Insert File
	Symbols and Special Characters
46	Header
	Save as Template
	Hanging Indent
Module 7 Graphics	
50	Pictures—Format
	Page Borders
	Online Video
51	SmartArt
	Shapes
	WordArt
52	Columns

See Appendix D: Command Summary for a detailed list of commands, the path, and button for each command.

Digital Citizenship

OVERVIEW

One search using a popular search engine and *digital citizenship* as keywords produced over three million results. A quick survey of the list of documents indicated that digital citizenship is a popular, if not required, topic in the curricula of K–12 schools. Many of the documents focused on digital citizenship research by Dr. Mike Ribble, on the framework developed by the Partnership for 21st Century Skills, and on the International Society for Technology in Education Standards for Students. A relatively small percentage of the documents listed referred to collegiate education or business and industry.

This article focuses on effective digital citizenship from four perspectives that can affect your career.

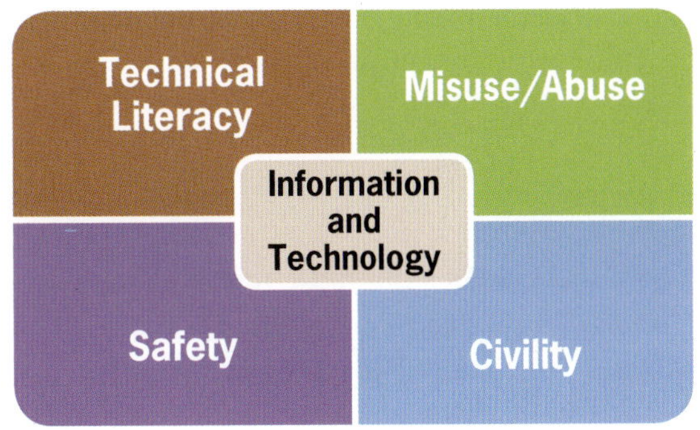

TECHNICAL LITERACY

Understanding how the Internet, social media applications, and other digital tools work enables you to use these tools creatively, responsibly, and safely. Technology is constantly evolving; things learned today can be outdated in a very short time. Therefore, continual learning is the only way to keep up with technology. Protecting your (or your company's) computer, network, and information from unauthorized access is critical. Many students and young employees who have grown up using all types of technology may be more technically savvy than their instructors or their managers. However, they often do not have the social skills and business savvy to be effective in using digital tools.

MISUSE/ABUSE

The Internet is a vast collection of information that can be accessed easily and at little or no cost. However, just because information has been posted on the Internet does not mean that it is accurate or valid.

Information Verification. Information should be analyzed carefully to determine the credibility of the writer, the source of the information, the accuracy of details, knowledge of the literature, and the currency of the information before relying on that information.

Plagiarism. Copyright laws protect material from unauthorized use. Request permission before using copyrighted materials. It is not acceptable to copy information from the Internet without properly documenting the source of the information and giving the writer proper credit. Software is available to check a paper and quickly determine if it has been plagiarized.

Piracy. Downloading of music, games, and movies and making copies of software without permission are illegal.

SAFETY

Privacy. Protecting private information and company proprietary information are key safety concerns. Protect your information and/or your company's information by using up-to-date antivirus software, antispyware, and firewalls.

Identity theft. Unauthorized persons may obtain information such as your Social Security number or credit card information and use it for criminal purposes. Posting private information on social networks can have serious negative consequences as shown in the following examples.

- Posting pictures of vacation sites and travel information alerted criminals that the family was away and their home was robbed.
- Posting pictures of children on the Internet and address information in other locations attracted predators to the home.
- Unprofessional information and pictures on a social network were viewed by a potential employer causing the person not to be hired. Many employers check out potential employees on social networks before hiring them.
- Negative information posted about a person's supervisor and company was viewed by company executives.

CIVILITY

Courtesy and good manners when posting information, sending emails, participating in a chat room, blogging, or posting on a social media site are always appropriate. The following tips are examples of good *netiquette*.

- Consider anything you post to be public information. Many people use technology to deliver messages that they would never send in a face-to-face situation.
- Use appropriate, non-offensive language and be sensitive to cultural issues.
- Avoid inflammatory messages and messages keyed in all capital letters.

Monkey Business Images/Shutterstock.com

- Be helpful to people who have less technical expertise than you do. They may have great ideas even though they are not technically savvy.
- Avoid texting and checking and sending emails, and place cell phones on vibrate during meetings and dining.

Know Your Computer

All-in-One Computer
Monitor and Processor Combined
Keyboard and Mouse Separate

Laptop Computer
Monitor, Processor, Keyboard, and Mouse Combined

Desktop Computer
Monitor, Processor, Keyboard, and Mouse Separate

Keys to Enter/Format Text

1. **Alphanumeric**—letters, numbers, and symbols.
2. **Tab**—positions text at fixed points.
3. **Caps Lock**—capitalizes all letters.
4. **Shift key**—capitalizes single letter; keys symbols.
5. **Space bar**—inserts space in text.
6. **Enter**—moves insertion point down to next line.
7. **Backspace**—deletes text to left of insertion point.
8. **Delete**—removes text to right of insertion point.
9. **Insert**—adds text or activates typeover.
10. **Numeric keypad**—numbers.

Keys to Execute Commands or Navigate

(Command keys often are used with other keys and vary with software.)

11. **Function (F1–F12) keys**
12. **Esc (Escape)**—cancel; stops action.
13. **Ctrl (Control)**
14. **Windows key**—displays Start menu and executes other commands.
15. **Alt (Alternate)**
16. **Arrow keys**—moves insertion point up, down, left, or right.
17. **Navigation keys**—Home, End, Page Up, and Page Down.

Keyboarding Assessment/Placement

Warmup

Key the paragraph using wordwrap (do not tap ENTER at the end of lines). Repeat if desired.

Good keyboarding skills are essential for almost all careers today. The time spent learning to key quickly and accurately is time well spent. Use good posture and good techniques to get you started on the right track. Then work diligently to achieve your speed and accuracy goals. Good keyboarding skills will save you time in preparing assignments for all of your classes. Also your work will impress your instructors.

Timed Writing

1. Take a 3' timed writing; use wordwrap (do not tap ENTER at the end of lines).
2. Tap TAB to begin.
3. Take a second 3' timed writing.

Note:
1' = 1 minute
30" = 30 seconds

LA ALL LETTERS

	gwam 1'	3'
Learning to key is just the first step toward developing a very	13	4
meaningful career skill. The next step is to build both speed and	26	9
accuracy. With basic keyboarding skills, you will be able to present	39	13
information in an attractive format that is quite easy to read. You will	54	18
also be able to develop your communication skills at the same time.	67	22
The next big step is to learn word processing. The software	12	26
most often used in business organizations is Word, which is much	25	31
more sophisticated than the basic word processor you used for	37	35
your warmup. With Word you will be able to create attractive	49	39
letters, memos, reports, and many other types of documents used	61	43
in business.	64	44
One of the exciting things about working diligently to develop	12	48
a skill is that you have the opportunity to set very specific goals	26	52
and challenge yourself to meet them. Nothing is more motivating	38	56
than being able to accomplish the goals that we set for ourselves.	52	61
The incremental goals that you meet each day will result in major	65	65
progress by the end of the course.	71	67

1'	1	2	3	4	5	6	7	8	9	10	11	12
3'		1			2			3			4	

Developing Keyboarding Skill

Learning Outcomes

Keyboarding

+ Key the alphabetic and numeric keys by touch.
+ Develop good keyboarding techniques.
+ Key fluently—at least 25 words per minute.
+ Develop reasonable accuracy.

Communication Skills

+ Develop proofreading skills.
+ Apply proofreaders' marks and revise text.

TIP

One way to divide the work is to ask each person to volunteer or be responsible for each of the five tips and expand on them. Secure pictures or video, or use other techniques to make the information interesting.

2. Make team assignments; then each members adds content to the file in a real-time editing session. Members will participate in editing each other's work. A brief in-person or telephone meeting prior to the editing session may be helpful in assigning roles. Often more than one editing session is needed to edit a complex document. The first session might include specifying the sections that need to be included and the types of illustrations that might work best. The next session may focus on editing the copy that each team member has added.
3. Remember to use the standard operating procedures for Palmetto Event Solutions. The standard theme is Office. Use your judgment on page numbering style, title and headings, borders, and other formats that are appropriate to use with Office styles. Ask one team member to be responsible for consistent and attractive formatting.
4. Each member of the team should save the document to his or her Module 9 files before exiting the real-time editing session. *(9-d4)*

9-d5

Memo

palmetto memo form

1. Your team will decide who will be designated Author 1 and who will make each of the edits suggested. Co-authoring with editing in real time should be used to create the document described.
2. Author 1 will open the Palmetto memo form from the data file, save it to the cloud, and share and invite all team members who will add their content to the form.
3. The first step is to outline the content of the memo and then decide on which team member will develop each section of the memo. Leave the To: and From: sections of the memo heading blank.
4. After the memo has been finalized, save and close. *(9-d5)*

The first part of the memo should inform business instructors that Palmetto Event Solutions has expanded and enriched its internship program. Use the information in the project setting on the previous page to describe the internship and the benefits it provides to students. Emphasize the learning, training, and relevant experience that interns will receive. Point out the pay and the advancement opportunities for students who perform well.

Describe how working for a week in another office in a different location helps to develop conceptual skills and seeing how the various segments of a business fit together. Describe how this opportunity follows the module for preparing for career success in document *9-d1*. What value does the community or four-year college receive from having its students participate in this type of program? Build a case why instructors should recommend outstanding students to apply for the internship.

MODULE 1

Alphabetic Keys

Lessons 1–10 *Alphabetic and Basic Punctuation Keys*

Lessons 11–13 *Review*

LEARNING OUTCOMES

- Key the alphabetic keys by touch.
- Key using proper techniques.
- Key at a rate of 14 *gwam* or more.

Lesson 1 Home Row, Space Bar, Enter, I

Keyboarding *A Wise Investment Now and For Your Career*

As you begin your keyboarding course, think about these two questions:

1. Why is keyboarding a great investment?

The ability to key rapidly and accurately is a lifelong skill. Instructors in virtually all courses expect you to submit papers and other assignments that have been keyed accurately and formatted attractively. Good keyboarding skills will result in time saved and will also give you a competitive advantage in courses such as *Word*, *Excel*, and *PowerPoint* as well as in many other courses, part-time jobs, and ultimately your career.

2. How can I get the best return on my investment?

Keyboarding is a psychomotor skill that requires muscle memory development with corrective drills and practice just as a pianist preparing for a concert or an athlete preparing for a sporting event has to develop basic skills. Your ultimate success in keying effectively is determined by the keyreach techniques you develop. You build muscle memory by reinforcing correct reaches over and over. Position is the constant point of reference for successful typists. Your textbook, software, and instructor will serve as your coach in developing the correct:

- Body position
- Finger position
- Wrist position
- Eyes position on screen/copy

Project Setting

Module 9

Mr. Tremblay's request to host the Senior Management Team Retreat in Yorkville, Canada, was granted. The six executive assistants met again this year during the retreat. In a joint session, senior managers and executive assistants approved the internship program enhancement.

The headquarters office and the four regional offices will each recruit four paid internships for up to 20 hours per week each semester and for the summer. Interns could hold a position for all three sessions if their evaluations merited continuing the relationship and if the interns wanted to continue in the positions. Interns would receive a 10 percent pay raise at the beginning of both the second and the third sessions.

The Senior Management Team also approved 10 hours of training for interns based on the *Skills Required for Career Success* document (see *9-d1*) during the first few weeks of the internship. Interns who completed the three-semester internship would have an expense-paid trip to work for a week in their choice of a regional or the headquarters office. The reason for this opportunity is that management wants to appeal to some of the most qualified students in the community, and they want to develop them as potential future employees.

The executive assistants agreed to develop the training program. They were asked to focus on soft skills. Many of the technical skills will be developed in their classes, and the conceptual skills will be developed during their internship work. Your team will start with one aspect of communication—making a good first impression.

9-d4

Article

first impression

1. Your instructor will determine if you will work in teams of two, three, or four for this project. The team will decide who will be designated Author 1 and who will make each of the edits suggested in this document. Co-authoring with editing in real time should be used to create the document described.
2. Author 1 will open *first impression* from the data file, save it to the cloud, and then share it and invite all team members, who will share their changes with the team.

Your team goal is to complete the training document on making first impressions.

1. Review the article and decide as a team what new materials are needed to enhance this training material. For example, include sections addressing questions such as these: What are the characteristics of a powerful handshake? What are ineffective handshakes? Can you locate or take pictures yourself and add pictures or video illustrating effective handshakes? Why is eye contact important? What is appropriate posture? Why is a smile important? Why is dress important? What type of dress is appropriate for employees at Palmetto Event Solutions? How does a person's dress affect your first impression of the person? What makes you nervous or uncomfortable using the techniques or styles suggested? Can you find pictures, graphics, video, or other means of illustrating the good and bad aspects of the concepts discussed?

STANDARD PLAN For Learning New Keyreaches

1. Find the new key on the illustrated keyboard. Then find it on your keyboard.
2. Watch your finger make the reach to the new key a few times. Keep other fingers curved in home position. For an upward reach, straighten the finger slightly; for a down reach, curve the finger a bit more.
3. Use these directions for learning all new keyreaches.

New Keys

1a Learn Home Row

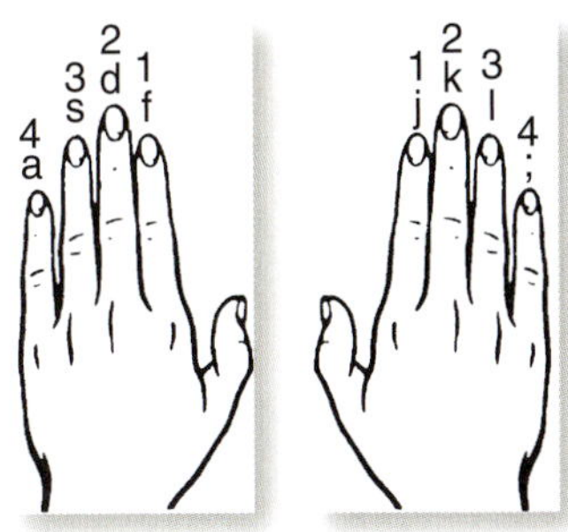

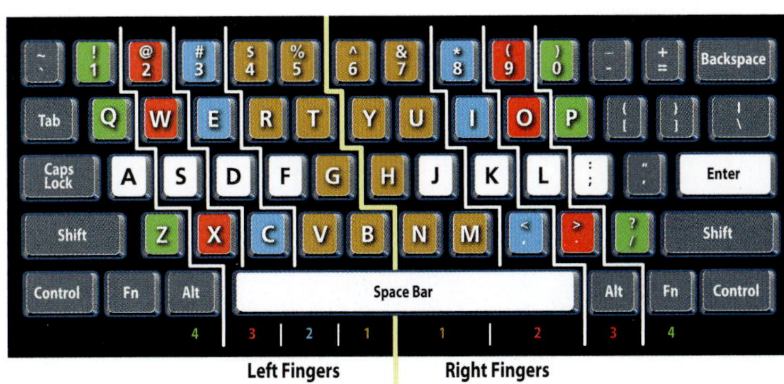

HOME-ROW POSITION

1. Drop your hands to your side. Allow your fingers to curve naturally. Maintain this curve as you key.
2. Lightly place your left fingers over the **a s d f** and the right fingers over the **j k l ;**. You will feel a raised element on the **f** and **j** keys, which will help you keep your fingers on the home-row position. You are now in home-row position.

© Cengage Learning, Courtesy of Meg Shanahan

© Cengage Learning

Note the curve of your fingers when your arms are hanging loosely at your side. Maintain this same curve when you place your hands on the home row.

Critical Thinking, Decision Making, and Problem Solving

Critical thinking, decision making, and problem solving are soft skills that businesses frequent list as requirements in job postings. They may be listed together, separately, or only one or two of the skills may be listed on a particular job posting.

Should critical thinking, decision making, and problem solving be considered as the same concept, or should they be thought of as different concepts, or should they be considered related concepts? Business executives tend to think of them as related but not identical concepts. The following chart show some of the typical ways of thinking about these concepts.

Critical Thinking	•Ability to think rationally, logically, and clearly •Ability to connect and interpret ideas
Decision Making	•A mental process that involves analyzing and choosing among alternatives •A process that leads to a final conclusion
Problem Solving	•A method of analyzing and correcting a problem–the inference that something is wrong • A method that focuses on what's causing a problem and how can it best be corrected

The ability to think critically helps you to make wise decisions that impact your work and your everyday life. Often decisions have to be made that result in correcting a problem-type situation. Follow these five basic steps to make effective decisions.

1. Identify the decision and collect facts. Analyze objectively the situation or problem requiring the decision. Get all the facts. Avoid making assumptions colored by stereotypes and preconceptions.
2. Determine the options available. Be creative in generating as many options as possible. In some cases, options are predetermined.
3. Analyze options carefully. Try to view the situation from the perspective of everybody involved and from the organization. Examine consequences for each person and for the organization.
4. Select the best option and implement it. Evaluate all of the options and get more facts if needed. Also consider what is necessary for the option to be successful. The way a decision is implemented often determines its success.
5. Evaluate the effectiveness of the decision implemented. Did it produce the desired results? Should you continue going through the process to improve the decision?

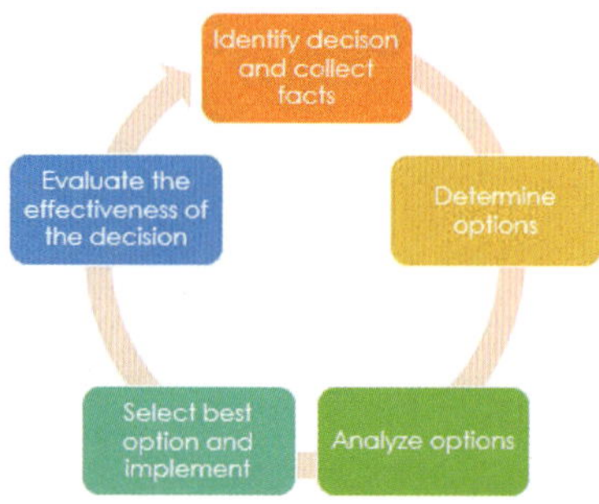

The use of the continuous cycle graphic implies that frequently the evaluation reveals that more adjusting or tweaking the decision may be decision may be necessary. In some cases, the entire decision-making process may need to be repeated.

1b Learn Space Bar and ENTER

SPACE BAR AND ENTER

Tap the Space Bar, located at the bottom of the keyboard, with a down-and-in motion of the right thumb to space between words.

© Cengage Learning

Enter Reach with the fourth (little) finger of the right hand to ENTER. Tap it to return the insertion point to the left margin. This action creates a **hard return**. Use a hard return at the end of all drill lines. Quickly return to home position (over ;).

© Cengage Learning

```
1 j jj f ff k kk d dd l ll s ss ; ;; a aa jkl; fdsa
2 a aa ; ;; s ss l ll d dd k kk f ff j jj fdsa jkl;
```

1c Master New Keys

Key each line once. Tap ENTER at the end of each line.

```
3 ff  jj  ff  jj  fj  fj  fj  dd  kk  dd  kk  dk  dk  dk
4 ss  ll  ss  ll  sl  sl  sl  aa  ;;  aa  ;;  a;  a;  a;
5 fj  fj  dk  dk  sl  sl  a;  fjdk  sla;  fjkd  ls;a
6 fff  jjj  fjf  fff  jjj  fjf  fjf  jfj  jfj  fjf
7 ddd  kkk  dkd  ddd  kkk  dkd  dkd  kdk  kdk  dkd
8 sss  lll  sls  sss  lll  sls  sls  lsl  lsl  sls
9 aaa  ;;;  a;a  aaa  ;;;  a;a  a;a  ;a;  ;a;  a;a
10 f  j  d  k  s  l  a  ;  ;  a  l  s  k  d  j  f
11 ff jj dd kk ss ll aa ;; jj ff kk dd ll ss aa ;;
12 fff  jjj  ddd  kkk  sss  lll  aaa  jjj  ;;;  fjdk  sla;
```

Keep your eyes on the textbook as you key each line.

1d Improve Keystroking

Key each line once. Tap ENTER at the end of each line.

```
13 a  a;  al  ak  aj  s  s;  sl  sk  sj  d  d;  dl  dk  dj
14 j  ja  js  jd  jf  k  ka  ks  kd  kf  l  la  ls  ld  lf
15 a;  sl  a;sl  dkfj  a;sl  dkfj  a;sl  dkfj  asdf  jk
16 a;  sl  a;sl  dk  fj  dkfj  a;sl  dkfj  fjdk  a;a
17 f  ff  j  jj  d  dd  k  kk  s  ss  l  ll  a  aa  ;  ;;  fj
18 afj;  a  s  d  f  j  k  l  ;  asdf  jkl;  fdsa  jkl;
```

7. Insert a Continuous Cyle SmartArt layout after the five basic steps to make effective decisions and key the following information in the Text pane. Change colors to Colorful.

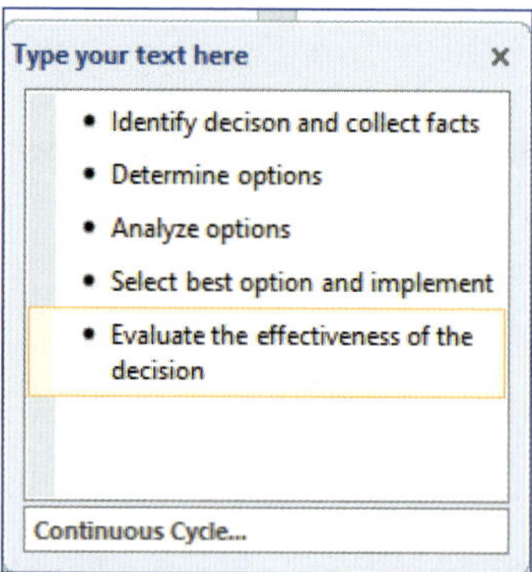

8. Select the five bulleted steps and convert bullets to numbers.
9. Apply a 3 point, Gold, Accent 3, Darker 25% box page border to all pages.
10. See the Quick Check on the next page; save a copy of the document in your Module 9 files and exit. *(9-d3)*

7. Key the last paragraph after the Continuous Cycle graphic.

   The use of the continuous cycle graphic implies that frequently the evaluation reveals that more adjusting or tweaking the decision may be necessary. In some cases, the entire decision-making process may need to be repeated.

8. Insert Round Rectangle page numbers at the top of the page. Do not show numbers on first page.
9. See the Quick Check on the next page; save a copy in your Module 9 files and exit. *(9-d3)*

1e i

© Cengage Learning

i Reach *up* with *right second* finger.

```
19 i ik ik ik is is id id if if ill i ail did kid lid
20 i ik aid ail did kid lid lids kids ill aid did ilk
21 id aid aids laid said ids lid skids kiss disk dial
```

Use good posture; back and body erect; feet flat on the floor.

1f Master New Keys

i

```
22 id aid ail fail sail jail ails slid dill sill fill
23 aid lads; if a kid is; a salad lid; kiss a sad dad
24 as ad all ask jak lad fad said ill kill fall disks
25 is all sad lass a lid; is silk; silk disk; dad is;
```

1g Build Skill

```
26 as as ask ask ad ad lad lad all all fall fall asks
27 as asks did disk ail fail sail ails jail sill silk
28 ask dad; dads said; is disk; kiss a lad; salad lid
29 fill a sail; aid a lad; is silk; if a dial; a jail
30 is a disk; dads said; did fall ill; if a lass did;
```

AVAVA/Shutterstock.com

WORKPLACE SUCCESS

Keyboarding: The Survival Skill

Keyboarding is a valuable and necessary skill for everyone in this technological world. It is an expected tool for effective communication throughout one's life.

Students who resort to "hunting and pecking" to key their school assignments are constantly searching for the correct letter on the keyboard. Frustration abounds for students who wish to key their research reports into the computer but do not have the touch keyboarding skills required to accomplish the task quickly and proficiently. Students who can key by touch are much more relaxed because they can keep their eyes on the screen and concentrate on text editing and composing.

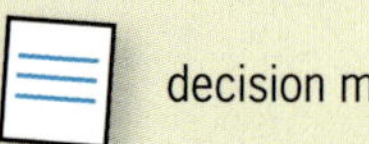

Article

decision making

The student who was Author 1 of the first document serves as Author 2 on this document.

The student who was Author 2 of the first document serves as Author 1 on this document.

The article you will co-author is part of a training program trying to help young, inexperienced employees improve their soft skills. The first article deals with critical thinking and decision making. With this article, you will format, add content, and make the content easier to read and understand.

Since team members reversed their authoring and editing roles, it would be helpful for both team members to review the steps used to prepare and set up a co-authoring setting in real time. The details provided prior to completing the last real-time editing session are not repeated for editing this document.

It would also be helpful to review and become familiar with the data file.

Instructions for Author 1

1. Open *decision making* from your data files and click Share. Then click Save to cloud.
2. Select OneDrive and Module 9 folder and click Save and name the document **9-d3**.
3. In the Invite people text box, key the email address of Author 2.
4. Click Always in the Automatically share changes box and start editing.
5. Follow the editing instructions for Author 1 shown below.
6. Key the following paragraph between the first and second paragraphs of the data file.

   Should critical thinking, decision making, and problem solving be considered as the same concept, or should they be thought of as different concepts, or should they be considered related concepts? Business executives tend to think of them as related but not identical concepts. The following chart show some of the typical ways of thinking about these concepts.

Instructions for Author 2

1. Check your email and follow the link sent to you by Author 1. If the document opens in *Word Online*, click OPEN IN WORD.
2. Click Yes in the Automatically share changes pane that opens.
3. When you click in the document to edit it, a colored flag will appear at the insertion point. You should also be able to see a flag where Author 1 is editing. Begin editing.
4. Follow the editing instructions for Author 2 shown below.
5. Apply the Vapor Trail theme; apply Title format to the title and decrease the font size to fit on one line.
6. Insert a Vertical Block List SmartArt layout after Author 2 finishes keying the new second paragraph, then key the following information in the Text pane.

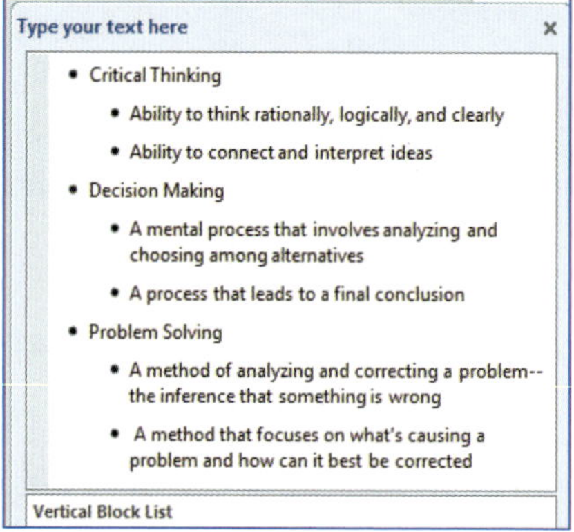

(continued)

Lesson 1R Review

Warmup *Lesson 1Ra Warmup*

Fingers curved and upright

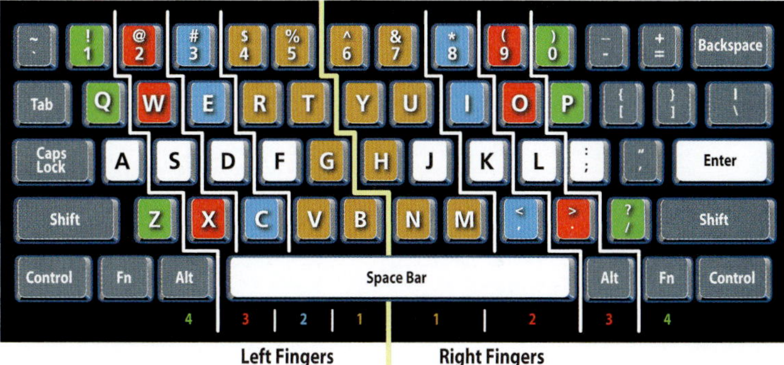

1 ff dd ss aa ff dd ss aa jj kk ll ;; fj dk sl a; a;
2 fj dk sla; fjdk sla; a;sl dkfj fjdk sla; fjdk sla;
3 aa ss dd ff jj kk ll ;; aa ss dd ff jj kk ll ;; a;
4 if a; as is; kids did; ask a sad lad; if a lass is

Skill Building

1Rb Improve Techniques

Key each line once.

Move fingers without moving your hands; eyes on textbook.

5 f j fjf jj fj fj jf dd kk dd kk dk dk dk
6 s ; s;s ;; s; s; s; aa ;; aa ;; a; a; a;
7 fj dk sl a; fjdk sla; jfkd lsa; ;a ;a ;s
8 f j fjf d k dkd s l sls a ; fj dk sl a;a
9 a; al aka j s s; sl sk sj d d; dl dk djd
10 ja js jd jf k ka ks kd kf l la ls ld lfl

1Rc Improve Keystroking

11 f fa fad s sa sad f fa fall fall l la lad s sa sad
12 a as ask a ad add j ja jak f fa fall; ask; add jak
13 ik ki ki ik is if id il ij ia ij ik is if ji id ia
14 is il ill sill dill fill sid lid ail lid slid jail
15 if is il kid kids ill kid if kids; if a kid is ill

Collaboration—A Key Business Requirement

In today's environment, teams work collaboratively on numerous projects. A written report generally is required at the completion of each project. Team writing presents numerous challenges because the report is usually divided into sections written by different people. When the sections are put together, inconsistencies, duplication of information, omission of needed information, and content that does not flow smoothly often results. Careful strategies need to be established and followed to ensure that the report reads as though it was written by one person, and the entire team should be responsible for editing the report.

Productivity Tools for Collaboration

Cloud-based storage and new editing tools enable teams to produce well-written reports more efficiently and effectively by working on the document at the same time. They also enable a team member who is not available at the time to work individually and remotely at another time and sync additions and edits to the document.

OneDrive

The OneDrive, cloud-based storage enables an author to share documents securely with other users in different locations. Team members can access the documents using different devices—desktop, laptop, tablet, or other mobile device.

Real-Time Co-Authoring

Co-authoring introduced in earlier versions of *Word* enabled multiple writers to work on the same document, but not on the same content at the same time. New features in *Word 2016* enable multiple authors to create and edit a document at the same time. When two or more authors are editing a document in real-time, each author can see the work of other authors.

"How to" Concepts for Real-Time Co-Authoring

It is easier to begin with an editing task rather than a new document. However, both approaches can be used. The following 10 steps outline the basic real-time co-authoring process.

1. One author has to start the co-authoring session.
2. Open an existing *Word 2016* document, and click Share.
3. Click "Save to Cloud" and select OneDrive as the location and click Save to display the Share pane. In a business setting, the location may be SharePoint Online.
4. In the invite people text box, key the email addresses of the users you want to invite.
5. Set the permissions to Can edit.

AUTHOR 1 AND AUTHOR 2 1

6. Key a message if desired. An example might be: As we agreed, let's begin editing at 2:30 pm today.
7. Start working on the document. If you have not already agreed to let others see your changes, select **Yes** to automatic sharing.
8. When authors follow the link you sent them, your document will open in their *Word 2016*. Each author must agree to automatic sharing by selecting **Yes**.
9. When authors begin work on your document, colored flags will appear at the spot each author is working. All authors can see each other's work.
10. You will be alerted when an author leaves the document.

Co-authoring in real time truly improves productivity and the quality of team reports. It is an excellent skill to develop.

AUTHOR 1 AND AUTHOR 2 2

Lesson 2 E and N

Warmup Lesson 2a Warmup

```
1 ff dd ss aa ff dd ss aa jj kk ll ;; fj dk sl a; a;
2 fj dk sl a; fjdk sla; a;sl dkfj dk sl a; fjdk sla;
3 aa ss dd ff jj kk ll ;; aa ss dd ff jj kk ll ;; a;
4 if a; as is; kids did; ask a sad lad; if a lass is
```

New Keys

2b e and n

e Reach *up* with *left second* finger.

n Reach *down* with *right first* finger.

e

```
5 e ed ed led led lea lea ale ale elf elf eke eke ed
6 e el el eel els elk elk lea leak ale kale led jell
7 e ale kale lea leak fee feel lea lead elf self eke
```

n

```
8 n nj nj an an and and fan fan and kin din fin land
9 n an fan in fin and land sand din fans sank an sin
10 n in ink sink inn kin skin an and land in din dink
```

2c All Reaches Learned

```
11 den end fen ken dean dens ales fend fens keen knee
12 if in need; feel ill; as an end; a lad and a lass;
13 and sand; a keen idea; as a sail sank; is in jail;
14 an idea; an end; a lake; a nail; a jade; a dean is
```

7. Select the ten steps that outline the basic co-authoring process and apply numbers to them. 8. Key the following below step 10 as a paragraph: **Co-authoring in real time truly improves productivity and the quality of team reports.**	8. Insert the Retrospect footer using Aqua, Accent 1, 25% Darker color. If only one name is listed in the footer, key the second name in the footer. 9. Add the following sentence to finish the paragraph that Author 1 keyed: **It is an excellent skill to develop.**

Both authors should check to ensure that all edits were made and that no other errors exist. Note that Author 1 is the owner of the document. Author 2 can use Save as to save a copy of the document to his or her files. Author 1 could also email a copy of the report to Author 2. Note that when Author 2 closes the document and exits Author 1 is notified that Author 2 is no longer editing the document.

Save and close. *(9-d2)*

Skill Building

2d Improve Techniques

1. Key each line once.
2. Keep your eyes on the copy.

Reach with little finger; tap ENTER; return to home key.

```
15 if a lad;
16 is a sad fall

17 if a lass did ask
18 ask a lass; ask a lad

19 a;sldkfj a;sldkfj a;sldkfj
20 a; sl dk fj fj dk sl a; a;sldkfj

21 ik ik if if is is kid skid did lid aid laid said
22 ik kid ail die fie did lie ill ilk silk skill skid
```

2e Improve Keystroking

i

```
23 ik ik ik if is il ik id is if kid did lid aid ails
24 did lid aid; add a line; aid kids; ill kids; id is
```

n

```
25 nj nj nj an an and and end den ken in ink sin skin
26 jn din sand land nail sank and dank skin sans sink
```

e

```
27 el els elf elk lea lead fee feel sea seal ell jell
28 el eke ale jak lake elf els jaks kale eke els lake
```

2f Build Skill

```
29 dine in an inn; fake jade; lend fans; as sand sank
30 in nine inns; if an end; need an idea; seek a fee;
31 if a lad; a jail; is silk; is ill; a dais; did aid
32 adds a line; and safe; asks a lass; sail in a lake
```

Keep your eyes on copy; key words at a steady pace.

2g Improve Techniques

Key each line once.

```
33 send land skin faded sand kind line nine sale fail
34 dense sales lakes jaded likes jails salad kale inn
35 lad likes kale; lass likes silk; add a fee; is ill
36 kids in a lake; if in need; ask a lass; lad is ill
```

Apply It

9-d1

Save Document to OneDrive

 success skills

1. Open the data file success skills, and then click Save As and select OneDrive.
2. Create a new folder named **Module 9**; then open the folder and save the document.
3. Name the file **9-d1**.

9-d2

Co-authoring and Editing in Real Time

 collaboration

1. Prepare for a co-authoring session in real time.
   a. Begin with a team of two students. One student will be listed as Author 1, and the other will be listed as Author 2.
   b. Both authors must be signed in to a OneDrive account and use *Word 2016* for all documents in this module. Authors must have each other's email address.
   c. Review the information on the previous two pages carefully and refer to it as needed.
   d. Read the *collaboration* document that you will edit carefully. It provides a summary of the steps that you must follow to edit this document.
   e. Set up a time that you both are available to edit the document.
   f. The remaining instructions are divided into two sections—Author 1 and Author 2.
2. Get started. Follow the instructions for your role—either as Author 1 or Author 2.

TIP

You may see a bracket display while the other author is keying or making an edit. Be patient—sometimes the edits take a few seconds before they display on your screen. The speed of your Internet affects the length of the brief delays.

Instructions for Author 1

1. Open *collaboration* from your data files and click Share. Then click Save to cloud.
2. Select OneDrive and the Module 9 folder. If you cannot locate the Module 9 folder on OneDrive, create a new folder name it **Module 9**, then click Save and name the document **9-d2**.
3. In the Invite people text box, key the email address of Author 2.
4. Make sure the Automatically share changes box is on either Ask me or Always. If you click Always, sharing will take place automatically.
5. Read the document and then start editing. Make the edits listed for Author 1 below.
6. Apply Headlines theme. Then apply Title style and decrease the font size to fit on one line; tap ENTER.

Instructions for Author 2

1. Check your email and follow the link sent to you by Author 1. If the document opens in *Word Online*, click OPEN IN WORD.
2. Click Yes in the Automatically share changes pane that opens.
3. When you click in the document to edit it, a colored flag will appear at the insertion point. You should also be able to see a flag where Author 1 is editing.
4. Read the document and then start editing. Make the edits listed for Author 2 below.
5. Apply Heading 1 style to the first and last headings.
6. Apply Heading 2 style to the two headings below Productivity Tools for Collaboration.
7. Locate and correct the error in Step 7.

(continued)

Lesson 3 Review

Warmup *Lesson 3a Warmup*

© Cengage Learning

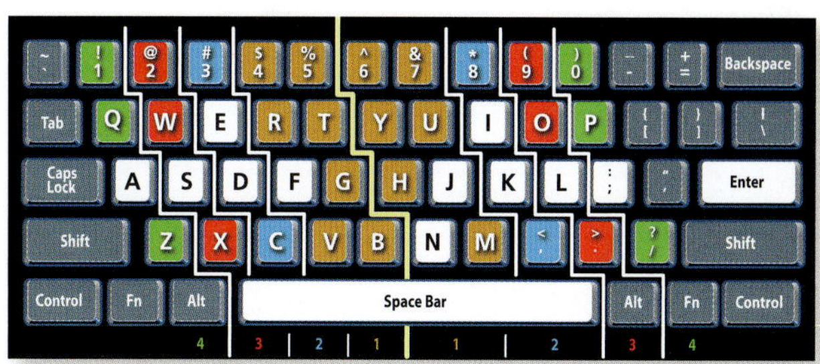

home 1 ad ads lad fad dad as ask fa la lass jak jaks alas
n 2 an fan and land fan flan sans sand sank flank dank
i 3 is id ill dill if aid ail fail did kid ski lid ilk
all 4 ade alas nine else fife ken; jell ink jak inns if;

Skill Building

3b Build Skill

Key each line once.

Lines 5–8: Think and key words. Make the space part of the word.

Lines 9–12: Think and key phrases. Do not key the vertical rules separating the phrases.

easy words

5 if is as an ad el and did die eel fin fan elf lens
6 as ask and id kid and ade aid eel feel ilk skis an
7 ail fail aid did ken ale led an flan inn inns alas
8 eel eke nee kneel did kids kale sees lake elf fled

easy phrases

9 el el | id id | is is | eke eke | lee lee | ale ale | jill jak
10 is if | is a | is a | a disk | a disk | did ski | did ski | is a
11 sell a | sell a | sell a sled | fall fad | fall fad | fad is
12 sees a lake | sees a lake | as a deal | sell sled | a sale

3c Improve Keystroking

home row: fingers curved and upright

13 jak lad as lass dad sad lads fad fall la ask ad as
14 asks add jaks dads a lass ads flak adds sad as lad

upward reaches: straighten fingers slightly; return quickly to home position

15 fed die led ail kea lei did ale fife silk leak lie
16 sea lid deal sine desk lie ale like life idea jail

double letters: stroke double letters at a steady, unhurried pace

17 fee jell less add inn seek fall alee lass keel all
18 dill dell see fell eel less all add kiss seen sell

Skills Required for Career Success

The skills required for specific jobs vary significantly depending on your field of interest, the organization that hires you, the type of job, and the level of the job. Regardless of these factors, a common base of knowledge and a common set of skills are required for virtually every job. These skills can be grouped into three categories: technical skills, soft skills, and conceptual skills.

Technical Skills

Technical skills refer to the specific knowledge, expertise, and ability to do the job. The specific knowledge varies depending on the field, such as—manager, medical professional, or architect. The content courses taken at an educational institution or in an industry training program generally provide the knowledge required for a specific job. Examples of universal technical skills would be language skills, keyboarding skill, ability to use applications, such as Word, Excel, Outlook, and PowerPoint.

Expertise includes the ability to know when and how to apply the knowledge to solve specific problems or to perform specific tasks or procedures.

The ability to do the job is developed through practice in appropriate settings and experience.

Soft Skills

Soft skills are personal attributes, interpersonal skills, and emotional intelligence. Soft skills relate to the way you interact with other employees. Ten frequently listed soft skills that are required in most jobs include:

1. Communication skills
2. Creativity/innovation
3. Critical thinking and decision making
4. Ethics, honesty, and integrity
5. Accountability and responsibility
6. Teamwork and collaboration
7. Time management and productivity
8. Work ethic
9. Analytical skills
10. Positive attitude

The first step in developing soft skills is to learn what skills are needed and why they are important. Generally, individuals have to take the initiative to improve the soft skills they need to be effective in the job desired. One effective way to develop soft skills is to observe how effective people in your organization apply the skills you need to improve.

SUSIE VANHUSS AND CONNIE FORDE 1

Conceptual Skills

Conceptual skills are the ability to see the big picture and how things fit together. Conceptual skills enable you to understand how your job fits into the overall business strategy of your organization. Conceptual skills begin with learning as much as possible about your organization. Effective industry conceptual skills development programs involve rotating employees to positions for several weeks in each of the divisions of the organization to learn what they do and to become familiar with the people who do the jobs in that division.

SUSIE VANHUSS AND CONNIE FORDE 2

3d Build Skill

19 and and land land el el elf elf self self ail nail
20 as as ask ask ad ad lad lad id id lid lid kid kids

phrases: think and key as phrases

21 if if | is is | jak jak | all all | did did | nan nan | elf elf
22 as a lad | ask dad | fed a jak | as all ask | sales fad

23 sell a lead | seal a deal | feel a leaf | if a jade sale
24 is a | is as if | a disk | aid all kids | did ski | is a silk

3e Improve Techniques

Key each line once.

Tap Space Bar with down-and-in motion.

reach review

25 ea sea lea seas deal leaf leak lead leas flea keas
26 as ask lass ease as asks ask ask sass as alas seas

27 sa sad sane sake sail sale sans safe sad said sand
28 le sled lead flee fled ale flea lei dale kale leaf

29 jn jn nj nj in fan fin an; din ink sin and inn an;
30 de den end fen an an and and ken knee nee dean dee

3f Timed Writing

Key lines 31–34 for 1'. If you finish before time is up, repeat the lines.

Note:
1' = 1 minute
30" = 30 seconds

31 el eel eld elf sell self el dell fell elk els jell
32 in fin inn inks dine sink fine fins kind line lain

33 an and fan dean elan flan land lane lean sand sane
34 sell a lead; sell a jade; seal a deal; feel a leaf

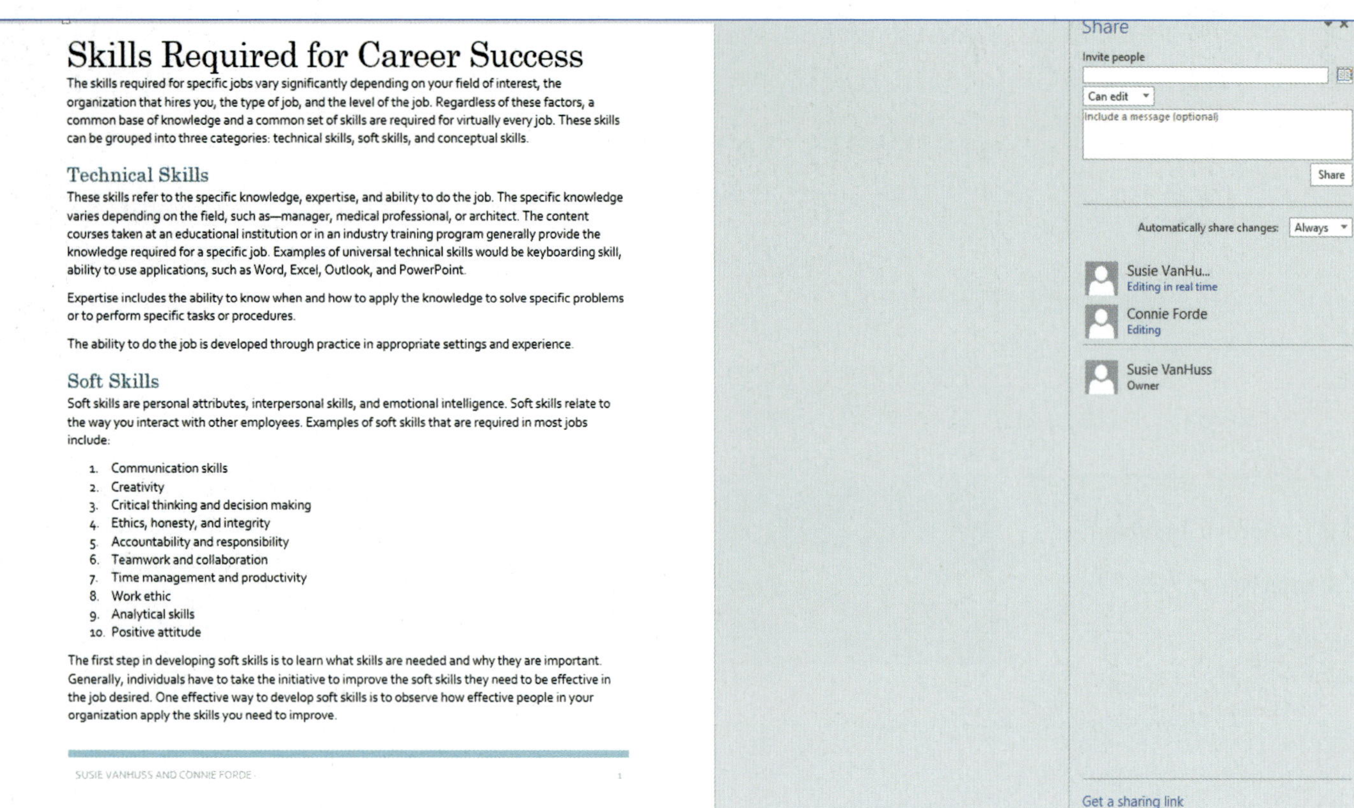
Skills Required for Career Success

The skills required for specific jobs vary significantly depending on your field of interest, the organization that hires you, the type of job, and the level of the job. Regardless of these factors, a common base of knowledge and a common set of skills are required for virtually every job. These skills can be grouped into three categories: technical skills, soft skills, and conceptual skills.

Technical Skills

These skills refer to the specific knowledge, expertise, and ability to do the job. The specific knowledge varies depending on the field, such as—manager, medical professional, or architect. The content courses taken at an educational institution or in an industry training program generally provide the knowledge required for a specific job. Examples of universal technical skills would be keyboarding skill, ability to use applications, such as Word, Excel, Outlook, and PowerPoint.

Expertise includes the ability to know when and how to apply the knowledge to solve specific problems or to perform specific tasks or procedures.

The ability to do the job is developed through practice in appropriate settings and experience.

Soft Skills

Soft skills are personal attributes, interpersonal skills, and emotional intelligence. Soft skills relate to the way you interact with other employees. Examples of soft skills that are required in most jobs include:

1. Communication skills
2. Creativity
3. Critical thinking and decision making
4. Ethics, honesty, and integrity
5. Accountability and responsibility
6. Teamwork and collaboration
7. Time management and productivity
8. Work ethic
9. Analytical skills
10. Positive attitude

The first step in developing soft skills is to learn what skills are needed and why they are important. Generally, individuals have to take the initiative to improve the soft skills they need to be effective in the job desired. One effective way to develop soft skills is to observe how effective people in your organization apply the skills you need to improve.

SUSIE VANHUSS AND CONNIE FORDE 1

Note the extensive format and text edits made in real-time editing by co-authors. The final edited document is also shown on the next page

Lesson 4 Left Shift, H, T, Period

Warmup *Lesson 4a Warmup*

home row 1 al as ads lad dad fad jak fall lass asks fads all;

e/i/n 2 ed ik jn in knee end nine line sine lien dies leis

all reaches 3 see a ski; add ink; fed a jak; is an inn; as a lad

easy 4 an dial id is an la lake did el ale fake is land a

New Keys

4b Left Shift and h

© Cengage Learning

left shift Reach *down* with *left fourth* (little) finger; shift, tap, release.

© Cengage Learning

h Reach to *left* with *right first* finger.

left shift

5 J Ja Ja Jan Jan Jane Jana Ken Kass Lee Len Nan Ned

6 and Ken and Lena and Jake and Lida and Nan and Ida

7 Inn is; Jill Ina is; Nels is; Jen is; Ken Lin is a

h

8 h hj hj he he she she hen aha ash had has hid shed

9 h hj ha hie his half hand hike dash head sash shad

10 aha hi hash heal hill hind lash hash hake dish ash

4c All Reaches Learned

11 Nels Kane and Jake Jenn; she asked Hi and Ina Linn

12 Lend Lana and Jed a dish; I fed Lane and Jess Kane

13 I see Jake Kish and Lash Hess; Isla and Helen hike

4d Improve Keystroking

Key the drill once. Strive for good control.

14 he she held a lead; she sells jade; she has a sale

15 Ha Ja Ka La Ha Hal Ja Jake Ka Kahn La Ladd Ha Hall

16 Hal leads; Jeff led all fall; Hal has a safe lead

17 Hal Hall heads all sales; Jake Hess asks less fee;

3. In the Invite people text box, key the email addresses of the authors you want to invite.
4. Make sure the Automatically share changes box is either on Ask me or Always and set the permission to Can edit; otherwise the author will only be able to view the document. If you click Always, sharing will take place automatically. See the illustration below. Then click Share.

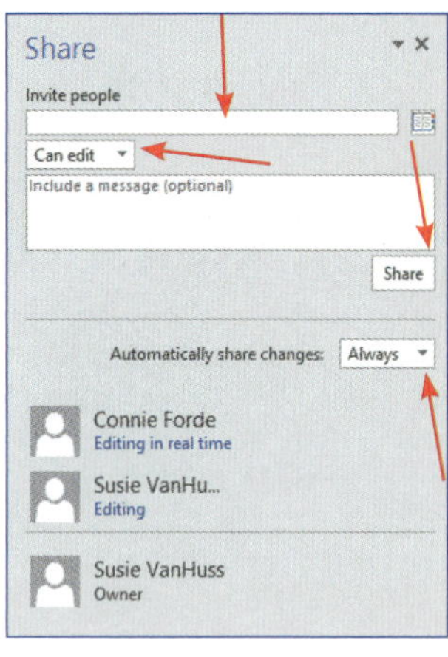

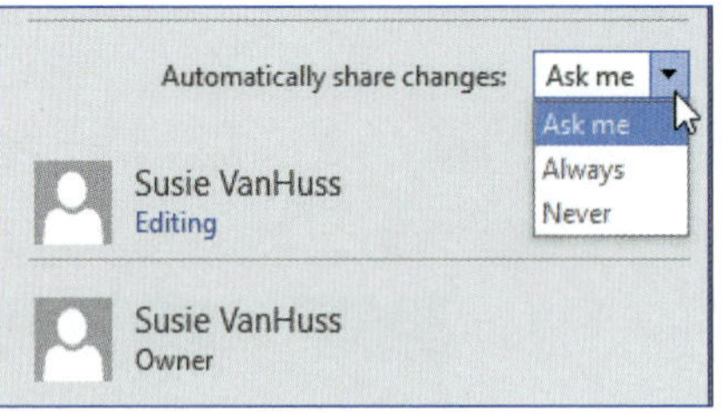

5. Start editing your document. If you have not already agreed to let others see your changes, select Yes to automatic sharing.

Getting Started—Author 2 (or more)

1. When your co-author follows the link you sent, your document will open in his or her *Word 2016*. If it opens in Office Online, click OPEN IN WORD as shown on the previous page.
2. Each author must agree to automatic sharing by selecting Yes. When authors begin working on your document, colored flags will appear at the location each author is working. All authors can see each other's work.

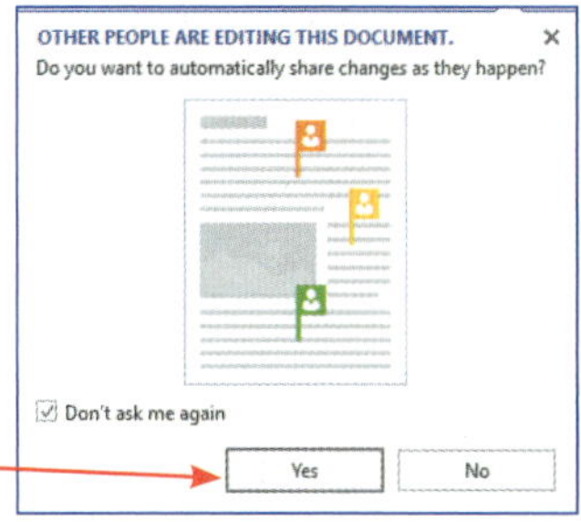

Authors Editing in Real Time

The illustrations below show both authors working in real time. When an author exits, others are notified.

Note that it is very important to read a document before you start editing it. Knowing what is in the document will help you to avoid duplication and detect things that may have been omitted. It will also help you to locate errors.

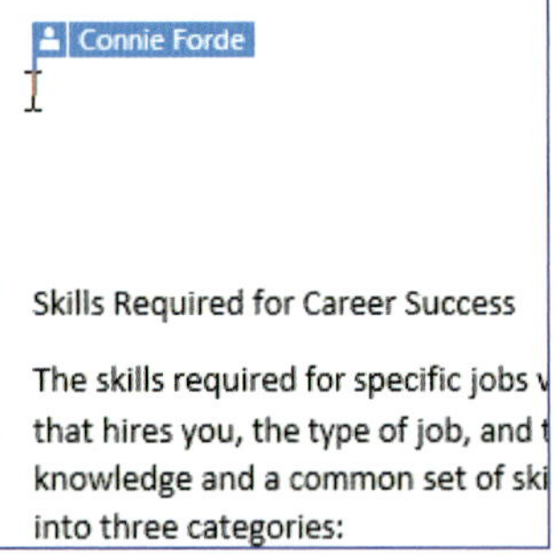

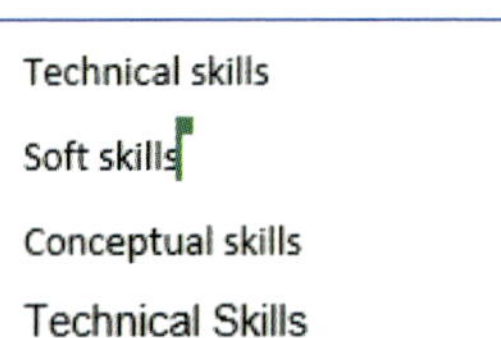

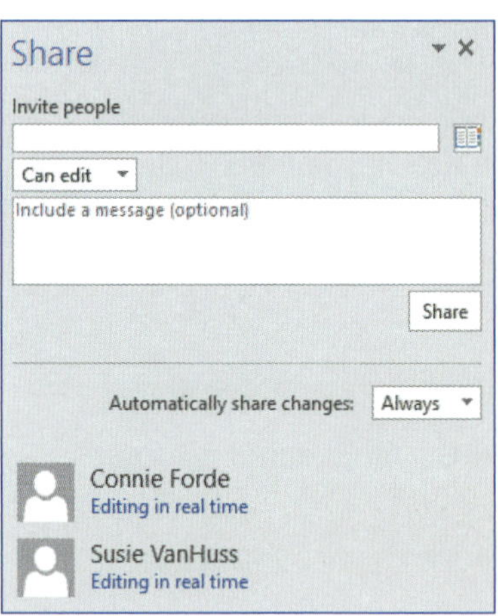

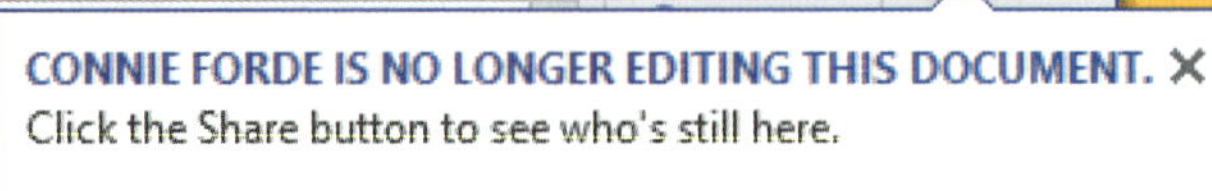

4e t and . (period)

t Reach *up* with *left first* finger.

t

18 t tf tf aft aft left fit fat fete tiff tie the tin
19 tf at at aft lit hit tide tilt tint sits skit this
20 hat kit let lit ate sit flat tilt thin tale tan at

Space once after a period.

. (period) Reach *down* with *right third* finger.

. (period)

21 .l .l l.l fl. fl. L. L. Neal and J. N. List hiked.
22 Hand J. H. Kass a fan. Jeff did. Hank needs ideas.
23 Jane said she has a tan dish; Jed and Lee need it.

4f Improve Keystroking

24 I did tell J. K. that Lt. Lee had left. He is ill.
25 tie tan kit sit fit hit hat; the jet left at nine.
26 I see Lila and Ilene at tea. Jane Kane ate at ten.
27 tf .l hj ft ki de jh tf ik ed hj de ft ki l. tf ik
28 elf eel left is sis fit till dens ink has delt ink
29 he he heed heed she she shelf shelf shed shed she
30 it is if id did lit tide tide tile tile list list

Skill Building

4g Build Skill

31 he has; he had; he led; he sleds; she fell; he is
32 it is; he hit it; he is ill; she is still; she is
33 Hal and Nel; Jade dishes; Kale has half; Jed hides
34 Hi Ken; Helen and Jen hike; Jan has a jade; Ken is

WORKING WITH WORD ON ONEDRIVE

Note that a number of Office Online apps are available on OneDrive. In this module, you will *not* be working with these apps. You will open *Word* from OneDrive as shown on the next page.

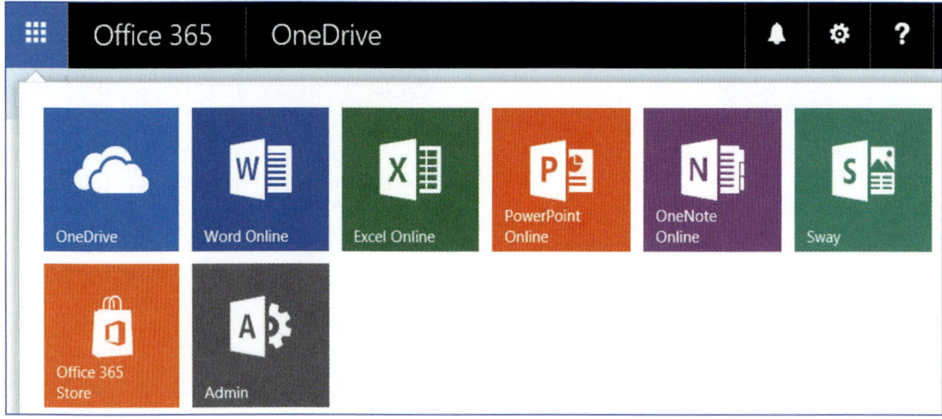

If a document opens in the *Word Online* app, you will need to open it in *Word* as shown below.

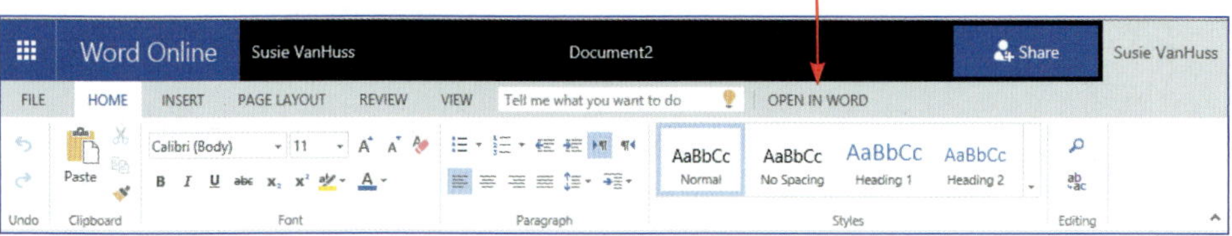

REAL-TIME CO-AUTHORING

In today's business environment, teams work collaboratively on numerous projects that require a final report. Real-time editing is a new productivity tool that combines storing and sharing a document on OneDrive with editing tools that enable multiple authors to work on the same document at the same time. It enhances and facilitates team writing.

Two students are required to work together on the first part of this module, and more students will work together on the project at the end of this module. Your instructor will help you form teams to get started. Both team members can work remotely as long as both are available at the same time for editing. Students will be referred to as authors during the editing session, and the first author will be shown as the owner of the document.

Getting Started—Author 1

Begin by having one author save a document online and invite others to work on it.

1. Open an existing *Word 2016* document and click Share and then Save to Cloud.
2. Select OneDrive, and select folder or create and name a new folder, and click Save.

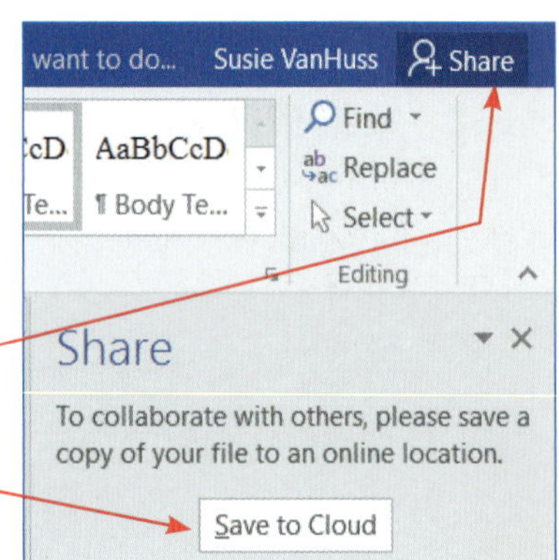

TIP

You only have to select OneDrive and the folder once for each document. The next time you open it, it will save back to the same folder.

Lesson 4R Review

Warmup *Lesson 4Ra Warmup*

home row 1 sad lad hall lad sale ask jak add aka fall fad ha;

review 2 H. Le Ki J. tan tin hit at tat nat hat nit Lt. hid

all reaches 3 Jed is in sales; Kate ate fish. Hank hit his head.

easy 4 sit dial and land fit then half din hand lend disk

Skill Building

4Rb Improve Keystroking

Key the drill once.

Think and key words and phrases.

words 5 slain tent Kent lent tea Jill Ned fed said laid he

phrases 6 he fakes | she hikes | his lead is safe | she and I fish

sentences 7 Nan is ill; He is at the lake; Jake is at the Inn.

sentences 8 Jed Hess did ski. Kit and I fished. Lisa ate fish.

sentences 9 Hank ate his salad. Jane has the disk in the tent.

sentences 10 He said that Nate left the lake and is at the Inn.

4Rc Build Skill

11 shelf lead jiff lead sand find dine kind fend tent

12 kale sake takes deal tended salad jaded dined left

13 if I sell it; seek a deal; find a tent; at the Inn

14 He asked Ken; I need a fan; He sells jade and land.

15 I like Hank and Jan; Leslie ate salad at the lake.

4Rd Timed Writing

1. Take two 1' timed writings. If you finish before time is up, begin again.
2. Use wordwrap.

Wordwrap:* *Text within a paragraph moves automatically from one line to the next; tap ENTER only to begin a new paragraph.

Use wordwrap

Janet sat in the tent; then she and I ate at the
lake. Janet and her dad did find the disk in the tent
at the lake. Helen and the dean ate a salad at the
Inn; then she asked the dean if he had a keen idea.
Jean said the dean had nine keen ideas.

MODULE 9

Real-Time Co-Authoring on OneDrive

Real-Time Co-Authoring on OneDrive
Palmetto Event Solutions, Inc.

LEARNING OUTCOMES

- Set up an account and use OneDrive.
- Upload *Word* documents to OneDrive.
- Share folders and documents.
- Edit documents using real-time co-authoring.

New Commands

GETTING STARTED WITH ONEDRIVE

OneDrive is an integral part of *Windows 10* that provides free online (cloud) storage for your documents, photos, videos, and audio files. You may already have set up your OneDrive when you downloaded *Windows 10*. If this is the first use of OneDrive on your computer, you may have to sign in with your Microsoft account. An Internet connection and a Microsoft account is required.

To access OneDrive

1. Open the Start menu, and click on OneDrive. If you do not see OneDrive, click All Apps and select OneDrive. You can also access OneDrive using the navigation menu of File Explorer.

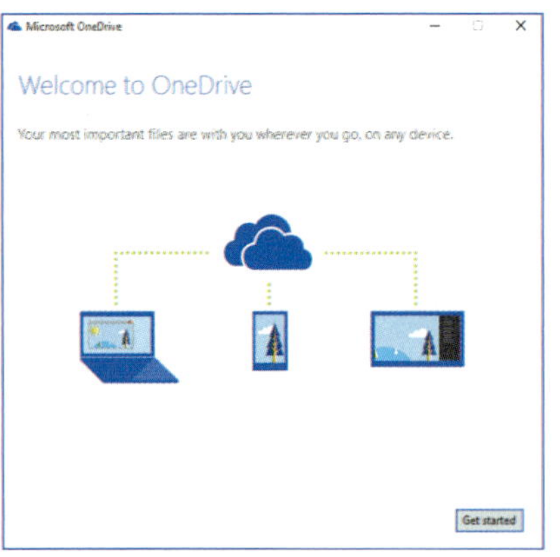

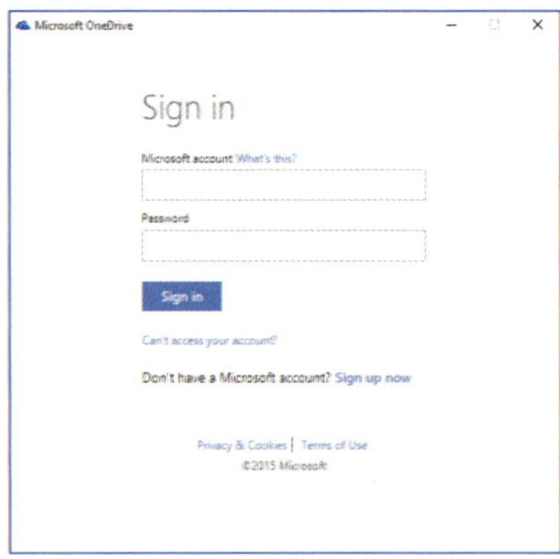

2. Click Get started on the bottom of the Welcome screen; then sign in or follow the directions to get a free Microsoft account.

You can copy or move files to OneDrive. When you create new files, you can use Save As to save them to OneDrive.

Lesson 5 R, Right Shift, C, O

Warmup *Lesson 5a Warmup*

home keys 1 a; ad add al all lad fad jak ask lass fall jak lad

t/h/i/n 2 the hit tin nit then this kith dint tine hint thin

left shift/. 3 I need ink. Li has an idea. Hank hit it. I see Kate.

all reaches 4 Jeff ate at ten; he left a salad dish in the sink.

New Keys

5b r and Right Shift

r Reach *up* with *left first* finger.

right shift Reach *down* with *right fourth* finger; shift, tap, release.

r

5 r rf rf riff riff fir fir rid ire jar air sir lair

6 rf rid ark ran rat are hare art rant tire dirt jar

7 rare dirk ajar lark rain kirk share hart rail tart

right shift

8 D D Dan Dan Dale Ti Sal Ted Ann Ed Alf Ada Sid Fan

9 and Sid and Dina and Allen and Eli and Dean and Ed

10 Ed Dana; Dee Falk; Tina Finn; Sal Alan; Anna Deeds

5c All Reaches Learned

11 Jane and Ann hiked in the sand; Asa set the tents.

12 a rake; a jar; a tree; a red fire; a fare; a rain;

13 Fred Derr and Rai Tira dined at the Tree Art Fair.

5d Improve Keystroking

Key each line once.

14 ir ir ire fir first air fair fire tire rid sir

15 fir jar tar fir flit rill till list stir dirt fire

16 Renee is ill. Fred read to her. Ed Finn left here.

17 All is still as Sarah and I fish here in the rain.

18 I still see a red ash tree that fell in the field.

19 Lana said she did sail her skiff in the dark lake.

8-d7

Compose Memo

palmetto memo form

1. Compose the memo; use subject **Wexford Information Requested**.
2. Read the report you printed in 8-d5 for reference in composing this memo. The report will be attached to the email along with this memo when it is sent to Jennifer Anderson.
3. Tell her that you have obtained the information about the Wexford Conference Center that she requested, and you think Wexford is ideal for her client.
4. Things to point out include how easy Julie Anders, the director, is to work with; the great facilities; and how cost-effective it will be. Include the options, but recommend the 80 percent room guarantee with all meals at Wexford if they have a need for that many rooms.
5. Note that the A/V situation is state-of-the-art (see report).
6. Remember the notes are rough and unorganized. Organize your thoughts, write complete sentences, and edit your memo very carefully. Check to see that you included all information requested. Remember to use the report for information as needed.
7. Save and close. (*8-d7*)

Please draft a memo for me to Jennifer Anderson in our Northwest Office. Be sure to include the recommendations we agreed on. My handwritten notes are shown below for your reference.

RB

Information based on client's estimate of 75 to 90 rooms needed.

Options:

- *Guarantee 70% rooms get 50% discount—A/V, media and equipment needed and use of Oak Room & computer lab. 80%—A/V free.*
- *80% all rooms plus all meals for participants; entire facility limited to your group except remaining residence rooms.*
- *Best food deals—buffet in dining room best breakfast & lunch; combination of themed buffets and seated dinners night meals. Outdoor recpts—especially gazebo area super if weather OK.*

Julie Anders will provide negotiated room rate by email tomorrow. Might get suites for senior managers at same rate as room with 80% guar. Also requested discounted rates golf and tennis for one afternoon; menus for food selection and pricing.

5e c and o

© Cengage Learning

c Reach *down* with *left second* finger.

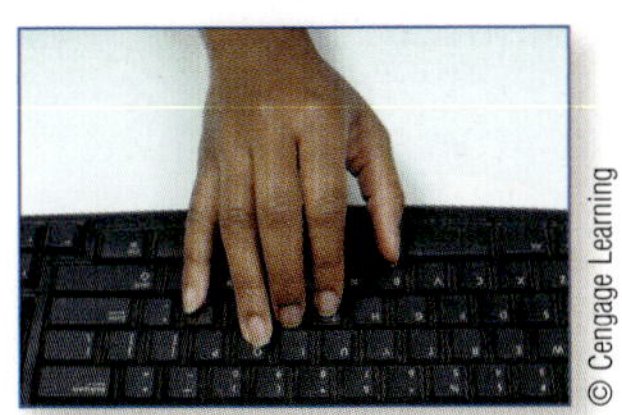
© Cengage Learning

o Reach *up* with *right third* finger.

c

20 c c cd cd cad cad can can tic ice sac cake cat sic
21 clad chic cite cheek clef sick lick kick dice rice
22 call acid hack jack lack lick cask crack clan cane

o

23 o ol ol old old of off odd ode or ore oar soar one
24 ol sol sold told dole do doe lo doll sol solo odor
25 onto door toil lotto soak fort hods foal roan load

Skill Building

5f Improve Keystroking

o/r
26 or or for for nor nor ore ore oar oar roe roe sore
27 a rose|her or|he or|he rode|or for|a door|her doll

e/n
28 en en end end ne ne need need ken ken kneel kneels
29 lend the|lend the|at the end|at the end|need their

c/o
30 ch ch check check ck ck hack lack jack co co cones
31 the cot|the cot|a dock|a dock|a jack|a jack|a cone

all reaches
32 Carlo Rand can call Rocco; Cole can call Doc Cost.
33 Trina can ask Dina if Nick Corl has left; Joe did.
34 Case sent Carole a nice skirt; it fits Lorna Rich.

5g Build Skill

i/t
35 is is tis tis it it fit fit tie tie this this lits
36 it is|it is|it is this|it is this|it sits|tie fits

all reaches
37 Jack and Rona did frost nine of the cakes at last.
38 Jo can ice her drink if Tess can find her a flask.
39 Ask Jean to call Fisk at noon; he needs her notes.

3. Key and format the following table; place it below the paragraph in which it is referenced in the report. Insert an en dash from Special Characters.

Lunch buffet in dining room	$10.00
Lunch in a separate meeting room	$12.00–$18.50
Theme buffet in the evening	$20.00
Seated dinners in the dining room	$25.50–$75.00
Indoor and outdoor receptions	$15.50–$50.00

   a. Size column A 4.5" wide and column B 2" wide.
   b. Add a row above row 1 and merge the cells; increase row height to 0.4".
   c. Key the table title **Meal Charges Per Person**; apply 16-point font.
   d. Apply Grid Table 4 – Accent 1 table style. Apply Align Center format to the title and Align Center Left to the remaining cells.
   e. Apply 0.3" row height to the rows with data.
   f. In the Table Style Options group on the Design tab, remove the check from the first column. Then center the table horizontally and print.

4. Print a copy of this report; you will use it in *8-d7*.
5. Save and close. (*8-d5*)

8-d6

Newsletter

pen newsletter
pen
new office

Format the open *pen* data file as follows:

1. Open *pen newsletter* from the data files and insert *pen* from the data files. Size it .05" high. Position in Top Left with Square Text Wrapping. See the illustration at the right.
2. Insert Fill – Black, Text 1, Outline – Background 1, Hard Shadow – Accent 1 WordArt (second icon in bottom row). Select the text and key **The Pen—Kansas City News**. Reduce the font size to 28 point. Position in Top Right with Square Text Wrapping.
3. Select the text and apply two-column format.
4. Apply Heading 1 format to each of the headings.
5. Insert the *new office* picture from the data files. Size it 2" high. Position in Bottom Right with Square Text Wrapping. Then drag it to the center of the column.
6. Save and close. (*8-d6*)

The Newsletter Committee has written the articles for The Pen; please format so we can send it to Hilton Head.

RB

TIP

If Heading 3 is not displayed in the Styles group on the Home tab, click Heading 2. Note that Heading 3 will then display.

The Pen—Kansas City News

The Kansas City office is celebrating its best quarter since the regional office was established two years ago. All of our major success indicators—revenue, events managed, expense control, new clients, support of other regions, and community engagement—are at all-time highs. You will receive our standard quarterly report in a few days.

Team Support

This month we are providing support for one or more projects in each of our regional offices. Our newest project is helping our Portland team secure the Wexford Conference Center for a client with offices throughout the United States for the first of several three-day leadership seminars for its senior managers. The Wexford Center is ideal for that type of event, and we are confident that we will be able to attract many more events with the relationship we have established with Julie Anders, the director of the center. The team concept that was envisioned when the regional offices were established is really paying off. The synergy created is primarily responsible for our increased success.

Congratulations Ryan Ellison

Ryan, the creative director in our office, won the company-wide contest to name our newsletter, The Pen. He also provided the logo to emphasize that we have a strong heritage, but at the same time we are a leading edge, technology savvy company. The pen represents both the traditional pen and the computer pen. Ryan received a $500 bonus for his creative work.

Thanks Hilton Head HR

The Hilton Head human resources staff has agreed to coordinate the newsletter with each regional office providing one page of articles each month. This really simplifies the task for all of us, and we appreciate the support.

New Office Location

Space in the building across the street from our current offices opened up this week. We were able to lease new facilities very similar to our current offices, but a little larger. We gained a large conference room, three additional offices, and a very large team work and meeting space. The new building, shown below, is owned by the same company that owns our current building so they are making our transition to the new offices very easy. They released us from our current lease, and we negotiated the same rate for the new facilities. The actual move is scheduled to occur in two weeks

Lesson 5R Review

Warmup *Lesson 5Ra Warmup*

r/c/o/right shift 1	circle order record Frank Sarah Tonia Carlo candor
r/c/o 2	effort trick scroll control clone donor salon corn
right shift 3	Sandra Forde Addie Crone Stan Allison Rhonda candor
all reaches 4	Jeff drank his cold tea and ate cookies in a tent.

Skill Building

Think and key words and phrases as units.

5Rb Improve Keystroking

1. Key each line once.
2. Keep your eyes on the copy.

words 5	choice rejoice north crank drank cross craft order
6	creaked kitchen store lost frost train rained horn
phrases 7	to the east | I left at noon | reach it | he liked Janet
8	Fred chose one | Connie cooked | Daniel ate fried food
sentences 9	Carl and Jack left for a short train ride at noon.
10	Lee and Jo can cook for their friends in the tent.

5Rc Build Skill

o/r 11	or cork for nor sore tore rote lore snore ore core
12	his or her | she rode | at the door | she tore her skirt
c/o 13	close choose color cork corn coal ocean cold scorn
14	close the door | choose a color | for a dock | cook corn
all reaches 15	Joan and Clark selected a nice color for the dock.
16	Dick sent Lori a nice skirt and Frank a red shirt.

5Rd Timed Writing

1. Key a 1' timing; use wordwrap—do not return at the end of the line. If you finish before time is up, begin again.
2. Key a 1' timed writing at a slower but fluent pace.

wordwrap

Connie said that her son can cook for her friends at noon. He is a trained chef and likes to cook for others. He can locate and choose the food. Harold offered to do all of the dishes. I think that is also a nice offer.

8-d5

Report with Table

wexford facilities

Prepare a draft of the following report:

1. Apply the following formats in the open document:
   a. Apply Title style to the title.
   b. Apply Heading 1 style to all headings except for the specific meeting and training rooms that follow the meeting facilities paragraph.
   c. Apply Heading 2 to the meeting and training rooms listed.
   d. Number the pages at the top of the page using Plain Number 3. Do not number the first page.
2. Key Insert #1 after the paragraph below the Guest Accommodations heading and Insert #2 after the paragraph below the Summit and Lakeview Rooms. Apply Heading 1 format to the headings in Insert #2.

Our Northwest Regional VP requested a report on the Wexford Center for a three-day leadership seminar for one of her Portland clients. I talked with her today, and she agreed Wexford is the best choice for her client.

RB

<u>Insert #1</u>

In addition to the on-site fitness center, extensive fitness and recreational facilities are available at the nearby Oak Park SportsPlex. Guests can access tennis, swimming, golf, walking trails, and a host of other activities with less than a five-minute ride on the free Wexford shuttle.

<u>Insert #2</u>

Outdoor Functions

The patios and large gazebo area provide excellent venues for receptions and picnics when the weather is appropriate for outdoor functions. Large climate-controlled tents can also be rented for special functions.

Food Service

The Wexford dining room provides full breakfast and lunch buffets for residential guests and for conference functions that do not have group meals for participants. Chef Pat receives rave reviews for the theme buffets he offers in the evening. The Wexford lounge is open daily from 5:00 p.m. until 11:00 p.m.

Meals are competitively priced. The following table shows the meal prices per person. Prices shown in ranges vary depending on the menu selection.

The chef requests that the number of participants for meal events be confirmed at least 24 hours in advance.

(continued)

Lesson 6 W, Comma, B, P

Warmup *Lesson 6a Warmup*

home row 1 ask a lad; a fall fad; had a salad; ask a sad jak;

o/t 2 to do it; to toil; as a tot; do a lot; he told her

c/r 3 cots are; has rocks; roll cot; is rich; has an arc

all reaches 4 Holt can see Dane at ten; Jill sees Frank at nine.

New Keys 

6b w and , (comma)

w Reach *up* with *left third* finger.

, (comma) Reach *down* with *right second* finger.

w

5 w ws ws was was wan wit low win jaw wilt wink wolf

6 sw sw w sow ow now now row row own own wow wow owe

7 to sew; to own; was rich; was in; is how; will now

, (comma)

8 k, k, k, irk, ilk, ask, oak, ark, lark, jak, rock,

9 skis, a dock, a fork, a lock, a fee, a tie, a fan,

10 Joe, Ed, and I saw Nan, Ann, and Wes in a new car.

6c All Reaches Learned

11 Win, Lew, Drew, and Walt will walk to West Willow.

12 Ask Ho, Al, and Jared to read the code; it is new.

13 The window, we think, was closed; we felt no wind.

6d Improve Techniques

Key each line once.

Good posture builds an attitude of preciseness.

14 walk wide sown wild town went jowl wait white down

15 a dock, a kit, a wick, a lock, a row, a cow, a fee

16 Joe lost to Ron; Fiji lost to Cara; Don lost to Al

17 Kane will win; Nan will win; Rio will win; Di wins

18 Walter is in Reno; Tia is in Tahoe; then to Hawaii

8-d4

Table

Prepare the following budget to present to Ms. Miguel for approval.

1. Tap ENTER three times, and key the table shown below; then apply the following formats.
2. Add a column between columns B and C and key the following data: **Unit Cost, $24.50, 65.75, 250.00, 4.25,** and **3.75.**
3. Insert a row above the column heads; merge all cells in the row. Set the row height at 0.5". Key the table title **Pre-Grand Opening Celebration Budget** using 16-point font.
4. Apply Grid Table 4 – Accent 1. Apply Align Center to Table title.
5. Change the row height of rows 2–8 to 0.3". Apply Align Center and bold to the column heads.
6. Align text in the columns as follows—A: Align Center Left, B: Align Center, C and D: Align Center Right.
7. Save and close. (*8-d4*)

Description	Quantity/Number	Estimated Cost
Food/beverage	120	$2,940.00
Floral arrangements	4	263.00
Decorations	1	250.00
Party favors	125	531.25
Invitations/mailing	150	562.50
Total cost		$4,546.75

QUICK ✓

Check your document against the illustration below.

Pre-Grand Opening Celebration Budget			
Description	**Quantity/Number**	**Unit Cost**	**Estimated Cost**
Food/beverage	120	$24.50	$2,940.00
Floral arrangements	4	65.75	263.00
Decorations	1	250.00	250.00
Party favors	125	4.25	531.25
Invitations/mailing	150	3.75	562.50
Total cost			$4,546.75

6e b and p

© Cengage Learning

b Reach *down* with *left first* finger.

© Cengage Learning

p Reach *up* with *right fourth* (little) finger.

b

19 bf bf bf biff fib fib bib bib boa boa fib fibs rob
20 bf bf bf ban ban bon bon bow bow be be rib rib sob
21 a dob, a cob, a crib, a lab, a slab, a bid, a bath

p

22 p; p; pa pa; pal pal pan pan pad par pen pep paper
23 pa pa; lap lap; nap nap; hep ape spa asp leap clap
24 a park, a pan, a pal, a pad, apt to pop, a pair of

Skill Building

6f Improve Keystroking

all reaches learned

25 Barb and Bob wrapped a pepper in paper and ribbon.
26 Rip, Joann, and Dick were all closer to the flash.
27 Bo will be pleased to see Japan; he works in Oslo.

reach review

28 ki kid did aid lie hj has has had sw saw wits will
29 de dell led sled jn an en end ant hand k, end, kin

s/w

30 ws ws lows now we shown win cow wow wire jowl when
31 Wes saw an owl in the willow tree in the old lane.

b/p

32 bf bf fib rob bid ;p p; pal pen pot nap hop cap bp
33 Rob has both pans in a bin at the back of the pen.

6g Build Skill

34 to do | can do | to bow | ask her | to nap | to work | is born
35 for this | if she | is now | did all | to see | or not | or if

all reaches

36 Dick owns a dock at this lake; he paid Ken for it.
37 Jane also kept a pair of owls, a hen, and a snake.

38 Blair soaks a bit of the corn, as he did in Japan.
39 I blend the cocoa in the bowl when I work for Leo.

8-d2

Memo

palmetto memo form

1. Prepare the following memo:
   a. Use the information provided below to complete the heading on the memo.
   b. Use Find and Replace to locate *contract* each time it is used and replace it with **agreement**.
2. Save and close. (*8-d2*)

This memo will be distributed to Haley Edwards, Jackson Moore, Lance Davis, and Cristina Kulchar with a copy to Karl Metze.

RB

To: Senior Executives | Subject: Miguel Contract

Miguel Enterprises accepted the Palmetto Event Solutions proposal to manage the grand opening and marketing of the new Miguel Emporium. Elena Miguel called me today to indicate that she had signed the contract without any modifications whatsoever, and she was having it hand delivered to us today.

Ms. Miguel also requested that our senior staff, as well as the Miguel Enterprises senior account manager, meet with her next Tuesday at 10:30 a.m. in our offices. Please plan to attend this important session, which will take place in the Board Room.

Marlene Delhomme, who is no longer with us, was the account manager responsible for the last two Miguel events. Karl Metze has been assigned as the senior account manager for the Miguel account. Please work with Karl on the proposed plan that we will present at the meeting.

c Karl Metze

8-d3

Invitation

invitation
miguel logo

Format the invitation as follows:

1. Open *invitation* from the data files and center each line except the *rsvp*, which should be left-aligned. *Note:* Miguel uses the Depth theme.
2. Apply Lucida Calligraphy 16-point font and Light Green, Accent 2, Darker 50% color to all text; use 2.5 line spacing.
3. Remove the space after the paragraph on each line, and change orientation to landscape.
4. Use the Insert Picture command to insert the company logo, *miguel logo*, at the top of the page. Change the size of the logo to 1" high, and use Center alignment on the Home tab to position the logo.
5. Save and close. (*8-d3*)

Please format the draft invitation Sarah created. It is saved as invitation in the data files.

RB

Lesson 7 Review

Warmup *Lesson 7a Warmup*

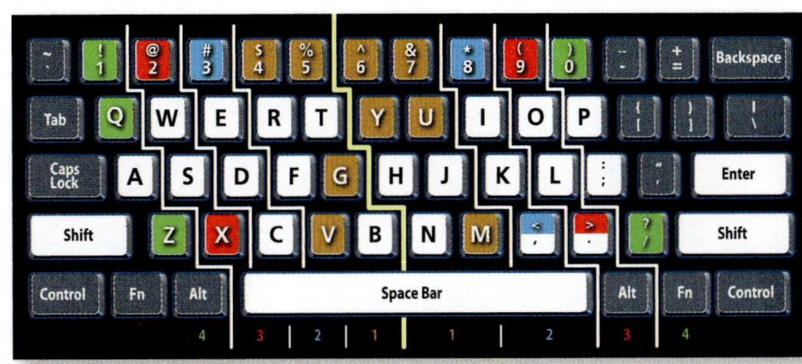

all 1 We often can take the older jet to Paris and back.
home 2 a; sl dk fj a;sl dkfj ad as all ask fads adds asks
1st row 3 Ann Bascan and Cabal Naban nabbed a cab in Canada.
3rd row 4 Rip went to a water show with either Pippa or Pia.

7b Improve Keystroking

5 ad la as in if it lo no of oh he or so ok pi be we
6 an ace ads ale aha a fit oil a jak nor a bit a pew
7 ice ades born is fake to jail than it and the cows
8 Ask Jed. Dr. Hand left at ten; Dr. Crowe, at nine.

Skill Building

7c Improve Techniques

Key each line once.

Keep your eyes on the textbook copy as you key.

9 ws ws was was wan wan wit wit pew paw nap pop bawl
10 bf bf fb fb fob fob rib rib be be job job bat back
11 p; p; asp asp pan pan ap ap ca cap pa nap pop prow
12 Barb and Bret took an old black robe and the boot.
13 Walt saw a wisp of white water renew ripe peppers.
14 Pat picked a black pepper for the picnic at Parks.

7d Build Skill

15 Jake held a bit of cocoa and an apricot for Diane.
16 Dick and I fish for cod on the docks at Fish Lake.
17 Kent still held the dish and the cork in his hand.
18 As far as I know, he did not read all of the book.

Do not prepare envelopes. In this office, most documents are distributed as attachments to email. Documents will be distributed after Ms. Barnett adds her electronic signature or initials.

KANSAS CITY OFFICE

You will report to Ms. Rachel Barnett, the Midwest Regional Vice President. She follows the SOPs and often leaves directions on yellow sticky notes. Check each document to make sure you have used or done the following:

- Office theme for all documents.
- Use the Kansas City letterhead and the standard memo form for all letters and memos. Use block letter style with open punctuation.
- Note the standard for bulleting items has been changed. Use the new square bullet style with Blue, Accent 5 color.
- Unless directed otherwise, use the salutation *Dear + personal title and last name*, such as Dear Ms. Miguel.
- Unless otherwise directed, use: **Sincerely** | **Rachel C. Barnett** | **Regional Vice President** for the closing lines. Position the name and title on two lines; do not use a title on any documents sent to Palmetto Event Solutions offices.
- Provide an appropriate subject line for memos and emails if one is not provided.
- Use the current date unless instructed otherwise.
- Add your reference initials, attachment notation, and copy notations as needed.
- Ensure that all documents are error-free. Use proofing tools and then edit, proofread, and correct errors. Verify dates and numerical data against the source.

8-d1

Letter

palmetto letterhead - kansas city

1. Prepare the following letter for Ms. Barnett with all necessary letter parts.
2. Save and close. (*8-d1*)

Send the letter to:

Ms. Elena T. Miguel,
President

Miguel Enterprises, Inc.

One Ward Parkway

Kansas City, MO 64114-2601

Ms. Barnett does not put the name of the attachment on the letter because it will be displayed on the email used to transmit the letter and attachment. Just key *Attachment* to call attention to it.

Thank you for accepting our proposal to manage the grand opening and marketing of your new gift shop, Miguel Emporium. We are very pleased to have the opportunity to work with you on another new store opening.

The senior staff of Palmetto Event Solutions, Inc. would be happy to meet with you next Tuesday at 10:30 a.m. in our offices as you requested. Prior to that meeting, we will prepare a proposed plan for the grand opening event. As we discussed, we will build on the same model that we used on your previous store openings.

Please sign the attached agreement and return one copy to us. We look forward to helping you make this a memorable event.

7e Textbook Keying

Key each line once.

Words: key as single unit; phrases: say and key fluently; sentences: work for fluency.

words 19 a an pan so sot la lap ah own do doe el elf to tot
phrases 20 if it | to do | it is | do so | for the | he works | if he bid
sentences 21 Jess ate all of the peas in the salad in the bowl.

words 22 bow bowl pin pint for fork forks hen hens jak jaks
phrases 23 is for | did it | is the | we did a | and so | to see | or not
sentences 24 I hid the ace in a jar as a joke; I do not see it.

words 25 chap chaps flak flake flakes prow prowl work works
phrases 26 as for the | as for the | and to the | to see it | and did
sentences 27 As far as I know, he did not read all of the book.

7f Timed Writing

1. Take two 1' timed writings. If you finish before time is up, begin again.
2. Use wordwrap; do not tap ENTER at the ends of the lines.

Goal: 12 *gwam*

wordwrap

gwam 1'

It is hard to fake a confident spirit. We will do 10
better work if we approach and finish a job and 19
know that we will do the best work we can and then 29
not fret. 31

| 1 | 2 | 3 | 4 | 5 | 6 | 7 | 8 | 9 | 10 |

7g Build Speed

STANDARD PLAN For Building Speed

You can build speed by practicing diligently and purposefully.

1. Focus on short timings and gradually increase the length.
2. Ignore errors.
3. Key the line first striving for fluency; do not time.
4. Take short timings (30") and gradually increase the length.
5. Strive to increase speed on each timing.

1. Key each line once for fluency.
2. Take two 30" writings on each line. Do not save the timings.

Goal: Reach the end of the line before time is up.

28 Dan took her to the show.
29 Jan lent the bowl to the pros.
30 Hold the wrists low for this drill.
31 Jessie fit the black panel to the shelf.
32 Patrick cooked breakfast for Jill and her friends.

MODULE 8

Palmetto Event Solutions, Inc.

Lessons 54–55 *Palmetto Event Solutions, Inc.*

LEARNING OUTCOMES

- Apply keying, formatting, and word processing skills.
- Work independently with few instructions.

Warmup *Lesson 54a Warmup*

lesson 54a warmup

Skill Building

54b Timed Writing

Key two 3' timed writings. Strive for control.

gwam 3'

Voting is a very important part of being a good citizen. However, 4 | 81
many young people who are eligible to vote choose not to do so. When 9 | 86
asked to explain or justify their decision, many individuals simply 13 | 90
shrug their shoulders and reply that they have no particular reason 18 | 95
for not voting. The explanation others frequently give is that they 22 | 99
just did not get around to going to the polls. 25 | 102
A good question to consider concerns ways that we can motivate 29 | 107
young people to be good citizens and to go to the polls and to vote. 34 | 111
Some people approach this topic by trying to determine how satisfied 39 | 116
people who do not vote are with the performance of their elected 43 | 120
officials. Unfortunately, those who choose not to vote are just as 47 | 124
satisfied with their elected officials as those who voted. 51 | 128
One interesting phenomenon concerning voting relates to the job 55 | 132
market. When the job market is strong, fewer young people vote than 60 | 137
when the job market is very bad. They also tend to be less satisfied 64 | 141
with their elected officials. Self-interest seems to be a powerful 69 | 146
motivator. Unfortunately, those who do not choose to vote miss the 73 | 150
point that it is in their best interest to be a good citizen. 77 | 154

3' | 1 | 2 | 3 | 4 |

Project Setting

PALMETTO EVENT SOLUTIONS, INC.

In this project, you are an executive assistant in the Kansas City office. This experience gives you an opportunity to apply the document formatting and word processing skills that you learned in Modules 3–7. Review the SOPs that are summarized on the next page, and apply them to your work.

Saving and Naming Documents

Set up a folder named Palmetto Event Solutions. Save each document as 8-d + the document number. (*8-d1*, *8-d2*, *8-d3*, etc.)

Lesson 8 G, Question Mark, X, U

Warmup *Lesson 8a Warmup*

all 1 Dick will see Job at nine if Rach sees Pat at one.
w/b 2 As the wind blew, Bob Webber saw the window break.
p/, 3 Pat, Pippa, or Cap has prepared the proper papers.
all 4 Bo, Jose, and Will fed Lin; Jack had not paid her.

New Keys

8b g and ? (question mark)

g Reach to *right* with *left first* finger.

? Left SHIFT; reach *down* with *right fourth* finger.

Question mark: The question mark is followed by one space.

g

5 g g gf gaff gag grog fog frog drag cog dig fig gig
6 gf go gall flag gels slag gala gale glad glee gals
7 golf flog gorge glen high logs gore ogle page grow

? (question mark)

8 ? ?; ?; ? ? Who? When? Where? Who is? Who was she?
9 Who is here? Was it she? Was it he? Did Pablos go?
10 Did Geena? Did he? What is that? Was Joe here too?

8c All Reaches Learned

11 Has Ginger lost her job? Were her last bills here?
12 Phil did not want the boats to get here this soon.
13 Loris Shin has been ill; Frank, a doctor, saw her.

8d Improve Keystroking

1. Key each line once.
2. Keep your eyes on the textbook copy.

reach review
14 ws ws hj hj tf tf ol ol rf rf ed ed cd cd bf bf p;
15 wed bid has old hold rid heed heed car bed pot pot

g
16 gf gf gin gin rig ring go gone no nog sign got dog
17 to go | to go | go on | go in | go in | to go in | in the sign

?
18 ?; ?;? who? when? where? how? what? who? It is he?
19 Is she? Is he? Did I lose Paul? Is Gabe all right?

Day Three Highlights

On this day, you go back in time about 2,000 years to visit the ancient city, Pompeii. It is often called the forgotten city because the volcano Mount Vesuvius erupted and buried residences, temples, artwork, and many other objects. You will have a full-day tour to visit the ruins and excavations as well as the surrounding areas.

Day Four Highlights

On this day, you select the surrounding city or town from a number of options that you would like to tour. Our staff will provide you with information about the many alternatives and will arrange your transportation to the desired destination.

Day Five Highlights

You can relax, swim, golf, play tennis, visit the spa, shop, or do whatever you would like as you prepare for your departure. Our final evening is a memorable banquet and gala with the award presentations followed by dancing.

Discover

Remove Space Before Paragraph

Home/Paragraph/Line and Paragraph Spacing

1. Position the insertion point in the heading.
2. Click Remove Space Before Paragraph.

3. Select the text and format it in two equal-width columns. Insert a Continuous section break at the end of the second column to balance the columns.
4. Apply Heading 1 format to each of the headings; then remove the space before each of the headings.
5. Key the title, **Amalfi Coast—Here We Come** at the second paragraph marker above the Continuous section break; apply 28-point Heading font.
6. Apply Text Effects: Fill – Blue, Accent 1, Shadow. Center the title.
7. Insert the *isle of capri boat trip* data file; size it 2.5" high. Position in Middle Center with Square Text Wrapping.
8. Save and close. (*53-d3*)

53-d4

Compose

palmetto memo form

Several employees have suggested that it would be nice to have an electronic employee newsletter with information supplied by each office. You talked with Mr. Tremblay about it, and he asked you to compose a memo to all Palmetto executive assistants.

1. Tell them about the suggestion and ask them to discuss it with their colleagues to determine the level of interest.
2. List questions that would need to be answered and ask everyone to share their thoughts on each question. The following examples are just to help you get started.
   a. What types of information would be included? Business activities and results from each office? Information about employees and their families? Company news? Tips for being more effective, etc.
   b. Who would report news from each office? Who would coordinate and distribute it?
   c. How often? How long would it be? What would it be named?
3. Save and close. (*53-d4*)

New Keys

8e x and u

x Reach *down* with *left third* finger.

u Reach *up* with *right first* finger.

Concentrate on correct reaches.

x

```
20 x x xs xs ox ox lox sox fox box ex hex lax hex fax
21 sx six sax sox ax fix cox wax hex box pox sex text
22 flax next flex axel pixel exit oxen taxi axis next
```

u

```
23 u uj uj jug jut just dust dud due sue use due duel
24 uj us cud but bun out sun nut gun hut hue put fuel
25 dual laud dusk suds fuss full tuna tutus duds full
```

Skill Building

8f Improve Keystroking

Think and key phrases.

```
26 Paige Power liked the book; Josh can read it next.
27 Next we picked a bag for Jan; then she, Jan, left.
28 Is her June account due? Has Jo ruined her credit?
29 nut cue hut sun rug us six cut dug axe rag fox run
30 out of the sun|cut the action|a fox den|fun at six
31 That car is not junk; it can run in the next race.
```

8g Timed Writing

1. Take two 1' timed writings. If you finish before time is up, begin again. (The dot above various words equals 2 *gwam*; each number is another 4 *gwam*.)
2. Use wordwrap; do not tap ENTER at the end of lines.

Goal: 14 *gwam*

wordwrap

```
How a finished job will look often depends on how
we feel about our work as we do it. Attitude has
a definite effect on the end result of work we do.
```

Tap ENTER once

```
When we are eager to begin a job, we relax and do
better work than if we start the job with an idea
that there is just nothing we can do to escape it.
```

Begin new paragraph →

I also encourage you to add an extra day to the length of the retreat and devote it to an intensive seminar entitled Upscale Corporate Marketing. This past quarter, our marketing team worked with a marketing consultant focusing on using an upscale, in-home event for senior executives of our top ten clients. We experimented with one event that produced very interesting results that we would like to share at the retreat. The setting for the event is shown below.

53-d3

Newsletter

isle of capri boat trip

You are working with Mason James, the senior event planning manager in the Toronto office, on a reward trip for one of your major clients, Market Trust Insurance Company. This is the third time the Toronto team has planned the annual reward trip. It is an all-expense paid trip for the 25 CEOs and their spouses of insurance companies that provide Market Trust the most revenue for the previous year. Your job is to prepare a one-page newsletter providing a few trip highlights that will be emailed to each attendee one week before their departure to get participants excited about the trip. They will have a complete packet of information when they arrive at the resort.

1. Apply Moderate margins. Turn Show/Hide on. Tap ENTER three times.
2. Key the newsletter shown below. Then follow directions to format the document.

One week from today you will arrive at the five-star Palazzo Ravello on the cliffs of the medieval town of Ravello for five exciting days on the Amalfi Coast of Italy! The spectacular view from your balcony high above the Mediterranean is simply breathtaking. Luxurious rooms with exquisite furnishings; impeccable service; a rooftop sun terrace; gym; spa; outdoor pool; three restaurants including a world-renowned, highly rated fine dining restaurant; and many other amenities await you.

Day One Highlights

Your first day is designed to be a relaxing one. You can have a delightful lunch on the Cliff Terrace overlooking the Mediterranean or at the Grille near the pool. A ten-minute walk will bring you to the Town Square with shops featuring hand-painted china and a variety of other art objects as well as a panoramic view of the area. The day ends with a reception and dinner so that you will have the opportunity to meet all of the President's Award Trip winners.

Day Two Highlights

Get your camera ready for a sightseeing boat trip around the Amalfi Coast and to the Isle of Capri. Bring your bathing suit if you want to swim in the Mediterranean near one of the famous grottos on the mountainous side of the island or at the Isle of Capri beach. You will have a sightseeing tour in a convertible and a delightful lunch. In the evening, transportation will be provided to some of the local dinner and entertainment places.

(continued)

Lesson 8R Review

Warmup *Lesson 8Ra Warmup*

```
reach review  1 Jack is glad about the response to the fundraiser.
           p  2 The local paper printed their public opinion poll.
           b  3 Four babies babbled as big bears rode brown bikes.
        easy  4 The newest prices were not shown to her and to me.
```

Skill Building

8Rb Improve Techniques

1. Key each line once.
2. Keep your eyes on the copy.

Move fingers up and down without moving your hands.

```
home row     5 add hash shall slash salads flags alfalfa fall ask
             6 A fresh salad dish was added for staff and guests.

third row    7 tire wrote rewrite ripe proper papers trip picture
             8 A reporter edited the newspaper stories with ease.

1st/2nd      9 returned guest changes kicked tonight flight drink
fingers     10 Ed kept doing kind deeds for the children in need.
```

8Rc Timed Writing

1. Take two 1' timed writings. If you finish before time is up, begin again.
2. Use wordwrap; do not tap ENTER at the ends of the lines.

```
                                                        gwam 1'
Luck looks at those who are prepared for it. Think          10
about what is needed to be where one should be in a         21
decade. What will it take? Will it take additional          31
education or perhaps just other experience? One sets        41
a large goal and then works through a series of other      52
lesser goals to get there. One needs to be able to          62
know what success looks like as one finishes one of         73
the goals to get to the next one. If one does it            83
well, people will think it was all luck.                    91
| 1 | 2 | 3 | 4 | 5 | 6 | 7 | 8 | 9 | 10 |
```

8Rd Build Speed

Key two 30" timings on each line. Try to increase your speed the second time.

```
We use the web and work online.
We shop online and use social networks.
The web helps us as we work and share data.
While working online, we need to keep our data safe.
```

53-d1

Organization Chart

A client who is considering a proposal for a project that Mr. Tremblay submitted has requested an organization chart showing the Senior Management Team. Abbreviate Vice President (VP) on the chart. Note from the Quick Check that you will need to add additional shapes.

1. Insert a SmartArt Name and Title Organization chart from the Hierarchy category, and include the members of the Senior Management Team:
   a. **Garrett Russell, President and CEO**
   b. **Ellen Miller, Executive Assistant**
   c. **Jennifer Anderson, Northwest Regional VP**
   d. **Rachel Barnett, Midwest Regional VP**
   e. **Aydyn Ellison, Chief Financial Officer**
   f. **Gabriel Tremblay, Canada Regional VP**
   g. **Carlos Torres, Southwest Regional VP**
2. Size the chart 3.5" high and 6.5" wide; position it in the Top Center with Square Text Wrapping.
3. Save and close. (*53-d1*)

Compare your document to the one shown below.

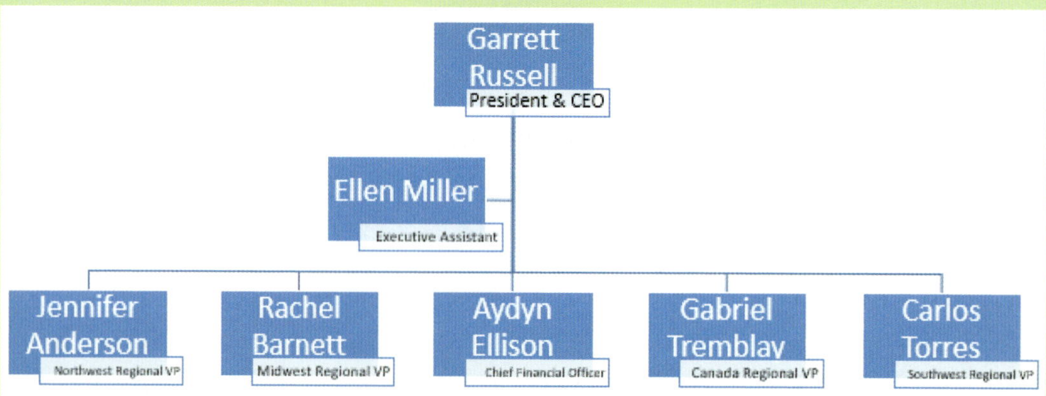

53-d2

Memo with Graphics

upscale in-home event
palmetto memo form

Prepare the memo below for Mr. Tremblay; he will attach it to an email to the Senior Management Team.

1. Use the current date and subject line: **Senior Management Team Retreat.**
2. Tap ENTER after the last paragraph and insert the *upscale in-home event* picture from the data files. Size it 3.5" high and apply Center from the Home tab.
3. Save and close. (*53-d2*)

The last Senior Management Team Retreats were in Portland and Hilton Head. Please let the Canada Region host this year's Senior Management Team Retreat in Yorkville, a vibrant cultural district of Toronto known for its visual and performing arts, restaurants, upscale shopping, and award-winning Village of Yorkville Park.

(continued)

Lesson 9 Q, M, V, Apostrophe

Warmup *Lesson 9a Warmup*

all letters 1 Lex gripes about cold weather; Fred is not joking.

space bar 2 Is it Di, Jo, or Al? Ask Lt. Coe, Bill; She knows.

easy 3 We did rush a bushel of cut corn to the six ducks.

easy 4 He is to go to the Tudor Isle of England on a bus.

New Keys

9b q and m

© Cengage Learning

q Reach *up* with *left fourth* finger.

© Cengage Learning

m Reach *down* with *right first* finger.

q

5 q qa qa quad quad quaff quant queen quo quit quick

6 qa qu qa quo quit quod quid quip quads quote quiet

7 quite quilts quart quill quakes quail quack quaint

m

8 m mj mj jam man malt mar max maw me mew men hem me

9 m mj ma am make male mane melt meat mist amen lame

10 malt meld hemp mimic tomb foam rams mama mire mind

9c All Reaches Learned

11 Quin had some quiet qualms about taming a macaque.

12 Jake Coxe had questions about a new floor program.

13 Max was quick to join the big reception for Lidia.

9d Improve Keystroking

1. Key each line once; keep your elbows at your side.
2. Keep your eyes on the textbook copy.

m/x

14 me men ma am jam am lax, mix jam; the hem, six men

15 Emma Max expressed an aim to make a mammoth model.

q/u

16 qa qu aqua aqua quit quit quip quite pro quo squad

17 Did Quin make a quick request to take the Qu exam?

g/n

18 fg gn gun gun dig dig nag snag snag sign grab grab

19 Georgia hung a sign in front of the union for Gib.

Lesson 53 Palmetto Event Solutions, Inc.

Learning Outcomes

- Apply keying, formatting, and word processing skills.
- Prepare documents with columns and graphics.
- Work independently with few specific instructions.

Warmup *Lesson 53a Warmup*

lesson 53a warmup

Skill Building

53b Timed Writing

Key two 3' timed writings.

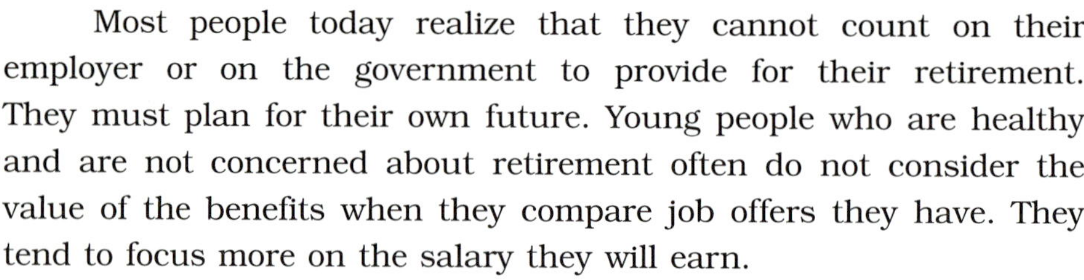

gwam 3'

Most people today realize that they cannot count on their 4 78
employer or on the government to provide for their retirement. 8 82
They must plan for their own future. Young people who are healthy 12 87
and are not concerned about retirement often do not consider the 17 91
value of the benefits when they compare job offers they have. They 21 95
tend to focus more on the salary they will earn. 24 98

Most companies provide some type of health benefits. The 28 102
portion that the employee has to pay tends to vary widely, however. 32 107
Therefore, it is wise to analyze the quality, the type of 36 110
coverage provided, and the cost of the benefits to the employee. 40 115
A lower salary with benefits paid by the company may produce more 45 119
net income than a higher salary with high benefit costs to the 49 123
employee. 49 124

To recruit bright young people who are likely to change jobs 53 128
many times, companies set up portable savings plans that defer 58 132
taxes on income. The company matches a certain percentage of the 62 136
savings to provide incentives for the employee to contribute to 66 140
the plan. Usually the plan vests in less than five years, and 70 144
employees can take the entire amount with them when they leave. 74 149

3' | 1 | 2 | 3 | 4 |

Project Setting

PALMETTO EVENT SOLUTIONS, INC.

For the project in this module, you will be preparing documents for Gabriel Tremblay our Canada Regional Vice President in Toronto. You will use the Toronto letterhead and the standard memo form. You may wish to review the SOPs for Palmetto Events Solutions, the letterhead for contact information, and the *About Us* section on pages 2-36 and 2-37. Do not prepare envelopes or emails to transmit the documents at this time.

As you work through each job and after all jobs are completed, make sure that you have used or done the following:

- Correct letterhead or the memo form for letters and memos.
- Block letter style for letters.
- Office theme for all documents.
- Previewed and proofread documents carefully.

9e v and ' (apostrophe)

v Reach *down* with *left first* finger.

' Reach to the *right* with the *right fourth* finger.

Apostrophe: The apostrophe shows either omission (as Rob't for Robert or it's for it is) or possession when used with nouns (as Joe's hat).

v

20 v vf vf vie vie via via vim vat vow vile vale vote
21 vf vf ave vet ova eve vie dive five live have lave
22 cove dove over aver vivas hive volt five java jive

' (apostrophe)

23 '; '; it's it's Rod's; it's Bo's hat; we'll do it.
24 We don't know if it's Lee's pen or Norma's pencil.
25 It's ten o'clock; I won't tell him that he's late.

Skill Building

9f Improve Keystroking

26 It's Viv's turn to drive Iva's van to Ava's house.
v/? 27 Qua, not Vi, took the jet; so did Owen. Didn't he?
28 Wasn't Vada Baxter a judge at the post garden show?
29 Viola said she has moved six times in five months.
30 Does Dave live on Vines Avenue? Must he leave now?
q/? 31 Did Viv vote? Can Paque move it? Did Valerie quit?
32 Didn't Raquel quit Carl Quent after their quarrel?

9g Timed Writing

Take a 1' timing on each paragraph. If you finish before time is up, start the paragraph again. The dots equal 2 words. Use wordwrap.

wordwrap

The questions of time use are vital ones; we miss so much just because we don't plan. If we structure our week, we save time for those extra premium things we long to do.

List the tasks to be done for the week and then place importance on each one. Complete the tasks in order of importance.

8. Insert an Alternating Flow SmartArt graphic (second icon in the second row) from the Process category.
    a. Click in the line below the Continuous section break and change the column format to one column.
    b. Size the entire graphic 2.25" high and 6.0" wide.
    c. Position it in the Bottom Center with Square Text Wrapping.
    d. Key the text shown below in the SmartArt text pane.
9. Save and close. *(52-d1)*

Architectural Plans
    Contract 6/25
    Approved 3/3
Next Steps
    Groundbreaking 3/18
    Cornerstone Club 3/18
Grand Opening
    Construction contract 6/15
    Completion 12 to 15 months

QUICK ✓

Check your document against the illustration below.

52-d2

Composition

cornerstone club memo form

1. Use the following information to compose a memo to Robbie Holiday from Jeff Crane inviting him to represent the Cornerstone Club at the groundbreaking ceremony. Date it March 5, 201-; add an appropriate subject line. Ask him to confirm his acceptance.
    a. Five people will participate in the ceremony; use the Arena Update for time, date, site, and other information as needed.
    b. Shovels and hardhats will be provided.
    c. Media will be present and may interview participants. Business attire is requested.
2. Edit and proofread to ensure that you used complete sentences and well-formed paragraphs.
3. Save and close. *(52-d2)*

Lesson 9R Review

Warmup *Lesson 9Ra Warmup*

all reaches	1	Quij produces both fine work and excellent volume.
g/?	2	Did he go? Where is Gianna? Did George go golfing?
b/p	3	Paul has pictures of bears, bats, pigs, and bison.
easy	4	Paige is to go in a taxi to the address we stated.

Skill Building

9Rb Improve Techniques

1. Key each line once.
2. Keep your eyes on the copy.

Work for smoothness, not speed.

Apostrophe	5	I’ll she’ll o'clock we’re didn’t she’s isn’t don’t
	6	one’s job; Donnel's, gov’t, it’s time; p’s and q’s
	7	Spell out it’s, doesn’t, can’t, gov’t, and she’ll.
q	8	netiquette queue quench quad FAQ quotes quit quest
	9	Quen asked a question; eat a quince; make it quick
	10	Quotes on quotas of useful equipment are required.
v	11	voice invert evoke vital prove event vacuum valid
	12	improve best speed; strive high; have clear vision
	13	Dev found five favorite websites for French class.

9Rc Timed Writing

1. Take two 1' timings on paragraph 1. If you finish before time is up, begin again.
2. Take a 2' timing on both paragraphs.

Goal: 13 *gwam*

wordwrap	*gwam* 1'	2'
Drill practice is a good thing to do to help with	10	5
speed and control. To get the most out of practice,	20	10
use the drills that help with the most common	30	15
problems. Finger and row drills are often used. Work	40	20
is often needed with the first, second, third, and	50	25
fourth fingers and rows. Work on the use of the shift	61	31
for capital letters as needed.	67	34
Work with double letters and letters next to each	10	39
other, as these letters often cause problems in	20	43
words. Spacing can also be a major concern, so	29	48
practice in the use of the space bar will help. Be	39	53
sure to review the required drills, and work on what	50	59
seems to help the most.	54	61

1' | 1 | 2 | 3 | 4 | 5 | 6 | 7 | 8 | 9 | 10
2' | 1 | 2 | 3 | 4 | 5

Cornerstone Club Named

Robbie Holiday of the Cougars Club submitted the winning name for the premium seating and club area of the new arena. Thanks to all of you who submitted suggestions for naming the new club. For his suggestion, which was selected from over 300 names submitted, Robbie has won season tickets for next year and the opportunity to make his seat selection first. The Cornerstone Club name was selected because members of our premium club play a crucial role in making our new arena a reality. Without the financial support of this group, we could not lay the first cornerstone of the arena.

Cornerstone Club members have first priority in selecting their seats for both basketball and hockey. Club members also have access to the Cornerstone Club before the event, during halftime, and after the event. They also receive a parking pass for the lot immediately adjacent to the arena. If you would like more information about the Cornerstone Club and how you can become a charter member, call the Cougars Club office during regular business hours.

What View Would You Like?

Most of us would like to sit in our seats and try them out before we select them rather than look at a diagram of the seating in the new arena. Former Cougar players make it easy for you to select the perfect angle to watch the ball go in the basket. Mark McKay and Jeff Dunlap, using their patented Real View visualization software, make it possible for you to experience the exact view you will have from the seats you select. In fact, they encourage you to try several different views. Most of the early testers of the new seat selection software reported that they came in with their minds completely made up about the best seats in the house. However, after experiencing several different views with the Real View software, they changed their original seat location request.

You must have either a blank paragraph marker or an unselected title for the system to add a Continuous section break above the columns.

3. Select the text; change the font size to 10 point, and format it into two equal-width columns. Note that a Continuous section break is positioned above the columns.
4. Apply Heading 1 to both headings.
5. Apply a Dark Red, Accent 1, 1½-point box border.
6. Insert Fill – Dark Red, Accent 1, Shadow WordArt.
   a. Size WordArt 0.8" high.
   b. Key the title **Arena Update**. Apply Dark Red, Accent 1, Darker 25% font color.
   c. Position in the Top Center with Square Text Wrapping. Note that it should be between the top border and the Continuous section break.
7. Position the picture described in the following steps after the third line under the last heading.
   a. Insert *arena seats* picture from the data files, and apply Top and Bottom Text Wrapping.
   b. Size it 2.25" high and drag to the center of the column.

(continued)

Lesson 10 Z, Y, Quotation Mark, Tab

Warmup *Lesson 10a Warmup*

all letters 1 Quill owed those back taxes after moving to Japan.

spacing 2 Didn't Vi, Max, and Quaid go? Someone did; I know.

q/v/m 3 Marv was quite quick to remove that mauve lacquer.

easy 4 Lana is a neighbor; she owns a lake and an island.

New Keys

10b Learn z and y

© Cengage Learning

z Reach *down* with *left fourth* finger.

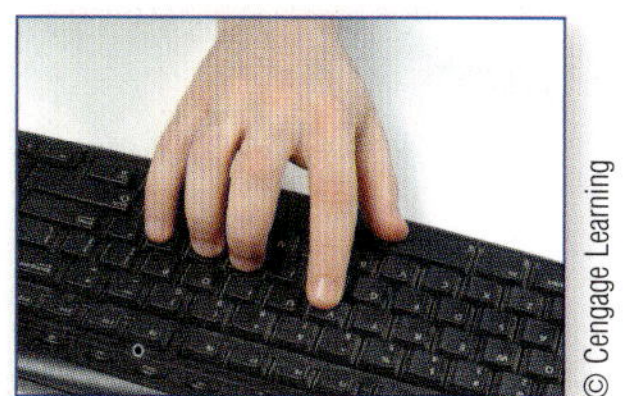

© Cengage Learning

y Reach *up* with *right first* finger.

Curve the little finger tightly to reach down and in for the z key.

z

5 za za zap zap zing zig zag zoo zed zip zap zig zed

6 doze zeal zero haze jazz zone zinc zing size ozone

7 ooze maze doze zoom zarf zebus daze gaze faze adze

y

8 y yj yj jay jay hay hay lay nay say days eyes ayes

9 yj ye yet yen yes cry dry you rye sty your fry wry

10 ye yen bye yea coy yew dye yaw lye yap yak yon any

10c All Reaches Learned

11 Did you say Liz saw any yaks or zebus at your zoo?

12 Relax; Jake wouldn't acquire any favorable rights.

13 Has Zack departed? Alex, Joy, and I will go alone.

10d Improve Keystroking

Key each line once.

14 Cecilia brings my jumbo umbrella to every concert.

direct reach 15 John and Kim recently brought us an old art piece.

16 I built a gray brick border around my herb garden.

17 sa ui hj gf mn vc ew uy re io as lk rt jk df op yu

Adjacent reach 18 In Ms. Lopez' opinion, the opera was really great.

19 Polly and I were joining Walker at the open house.

DRILL 3 REMOVE LINE AND ADD GRAPHICS

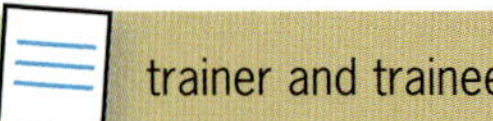
trainer and trainee

1. Open *52-drill2* and remove the line between the columns.
2. Insert *trainer and trainee* from the data files; size the picture 2" high and position it in the Middle Center with Square Text Wrapping.
3. Apply an Orange – Accent 1 thick and thin, 3-point box page border. See Quick Check below.
4. Save and close. (*52-drill3*)

Check your document against the illustration below.

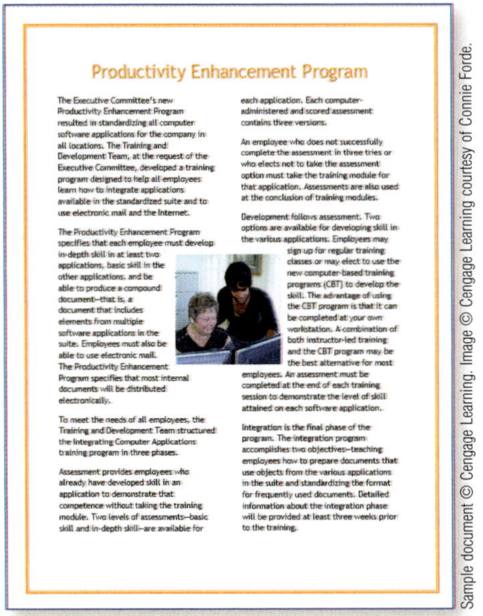

Productivity Enhancement Program

The Executive Committee's new Productivity Enhancement Program resulted in standardizing all computer software applications for the company in all locations. The Training and Development Team, at the request of the Executive Committee, developed a training program designed to help all employees learn how to integrate applications available in the standardized suite and to use electronic mail and the Internet.

The Productivity Enhancement Program specifies that each employee must develop in-depth skill in at least two applications, basic skill in the other applications, and be able to produce a compound document—that is, a document that includes elements from multiple software applications in the suite. Employees must also be able to use electronic mail. The Productivity Enhancement Program specifies that most internal documents will be distributed electronically.

To meet the needs of all employees, the Training and Development Team structured the Integrating Computer Applications training program in three phases.

Assessment provides employees who already have developed skill in an application to demonstrate that competence without taking the training module. Two levels of assessments—basic skill and in-depth skill—are available for each application. Each computer-administered and scored assessment contains three versions.

An employee who does not successfully complete the assessment in three tries or who elects not to take the assessment option must take the training module for that application. Assessments are also used at the conclusion of training modules.

Development follows assessment. Two options are available for developing skill in the various applications. Employees may sign up for regular training classes or may elect to use the new computer-based training programs (CBT) to develop the skill. The advantage of using the CBT program is that it can be completed at your own workstation. A combination of both instructor-led training and the CBT program may be the best alternative for most employees. An assessment must be completed at the end of each training session to demonstrate the level of skill attained on each software application.

Integration is the final phase of the program. The integration program accomplishes two objectives—teaching employees how to prepare documents that use objects from the various applications in the suite and standardizing the format for frequently used documents. Detailed information about the integration phase will be provided at least three weeks prior to the training.

Apply It

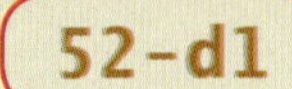

Newsletter

arena seats

1. In a new document, apply Ion theme and Narrow margins.
2. Tap ENTER four times; then key the newsletter as it is shown. Do not format as you key.

The architects have put the final touches on the arena plans, and the groundbreaking has been scheduled for March 18. Put the date on your calendar and plan to be a part of this exciting time. The Groundbreaking Ceremony will begin at 5:00 at the new arena site. After the ceremony, you will join the architects in the practice facility for refreshments and a thrilling video presentation of the new arena. The party ends when we all join the Western Cougars as they take on the Central Lions for the final conference game.

(continued)

New Keys

10e Learn " (quotation mark) and TAB

© Cengage Learning

" Left shift; then reach to the *right* with the *right fourth* finger.

© Cengage Learning

TAB Reach *up* with *left fourth* finger.

" (quotation mark)

20 "; "; " " "web" "media" "videos" I like "texting."

21 "I am not," she said, "going." I just said, "Why?"

TAB key

22 The tab key is used for indenting paragraphs and aligning columns.

23 Tabs that are set by the software are called default tabs, which are usually a half inch.

Skill Building

10f Build Skill

Key each line once. Tap TAB to indent each paragraph. Use wordwrap, tapping ENTER only at the end of each paragraph.

24 The expression "I give you my word," or put another
25 way, "Take my word for it," is just a way I can say, "I
26 prize my name; it clearly stands in back of my words."
27 I offer "honor" as collateral.

tab 28 Tap the tab key and begin the line without a pause to maintain fluency.

29 She said that this is the lot to be sent; I agreed with her.

30 Tap Tab before starting to key a timed writing so that the first line is indented.

10g Timed Writing

Take two 1' timed writings. If you finish before time is up, begin again.

Goal: 15 *gwam*

wordwrap *gwam* 1'

Tab → All of us work for progress, but it is not 9
always easy to analyze "progress." We work hard for 19
it; but, in spite of some really good efforts, we may 29
fail to get just exactly the response we want. 39

Tab → When this happens, as it does to all of us, it 9
is time to cease whatever we are doing, have a quiet 20
talk with ourselves, and face up to the questions 29
about our limited progress. How can we do better? 39

| 1 | 2 | 3 | 4 | 5 | 6 | 7 | 8 | 9 | 10 |

To format equal-width columns:

Layout/Page Setup/Columns

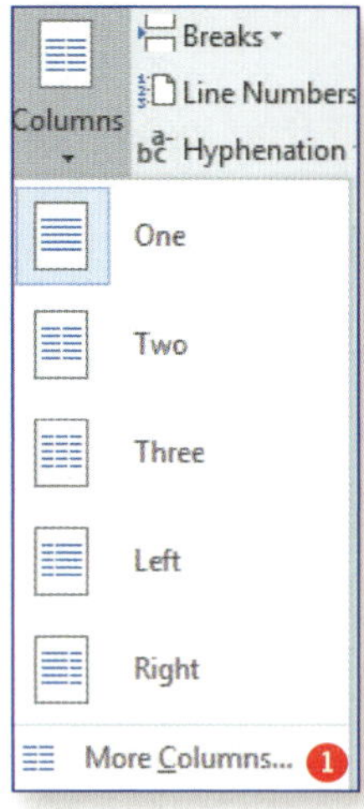

1. Select the text you want to format in columns; click Columns and select the desired number of columns from the options that display.
2. To balance columns on a page, click at the end of the columns and insert a Continuous section break.

DRILL 1 COLUMNS

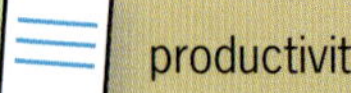

productivity

1. Open the *productivity* data file and apply Berlin Theme.
2. Select the title and apply Orange, Accent 1 from the Font group on the Home tab.
3. Select the text, click Columns, and select Three.
4. Preview the document and then revise the column structure; select the text again and click Two columns.

Layout/Page Setup/Breaks

4. Add a Continuous section break at the end of the columns to balance them.
5. Save and close. (*52-drill1*)

To add a line between columns:

Layout/Page Setup/Columns

1. From the number of column options, as shown above for formatting equal-width columns, click More Columns ❶ to display the Columns dialog box.
2. Click Line between ❷. To remove the line, remove the check from the box.

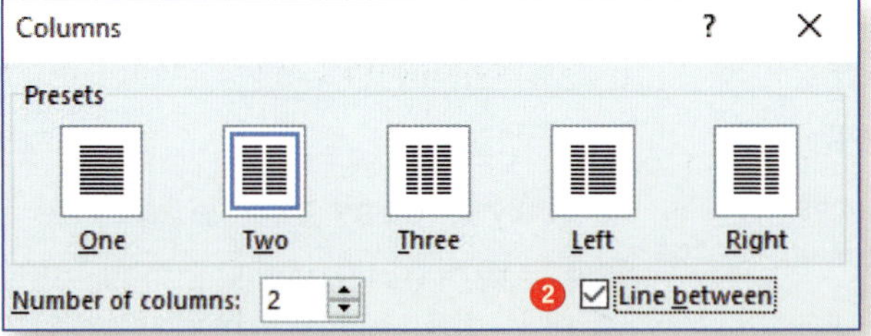

DRILL 2 LINE BETWEEN COLUMNS

1. Open *52-drill 1* and add a line between the columns.
2. Save and close. (*52-drill2*)

Lesson 11 Review

Warmup *Lesson 11a Warmup*

alphabet 1 Zeb had Jewel quickly give him five or six points.
“ (quote) 2 Can you spell “chaos,” “bias,” “bye,” and “their”?
y 3 Ty Clay may envy you for any zany plays you write.
easy 4 Did he bid on the bicycle, or did he bid on a map?

Skill Building

11b Improve Keystroking

Work for smoothness, not speed.

5 za za zap az az maze zoo zip razz zed zax zoa zone
6 Liz Zahl saw Zoe feed the zebra in an Arizona zoo.

7 yj yj jy jy joy lay yaw say yes any yet my try you
8 Why do you say that today, Thursday, is my payday?

9 xs xs sax ox box fix hex ax lax fox taxi lox sixes
10 Roxy, you may ask Jay to fix any tax sets for you.

11 qa qa aqua quail quit quake quid equal quiet quart
12 Did Enrique quietly but quickly quell the quarrel?

13 fv fv five lives vow ova van eve avid vex vim void
14 Has Vivi, Vada, or Eva visited Vista Valley Farms?

11c Build Skill

Key balanced-hand words quickly and as phrases to increase speed.

15 is to for do an may work so it but an with them am
16 am yam map aid zig yams ivy via vie quay cob amend

17 to do is for an may work so it but am an with them
18 for it | for it | to the | to the | do they | do they | do it

19 Pamela may go to the farm with Jan and a neighbor.
20 Rod and Ty may go by the lake if they go downtown.

Lesson 52 Documents with Columns

New Commands

- Equal-Width Columns
- Balance Columns
- Revise Column Structure
- Line between Columns
- Format Banner

Warmup *Lesson 52a Warmup*

lesson 52a warmup

Skill Building

52b Improve Techniques

1. Key each line once, concentrating on using good keying techniques.
2. Repeat the drill if time permits.

1st finger

1 Freddie just gave a friend that nice ring for her fifth birthday.
2 Ginger and Gretchen recently found three cute bunnies in my yard.

2nd finger

3 David decided to compete as a place kicker for the football team.
4 Cecilia and Kit decided to kill time playing on the deck at noon.

double letters

5 Jarrett cheerfully killed millions of bugs near the pool at noon.
6 All planning committees have four dinner meetings with key staff.

New Commands

52c

COLUMNS OF EQUAL WIDTH

Text formatted in multiple columns on a page is easier to read. The text flows down one column and then to the top of the next column. The heading on a document with multiple columns, called a banner or masthead, usually spans multiple columns. Newsletters, flyers, brochures, and programs are typically formatted in columns. Columns may be of equal or varying widths. Columns may be formatted before or after text is keyed, but generally, it is easier to format text in columns after it has been keyed. Columns are usually balanced or forced to end at approximately the same point on the page.

Productivity Enhancement Program

The Executive Committee's new Productivity Enhancement Program resulted in standardizing all computer software applications for the company in all locations. The Training and Development Team, at the request of the Executive Committee, developed a training program designed to help all employees learn how to integrate applications available in the standardized suite and to use electronic mail and the Internet.

The Productivity Enhancement Program specifies that each employee must develop in-depth skill in at least two applications, basic skill in the other applications, and be able to produce a compound document—that is, a document that includes elements from multiple software applications in the suite. Employees must also be able to use electronic mail. The Productivity Enhancement Program specifies that most internal documents will be distributed electronically.

To meet the needs of all employees, the Training and Development Team structured the Integrating Computer Applications training program in three phases.

Assessment provides employees who already have developed skill in an application to demonstrate that competence without taking the training module. Two levels of assessments—basic skill and in-depth skill—are available for each application. Each computer-administered and scored assessment contains three versions.

An employee who does not successfully complete the assessment in three tries or who elects not to take the assessment option must take the training module for that application. Assessments are also used at the conclusion of training modules.

Development follows assessment. Two options are available for developing skill in the various applications. Employees may sign up for regular training classes or may elect to use the new computer-based training programs (CBT) to develop the skill. The advantage of using the CBT program is that it can be completed at your own workstation. A combination of both instructor-led training and the CBT program may be the best alternative for most employees. An assessment must be completed at the end of each training session to demonstrate the level of skill attained on each software application.

Integration is the final phase of the program. The integration program accomplishes two objectives—teaching employees how to prepare documents that use objects from the various applications in the suite and standardizing the format for frequently used documents. Detailed information about the integration phase will be provided at least three weeks prior to the training.

11d Improve Techniques

Key each line once.

Key smoothly without looking at fingers.

```
21 Make the return snappily
22 and with assurance; keep
enter 23 your eyes on your source
24 data; maintain a smooth,
25 constant pace as you key.
```

When spacing, use a down-and-in motion.

```
space bar 26 us me it of he an by do go to us if or so am ah el
27 To enter the website, key "Guest" as the password.
```

Press Caps Lock key to toggle on or off.

```
caps lock 28 Use ALL CAPS for items such as TO, FROM, or SUBJECT.
29 Did Kristin mean Kansas City, MISSOURI, or KANSAS?
```

11e Timed Writing

Take two 1' timed writings. If you finish before time is up, begin again. The dot above words represents 2 *gwam*.

Goal: 16 *gwam*

wordwrap

	gwam 1'	2'
Have we thought of communication as a kind	8	4
of war that we wage through each day?	16	8
When we think of it that way, good language	24	12
would seem to become our major line of attack.	34	17
Words become muscle; in a normal exchange or in	43	22
a quarrel, we do well to realize the power of words.	53	27

11f Build Skill

1. Go to Skill Builder 1 on page 1-35.
2. Read the technique tip in the left column; concentrate on using the techniques listed.
3. Key Drill 1a from page 1-35. Key each line once, striving for good accuracy.

Compare your document to the illustration shown below.

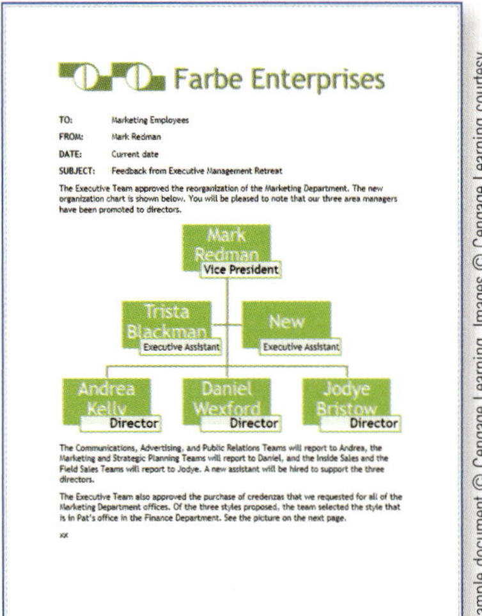

Farbe Enterprises

TO: Marketing Employees
FROM: Mark Redman
DATE: Current date
SUBJECT: Feedback from Executive Management Retreat

The Executive Team approved the reorganization of the Marketing Department. The new organization chart is shown below. You will be pleased to note that our three area managers have been promoted to directors.

The Communications, Advertising, and Public Relations Teams will report to Andrea, the Marketing and Strategic Planning Teams will report to Daniel, and the Inside Sales and the Field Sales Teams will report to Jodye. A new assistant will be hired to support the three directors.

The Executive Team also approved the purchase of credenzas that we requested for all of the Marketing Department offices. Of the three styles proposed, the team selected the style that is in Pat's office in the Finance Department. See the picture on the next page.

xx

Sample document © Cengage Learning. Images © Cengage Learning courtesy of Susie VanHuss.

Sample document © Cengage Learning. Image © Cengage Learning courtesy of Susie VanHuss.

51-d3

Announcement with Online Picture, WordArt, and Border

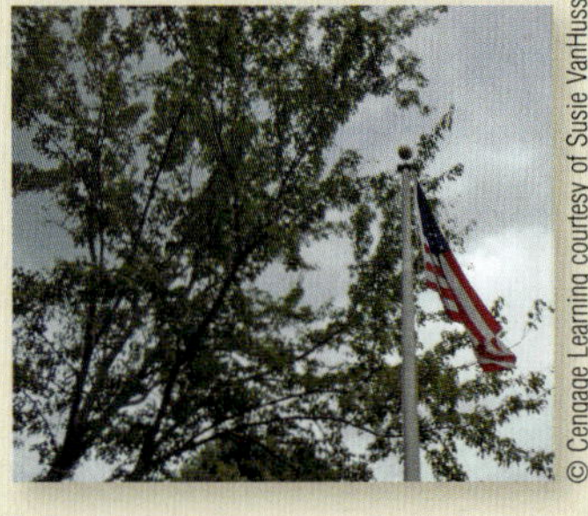

© Cengage Learning courtesy of Susie VanHuss.

 flag

1. Turn on Show/Hide. Apply Integral theme and Landscape orientation.
2. Apply Moderate margins.
3. Insert the flag from the data files; crop the flag as shown in the Quick Check below. Then size 2" high and add a standard red color picture border.
4. Insert WordArt Fill – White, Outline – Accent 2, Hard Shadow – Accent 2.
   a. Select text and replace with **Fourth of July Celebration**; apply Red from Standard Colors Text Fill.
   b. Size the WordArt 1.5" high and 7" wide.
   c. Apply Transform Stop Text Effects (second icon under Warp).
   d. Position in Top Right with Square Text Wrapping.
5. Tap ENTER three times below the picture and apply 36-point font size. Key the text shown below. Justify the text.
6. Apply a thick and thin page border, using Blue from the Standard Colors.
7. Save and close. (*51-d3*)

Fourth of July Celebration

Pack your lawn chairs or blankets and bring the entire family to join your friends and neighbors for the annual Fourth of July celebration at City Park. Music and festivities begin at 7:30 p.m. and end with a spectacular fireworks display at 10:30.

Lesson 12 Review

Warmup *Lesson 12a Warmup*

alphabet 1 Jack won five quiz games; Brad will play him next.
q 2 Quin Racq quickly and quietly quelled the quarrel.
z 3 Zaret zipped along sizzling, zigzag Arizona roads.
easy 4 Did he hang the sign by the big bush at the lake?

Skill Building

12b Improve Keystroking

b/f
5 bf bf fab fab ball bib rf rf rib rib fibs bums bee
6 Did Buffy remember that he is a brass band member?

z/y
7 za za zag zig zip yj yj jay eye day lazy hazy zest
8 Liz amazed us with the zesty pizza on a lazy trip.

q/u
9 qa qa quo qt. quit quay quad quarm que uj jug quay
10 Where is Quito? Qatar? Boqueirao? Quebec? Quilmes?

v/m
11 vf vf valve five value mj mj ham mad mull mass vim
12 Vito, enter the words vim, vivace, and avar; save.

all
13 I faced defeat; only reserves saved my best crews.
14 In my opinion, I need to rest in my reserved seat.

all
15 Holly created a red poppy and deserves art awards.
16 My pump averages a faster rate; we get better oil.

12c Improve Techniques

Key each line once.

Keep fingers curved and body aligned properly.

de/ed
17 ed fed led deed dell dead deal sled desk need seed
18 Dell dealt with the deed before the dire deadline.

ol/lo
19 old tolls doll solo look sole lost love cold stole
20 Old Ole looked for the long lost olive oil lotion.

op/po
21 pop top post rope pout port stop opal opera report
22 Stop to read the top opera opinion report to Opal.

we/ew
23 we few wet were went wears weather skews stew blew
24 Working women wear sweaters when weather dictates.

Apply It

51-d1

Memo Form with Graphics

farbe logo

Discover

Recolor

Picture Tools Format/ Adjust/Color

1. Click the drop-list arrow on Color to display the color options.
2. Click the desired color.

1. Apply Facet theme style to a new document and insert the *farbe logo* from the data files.
2. Farbe now distributes its documents electronically and wants to recolor the logo color to Green – Accent Color1 Light.
3. Insert Fill-Green – Accent 1, Shadow WordArt to the right side of the logo; select the text and key **Farbe Enterprises**; apply Cool Slant Bevel Text Effects (last bevel on first row).
4. Size the WordArt 1" high and 4.2" wide.
5. Key the memo headings as shown in the Quick Check on the next page.
6. Save and close. (*51-d1*)

51-d2

Document with Graphics

credenza

1. Open *51-d1* and key the memo shown below, inserting the SmartArt Name and Title Organization chart where noted.
2. Click in the top shape and add another Assistant shape. Use the Text Pane to key the names in the organization chart. Click in the Title boxes to key the titles. In the second Assistant shape, use **New** as the name.
3. Use In Line with Text wrapping and size the organization chart 3.8" high by 6.5" wide.
4. Tap ENTER after the reference initials and insert the *credenza* picture from the data files. Size it 5" high and position at Top Center with Square Text Wrapping. Compress the picture, accepting the defaults.
5. Save and close. (*51-d2*)

Marketing Employees | Mark Redman | Current date | Feedback from Executive Management Retreat

The Executive Team approved the reorganization of the Marketing Department. The new organization chart is shown below. You will be pleased to note that our three area managers have been promoted to directors.

(Insert Name and Title Organization Chart here. Key the names and titles shown below in the chart.)

Mark Redman Vice President | Trista Blackmon Executive Assistant | New Executive Assistant | Andrea Kelly Director | Daniel Wexford Director | Jodye Bristow Director

The Communications, Advertising, and Public Relations Teams will report to Andrea, the Marketing and Strategic Planning Teams will report to Daniel, and the Inside Sales and the Field Sales Teams will report to Jodye. A new assistant will be hired to support the three directors.

The Executive Team also approved the purchase of credenzas that we requested for all of the Marketing Department offices. Of the three styles proposed, the team selected the style that is in Pat's office in the Finance Department. See the picture on the next page.

xx

12d Improve Techniques

Key each line once.

Keep hands quiet; do not bounce. Keep fingers curved and upright.

```
25 a for we you is that be this will be a to and well
26 as our with I or a to by your form which all would
27 new year no order they so new but now year who may

28 This is Lyn's only date to visit their great city.
29 I can send it to your office at any time you wish.
30 She kept the fox, owls, and fowl down by the lake.

31 Harriette will cook dinner for the swimming teams.
32 Annette will call at noon to give us her comments.
33 Johnny was good at running and passing a football.
```

12e Timed Writing

1. Take a 2' timed writing. If you finish before time is up, begin again.
2. Use wordwrap.

Goal: 16 *gwam*

Copy Difficulty

What factors determine whether copy is difficult or easy? Research shows that difficulty is influenced by syllables per word, characters per word, and percent of familiar words. Carefully controlling these three factors ensures that speed and accuracy scores are reliable—that is, increased scores reflect increased skill.

In Level 1, all timings are easy. Note "E" inside the triangle at left of the timing. Easy timings contain an average of 1.2 syllables per word, 5.1 characters per word, and 90 percent familiar words. Easy copy is suitable for the beginner who is mastering the keyboard.

	gwam 2'	
There should be no questions, no doubt, about	5	35
the value of being able to key; it's just a matter	10	40
of common sense that today a pencil is much too slow.	15	45
Let me explain. Work is done on a keyboard	19	49
three to six times faster than other writing and	24	54
with a product that is a prize to read. Don't you	29	59
agree?	29	60

2' | 1 | 2 | 3 | 4 | 5 |

12f Build Skill

1. Go to Skill Builder 1 on page 1-35.
2. Focus on using good techniques.
3. Key Drill 1b from page 1-35. Key each line once, striving for good accuracy.

Compare your document to the illustration shown below.

Happy Birthday to You!

Communication

CAPITALIZATION

51d

1. Review the "Capitalization" section of Appendix C.
2. Key the sentences, correcting all capitalization errors. Use the Numbering command to number the sentences.
3. Save and close. (*51d*)

1. according to one study, the largest ethnic minority group online is hispanics.
2. the american author mark twain said, "always do right; this will gratify some people and astonish the rest."
3. the grand canyon was formed by the colorado river cutting into the high-plateau region of northwestern arizona.
4. the president of russia is elected by popular vote.
5. the hubble space telescope is a cooperative project of the european space agency and the national aeronautics and space administration.
6. the train left north station at 6:45 this morning.
7. the trademark cyberprivacy prevention act would make it illegal for individuals to purchase domains solely for resale and profit.
8. consumers spent $7 billion online between november 1 and december 31, 201-, compared to $3.1 billion for the same period in 2014.
9. new students should attend an orientation session on wednesday, august 15, at 8 a.m. in room 252 of the perry building.
10. the summer book list includes *where the red fern grows* and *the mystery of the missing baseball.*

Communicating Today

Electronic Document Distribution

Electronic document distribution is a key factor leading to the increased use of color and graphics in business documents today especially in small businesses. Previously, small businesses limited the use of color and graphics because they did not have the graphic arts staff or the budget to create effective color graphics. Although the cost of color printing has declined dramatically, it still costs significantly more than black-and-white printing. When documents are distributed electronically, printing costs are eliminated.

SmartArt and color digital pictures make it easy to create effective graphics that simplify complex concepts. Color and SmartArt not only make documents more interesting; used effectively, they help make documents more understandable.

Lesson 13 Review

Warmup *Lesson 13a Warmup*

alphabet 1 Bev quickly hid two Japanese frogs in Mitzi's box.

shift 2 Jay Nadler, a Rotary Club member, wrote Mr. Coles.

, (comma) 3 Jay, Ed, and I paid for plates, knives, and forks.

easy 4 Did the amendment name a city auditor to the firm?

Skill Building

13b Improve Fluency

Key each line once.

Key short, familiar words as units.

5 is to for do an may work so it but an with them am

6 Did they mend the torn right half of their ensign?

7 Hand me the ivory tusk on the mantle by the bugle.

Key more difficult words by letter.

8 only state jolly zest oil verve join rate mop card

9 After defeat, look up; gaze in joy at a few stars.

10 We gazed at a plump beaver as it waded in my pool.

Use variable speed; your fingers will feel the difference.

11 it up so at for you may was but him work were they

12 It is up to you to get the best rate; do it right.

13 Sami greeted reporters as stars got ready at home.

13c Improve Keystroking

14 Pat appears happy to pay for any supper I prepare.

15 Knox can relax; Alex gets a box of flax next week.

16 Vi, Ava, and Viv move ivy vines, leaves, or stems.

17 It's a question of whether they can't or won't go.

18 Did Jane go? Did she see Sofia? Who paid? Did she?

19 Ms. E. K. Nu and Lt. B. A. Walz had the a.m. duty.

20 "Who are you?" he asked. "I am," I said, "Jayden."

21 Find a car; try it; like it; work a price; buy it.

To insert WordArt:

Insert/Text/WordArt

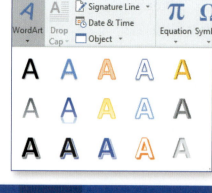

1. Click WordArt to display the WordArt gallery.
2. Preview and select the desired option.
3. Select the text in the text box that displays and replace it with your text.
4. Size and position the WordArt as desired.

WordArt can be formatted using the tools on the Drawing Tools Format tab.

- *Styles*—can be changed to any style in the gallery.
- *Text Fill*—used to add color or change the color of the interior of the letters.
- *Text Outline*—used to change the color, style, or weight of the lines of the exterior border of the letters.
- *Text Effects*—add depth or emphasis to text. See Text Effects and Transform options below.

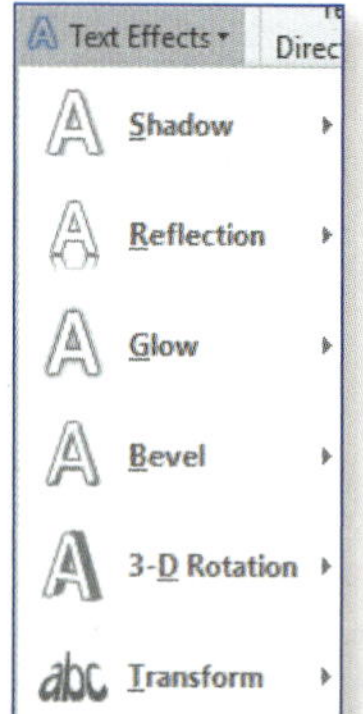

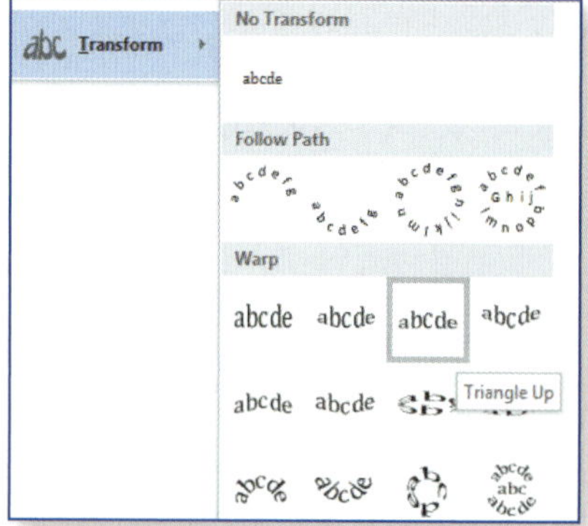

To apply WordArt formats:

Drawing Tools Format/WordArt Styles/Text Fill, Text Outline, Text Effects, or WordArt Styles

1. To change to a new WordArt style, preview and click the desired style.
2. To change Text Fill, Text Outline, or Text Effects, select the text, click the appropriate drop-list arrow, and select the desired color, line, or effect.

DRILL 3 WORDART

1. Display the WordArt gallery and select Fill – Black Text 1, Outline – Background 1, Hard Shadow – Background 1, and key **Happy Birthday to You!**
2. Select the text and apply Dark Red Standard Color fill.
3. Apply text effects: Art Deco Bevel (last icon) and Triangle Up Transform.
4. Size 1.5" high and 5.5" wide, and position in Top Center with Square Text Wrapping.
5. Compare your document to the Quick Check on the next page.
6. Save and close. (*51-drill3*)

13d Master Difficult Reaches

Key each line once.

Keep hands and arms still as you reach up to the third row and down to the first row.

t 22 at fat hat sat to tip the that they fast last slat
r 23 or red try ran run air era fair rid ride trip trap
t/r 24 A trainer sprained an arm trying to tame the bear.

m 25 am me my mine jam man more most dome month minimum
n 26 no an now nine once net knee name ninth know never
m/n 27 Many men and women are important company managers.

o 28 on or to not now one oil toil over only solo today
i 29 it is in tie did fix his sit like with insist will
o/i 30 Joni will consider obtaining options to buy coins.

a 31 at an as art has and any case data haze tart smart
s 32 us as so say sat slap lass class just sassy simple
a/s 33 Disaster was averted as the steamer sailed to sea.

e 34 we he ear the key her hear chef desire where there
i 35 it is in tie did fix his sit like with insist will
e/i 36 An expression of gratitude for service is desired.

13e Timed Writing

Take two 2' timed writings. If you finish before time is up, begin again.

Goal: 16 *gwam*

wordwrap *gwam* 2'

Some people think that the first impression made 5
in the first few seconds is the best method to find 10
out what a person is like. Think of meeting friends 15
for the first time. Was this true of them? In some 20
cases, one might be correct in judging a person in a 26
few seconds. However, in most cases, one will find 31
that it takes more than the first meeting to know 36
what a person is like. But the first time meeting a 41
person could give some idea, often if a person does 46
not show good qualities. For example, one might see 51
poor speaking skills, improper dress, and poor 56
personal traits when meeting a person for the first 61
time. 62

2' | 1 | 2 | 3 | 4 | 5 |

ADD SHAPES

Each SmartArt diagram offers a few shapes by default. You can add more shapes by tapping ENTER after the last entry or from the SmartArt Tools Design tab.

To add shapes to SmartArt:

SmartArt Tools Design/Create Graphic/Add Shape

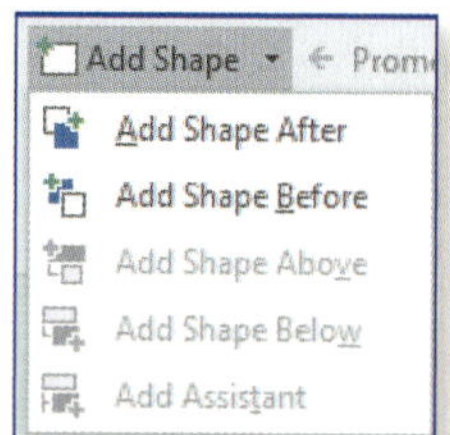

1. Click in the shape before or after which you want to add another shape.
2. Follow the path to add a shape, or click the drop-list arrow and select an option from the Add Shape options.
3. Repeat the process until you have as many shapes as you need in the layout.

TIP

The options available on the Add Shape list depend on the type of diagram you are working with.

DRILL 2 ADD SHAPES

1. Apply Slate theme and key **Effective Decision Making**; apply Title style and tap ENTER twice.
2. Insert a Block Cycle from the SmartArt Cycle category; add a shape after the last shape.
3. Key the text in the text pane.
4. Compare to the Quick Check; save and close. (*51-drill2*)

Identify decision to be made
Determine options
Analyze options
Select best option
Implement option
Evaluate decision

Compare your document to the illustration shown below.

Effective Decision Making

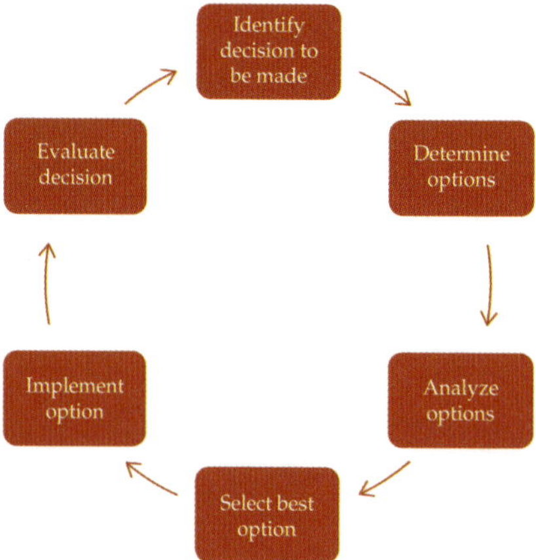

WORDART

WordArt adds special effects to text to make it more interesting. It is typically used in announcements, flyers, newsletters, and other casual documents.

Skill Builder 1

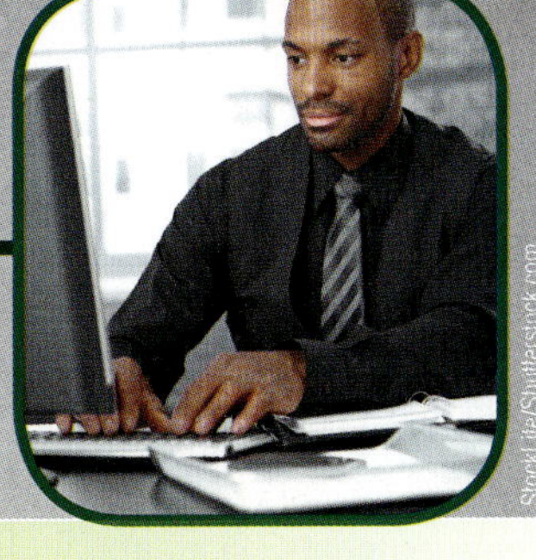

StockLite/Shutterstock.com

Skill Building *Emphasis on Improving Techniques*

For each drill, key each line once at a comfortable rate. Tap ENTER at the end of each line. Single-space the drill. Concentrate and key accurately. Repeat if desired.

DRILL 1

Goal: reinforce key locations

Key each line once at a comfortable, constant rate.

© Cengage Learning

TECHNIQUE TIP

Keep
- your eyes on source copy
- your fingers curved, upright
- your wrists low but not touching
- your elbows hanging loosely
- your feet flat on the floor

Drill 1a

A We saw that Alan had an alabaster vase in Alabama.
B My rubber boat bobbed about in the bubbling brook.
C Ceci gave cups of cold cocoa to Rebecca and Rocco.
D Don's dad added a second deck to his old building.
E Even as Ellen edited her document, she ate dinner.
F Our firm in Buffalo has a staff of forty or fifty.
G Ginger is giving Greg the eggs she got from Helga.
H Hugh has eighty high, harsh lights he might flash.

Drill 1b

I Irik's lack of initiative is irritating his coach.
J Judge J. J. Jore rejected Jeane and Jack's jargon.
K As a lark, Kirk kicked back a rock at Kim's kayak.
L Lucille is silly; she still likes lemon lollipops.
M Milt Mumm hammered a homer in the Miami home game.
N Ken Linn has gone hunting; Stan can begin canning.
O Jon Soto rode off to Otsego in an old Morgan auto.
P Philip helped pay the prize as my puppy hopped up.
Q Quiet Raquel quit quoting at an exquisite marquee.

Drill 1c

R As Mrs. Kerr's motor roared, her red horse reared.
S Sissie lives in Mississippi; Lissa lives in Tulsa.
T Nat told Betty not to tattle on her little sister.
U Ula has a unique but prudish idea on unused units.
V Eva visited every vivid event for twelve evenings.
W We watched as wayworn wasps swarmed by the willow.
X Tex Cox waxed the next box for Xenia and Rex Knox.
Y Ty says you may stay with Fay for only sixty days.
Z Hazel is puzzled about the azure haze; Zack dozes.

If desired, apply a document theme so that the SmartArt layout will use the appropriate colors of the theme.

The Text Pane options adjust to match each layout. If the text pane is not displayed, follow the path and click Text Pane.

SmartArt Tools Design/
Create Graphic/Text Pane

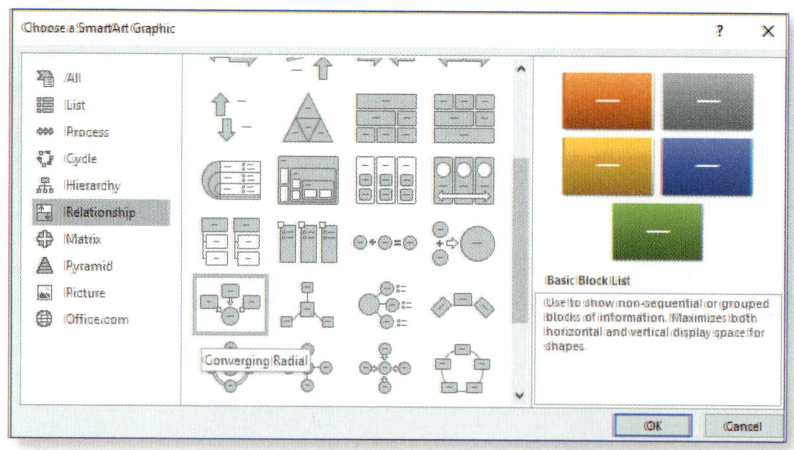

2. Click the category desired, or scroll through all layouts and click the desired layout, and OK to insert it.
3. Key text in the text pane that displays or directly in each shape. Note that the text size adjusts to fit the shape.

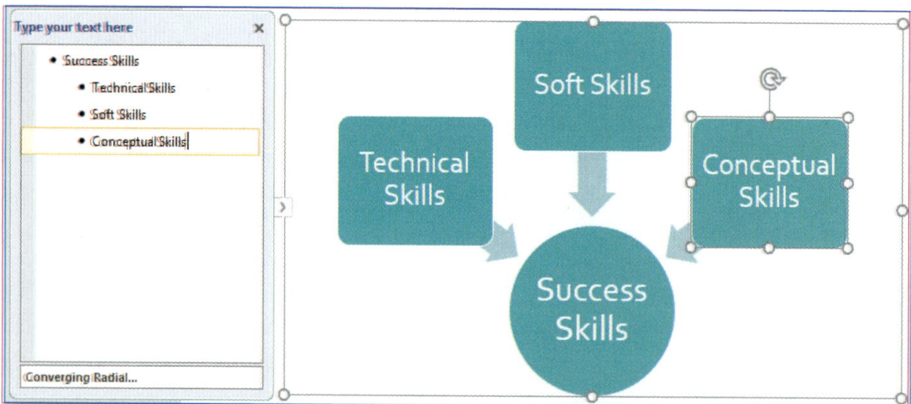

DRILL 1 SMARTART

1. In a new document, apply Depth theme and insert a SmartArt Converging Radial from the Relationship category.
2. Key the text shown at the right in the shapes using the Text pane.
3. Compare your solution to the illustration above; save and close. (*51-drill1*)

Success Skills
    Technical Skills
    Soft Skills
    Conceptual Skills

DRILL 2

Goal: strengthen up and down reaches

Keep hands and wrists quiet; fingers well curved in home position; stretch fingers up from home or pull them palmward as needed.

home position

1 Hall left for Dallas; he is glad Jake fed his dog.
2 Ada had a glass flask; Jake had a sad jello salad.
3 Lana Hask had a sale; Gala shall add half a glass.

down reaches

4 Did my banker, Mr. Mavann, analyze my tax account?
5 Do they, Mr. Zack, expect a number of brave women?
6 Zach, check the menu; next, beckon the lazy valet.

up reaches

7 Prue truly lost the quote we wrote for our report.
8 Teresa quietly put her whole heart into her words.
9 There were two hilarious jokes in your quiet talk.

DRILL 3

Goal: strengthen individual finger reaches

1st finger

1 Bob Mugho hunted for five minutes for your number.
2 Juan hit the bright green turf with his five iron.
3 The frigates and gunboats fought mightily in Java.

2nd finger

4 Dick said the ice on the creek had surely cracked.
5 Even as we picnicked, I decided we needed to diet.
6 Kim, not Mickey, had rice with chicken for dinner.

3rd/4th finger

7 Pam saw Roz wax an aqua auto as Lex sipped a cola.
8 Wally will quickly spell Zeus, Apollo, and Xerxes.
9 Who saw Polly? Pax Zais saw her; she is quiet now.

DRILL 4

Goal: strengthen special reaches

Emphasize smooth stroking. Avoid pauses, but do not reach for speed.

adjacent reaches

1 Falk knew well that her opinions of art were good.
2 Theresa answered her question; order was restored.
3 We join there and walk north to the western point.

direct reaches

4 Barb Nunn must hunt for my checks; she is in debt.
5 In June and December, Irvin hunts in Bryce Canyon.
6 We decided to carve a number of funny human faces.

double letters

7 Anne stopped off at school to see Bill Wiggs cook.
8 Edd has planned a small cookout for all the troop.
9 Keep adding to my assets all fees that will apply.

| 1 | 2 | 3 | 4 | 5 | 6 | 7 | 8 | 9 | 10 |

Lesson 51 SmartArt and WordArt

New Commands

- Insert SmartArt
- SmartArt Design Tools
- SmartArt Layout Tools
- Add Text to SmartArt
- Add Shapes
- Insert WordArt
- Format WordArt

Warmup *Lesson 51a Warmup*

lesson 51a warmup

Skill Building

51b Improve Techniques

1. Key each line once, concentrating on using good keying techniques.
2. Repeat the drill if time permits.

1st row
1 Max, Zam, and a local man saw an amazing cave on a long bus ride.
2 Janna came back home six times to visit the bat caves at the zoo.

3rd row
3 We wrote Terry to try to get a quote; Perry tried to get a quote.
4 Perry peeped at Terry's quote; were you there with Perry or Pete?

home row
5 Kala was glad Alyssa sold a glass flask at a gala sale in Dallas.
6 Jack Hall's dad was in Dallas at a glass sale; a sad lad saw him.

one hand
7 Jimmy saw him carve a great pumpkin; John deserved better awards.
8 Nikki saved a million as a minimum reserve on debt; Jimmy agreed.

balanced hand
9 Jamale Rodney, a neighbor, and Sydney may go to the lake by auto.
10 Bud got the tub of big worms to go to the dock to fish with them.

New Commands

51c

SMARTART

SmartArt consists of predesigned diagrams that help to simplify complex concepts. Note in the SmartArt graphic dialog box that SmartArt layouts are grouped into eight categories. You can view all of the layouts or the layouts in one category.

To insert and add text to SmartArt:

Insert/Illustrations/SmartArt

1. Position the insertion point where you want to add the graphic, and click SmartArt to open the Choose a SmartArt Graphic dialog box shown on the next page. Categories of SmartArt are listed on the left, layouts for each category display in the center, and the preview and description of the appropriate use appear in the right pane.

(continued)

DRILL 5

Goal: improve troublesome pairs

Use a controlled rate without pauses.

1 ad add did does dish down body dear dread dabs bad
d/k 2 kid ok kiss tuck wick risk rocks kayaks corks buck
3 Dirk asked Dick to kid Drake about the baked duck.

4 deed deal den led heed made needs delay he she her
e/i 5 kit kiss kiln kiwi kick kilt kind six ribs kill it
6 Abie had neither ice cream nor fried rice in Erie.

7 fib fob fab rib beg bug rob bad bar bed born table
b/v 8 vat vet gave five ever envy never visit weave ever
9 Vic and Bev gave five very big baby beds to a vet.

10 aft after lift gift sit tot the them tax tutu tyro
t/r 11 for far ere era risk rich rock rosy work were roof
12 In Toronto, Ruth told the truth about her artwork.

13 jug just jury judge juice unit hunt bonus quiz bug
u/y 14 jay joy lay you your only envy quay oily whey body
15 Willy usually does not buy your Yukon art in July.

DRILL 6

Goal: fluency

1 Dian may make cocoa for the girls when they visit.
2 Focus the lens for the right angle; fix the prism.
3 She may suspend work when she signs the torn form.
4 Augment their auto fuel in the keg by the autobus.
5 As usual, their robot did half turns to the right.
6 Pamela laughs as she signals to the big hairy dog.
7 Pay Vivian to fix the island for the eighty ducks.

DRILL 7

Goal: eyes on the copy

1. Key sentences 1–5 for fluency. Press ENTER after each line.
2. Take a 20" and then a 30" timed writing on each sentence.

Goal: Try to key 2–3 words more on the second timing on each line.

	words 30"	20"
1 Did she make this turkey dish?	12	18
2 Blake and Laurie may go to Dubuque.	14	21
3 Signal for the oak sleigh to turn right.	16	24
4 I blame Susie; did she quench the only flame?	18	27
5 She turns the panel dials to make this robot work.	20	30

  b. Size the picture 2.4" high and use the Center command on the Home tab to center it.

6. Insert the *closed for work focus* and the *open for interaction* picture data files on the line below the last paragraph.
   a. Compress both pictures; use document resolution.
   b. Size both pictures 2.4" high and apply Square Text Wrapping.
   c. Position the *closed for work focus* picture on the left and the *open for interaction* picture on the right.
7. Number the pages on the top of the page using Plain Number 3. Do not show the number on the first page.
8. Check the position of the photos against the illustration below.
9. Save and close. (*50-d1*)

50-d2

Document with Page Border

1. Open *50-d1* and apply a box page border.
2. Use a single line style with Brown, Text 2 theme color and 1-point line width.
3. Apply to the whole document.
4. Save and close. (*50-d2*)

QUICK ✓

The illustration on the left shows *50-d1* page 1; the one on the right shows *50-d2* page 2 with the border.

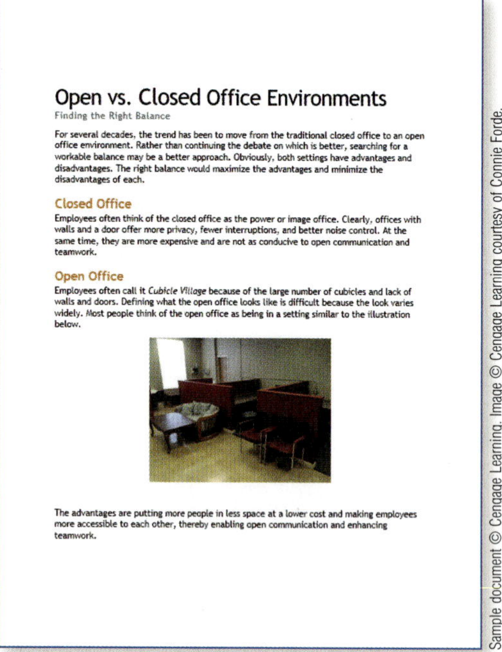

Open vs. Closed Office Environments

Finding the Right Balance

For several decades, the trend has been to move from the traditional closed office to an open office environment. Rather than continuing the debate on which is better, searching for a workable balance may be a better approach. Obviously, both settings have advantages and disadvantages. The right balance would maximize the advantages and minimize the disadvantages of each.

Closed Office

Employees often think of the closed office as the power or image office. Clearly, offices with walls and a door offer more privacy, fewer interruptions, and better noise control. At the same time, they are more expensive and are not as conducive to open communication and teamwork.

Open Office

Employees often call it *Cubicle Village* because of the large number of cubicles and lack of walls and doors. Defining what the open office looks like is difficult because the look varies widely. Most people think of the open office as being in a setting similar to the illustration below.

The advantages are putting more people in less space at a lower cost and making employees more accessible to each other, thereby enabling open communication and enhancing teamwork.

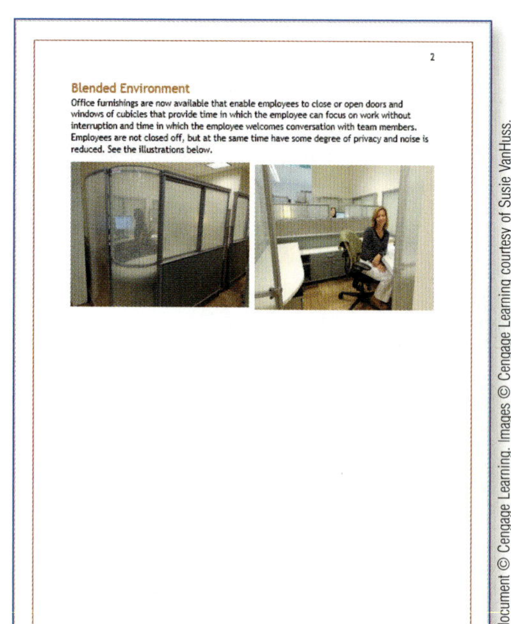

2

Blended Environment

Office furnishings are now available that enable employees to close or open doors and windows of cubicles that provide time in which the employee can focus on work without interruption and time in which the employee welcomes conversation with team members. Employees are not closed off, but at the same time have some degree of privacy and noise is reduced. See the illustrations below.

TO USE TIMED WRITINGS EFFECTIVELY:

1. Select the timed writing.
2. Select the paragraph and the timing length. For example,
    - Select Paragraph 1 and 1'. Key paragraph 1; if you finish before time is up, repeat the same paragraph. Always use wordwrap when keying timed writings.
    - Select Paragraph 2 and 1'. Key paragraph 2; repeat the same paragraph if you finish before time is up.
    - Select Entire Writing and 2'. Try to maintain your 1' rate. If you finish before time is up, start over, beginning with paragraph 1.

Goal: build staying power

1. Key each paragraph for fluency. Use wordwrap.
2. Key a 2' timing on both paragraphs. Use wordwrap.

gwam 2'

Writing 1: 18 *gwam*

Why spend weeks with some problem when just a few quiet 6
minutes can help us to resolve it. 9

If we don't take time to think through a problem, it will 15
swiftly begin to expand in size. 18

Writing 2: 20 *gwam*

We push very hard in our quest for growth, and we all think 6
that only excellent growth will pay off. 10

Believe it or not, one can actually work much too hard, 16
be much too zealous, and just miss the mark. 20

Writing 3: 22 *gwam*

A business friend once explained to me why he was often 6
quite eager to be given some new project to work with. 11

My friend said that each new project means he has to 16
organize and use the best of his knowledge and his skill. 22

Writing 4: 24 *gwam*

Just don't let new words get away from you. Learn how to spell 6
and pronounce new words and when and how to use them with skill. 13

A new word is a friend, but frequently more. New words 19
must be used lavishly to extend the size of your word power. 25

2' | 1 | 2 | 3 | 4 | 5 | 6 |

Apply It

50-d1

Document with Graphics

closed for work focus
open for interaction
cubicles online

If you do not have access to OneDrive, your instructor may provide access to an alternate drive.

1. Check to see if the *cubicles online* data file has been synced to your OneDrive. If it is not on OneDrive, upload it to your OneDrive.
2. Tap ENTER three times and key the title.
3. Key the report shown below and then apply the formats listed after the report.

Open vs. Closed Office Environments

Finding the Right Balance

For several decades, the trend has been to move from the traditional closed office to an open office environment. Rather than continuing the debate on which is better, searching for a workable balance may be a better approach. Obviously, both settings have advantages and disadvantages. The right balance would maximize the advantages and minimize the disadvantages of each.

Closed Office

Employees often think of the closed office as the power or image office. Clearly, offices with walls and a door offer more privacy, fewer interruptions, and better noise control. At the same time, they are more expensive and are not as conducive to open communication and teamwork.

Open Office

Employees often call it *Cubicle Village* because of the large number of cubicles and lack of walls and doors. Defining what the open office looks like is difficult because the look varies widely. Most people think of the open office as being in a setting similar to the illustration below.

The advantages are putting more people in less space at a lower cost and making employees more accessible to each other, thereby enabling open communication and enhancing teamwork.

Blended Environment

Office furnishings are now available that enable employees to close or open doors and windows of cubicles that provide time in which the employee can focus on work without interruption and time in which the employee welcomes conversation with team members. Employees are not closed off, but at the same time have some degree of privacy and noise is reduced. See the illustrations below.

4. Apply the Berlin theme.
5. Apply Title style to the title, Subtitle style to the subtitle, and Heading 1 to the three headings. Decrease the title font size to fit on one line.
6. Use the Online Pictures command and insert *cubicles online* from your OneDrive.
    a. Tap ENTER after the first paragraph under the *Open Office* heading and insert the *cubicles online* picture.

(continued)

Goal: build staying power

1. Key each paragraph for fluency. Use wordwrap.
2. Key a 2' timing on both paragraphs. Use wordwrap.

Note: The dot above text represents two words.

Writing 5: 26 *gwam*

gwam 2'

We usually get the best results when we know where 5
we are going. Just setting a few goals will help us quietly 12
see what we can do. 13

Goals can help measure whether we are moving at a good 19
rate or dozing along. You can expect a goal to help you find 25
good results. 26

Writing 6: 28 *gwam*

To win whatever prizes we want from life, we must plan to 6
move carefully from this goal to the next to get the maximum 12
result from our work. 14

If we really want to become skilled in keying, we must 19
come to see that this desire will require of us just a little 26
patience and hard work. 28

Writing 7: 30 *gwam*

Am I an individual person? I'm sure I am; still, in a 5
much, much bigger sense, other people have a strong voice in 12
thoughts I think and actions I take. 15

Although we are each a unique person, we work and 21
play in organized groups of people who just do not expect us to 26
dismiss their rules of law and order. 30

2' | 1 | 2 | 3 | 4 | 5 | 6 |

PAGE BORDER

Page borders can be formatted using a variety of settings, styles, colors, and line widths. They can be applied to the whole document or to various sections of the document.

TIP

Note that the line color displayed is determined by the theme colors, or you can select a standard color.

To apply a page border:

Design/Page Background/Page Borders

1. Click Page Borders to display the Borders and Shading dialog box.
2. Make sure the Page Border tab is active.
3. Choose the desired setting, style, color, and width.
4. In the Apply to box, choose the desired option.

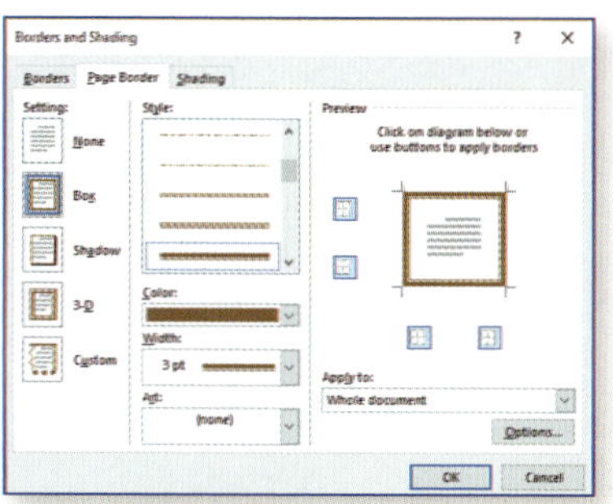

DRILL 6 PAGE BORDERS

leopard

1. Open *leopard* data file and apply a Box page border.
2. Choose the thick-and-thin line style, 3-point width shown in the illustration above.
3. Choose Gold, Accent 4, Darker 50% color.
4. Apply to the whole document.
5. Save and close. (*50-drill6*)

WORKPLACE SUCCESS

EDHAR/Shutterstock.com

Positive Attitude

What makes a successful employee? Employers say that "soft skills" are critical. A positive attitude is generally one of the top five soft skills required. Why? Because it enhances performance. People with positive attitudes tend to be problem solvers. They view problems as challenges with opportunities and find ways to solve them.

Self-confidence is also linked to a positive attitude. If you think you can do something, you are quite likely to do it. Workers with a poor self-image are more likely to look for faults than strengths.

Another important reason for developing a positive attitude is that other employees prefer to work with individuals who have a positive attitude. Most companies require employees to work on teams; thus, having a positive attitude enhances teamwork and contributes to the success of the team.

MODULE 2

Figure and Symbol Keys

LEARNING OUTCOMES

- Key the numeric keys by touch.
- Use symbol keys correctly.
- Build keying speed and accuracy.
- Apply proofreaders' marks.

Lesson 14 I and 8

Warmup *Lesson 14a Warmup*

lesson 14a warmup

New Keys

14b 1 and 8

1 Reach *up* with *left fourth* finger.

8 Reach *up* with *right second* finger.

Abbreviations: Do not space after a period within an abbreviation, as in U.S., C.O.D., a.m.

The digit "1" and the letter "l" have separate values; do not interchange.

1

1 1 1a a1 1 1; 1 and a 1; 1 add 1; 1 aunt; 1 ace; 1 arm; 1 aye
2 1 and 11 and 111; 11 eggs; 11 vats; Set 11A; May 11; Item 11
3 The 11 aces of the 111th Corps each rated a salute at 1 p.m.

8

4 8 8k k8 8 8; 8 kits; ask 8; 8 kites; kick 8; 8 keys; spark 8
5 OK 88; 8 bags; 8 or 88; the 88th; 88 kegs; ask 88; order 888
6 Eight of the 88 cars score 8 or better on our Form 8 rating.

7 She did live at 818 Park, not 181 Park; or was it 181 Clark?
8 Put 1 with 8 to form 18; put 8 with 1 to write 81. Use 1881.
9 On May 1 at 8 a.m., 18 men and 18 women left Gate 8 for Rio.

14c All Figures Learned

ONLINE VIDEO

Online video is used in industry to promote products or services, to showcase new products, to demonstrate procedures, and in many other ways. Video can be inserted in a *Word* document in several ways. The video you will insert and play is an example of a company promoting a new product.

To insert online videos:

Insert/Media/Online Video

TIP

The long embed code used to insert a video is provided in a data file so that you can copy and paste it in the text box. Note you need to use the paste short cut (CTRL + v) to paste it. Additional directions are also included in the data file.

Bing Video Search box

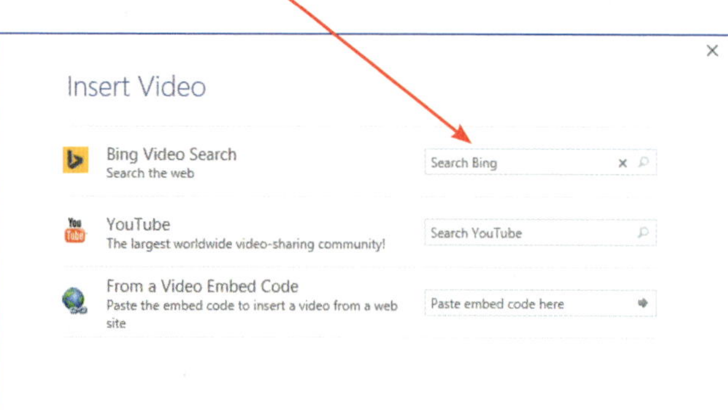

1. In a new document, click Online Video to display the Online Video dialog box.
2. Key the keywords in the Bing Video Search box or YouTube search box to search for the desired video or paste the Video Embed Code in the From a Video Embed Code text box. Use (CTRL + v) paste shortcut.
3. Click the search icon or arrow to insert the play box.
4. Click the play arrow in the center of the play box to display the selected video play box.

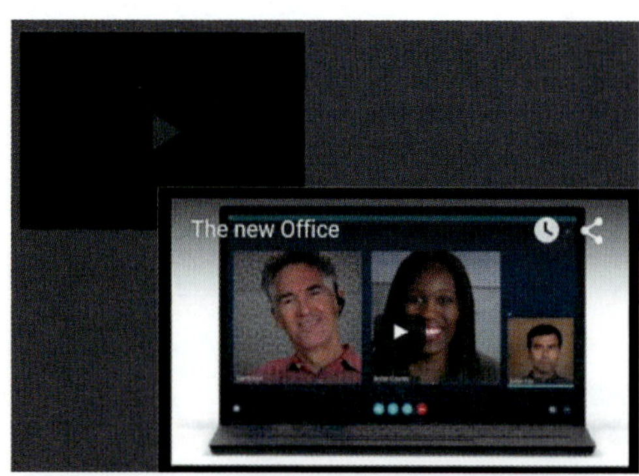

5. Click the arrow in the video box to play it. The line shows the progress in the video. The stop button, the volume, and the time are shown at the bottom of the screen.

DRILL 5 INSERT AND PLAY VIDEO

the new office video

1. In a new document, click the Online Video button and paste the Embed Code from the data file in the From a Video Embed Code text box.
2. Wait for the play box to display, then click the play arrow in the center of the box.
3. When The New Office video box appears, click the play arrow and play the video.
4. Save and close. (*50-drill5*)

Skill Building

14d Improve Fluency

Key each line once.

Work for fluency as you key these high-frequency words.

10 a an it been copy for his this more no office please service
11 our service than the they up was work all any many thank had
12 business from I know made more not me new of some to program
13 such these two with your about and have like department year
14 by at on but do had in letter most now one please you should
15 their order like also appreciate that there gentlemen letter
16 be can each had information letter may make now only so that
17 them time use which am other been send to enclosed have will
18 Please thank the department staff for the excellent program.
19 Therefore, send the information as they are very interested.
20 She sent a receipt and an invoice for the payment due today.
21 Our board and president are happy about the new tax service.
22 We appreciate the excellent help received from every office.
23 Please return the attached form prior to the second meeting.

14e Improve Keystroking

figures

24 Our 188 trucks moved 1881 tons on August 18 and December 18.
25 Send Mary 181 No. 188 panes for her home at 8118 Oak Street.
26 The 188 men in 8 boats left Docks 1 and 18 at 1 p.m., May 1.
27 pop was lap pass slaw wool solo swap Apollo wasp load plaque
28 Was Polly acquainted with the skillful jazz player in Texas?
29 The computer is a useful tool; it helps you to perform well.

14f Build Skill

Take two 30" timed writings on each line.

Goal: Key 2 or 3 more words on the second timed writing.

30 Did their form entitle them to the land?
31 Did the men in the field signal for us to go?
32 I may pay for the antique bowls when I go to town.
33 The auditor did the work right, so he risks no penalty.
34 The man by the big bush did signal us to turn down the lane.

| 1 | 2 | 3 | 4 | 5 | 6 | 7 | 8 | 9 | 10 | 11 | 12 |

ONLINE PICTURES

The Online Pictures command is used to access digital pictures and illustrations from sources other than your computer and your computer network. Note that some of the sources require you to set up an account if you do not already have one.

TIP

The free Microsoft account for your OneDrive provides storage for your photos.

The free Flickr account from Yahoo gives you access to the photo-sharing social media site. You can also access Flickr from a Facebook account.

To insert online pictures:

Insert/Illustrations/Online Pictures

1. Click Online Pictures to display the Online Pictures options. If you have used previous versions of *Word*, you will notice that Clip Art is no longer available.
2. Key the keywords in the Bing Image search box to search for the desired picture.
3. Select the desired picture and double-click it or click Insert to insert the picture.

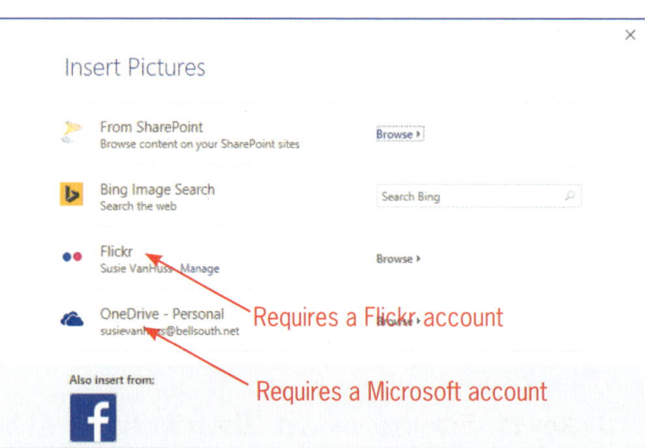

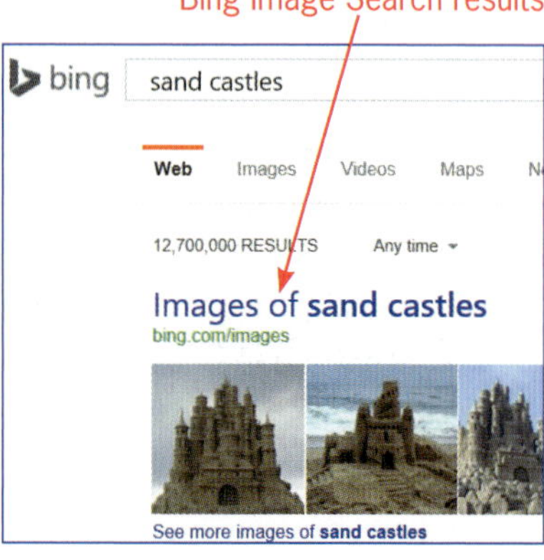

Note: You can format online pictures and illustrations using the commands on the Picture Tools Format tab.

DRILL 4 INSERT AND FORMAT ONLINE PICTURES

1. In a new document, use a Bing Image Search for *sand castles.*
2. Select the desired picture from the search results and insert it.
3. Size the picture 3" high, and apply Square Text Wrapping.
4. Crop the picture close to the sand castle.
5. Position the picture in the Middle Center with Square Text Wrapping.
6. Resize the picture to 3" if cropping affected the height of the picture.
7. Save and close. (*50-drill4*)

Lesson 15 5 and 0

Warmup *Lesson 15a Warmup*

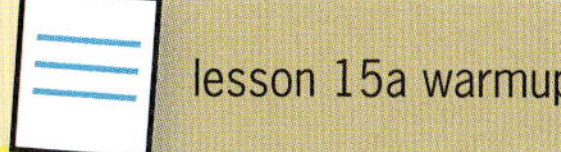
lesson 15a warmup

New Keys

15b 5 and 0

© Cengage Learning

5 Reach *up* with *left first* finger.

© Cengage Learning

0 Reach *up* with *right fourth* finger.

5

1 5 5f f5 5 5; 5 fans; 5 feet; 5 figs; 5 fobs; 5 frus; 5 flaws
2 5 o'clock; 5 a.m.; 5 p.m.; is 55 or less; buy 55; 5 and 5 is
3 Call Line 555 if 5 fans or 5 bins arrive at Pier 5 by 5 p.m.

0

4 0 0; ;0 0 0; skip 0; plan 0; left 0; is below 0; I scored 0;
5 0 degrees; key 0 and 0; write 00 here; the total is 0 or 00;
6 She laughed at their 0 to 0 score; but ours was 0 to 0 also.

15c All Figures Learned

7 I keyed 550 pages for Invoice 05, or 50 more than we needed.
8 Pages 15 and 18 of the program listed 150, not 180, members.
9 On May 10, Rick drove 500 miles to New Mexico in car No. 08.

Skill Building

15d Improve Keystroking

Key each line once.

Watch the copy, not the hands.

10 Read pages 5 and 8; duplicate page 18; omit pages 50 and 51.
11 We have Model 80 with 10 meters or Model 180 with 15 meters.
12 After May 18, French 050 meets in room 15 at 10 a.m. daily.

13 Barb Abver saw a vibrant version of her brave venture on TV.
14 Call a woman or a man who will manage Minerva Manor in Nome.
15 We were quick to squirt a quantity of water at Quin and West.

To compress a picture:

Picture Tools Format/Adjust/Compress Pictures

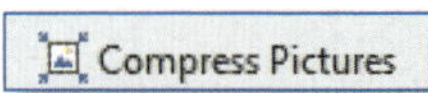

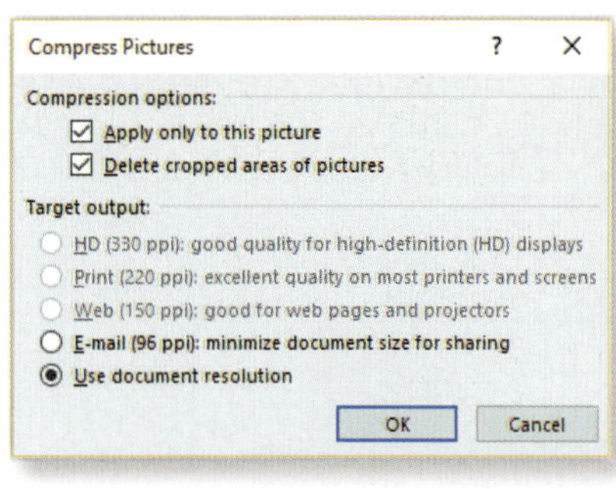

Compressing the picture reduces the file size; note that for email you can reduce the size even smaller.

1. Select the picture and click Compress Pictures to display the Compress Pictures dialog box.
2. Select *Use document resolution* unless you plan to email the picture.

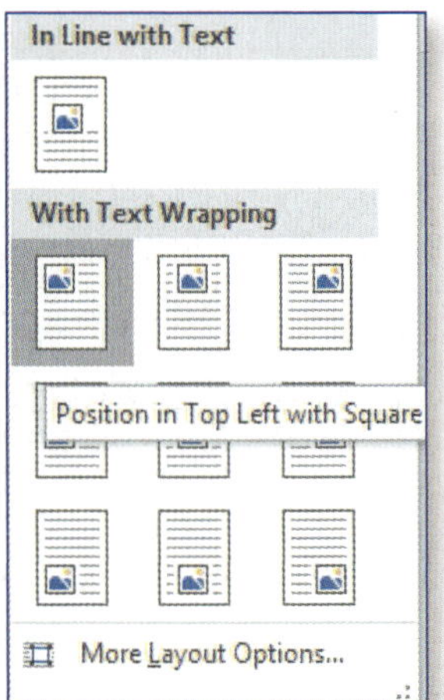

To move a picture:

Picture Tools Format/Arrange/Position

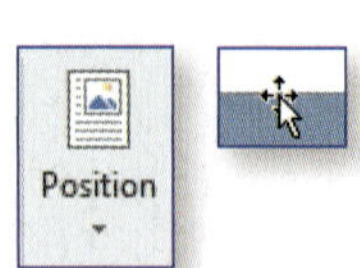

Pictures may be moved with the Position command or by dragging them with the mouse.

1. To position a picture, select the picture and click Position to display the position options.
2. Select the desired position as shown on the left. -or-
3. To move a picture with the mouse, select it and hover over the picture until the mouse turns to a four-headed arrow. Then drag the picture to the desired position.

TIP

Note that the default for wrapping text is In Line with Text as shown by the red arrow in the illustration.

To wrap text:

Picture Tools Format/Arrange/Wrap Text

Wrap Text

Wrap Text determines how text wraps around a selected object, such as a picture. Wrap Text can be applied by using the Layout Options button that displays when a picture is selected or by using the Wrap Text command.

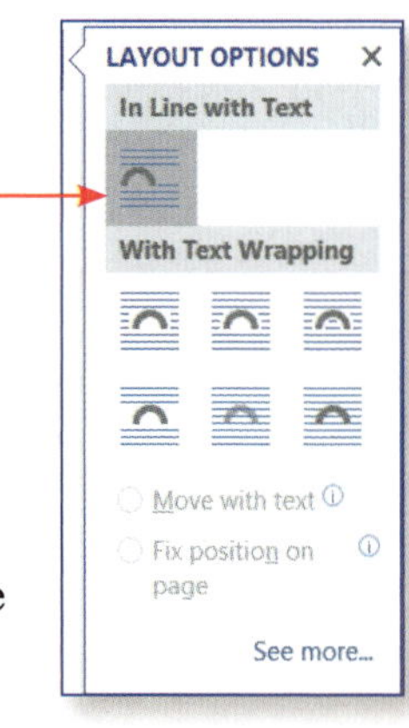

1. Select the picture and then click Layout Options button or the Wrap Text drop-list arrow to display the options.
2. Select the desired option, such as Square or Tight as shown on the right.

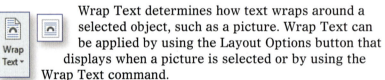

DRILL 3 FORMAT PICTURE

format pictures

1. With *format pictures* data file open, read the information in the document, and then complete the five numbered steps.
2. Save and close. (*50-drill3*)

15e Improve Techniques

Key each line once.

Build confidence—trust yourself to make the right reach.

pu/nv
16 pumps impulse campus invoices convey envy puck public canvas
17 Computer's input on environmental canvass confirms decision.

mb ey rk
18 embarked number climb eye obeying park remark thumb attorney
19 Ambitious people gambled money on unusual pieces of artwork.

tl ru pt
20 subtle apt capture excerpt adult abrupt brittle forums drug
21 Ruth opts to be greatly optimistic about seven new recruits.

ob rg un
22 objective lobster organize urge bounce tribunal global surge
23 Marge's hunger for mobile action targets frequent traveling.

15f Timed Writing

1. Take two 1' timed writings. If you finish before time is up, begin again.
2. Use wordwrap; do not tap ENTER at the end of lines.

wordwrap

gwam 1'

I thought about Harry and how he worked for me in my 11
family insurance business for 10 years; how daily at 8 he 23
parked his old car in the company lot; then, he left exactly 35
at 5. Every day was almost identical for him. 44

In a quiet way, he did an outstanding job, requesting 56
little attention. So I never recognized his thirst for travel. 68
I didn't expect to find all those travel brochures near his 80
workplace. 82

1' | 1 | 2 | 3 | 4 | 5 | 6 | 7 | 8 | 9 | 10 | 11 | 12 |

Communication

15g Composition

1. Compose one paragraph that describes travel that you have done or perhaps that you wish to take. Include at least two attractions you visited or hope to visit while on this trip. Use proper grammatical structure. Do not worry about keying errors at this time.
2. Save the document as *xx-15g*. (Replace *xx* with your initials.)

To size pictures:

Picture Tools Format/Size/Height or Width Arrows

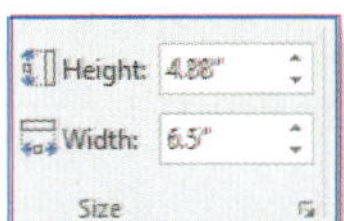

Pictures can be sized or cropped. Cropping removes unwanted portions of the picture. The file size of a picture can be reduced by compressing it.

1. To change the size of a picture, select it and use the height or width arrows to increase or decrease the size. -or-
2. Select the picture, position the mouse over the sizing handles; when the pointer turns to a double-headed arrow, drag to the size desired.

You can drag the square handle on the side of a picture or other graphic to size the image, but you will distort its size. Always drag a corner handle to maintain the image's proportion.

To crop pictures:

Picture Tools Format/Size/Crop

1. To crop one side of a picture, click Crop and drag the cropping handle on the side inward. The cropping line will illustrate what will be cut off.
2. To crop the same amount on two sides, press CTRL while you drag the handle.
3. To finish, click off the picture.

DRILL 2 SIZE PICTURE

1. Open *50-drill1*; size the picture to 2.5" high.
2. Crop the picture to focus only on the sand castles as shown above.
3. Click off the picture to finish it; then size it to 2" high.
4. Save and close. (*50-drill2*)

Lesson 16 2 and 7

Warmup *Lesson 16a Warmup*

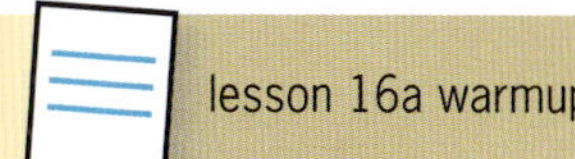

New Keys

16b 2 and 7

2 Reach *up* with *left third* finger.

7 Reach *up* with *right first* finger.

2

1 2 2s s2 2 2; has 2 sons; is 2 sizes; was 2 sites; has 2 skis
2 add 2 and 2; 2 sets of 2; catch 22; as 2 of the 22; 222 Main
3 Exactly at 2 on April 22, the 22nd Company left from Pier 2.

7

4 7 7j j7 7 7; 7 jets; 7 jeans; 7 jays; 7 jobs; 7 jars; 7 jaws
5 ask for 7; buy 7; 77 years; June 7; take any 7; deny 77 boys
6 From May 7 on, all 77 men will live at 777 East 77th Street.

16c All Figures Learned

7 I read 2 of the 72 books, Ellis read 7, and Han read all 72.
8 Tract 27 cites the date as 1850; Tract 170 says it was 1852.
9 You can take Flight 850 on January 12; I'll take Flight 705.

Skill Building

16d Improve Techniques

Key each line once. Keep fingers curved and relaxed; wrists low.

3rd/4th

10 pop was lap pass slaw wool solo swap apollo wasp load plaque
11 Al's quote was, "I was dazzled by the jazz, pizza, and pool."

1st/2nd

12 bad fun nut kick dried night brick civic thick hutch believe
13 Kim may visit her friends in Germany if I give her a ticket.

3rd/1st

14 cry tube wine quit very curb exit crime ebony mention excite
15 To be invited, petition the six executive committee members.

New Commands

50c

LEARNING ABOUT GRAPHICS

Many different types of graphics can be used to enhance documents. Typically, graphics are used in documents such as announcements, invitations, flyers, brochures, reports, and newsletters. However, they can be used in virtually any type of document to enhance the document and to clarify or simplify concepts. For example, a picture may convey a concept that would take many words to describe adequately. It is important to use graphics strategically and not to overuse them. The overuse of graphics can be distracting to the reader.

PICTURES

Word provides two different commands to insert pictures based on the source of the picture. The Pictures button enables you to insert pictures from your computer or other computers on your network. The Online Pictures button enables you to insert pictures from web searches, your OneDrive, or from Flickr—a photo-sharing social media site.

To insert pictures from your computer:

Insert/Illustrations/Pictures

1. Click at the position you wish to insert a picture and then click Pictures to display the Insert Pictures dialog box.
2. Browse through your files of digital pictures and select the one you wish to insert.
3. Double-click the picture or click the Insert button at the bottom of the dialog box to insert it.

Note that the size of the picture varies, but it is usually large.

DRILL 1 INSERT PICTURE

sand castles

1. In a new document, insert the *sand castles* picture from your data files.
2. Save and close. (*50-drill1*)

FORMAT PICTURES

Pictures are formatted using the tools on the Format tab that displays when you select a picture. These tools are used in a similar manner to the way you used Table tools in Module 5. Note that when you click the Picture Tools Format tab, the Ribbon displays with four groups of commands used to format pictures: Adjust, Picture Styles, Arrange, and Size. Remember you must select a picture before you apply any format.

16e Improve Keystroking

16 line 8; Book 1; No. 88; Seat 11; June 18; Cart 81; date 1881
17 take 2; July 7; buy 22; sell 77; mark 27; adds 72; Memo 2772
18 feed 5; bats 0; age 50; Ext. 55; File 50; 55 bags; band 5005
19 I work 18 visual signs with 20 turns of the 57 lenses to 70.
20 Did 17 boys fix the gears for 50 bicycles in 28 racks or 10?

16f Build Fluency

Key each line once.

Think and key the words and phrases as units rather than letter by letter.

words: *think, say,* and *key* words

21 is do am lay cut pen dub may fob ale rap cot hay pay hem box
22 box wit man sir fish also hair giant rigor civic virus ivory
23 laugh sight flame audit formal social turkey bicycle problem

phrases: *think, say,* and *key* phrases

24 is it | is it | if it is | if it is | or by | or by | or me | or me | for us
25 and all | for pay | pay dues and | the pen | the pen box | the pen box
26 such forms | held both | work form | then wish | sign name | with them

easy sentences

27 The man is to do the work right; he then pays the neighbors.
28 Sign the forms to pay the eight men for the turkey and hams.
29 The antique ivory bicycle is a social problem for the chair.

16g Timed Writing

Take two 2' timed writings. If you finish before time is up, begin again. Use wordwrap.

Goal: 16 *gwam*

	gwam 2'	3'
When choosing a password, do not select one you have	6	4
already used. Create a new one quite often, perhaps every	11	8
three to four weeks. Be sure to use a combination of both	17	11
letters and numbers.	19	13
Know your password; do not record it on paper. If you	25	17
must write it down, be sure the password is not recognized.	31	21
Don't let anyone watch you key. Just position yourself away	37	24
from the person or key a few extra strokes.	41	27

2' | 1 | 2 | 3 | 4 | 5 | 6
3' | 1 | 2 | 3 | 4

MODULE 7

Graphics

Lesson 50 *Pictures, Online Pictures, and Video*
Lesson 51 *SmartArt and WordArt*
Lesson 52 *Documents with Columns*
Lesson 53 *Palmetto Event Solutions, Inc.*

LEARNING OUTCOMES

- Learn and apply essential *Word 2016* commands.
- Create documents with pictures, video, SmartArt, WordArt, and borders.
- Create documents with equal-width columns and graphics.
- Build keyboarding skills.

Lesson 50 Pictures, Online Pictures, and Video

New Commands

- Insert Pictures
- Picture Tools Format
- Size Pictures
- Crop Pictures
- Compress Pictures
- Wrap Text
- Position Pictures
- Insert Online Pictures
- Page Borders
- Insert Video

Warmup *Lesson 50a Warmup*

lesson 50a warmup

Skill Building

50b Timed Writing

1. Key a 1' timed writing on each paragraph; work to increase speed.
2. Key a 3' timed writing on both paragraphs.

gwam 1' | 3'

Most of us know that having a good professional image can help us 13 | 4
to create a good first impression when we meet people. The same 26 | 9
general principle applies to the letters, memos, reports, and 38 | 13
other documents that we prepare and send to our business associates, 51 | 17
clients, or customers. The way that a document appears when 63 | 21
the recipient opens it and looks at it makes either a good or a 76 | 25
bad first impression. 80 | 27

The quality and the organization of the content are very 11 | 30
important when a document is examined in detail, but they are not 24 | 35
the factors that create the first impression. The general appearance 38 | 39
does that. The judicious use of color and certain types of 49 | 43
graphics can create a good visual impact, but using too much color 63 | 48
or the wrong type of color or graphic can do just the opposite. 75 | 52

Lesson 17 4 and 9

Warmup *Lesson 17a Warmup*

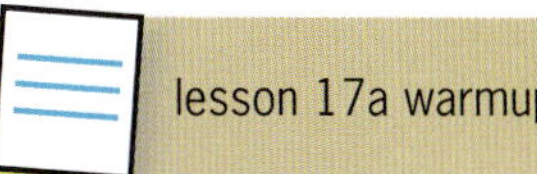

New Keys

17b 4 and 9

4 Reach *up* with *left first* finger.

9 Reach *up* with *right third* finger.

4

1 4 4f f4 f f f; if 4 furs; off 4 floors; gaff 4 fish; 4 flags
2 44th floor; half of 44; 4 walked 44 flights; 4 girls; 4 boys
3 I order exactly 44 bagels, 4 cakes, and 4 pies before 4 a.m.

9

4 9 91 l9 9 9 9; fill 9 lugs; call 9 lads; Bill 9 lost; dial 9
5 also 9 oaks; roll 9 loaves; 9.9 degrees; sell 9 oaks; Hall 9
6 Just 9 couples, 9 men and 9 women, left at 9 on our Tour 99.

17c All Figures Learned

7 4 feet; 4 inches; 44 gallons, 444 quarts, 4 folders, 44 fads
8 Lucky 99; 999 leaves; 9 lottery tickets; 9 losers; 9 winners
9 Memo 94 says 9 pads, 4 pens, and 4 ribbons were sent July 9.
10 Study Item 17 and Item 28 on page 40 and Item 59 on page 49.
11 Within 17 months he drove 85 miles, walked 29, and flew 490.

Skill Building

17d Improve Keystroking

Key each line once.

Keep hands quiet as you reach to the top row; do not bounce.

12 My staff of 18 worked 11 hours a day from May 27 to June 12.
13 There were 5 items tested by Inspector 7 at 4 p.m. on May 8.
14 Please send her File 10 today at 8; her access number is 97.
15 Car 947 had its trial run. The qualifying speed was 198 mph.
16 The estimated total score? 485. Actual? 390. Difference? 95.

49-d2

Leftbound Report

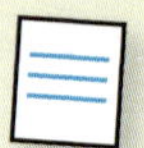

study

1. Open *study* from the data files. Key the remainder of the report shown below and format as a leftbound report.
2. Apply the Retrospect theme. Format the title and side headings with the appropriate style. Tap ENTER twice after the title.
3. Key the table below, placing it in the report below the paragraph that describes Table 1; apply the Grid Table 6 Colorful – Accent 3. Merge the cells as shown. Center the headings as shown. Insert a right tab at the approximate center of columns B–E to align the numbers in the approximate center of the column.
4. Choose the open circle bullet for the bulleted list.
5. Insert the second content footnote as marked in the report.
6. Number the pages at the top right using the Accent Bar 2 page number style.
7. Save and close. (*49-d2*)

Table 1
Comparison of Adherence of Dress Code Policy to Absenteeism and Tardiness

	Absenteeism		Tardiness	
	Male	Female	Male	Female
Adhered to policy	2%	2%	1%	0%
Did not adhere to policy	25%	30%	12%	10%

The findings clearly verify our review of the business literature that employees who dress more professionally are absent fewer days and are on time for work more often.

Recommendations

Although complete adherence to the dress code was not found, the findings of the study do show that the compliance to our policy (89%) is much better than companies included in the NABASW Study.[2] However, because the findings in our company show a correlation between absenteeism and tardiness, this subcommittee respectfully submits the following recommendations.

- Consider employing an image consultant to teach employees what is appropriate business casual and to plan the best business attire to project the image of our company.
- Prepare online materials that more clearly explain the areas of the dress code that appeared in the study as violations.

In summary, the current dress code is fulfilling the company philosophy to provide a comfortable work environment and to project a positive corporate image. Professional development is recommended in selected areas.

Footnote text:

[2] Study of 500 companies revealed that 80 percent of the companies reported a 60 percent level of compliance by employees to established company dress policy.

17e Improve Keystroking

first finger

17 buy them gray vent guy brunt buy brunch much give huge vying
18 Hagen, after her July triumph at tennis, may try volleyball.
19 Verna urges us to buy yet another of her beautiful rag rugs.

second finger

20 keen idea; kick it back; ice breaker; decide the issue; cite
21 Did Dick ask Cecelia, his sister, if she decided to like me?
22 Suddenly, Micki's bike skidded on the Cedar Street ice rink.

third/fourth finger

23 low slow lax solo wax zip zap quips quiz zipper prior icicle
24 Paula has always allowed us to relax at La Paz and at Quito.
25 Please ask Zale to explain who explores most aquatic slopes.

17f Timed Writing

Take a 2' timing on all the paragraphs. Repeat the timing. Use wordwrap.

	gwam 2'	3'
Many experts believe stress affects the mind as well as	6	4
the body. However, they are not quite sure just how much	11	8
damage can be caused. This may be because people deal with	17	12
stress in several different ways. Some learn to either shrug	23	16
it off or else put little thought to it.	27	19
Coping with stress is difficult but if one is willing to	34	23
make an effort, it can be handled easily. One way to deal	39	27
with stress is having a good diet as well as regular exercise.	46	31
Another way is to become involved with enjoyable activities	52	35
such as writing, painting, or running. Last, but certainly not	58	39
least, have a positive thought process, a great zest for life,	64	43
and a big cheerful smile.	67	45

17g Build Skill

1. Go to Skill Builder 1 on page 1-35.
2. Key Drill 2 from page 1-36. Key each line once; strive to improve accuracy.

Lesson 49 Assessment Modules 5 and 6

Warmup *Lesson 49a Warmup*

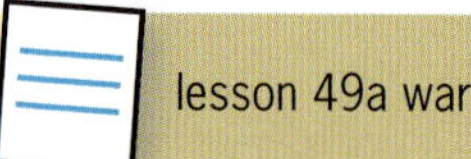
lesson 49a warmup

Apply It

49-d1

Table

1. Key the table shown below. Apply Grid Table 5 Dark – Accent 6 style to the table.
2. Insert a row at the beginning of the table. Key the title **Occupational Health and Safety Department Survey**. Merge the cells and center the title.
3. Change row height of row 1 to 0.4" and click Align Center to center the text vertically and horizontally in the row.
4. Save and close. (*49-d1*)

Safety and health is a primary concern in every operation at Areorbit Corporation, and our goal is to be in compliance with the state's job safety and health laws and regulations. A summary of the annual safety report is shown below. The necessary adjustments are being made to produce a safer working environment.

Safety Standard	Madison Facility	Central Park Facility
Adequate lighting in hallways and stairwells.	Pass	Pass
Aisles and passageways are sufficiently wide for easy movement and should be kept clear at all times.	Pass	Pass
Temporary electrical cords that cross aisles are taped or anchored to the floor.	Pass	Electrical cord to coffee maker needs to be anchored in kitchen.
Adequate lighting is provided during night hours.	Two exterior lights need to be replaced in front of the building.	Pass
Floor surfaces are even; no bulges in carpet that can cause tripping hazards.	Stretch carpet in employee lounge to eliminate bulges.	Pass
Signs leading to exits are posted and are easily visible in the dark.	Pass	Light needs to be replaced in exit sign 7.

Lesson 18 3 and 6

Warmup *Lesson 18a Warmup*

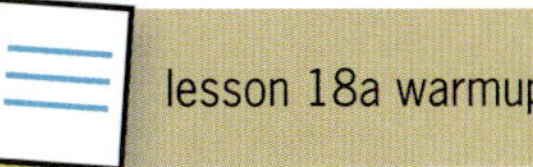

lesson 18a warmup

New Keys

18b 3 and 6

© Cengage Learning

3 Reach *up* with *left second* finger.

© Cengage Learning

6 Reach *up* with *right first* finger.

Note: Ergonomic keyboard users will use *left first* finger to key 6.

3

1 3 3d d3 3 3; had 3 days; did 3 dives; led 3 dogs; add 3 dips

2 we 3 ride 3 cars; take 33 dials; read 3 copies; save 33 days

3 On July 3, 33 lights lit 33 stands holding 33 prize winners.

6

4 6 6j 6j 6 6; 6 jays; 6 jams; 6 jigs; 6 jibs; 6 jots; 6 jokes

5 only 6 high; on 66 units; reach 66 numbers; 6 yams or 6 jams

6 On May 6, Car 66 delivered 66 tons of No. 6 shale to Pier 6.

18c All Figures Learned

7 At 6 p.m., Channel 3 reported the August 6 score was 6 to 3.

8 Jean, do Items 28 and 6; Mika, 59 and 10; Kyle, 3, 4, and 7.

9 Cars 56 and 34 used Aisle 9; Cars 2 and 87 can use Aisle 10.

18d Improve Fluency

Key each line once.

word response: *think* and *key* words

10 he el id is go us it an me of he of to if ah or bye do so am

11 Did she enamel emblems on a big panel for the downtown sign?

stroke response: *think* and *key* each stroke

12 kin are hip read lymph was pop saw ink art oil gas up as mop

13 Barbara started the union wage earners tax in Texas in July.

combination response: vary speed but maintain rhythm

14 upon than eve lion when burley with they only them loin were

15 It was the opinion of my neighbor that we may work as usual.

48-d3

Letter

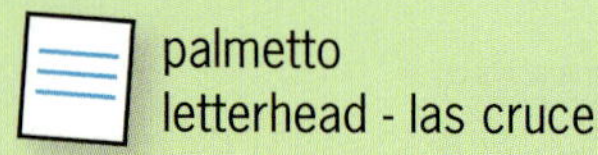

Much communication will be necessary between Mr. Torres and Mr. Romero, the president of Southwest Culinary Association. Open the palmetto letterhead from the data files and prepare the following letter.

1. Include all necessary letter parts. Address to **Mr. Jason Romero, President | Southwest Culinary Association | P.O. Box 3759 | Oklahoma City, OK 73101-3759**. Date the letter **January 15, 201-**.
2. Save and close. *(48-d3)*

Our office is very pleased to be working with you on event planning for the Southwest Culinary Association Convention to be held in San Antonio on February 1–4. We distributed the Request for Proposals yesterday to the lists provided by Ms. Janet Wiseman, the treasurer of your association.

Next we are focusing our attention on sponsorships for the following major events:

1. Board dinner on March 31
2. Opening reception on February 1
3. Morning and afternoon coffee breaks on February 2 and 3
4. Wine and cheese reception on February 3

Event proposal forms are attached for each of the events listed above. Please complete the forms and return by email to me at conference201@palmettoeventsolutions.com. Your return of these forms by next Monday will be greatly appreciated. Our goal is to solicit at least two sponsors for each event, and this information is valuable to us as we plan our campaign.

Thank you for your valuable input in our event planning.

48-d4

Compose Letter

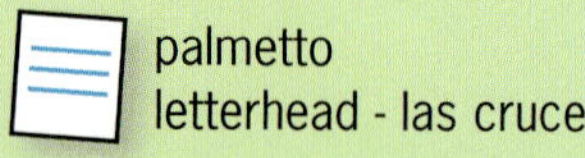

Mr. Torres has asked you to compose a draft of the letter to be emailed to the presenters whose proposals are being accepted for the Southwest Culinary Association Convention. Date the letter May 31 and key on the Southwest letterhead. The following details are important to include.

1. Congratulate the presenter for having a proposal accepted for the convention.
2. Explain that the assignment of day, time, and room are not complete and will be emailed within the month.
3. Attach the speaker form you prepared earlier and ask the speaker to complete and return to you by June 15. Also request a brief biographical sketch to be used in the convention program and by the session facilitator who will introduce the speaker.
4. End with a gracious thank-you for their willingness to speak at the convention.
5. Save and close. *(48-d4)*

18e Improve Keystroking

long reaches

16 ce cede cedar wreck nu nu nut punt nuisance my my amy mystic
17 ny ny any many company mu mu mull lumber mulch br br furbish
18 Cecil received a large brown umbrella from Bunny and Hunter.

number review

19 set 0; push 4; Car 00; score 44; jot 04; age 40; Billet 4004
20 April 5; lock 5; set 66; fill 55; hit 65; pick 56; adds 5665
21 Her grades are 93, 87, and 100; his included 82, 96, and 54.

18f Timed Writing

Key two 3' writings. Use wordwrap.

Lisa S./Shutterstock.com

gwam 3'

I am something quite precious. Though millions of people 4
in other countries might not have me, you likely do. I am very 8
powerful. I choose the new president every four years. I 12
decide if a tax should be levied or repealed. I even decide 16
questions of war and peace. I was acquired with great expense; 20
however, I am free to all citizens. But sadly enough, I am 24
often ignored; or, still worse, I am just taken for granted. I 28
can be lost, and in certain circumstances I can even be taken 33
away. What am I? I am your right to vote. Don't take me 36
lightly. Exercise your right to vote at every election; 40
consider it an opportunity and a privilege. 43

3' | 1 | 2 | 3 | 4 |

Communication

18g Composition

1. Compose two paragraphs, each having about three sentences, in which you introduce yourself to your instructor. Use proper grammatical structure. Disregard keying errors at this time.
2. Save the document as *xx-18g*; replace *xx* with your initials. You will edit this document later.

48-d2

Speaker Form

A speaker form will be sent to presenters of proposals that were accepted for the convention program.

1. Create the table below as a 2 × 10 table. Split the cells in rows 8 and 9 into five columns, then merge row 9 as shown.
2. Select the entire table and change the height of the table rows to 0.3".
3. In row 1, change the text to Align Center; for text in rows 2–10, change text to Align Center Left.
4. Save and close. (*48-d2*)

SPEAKER CONTACT INFORMATION					
Name:					
Professional Credentials:					
Title:					
Company:					
Address 1:					
Address 2:					
City:		State:		ZIP Code:	
Telephone:			Fax:		
Email:					

QUICK ✓

Check your document against the illustration below.

SPEAKER CONTACT INFORMATION					
Name:					
Professional Credentials:					
Title:					
Company:					
Address 1:					
Address 2:					
City:		State:		ZIP Code:	
Telephone:			Fax:		
Email:					

Lesson 18R Review

Warmup *Lesson 18Ra Warmup*

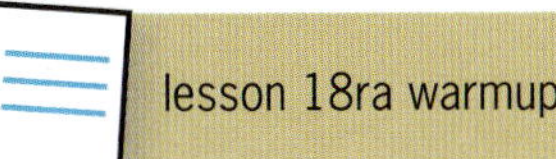

Skill Building

18Rb Improve Keystroking

Key each line once; work for fluency.

1 Jake may pay the sixty men for eighty bushels of blue forks.
2 We used software versions 1.01, 2.6, 7.2, 8.3, 8.5, and 9.4.
3 The big box by the lake held fish, duck, apricot, and a map.
4 Adding 123 and 345 and 567 and 80 and 62 and 5 totals 1,182.
5 Lana and Jay and Ken paid to sit by the lake to fish at six.
6 We can see you at 6:30, 7:30, 8:45, 9:00, or 12:15 tomorrow.

18Rc Timed Writing

Key a 3' timing on all paragraphs. Repeat.

gwam 3'

You want to be known as a person of good character. If 4
someone says that you have character, it usually means that 8
you are honest, have integrity, and are reliable and 12
responsible. On the other hand, if you lie, cheat, or steal, 16
or are lazy, you will be known as a person with poor 19
character. If others say that you are quite a character, it 23
usually means that you have good character. 26

You will be judged by your actions and expressions. What 30
you say and do to others affects how others will respond to 34
you. You need to be considerate of others and conscientious in 38
your work. Others will respect and trust you and want you 42
involved in their activities. 44

3' | 1 | 2 | 3 | 4 |

18Rd Improve Keystroking

1. Take a 30" timing on each line.
2. Try to maintain the same speed on each line.

7 Come work with us on this new job next month.
8 Jo will be 44 years 2 months and 24 days old.

9 I see you need some help with the new assignments.
10 I will be 44 years 2 months and 24 days old today.

11 Sixteen of us can come and help you today and tomorrow.
12 Order 99 cookies; at least have 33 sugar and 39 ginger.

13 Tell us how you want the work done; we will finish it today.
14 I delivered Order 6688 for 88 chairs and 66 tables by 6 p.m.

Session Descriptions

Convention participants will choose from four types of convention sessions. In preparing the proposal, use the following information to select the most appropriate type of session for the proposed session content.

Type	Length	Room Setup	Audience Size
Lecture (L)	60 minutes	Tables	50
Roundtable (RT)	60 minutes (20 minutes per rotation)	Roundtables	8 per table
Hands-on Computer Workshop (W)	90 minutes	Lab with 20 laptop computers	20
Demonstrations (D)	60 minutes	Theater seating in teaching kitchen	100

Submission Information and Deadlines

Email proposals to Carlos Torres carlos.torres@palmettoeventsolutions.com by May 15 at 5 p.m. If you have questions, please call Carlos Torres at 505.555.0152.

Guidelines

The proposal must be no more than four single-spaced pages and must include the following information:

1. Cover Page that includes the title of presentation, type of session (Lecture, Roundtable, Hands-on Computer Workshop, or Demonstration), names of all presenters, and contact information for all presenters (company name, mailing address, email address, and telephone numbers)
2. Title of Presentation with description of presentation for program (limit to 50 words)
3. Purpose of Presentation and Justification for Acceptance
4. Topical Outline

Notification

Authors of accepted proposals will be notified on June 15.

Lesson 19 $ and – (hyphen)

Warmup *Lesson 19a Warmup*

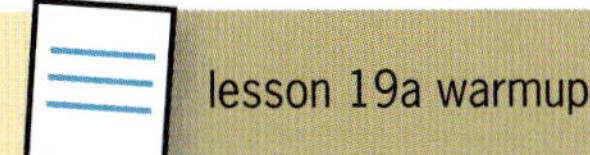

19b Learn $ and -

$ Right shift; then reach *up* with *left first* finger.

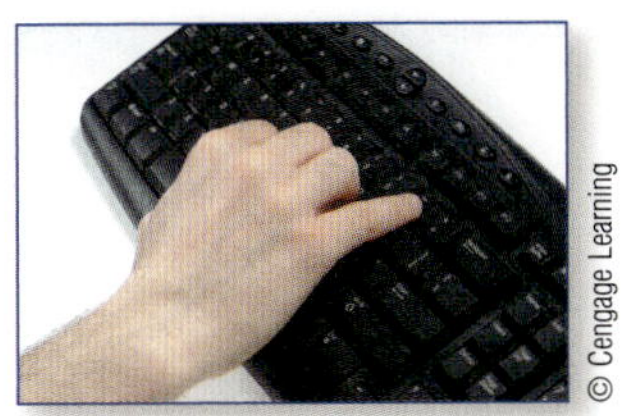

- (hyphen) Reach *up* with *right fourth* finger.

- = hyphen
-- = dash
Do not space before or after a hyphen or a dash.

$

1 $ $f f$ $ $; if $4; half $4; off $4; of $4; $4 fur; $4 flats
2 for $8; cost $9; log $3; grab $10; give Rolf $2; give Viv $4
3 Since she paid $45 for the item priced at $54, she saved $9.

- (hyphen)

4 - -; ;- - - -; up-to-date; co-op; father-in-law; four-square
5 pop-up foul; big-time job; snap-on bit; one- or two-hour ski
6 You need 6 signatures--half of the members--on the petition.

19c All Symbols Learned

7 I paid $10 for the low-cost disk; high-priced ones cost $40.
8 Le-An spent $20 for travel, $95 for books, and $38 for food.
9 Mr. Loft-Smit sold his boat for $467; he bought it for $176.

Skill Building

19d Improve Keystroking

10 Edie discreetly decided to deduct expenses in making a deal.
11 Working women wear warm wool sweaters when weather dictates.
12 We heard very rude remarks regarding her recent termination.
13 Daily sudden mishaps destroyed several dozens of sand dunes.
14 Beverley voted by giving a bold beverage to every brave boy.

Project Setting

PALMETTO EVENT SOLUTIONS, INC.

For the project in this module, you will be preparing documents for Carlos Torres, the regional vice president in the Southwest office in Las Cruces. The Southwest office was recently contracted to coordinate events for the Southwest Culinary Association Convention to be held in San Antonio next year. You have been assigned exclusively to this project.

As you work through each job, make sure you do the following:

- Use Southwest letterhead for all letters and the block letter style with open punctuation.
- Key **Mr. Torres** as the author of all letters and format the signature line as follows: **Sincerely | Carlos Torres | Regional Vice President**. Letters are generally emailed as attachments unless otherwise directed. Items attached to the letter would be considered attachments.
- Apply the Grid Table 4 – Accent 5 table style for all tables.
- Use the Accent Bar 2 page number style for all reports.

48-d1

Request for Proposals

Prepare the Request for Proposals below as an unbound report.

1. Apply the Title style to the title and Heading 1 style to side headings.
2. Format the table appropriately and number the pages.
3. Save and close. (*48-d1*)

Request for Proposals

The purpose of this Request for Proposals (RFP) is to solicit speakers for the Southwest Culinary Association Convention to be held on February 1–4, 201-, in San Antonio, Texas, at the San Antonio Hotel. Approximately 2,000 members, exhibitors, and guests are expected to attend this annual convention.

The Southwest regional office of Palmetto Event Solutions, Inc. is the official event planner of this conference and will oversee the RFP and the final selection program presenters. Send all questions to the following address before May 1:

Mr. Carlos Torres

Regional Vice President

Palmetto Event Solutions, Inc.

590 S. Solano Drive

Las Cruces, NM 88001-3290

575.555.0152

Press SHIFT + ENTER for these short lines.

The conference speakers will be carefully selected individuals who have expertise in the current trends and issues, use of cutting edge technology needed by today's chefs, and a showcase of best practices in the field.

(continued)

19e Build Speed

1. Key each line once.
2. When keying easy words and phrases:
   - Think and key words and phrases rather than letter by letter.
   - Make the space part of the word.

easy words

15 am it go bus dye jam irk six sod tic yam ugh spa vow aid dug
16 he or by air big elf dog end fit and lay sue toe wit own got
17 six foe pen firm also body auto form down city kept make fog

easy phrases

18 it is | if the | and also | to me | the end | to us | if it | it is | to the
19 if it is | to the end | do you wish | to go to | for the end | to make
20 lay down | he or she | make me | by air | end of | by me | kept it | of me

easy sentences

21 Did the chap work to mend the torn right half of the ensign?
22 Blame me for their penchant for the antique chair and panel.
23 She bid by proxy for eighty bushels of a corn and rye blend.

19f Practice Numbers

1. Key lines 24–29, focusing on good techniques.
2. Key lines 24–29 again, striving for fluency.

Key numbers without watching your fingers.

24 Jan will come by at 4 o'clock to pick up the 3 girls.
25 Lauren and Paul invited 200 guests to the reception.
26 We have 3 more days to finish 66 percent of the plan.
27 Tish sent 7 24-pound boxes and 10 3-ounce envelopes.
28 I deposited 15 quarters, 10 dimes, and 4 nickels in the ATM.
29 A quorum was established; 7 of the 12 members voted.

19g Build Speed

1. Go to Skill Builder 1 that starts on page 1-35.
2. Take a 1' timed writing on Writing 2 from page 1-38.
3. Key it again. Strive to increase speed by 2 *gwam* the second time.

Lesson 48 Palmetto Event Solutions, Inc.

Warmup *Lesson 48a Warmup*

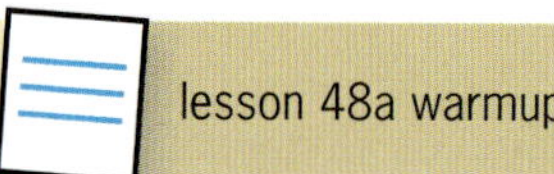

Skill Building

48b Improve Keystroking

caps
1 James Carswell plans to visit Austin and New Orleans in December.
2 Will Peter and Betsy go with Mark when he goes to Alaska in June?
3 John Kenny wrote the book *Innovation and Timing—Keys to Success.*

double letters
4 Jeanne arranges meeting room space in Massey Hall for committees.
5 Russell will attend to the bookkeeping issues tomorrow afternoon.
6 Todd offered a free book with all assessment tools Lynette sells.

balanced hand
7 Jane, a neighbor and a proficient auditor, may amend their audit.
8 Blanche and a neighbor may make an ornament for an antique chair.
9 Claudia may visit the big island when they go to Orlando with us.

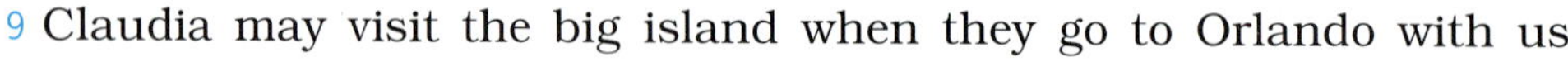

48c

Timed Writing

1. Key a 1' timing on each paragraph; work to increase speed.
2. Key a 3' timing on all paragraphs.

	gwam 1'	3'
Whether any company can succeed depends on how well it fits into	13	4
the economic system. Success rests on certain key factors that are	26	9
put in line by a management team that has set goals for the company	39	13
and has enough good judgment to recognize how best to reach these	52	17
goals. Because of competition, only the best-organized companies	65	22
get to the top.	68	23
A commercial enterprise is formed for a specific purpose: that	12	27
purpose is usually to equip others, or consumers, with whatever	25	31
they cannot equip themselves. Unless there is only one provider,	38	35
a consumer will search for a company that returns the most value	51	40
in terms of price; and a relationship with such a company, once	63	44
set up, can endure for many years.	70	46
Thus our system assures that the businesses that manage to survive	13	50
are those that have been able to combine successfully an excellent	26	55
product with a low price and the best service—all in a place that	39	59
is convenient for the buyers. With no intrusion from outside forces,	53	64
the buyer and the seller benefit both themselves and each other.	66	68

Lesson 20 # and /

Warmup *Lesson 20a Warmup*

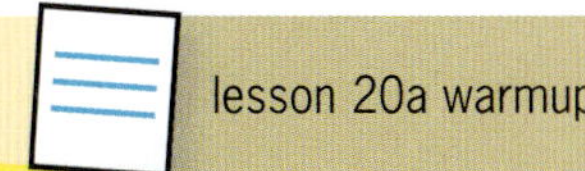

New Keys

20b Learn # and /

Right shift; then reach *up* with *left second* finger.

/ Reach *down* with *right fourth* finger.

 # = number sign, pounds
/ = diagonal, slash

#

1 # #e e# # # #; had #3 dial; did #3 drop; set #3 down; Bid #3
2 leave #82; sold #20; Lyric #16; bale #34; load #53; Optic #7
3 Notice #333 says to load Car #33 with 33# of #3 grade shale.

/

4 / /; ;/ / / /; 1/2; 1/3; Mr./Mrs.; 1/4/12; 22 11/12; and/or;
5 to/from; /s/ William Smit; 2/10, n/30; his/her towels; 6 1/2
6 The numerals 1 5/8, 3 1/4, and 60 7/9 are "mixed fractions."

20c All Symbols Learned

7 Invoice #737 cites 15 2/3# of rye was shipped C.O.D. 4/6/14.
8 B-O-A Company's Check #50/5 for $87 paid for 15# of #3 wire.
9 Our Co-op List #20 states $40 for 16 1/2 crates of tomatoes.

Skill Building

20d Build Skill

Strive to maintain your speed on the second line in the pair.

10 She did the key work at the height of the problem.
11 Form #726 is the title to the island; she owns it.

12 The rock is a form of fuel; he did enrich it with coal.
13 The corn-and-turkey dish is a blend of turkey and corn.

14 It is right to work to end the social problems of the world.
15 If I sign it on 3/19, the form can aid us to pay the 40 men.

16 Profit problems at the firm may cause it to take many risks.
17 Dale discovered that Invoice #238 for $128.83 is dated 8/15.

Apply It

47-d1

APA Template

1. In a new document, click No Spacing style and change line spacing to 2.0.
2. Change to 12-point Times New Roman font.
3. Double-click in the header section and change to 12-point Times New Roman font. Key **TITLE OF PAPER** at the left margin. Tap TAB twice and insert page number. Close the Header & Footer.
4. Key **Title of Paper** at 1" and center.
5. Save as a Word Template and close. *(47-d1)*

47-d2

APA Report

1. Open the file *(47-d1)* that you created in the previous exercise and key the APA report shown on pages 2-119 and 2-200 using the template with the APA formatting already applied. Do not key the Bibliography page.
2. Double click in the header and change *TITLE OF PAPER* to **WRITING A SCHOLARLY REPORT**. Close the header.
3. In the title line, replace *Title of Paper* with **Writing a Scholarly Report**.
4. Click Increase Indent once to indent the long quotation 0.5" from the left margin.
5. Check that side headings are not alone at the bottom of the page. Use the Keep with next command if needed.
6. Save and close. *(47-d2)*

47-d3

Bibliography

1. Open the file *(47-d2)* that you created in the previous exercise. Position the insertion point at the end of the report. Press CTRL + ENTER to begin a new page.
2. Begin at 1" and key the bibliography shown below. DS and format the references in hanging indent style.
3. Save and close. *(47-d3)*

Capitalize only the first word and proper nouns in book titles and journal titles.

Italicize journal name and volume number.

Bibliography

Millsaps, J. T. (2018). *Report writing handbook: An essential guide.* Columbus: Wellington Books.

Quattlebaum, S. (2016). Apply reference styles correctly. *The Quarterly Reference Journal*, 27(1), 35-42.

20e Build Fluency

Key each line once. Notice the difference in the rhythm of your keying.

one hand
18 lip ere him bat lion date pink face pump rear only brag fact
19 at my; oh no; add debt; extra milk; union agreed; act faster

balanced hand
20 so it is | now is the | do so when | sign the forms | is it downtown
21 He may wish to go to town with Pamela to sign the amendment.

combination
22 was for | in the case of | they were | to down | pink bowls | wet rugs
23 They were to be down in the fastest sleigh if you are right.

20f Timed Writing

1. Key a 1' timing on each paragraph; work to increase speed.
2. Key a 3' timing on all paragraphs.

	gwam 1'	3'
Most people want to be socially acceptable. In some	11	4
cases, the need for attention can lead to difficulties. Some	23	8
of us think that the best way to get attention is to try a new	36	12
style, or to look quixotic, or to be different somehow.	47	16
Perhaps we are looking for nothing much more than acceptance	59	20
from others of ourselves just the way we now are.	68	23
There is no question about it; we all want to look our	12	27
best to impress other people. How this is achieved may mean	24	31
that we try something new, or perform things differently.	35	34
Regardless, our basic objective is to continue to build	46	38
character with zeal from our raw materials, you and me.	57	42

1' | 1 | 2 | 3 | 4 | 5 | 6 | 7 | 8 | 9 | 10 | 11 | 12 |
3' | 1 | 2 | 3 | 4 |

Communication

20g Composition

A major employer spoke at a career day at your school and indicated his company preferred to hire new employees who have had experience working in teams. He felt that teams completed projects more effectively and more efficiently than individuals and encouraged instructors to engage students in teamwork in their classes.

1. Compose a paragraph of at least three sentences describing what you think are the advantages of working on a team of four or five students to complete class projects.
2. Then compose a second paragraph of at least three sentences describing what you think are the disadvantages of working on a team of four or five students to complete class projects.
3. Save as *xx-20g*.

INTERNAL CITATIONS IN APA STYLE

1. When cited information is paraphrased, the last name of the author(s) and the publication year of the paraphrased material are shown in parenthesis. Example: *Podcasts are effectively used by distance faculty (Crawford, 2018).*
2. When the author(s) names are used in the text, the publication year is keyed after the author name(s). Example: *According to Crawford (2018), podcasts are effectively used by distance faculty.*
3. When the citation is a direct quote, the page number appears in parenthesis after the quote. Example: *Crawford (2018) said, "Faculty are uploading podcast lectures" (p. 134).*
4. Long quotations of 40 words or more are indented 0.5" from the left margin and DS. Tap ENTER once before and after the long quotation. See the example below.

Probably no successful enterprise exists that does not rely upon the ability of its members to communicate for its success. Shaefer (2018) adds:

> Make no mistake, both written and verbal communication are the stuff upon which success is built in all types of organizations. Both forms deserve careful study by any business that wants to grow. Successful businesspeople must read, write, speak, and listen with skill. Often professional development in these areas is needed. (p. 28)

Communicating Today

Why Styles Cannot Be Overlooked

Styles provide consistent and attractive formatting with a quick click. The Format Painter can even be used to copy a style once it has been applied. Most importantly, when styles are applied, the headings are listed in the navigation bar for easy movement within a large document.

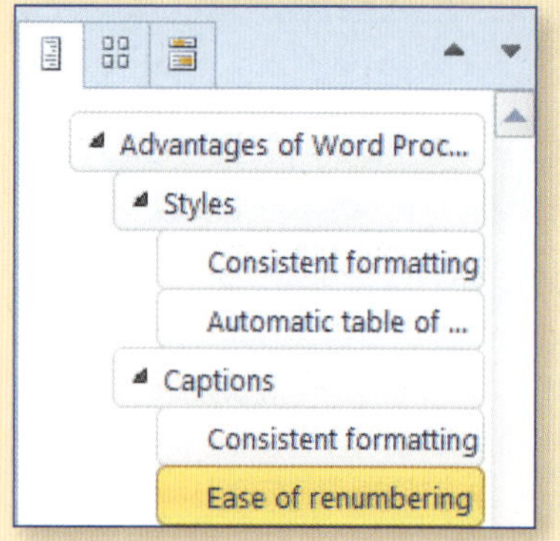

At the right you can see the Level 1 heading displayed at the far left. The two Level 2 headings are indented beneath that, and Level 3 headings are indented again. Simply click on the heading to go to that section of the paper. No more time-consuming scrolling is needed.

Another major advantage of using styles, especially in a long report, is the ability to generate an automatic table of contents. Once the proper level of heading styles is applied, one click of the mouse creates a beautifully formatted table of contents. If changes are made in the report, one click updates the table of contents.

Lesson 21 % and !

Warmup *Lesson 21a Warmup*

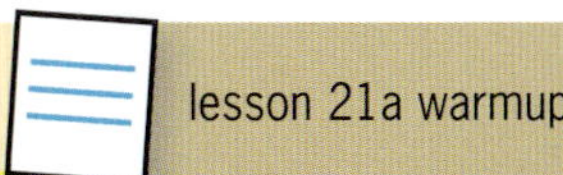

New Keys

21b % and !

% Right shift; then reach *up* with *left first* finger.

- Do not space between a figure and the % or $ sign.
- Do not space before or after the dash.

% = percent sign: Use % with business forms or where space is restricted; otherwise use the word "percent."

Space once after the exclamation point.

% right shift; then reach up with left first finger

1 % %f f% % %; off 5%; if 5%; of 5% fund; half 5%; taxes of 5%
2 7% rent; 3% tariff; 9% F.O.B.; 15% greater; 28% base; up 46%
3 Give discounts of 5% on rods, 50% on lures, and 75% on line.

! right shift; then reach up with the left fourth finger

4 ! !a a! ! ! !; Eureka! Ha! No! Pull 10! Extra! America! Yea!
5 Attention! Now! Ready! On your mark! Get set! Go! Good show!
6 We need it now, not next week! I am sure to lose 50% or $19.

21c All Symbols Learned

7 The ad offers a 10% discount, but this notice says 15% less!
8 He got the job! With Loehman's Supermarket! Please call Mom!
9 Bill #92-44 arrived very late from Zyclone; it was paid 7/4.

21d Improve Keystroking

all symbols

10 As of 6/28, Jeri owes $31 for dinner and $27 for cab fare.
11 Invoice #20--it was dated 3/4--billed $17 less 15% discount.
12 He deducted 2% instead of 6%, a clear saving of 6% vs. 7%.

combination response

13 Look at my dismal grade in English; but I guess I earned it.
14 Kris started to blend a cocoa beverage for a shaken cowhand.
15 Jan may make a big profit if she owns the title to the land.

Running head → WRITING A SCHOLARLY REPORT 2

a hanging indent in both MLA and APA, but be cautious of the differences in the formatting of authors' names and book and article titles" (p. 40).

Summary

Experienced writers understand the importance of selecting credible resources, documenting references, and applying the exact reference style required in the report. Learning to document your references accurately is an important step toward becoming an experienced writer.

WRITING A SCHOLARLY REPORT

3

Bibliography

Millsaps, J. T. (2018). *Report writing handbook: An essential guide*. Columbus: Wellington Books.

Quattlebaum, S. (2016). Apply reference styles correctly. *The Quarterly Reference Journal, 27*(1), 35-42.

APA Report Style

21e Improve Techniques

Key each line once.

1st finger

16 by bar get fun van for inn art from gray hymn July true verb

17 brag human bring unfold hominy mighty report verify puny joy

18 You are brave to try bringing home the van in the bad storm.

2nd finger

19 ace ink did cad keyed deep seed kind Dick died kink like kid

20 cease decease decades kick secret check decide kidney evaded

21 Dedre likes the idea of ending dinner with cake for dessert.

3rd finger

22 oil sow six vex wax axe low old lox pool west loss wool slow

23 swallow swamp saw sew wood sax sexes loom stew excess school

24 Wes waxes floors and washes windows at low costs to schools.

4th finger

25 zap zip craze pop pup pan daze quote queen quiz pizza puzzle

26 zoo graze zipper panzer zebra quip partizan patronize appear

27 Czar Zane appears to be dazzled by the apple pizza and jazz.

21f Timed Writing

1. Key a 1' timing on each paragraph.
2. Key a 3' timing on both paragraphs.

	gwam 1'	3'
Teams are the basic unit of performance for a firm. They	12	4
are not the solution to all the problems and needs of the	24	8
organization. However, they can perform at a higher rate	35	12
compared to other groups. Their support has great impact on	47	16
changes that are crucial to a firm.	54	18
Teams are not established just by joining people together	13	22
in a group. Team members should have a clear purpose and they	25	26
should also work with each other to reach a common goal. In	37	30
order to make a quality working plan, the team must maximize	49	38
their time and their abilities. They need to learn how to help	62	39
one another and make an effort to coordinate the tasks.	73	42

21g Build Skill

Take two 1' writings; the last number you key is your approximate *gwam*.

Reach for numbers with a minimum of hand movement.

1 and 2 and 3 and 4 and 5 and 6 and 7 and 8 and 9 and 10 and 11 and 12 and 13 and 14 and 15 and 16 and 17 and 18 and 19 and 20 and 21 and 22 and 23 and 24 and 25 and 26 and 27 and

Running head on each page with title of page and page number

WRITING A SCHOLARLY REPORT 1

1"

Writing a Scholarly Report

Title

Preparing a thorough and convincing scholarly report requires excellent research, organization, and composition skills as well as extensive knowledge of documenting referenced materials. The purpose of this report is to present the importance of documenting a report with credible references and the techniques for creating accurate citations.

Well-Cited References

1"

For a report to be believable and accepted by its readers, a thorough review of related literature is essential. The background information is an important part of the report and shows integrity of the report.

Good writers must learn quickly how to evaluate many printed and electronic references located to support the theme of any report being written. Those references judged acceptable are then cited in the report. Millsaps (2018) shares this simple advice:

Long quotation indented 0.5"

> Today writers can locate a vast number of references in very little time. Electronic databases and Web pages . . . provide a multitude of information. The novice writer will be quick to include all these references in a report without verifying their credibility. Writers check electronic sources as well. (p. 12)

Correct Styles Applied

The *MLA Handbook for Writers of Research Papers* and the *Publication Manual of the American Psychological Association* are two popular style manuals. Knowing the required styles for the manuscript being produced is critical. For example, a running head with the paper title and page number is required in APA while MLA requires the last name of the author and the page number. Quattlebaum (2016) writes, "Be sure to check that the reference list is formatted as

1"

APA Report Style

Lesson 22 (and) and Backspace Key

Warmup *Lesson 22a Warmup*

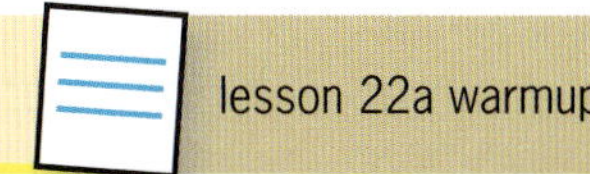

lesson 22a warmup

New Keys

22b (and)

( ) = parentheses
Parentheses indicate off-hand, aside, or explanatory messages.

(Left shift; then reach *up* with the *right third* finger.

) Left shift; then reach *up* with the *right fourth* finger.

1 ((l l((; (; Reach from l for the left parenthesis; as, ((.
2)); ;))); Reach from ; for the right parenthesis; as,)).

( )

3 Learn to use parentheses (plural) or parenthesis (singular).
4 The red (No. 34) and blue (No. 78) cars both won here (Rio).
5 We (Galen and I) dined (bagels) in our penthouse (the dorm).

22c All Symbols Learned

6 The jacket was $35 (thirty-five dollars)--the tie was extra.
7 Starting 10/29, you can sell Model #49 at a discount of 25%.
8 My size 8 1/2 shoe--a blue pump--was soiled (but not badly).

22d Improve Keystroking

Key each line once.

Build confidence—trust yourself to make the correct reach.

9 Jana has one hard-to-get copy of her hot-off-the-press book.
10 An invoice said that "We give discounts of 10%, 5%, and 3%."
11 The company paid bill 8/07 on 5/2/14 and bill 4/9 on 3/6/14.
12 The catalog lists as out of stock Items #230, #710, and #13.
13 Ellyn had $8; Sean, $9; and Cal, $7. The cash total was $24.
14 A representative from the 16th District (Tom Law) will come.
15 The oldest family member (May Gray) will attend the reunion.

Lesson 47 Reports in APA Style

Warmup *Lesson 47a Warmup*

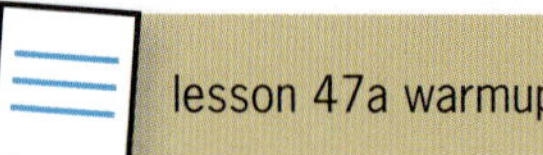

lesson 47a warmup

Document Design

47b

APA REPORT STYLE

Study the guidelines shown below for an academic report formatted in APA style. Refer to the full-page model on pages 2-119 and 2-200 and always check the *Publication Manual of the American Psychological Association* and your teacher's instructions.

- Use 12-point Times New Roman font.
- Use 1" margins (top, bottom, left, and right).
- DS paragraphs and indent 0.5".
- DS long quotations of 40 or more words and indent 0.5" from the left margin.
- Key a running head in ALL CAPS at the top of each page that includes the title of paper (limited to 50 characters) at the left margin and page number aligned at the right.
- Center the report title and capitalize all main words.
- Include a complete alphabetical listing of all references cited in the report and label it **Bibliography**; DS.

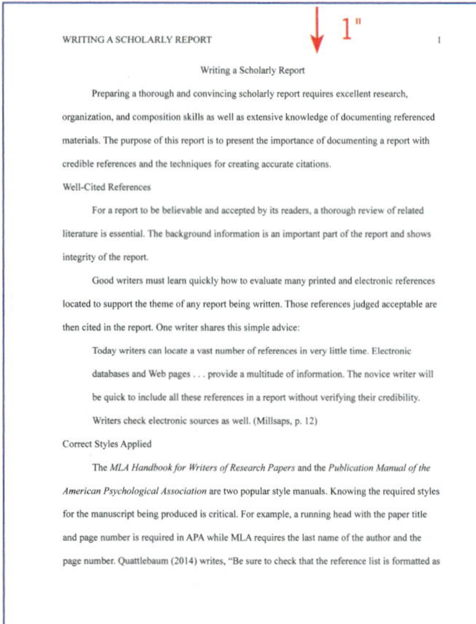

WRITING A SCHOLARLY REPORT 1

Writing a Scholarly Report

Preparing a thorough and convincing scholarly report requires excellent research, organization, and composition skills as well as extensive knowledge of documenting referenced materials. The purpose of this report is to present the importance of documenting a report with credible references and the techniques for creating accurate citations.

Well-Cited References

For a report to be believable and accepted by its readers, a thorough review of related literature is essential. The background information is an important part of the report and shows integrity of the report.

Good writers must learn quickly how to evaluate many printed and electronic references located to support the theme of any report being written. Those references judged acceptable are then cited in the report. One writer shares this simple advice:

Today writers can locate a vast number of references in very little time. Electronic databases and Web pages . . . provide a multitude of information. The novice writer will be quick to include all these references in a report without verifying their credibility. Writers check electronic sources as well. (Millsaps, p. 12)

Correct Styles Applied

The *MLA Handbook for Writers of Research Papers* and the *Publication Manual of the American Psychological Association* are two popular style manuals. Knowing the required styles for the manuscript being produced is critical. For example, a running head with the paper title and page number is required in APA while MLA requires the last name of the author and the page number. Quattlebaum (2014) writes, "Be sure to check that the reference list is formatted as

Page 1

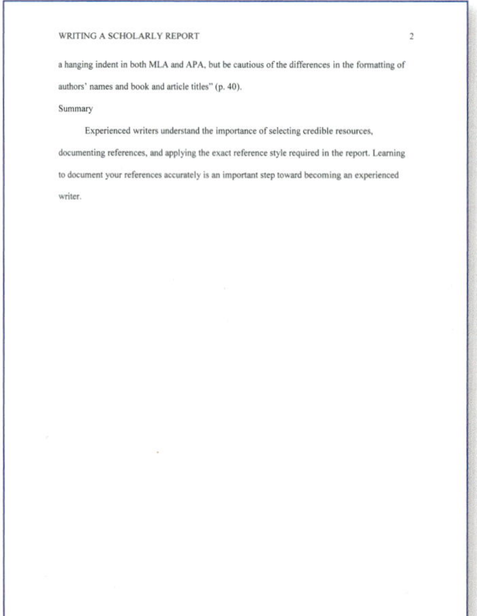

WRITING A SCHOLARLY REPORT 2

a hanging indent in both MLA and APA, but be cautious of the differences in the formatting of authors' names and book and article titles" (p. 40).

Summary

Experienced writers understand the importance of selecting credible resources, documenting references, and applying the exact reference style required in the report. Learning to document your references accurately is an important step toward becoming an experienced writer.

Page 2

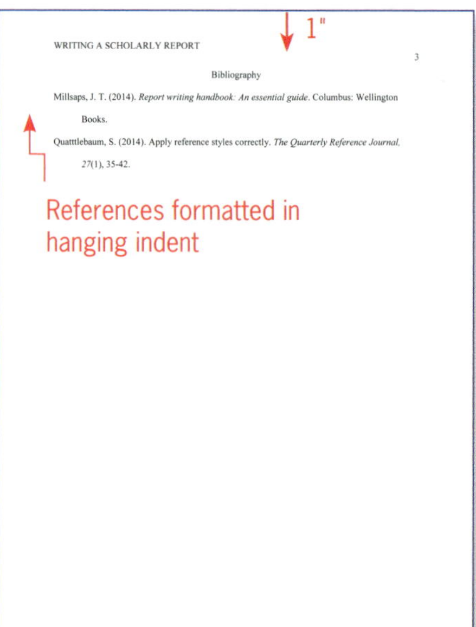

WRITING A SCHOLARLY REPORT 3

Bibliography

Millsaps, J. T. (2014). *Report writing handbook: An essential guide*. Columbus: Wellington Books.

Quatttlebaum, S. (2014). Apply reference styles correctly. *The Quarterly Reference Journal, 27*(1), 35-42.

Bibliography Page

22e Backspace Key

Key sentences 16–21: use the Backspace key to correct errors as they occur.

Use the Backspace key effectively.

Backspace reach up with the right fourth finger

16 You should be interested in the special items on sale today.
17 If she is going with us, why don't we plan to leave now?
18 Do you desire to continue working on the memo in the future?
19 Did the firm or their neighbors own the autos with problems?
20 Juni, Vec, and Zeb had perfect grades on weekly query exams.
21 Jewel quickly explained to me the big fire hazards involved.

Skill Building

22f Timed Writing

1. Take two 3' timings on both paragraphs.
2. Use the Backspace key to correct errors.

gwam 3'

It is our obligation to preserve the planet and hand it 4
down to our children and grandchildren in a better condition 8
than when we first found it. We must take extra steps just to 12
make the quality of living better. Unless we change our ways 16
and stop damaging the environment, the world will not be a 20
good place to live. 22

To help save our ozone layer, we should not use any 25
products that may have harmful gas in them. There are many 29
simple and easy ways to clean the air such as planting more 33
trees and reusing materials. Also as important is the proper 37
disposal of our garbage in order to stop our water from 41
getting more and more polluted. 43

3' | 1 | 2 | 3 | 4 |

Apply It

46-d1

MLA Template

1. In a new document, click No Spacing style and change line spacing to 2.0.
2. Change to 12-point Times New Roman font.
3. Key the following heading at 1":

   Student's Full Name

   Instructor's Full Name

   Name of Assignment
4. Tap ENTER after *Name of Assignment and* insert the current date using the MLA-required date format (9 September 2018); click option to update automatically.
5. Double-click in the header section and change to 12-point Times New Roman font.
6. Click Align Right and key **LName**, space one time, and insert Page number command (Insert/Header & Footer/Page Number/Current Position. Click Plain Number). Close the Header & Footer.
7. Save as a Word Template and close. (*46-d1*)

46-d2

MLA Report

1. Open the file (*46-d1*) that you created in the previous exercise and key the MLA report shown on pages 2-115 and 2-116.
2. Highlight the long quotation and click Increase Indent twice to indent it 1" from the left margin. Key a space after each period in the ellipsis.
3. Click Decrease Indent twice to return the insertion point back to the left margin.
4. Double-click in the header and change *LName* to **Watson**.
5. Edit the information at the top of page 1 with Watson's information.
6. Check that side headings are not alone at the bottom of the page. Use the Keep with next command if needed.
7. Save and close. (*46-d2*)

Discover

Increase Indent

Home/Paragraph/ Increase Indent or Decrease Indent

46-d3

Works Cited Page

1. Open the file (*46-d2*) that you created in the previous exercise. Position the insertion point at the end of the report. Press CTRL + ENTER to begin a new page.
2. Key the works cited shown below with hanging indent formatting. Try the shortcut, CTRL + T.
3. Save and close. (*46-d3*)

Discover

Page Break

Insert/Pages/Page Break

Shortcut: CTRL + ENTER

To remove a manual page break, position insertion point at the beginning of the page break (with Show/Hide on) and tap DELETE.

Works Cited

Millsaps, John Thomas. *Report Writing Handbook: An Essential Guide.* Columbus: Wellington Books, 2014. Print.

Quattlebaum, Sarah. "Apply Reference Styles Correctly." *The Quarterly Reference Journal* 27.1 (2014): 35-42. Print.

Lesson 23 & and : (colon), Proofreaders' Marks

Warmup *Lesson 23a Warmup*

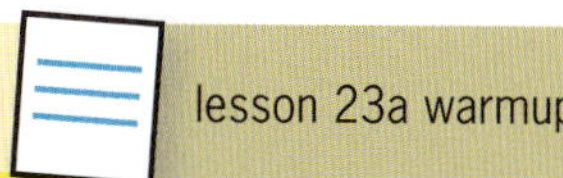

New Keys

23b & and : (Colon)

& Left shift; then reach *up* with *right first* finger.

: (colon) Left shift; then tap key with *right fourth* finger.

& = ampersand: The ampersand is used only as part of company names.

Colon: Space once after a colon except when used within a number for time.

& (ampersand)

1 & &j j& & & &; J & J; Haraj & Jay; Moroj & Jax; Torj & Jones
2 Nehru & Unger; Mumm & Just; Mann & Hart; Arch & Jones; M & J
3 Rhye & Knox represent us; Steb & Doy, Firm A; R & J, Firm B.

: (colon)

4 : :; ;: : : :; as: for example: notice: Dear Sir: Gentlemen:
5 In stock: 10:30; 7:45; Age: Address: Read: Cell: Attachment:
6 Space once after a colon, thus: Telephone: Home Address: To:

23c All Symbols Learned

7 Consider these companies: J & R, Brand & Kay, Upper & Davis.
8 Memo #88-829 reads as follows: "Deduct 15% of $300, or $45."
9 Bill 32(5)--it got here quite late--from M & N was paid 7/3.

Skill Building

23d Improve Keystroking

Key each line once.

10 *Jane may work with an auditing firm if she is paid to do so.*
11 *Pam and eight girls may go to the lake to work with the dog.*
12 *Clancy and Claudia did all the work to fix the sign problem.*
13 *Did Lea visit the Orlando land of enchantment or a neighbor?*
14 *Ana and Blanche made a map for a neighbor to go to the city.*
15 *Sidney may go to the lake to fish with worms from the docks.*
16 *Did the firm or the neighbors own the auto with the problem?*

for the manuscript being produced is critical. For example, a running head with the paper title and page number is required in APA while MLA requires the last name of the author and the page number. Quattlebaum (2014) writes, “Be sure to check that the reference list is formatted as a hanging indent in both MLA and APA, but be cautious of the differences in the formatting of authors’ names as well as the capitalization of book and article titles” (40).

Summary

Experienced writers understand the importance of selecting credible resources, documenting references, and applying the exact reference style required in the report. Learning to document your references accurately is an important step toward becoming an experienced writer.

MLA Report Style

23e Improve Keystroking

double letters

17 Do Bennett was puzzled by drivers exceeding the speed limit.
18 Bill needs the office address; he will cut the grass at ten.
19 Todd saw the green car veer off the street near a tall tree.

figures and symbols

20 Invoice #84 for $672.90, plus $4.38 tax, was due February 3.
21 Do read Section 4, pages 60–74 and Section 9, pages 198–225.
22 Enter as follows: (a) name, (b) address, and (c) cell phone.

23f Timed Writing

Take two 3' timings. Use wordwrap.

gwam 3'

Is how you judge my work important? Does your honest 4
opinion or feedback really matter? It does, of course; I hope 8
you appreciate the effort and recognize some basic merit in 12
it. We all expect to get credit for the hard work we put forth 16
and the good work we conclude. After all, we are all working 20
together to accomplish the goals of the company. 23

As a human being, I want approval for the ideas 27
presented, things written, and tasks completed. I always look 31
forward to your evaluations so I can learn more and continue 35
to grow. My work does not define me, but it shows my abilities 39
and skills. Through my work, I am my very own unique self. 43

3' | 1 | 2 | 3 | 4 |

Communication

23g Edit Text

1. Key your name, class, and **23g** at the left margin. Then key lines 23–28, making the revisions as you key. Use the Backspace key to correct errors.
2. Proofread and correct errors.
3. Save as *xx-23g*.

Symbol	Meaning	Symbol	Meaning
___	Italic	○ sp	Spell out
~~	Bold	¶	Paragraph
Cap or ≡	Capitalize	#	Add horizontal space
^	Insert	/ or lc	Lowercase
℘	Delete	⁀	Close up space
[	Move to left	∼	Transpose
]	Move to right	stet	Leave as originally written

23 We miss 50% in life's rowards by refusingto new try things.
24 do it now--today--then tomorrow's load will be 100% lighter.
25 Satisfying work-whether it pays $40 or $400-is the pay off.
26 Avoid mistakes: confusing a #3 has cost thousands.
27 Pleased most with a first rate job is the person who did it.
28 My wife and/or me mother will except the certifi cate for me.

Watson 1

Daniel Watson

Dr. Caroline Kennedy

Assignment 1

14 February 2013 ↓ 1

Writing a Scholarly Report

1" Preparing a thorough and convincing scholarly report requires excellent research, organization, and composition skills as well as extensive knowledge of documenting referenced materials. The purpose of this report is to present the importance of documenting a report with credible references and the techniques for creating accurate citations. 1"

Well-Cited References

For a report to be believable and accepted by its readers, a thorough review of related literature is essential. This background information is an important part of the report and shows integrity of the report.

Good writers must learn quickly how to evaluate many printed and electronic references located to support the theme of any report being written. Those references judged acceptable are then cited in the report. Millsaps shares this simple advice:

Long quotation indented 1"

> Today writers can locate a vast number of references in very little time. Electronic databases and Web pages . . . provide a multitude of information. The novice writer will be quick to include all these references in a report without verifying their credibility. Writers check electronic sources as well. (Millsaps 12)

Correct Styles Applied

The *MLA Handbook for Writers of Research Papers* and the *Publication Manual of the American Psychological Association* are two popular style manuals. Knowing the required styles

1"

MLA Report Style

Lesson 24 Other Symbols

Warmup *Lesson 24a Warmup*

New Keys

24b Textbook Keying

@ * + =

Be confident—watch the copy, not the hands.

@	at
*	asterisk
+	plus sign (use a hyphen for minus and x for "times")
=	equals

@ **shift; reach *up* with *left third* finger to @**

1 @ @s s@ a a; 24 @ .15; 22 @ .35; sold 2 @ .87; were 12 @ .95

2 You may contact Calvin @: CEP@rpx.com or fax @ 602.555.0101.

3 E-mail Al ajj@crewl.com and Matt mrw10@scxs.com by 9:30 p.m.

* **shift; reach *up* with *right second* finger to ***

4 * *k k8* * *; aurelis*; May 7*; both sides*; 250 km.**; aka*

5 Note each *; one * refers to page 29; ** refers to page 307.

6 Use *.* to search for files; the * looks for all characters.

+ **shift; reach *up* with *right fourth* finger to +**

7 + ;+ +; + + +; 2 + 2; A+ or B+; 70+ F. degrees; +xy over +y;

8 The question was 8 + 7 + 51; it should have been 8 + 7 + 15.

9 My grades on the tests and final exam are B+, C+, B+, and A.

= **reach *up* with *right fourth* finger to =**

10 = =; = = =; = 4; If 14x = 28, x = 2; if 8x = 16, then x = 2.

11 Change this solution (where it says "= by") to = bx or = BX.

12 Key the formula =(a2+b2)*d5/4 in the formula bar; tap Enter.

INTERNAL CITATIONS IN MLA STYLE

The last name of the author(s) and the page number of the cited material are shown in parentheses within the body of the report (Crawford 134). When the author's name is used in the text to introduce the quotation, only the page number appears in parentheses: *Crawford said, "Faculty are uploading podcast lectures to their distance website" (134).*

Short, direct quotations of three lines or fewer are enclosed within quotation marks. Long quotations of four lines or more are indented 1" from the left margin and DS. Tap ENTER once before and after the long quotation.

→ According·to·Estes,·"Successful·business·executives·have·long·known·the·importance·of·good·verbal·communication"·(29).¶

Short Quotation

Probably no successful enterprise exists that does not rely upon the ability of its members to communicate for its success. Shaefer adds

> Make no mistake, both written and verbal communication are the stuff upon which success is built in all types of organizations. Both forms deserve careful study by any business that wants to grow. Successful businesspeople must read, write, speak, and listen with skill. Often professional development in these areas is needed (p. 28)

Long Quotation

WORKS CITED PAGE IN MLA STYLE

References cited in the report are listed at the end of the report in alphabetical order by authors' last name. Study the guidelines and the model shown below.

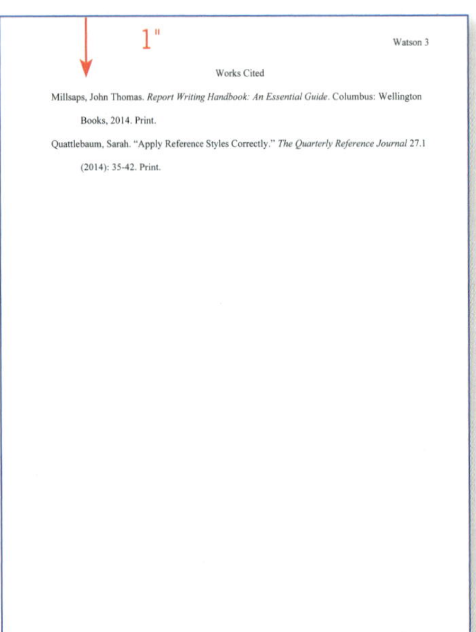

Watson 3

Works Cited

Millsaps, John Thomas. *Report Writing Handbook: An Essential Guide*. Columbus: Wellington Books, 2014. Print.

Quattlebaum, Sarah. "Apply Reference Styles Correctly." *The Quarterly Reference Journal* 27.1 (2014): 35-42. Print.

- Begin the references on a new page (insert manual page break at the end of the report).
- Center the title at the top of the page (1") with main words capitalized.
- Double-space the references. DS is 2.0 line spacing.
- Format references with hanging indent.
- Number the reference page at the top right of the page using same format as the report.

Skill Building

24c Improve Keystroking

double letters

13 feel pass mill good miss seem moons cliffs pools green spell

14 Assets are being offered in a stuffy room to two associates.

balanced hand

15 is if of to it go do to is do so if to the to sign it vie to

16 Pamela or Jen may also go to town with Blanche if she works.

24d Timed Writing

Take two 3' timings.
Use wordwrap.

	gwam 3'
Why do we resist change so much? Do you think perhaps it	4
is because it requires more time and effort learning new	8
things and making difficult decisions? Is it also because we	12
are set in our ways, afraid to take chances and dislike being	16
told what to do? Besides, what is the point of trying to	20
improve something that works just fine?	22
We know change can and does extend new areas of	26
enjoyment, areas we might never have known existed. If we stay	30
away from all change, we could curtail our quality of life.	34
People who are open to change are more zealous and more	38
productive than those who aren't. They are also better at	42
coping with the hardships and challenges that life often	46
brings.	46

3' | 1 | 2 | 3 | 4 |

Communication

24e Composition

1. Open the file *xx-profile* that you created in Lesson 18.
2. Position the insertion point at the end of the last paragraph. Tap ENTER twice.
3. Key an additional paragraph that begins with the following sentence:

   Thank you for allowing me to introduce myself.
4. Finish the paragraph by adding two or more sentences that describe your progress and satisfaction with keyboarding.
5. Use the Backspace key to correct errors as you key the document.

24f Edit Copy

1. Key your name, class, and date at the left margin on separate lines.
2. Key each line, making the corrections marked with proofreaders' marks.
3. Proofread and correct errors using the Backspace key.
4. Save as *xx-24f*.

```
17 Ask Group 1 to read Chater 6 of Book 11 (Shelf 19,Room 5).
18 All 6 of us live at One Bay road, not at 126 -56th Street.
19 AT 9 a.m. the owners decided to close form 12 noon to 1 p.m.
20 Ms. Vik leaves June 9; she r eturns the 14 or 15 of July.
21 The 16 per cent discount saves 115. A stamp costs 44 cents.
22 Elin gave $300,000,000; our gift was only 75 cents.
```

Document Design

46c

MLA REPORT STYLE

Study the guidelines shown below for an academic report formatted in MLA style. Refer to the full-page model on pages 2-115 and 2-116 and always check the *MLA Handbook for Writers of Research Papers* and your teacher's instructions.

- Use 12-point Times New Roman font.
- Use 1" margins (top, bottom, left, and right).
- DS paragraphs and indent 0.5".
- DS long quotations of 40 or more words and indent 1" from the left margin.
- Key heading information beginning at 1"; include full name, instructor's name, assignment name, and current date.
- Center the report title and capitalize all main words.
- Place page numbers at the top right of every page. Include the writer's last name and the page number (Last Name 1).
- Include a complete alphabetical listing of all references cited in the report and label it **Works Cited;** DS.

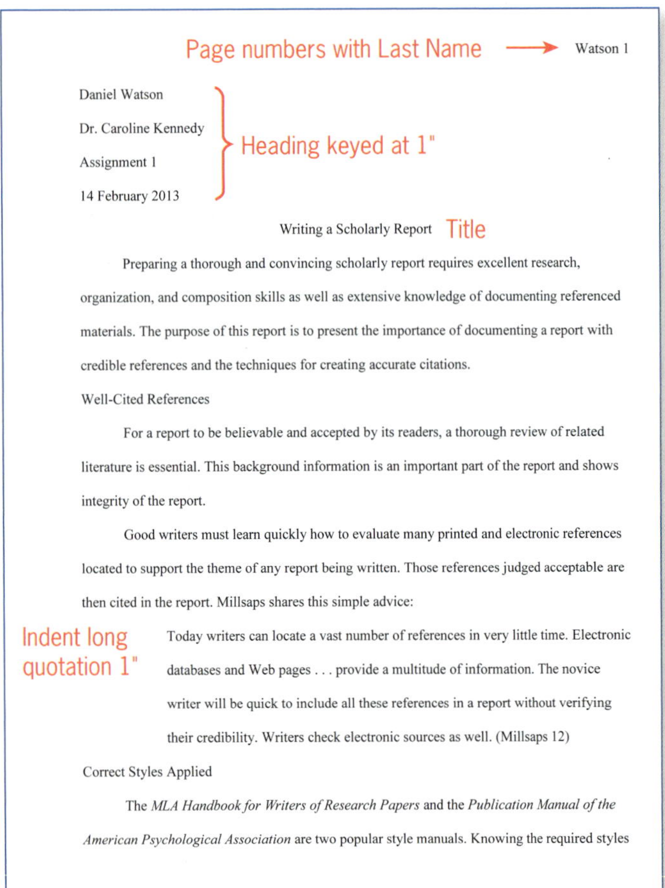

Page numbers with Last Name → Watson 1

Daniel Watson
Dr. Caroline Kennedy
Assignment 1
14 February 2013

Heading keyed at 1"

Writing a Scholarly Report   Title

Preparing a thorough and convincing scholarly report requires excellent research, organization, and composition skills as well as extensive knowledge of documenting referenced materials. The purpose of this report is to present the importance of documenting a report with credible references and the techniques for creating accurate citations.

Well-Cited References

For a report to be believable and accepted by its readers, a thorough review of related literature is essential. This background information is an important part of the report and shows integrity of the report.

Good writers must learn quickly how to evaluate many printed and electronic references located to support the theme of any report being written. Those references judged acceptable are then cited in the report. Millsaps shares this simple advice:

Indent long quotation 1"

> Today writers can locate a vast number of references in very little time. Electronic databases and Web pages . . . provide a multitude of information. The novice writer will be quick to include all these references in a report without verifying their credibility. Writers check electronic sources as well. (Millsaps 12)

Correct Styles Applied

The *MLA Handbook for Writers of Research Papers* and the *Publication Manual of the American Psychological Association* are two popular style manuals. Knowing the required styles

Page numbers with Last Name → Watson 2

for the manuscript being produced is critical. For example, a running head with the paper title and page number is required in APA while MLA requires the last name of the author and the page number. Quattlebaum (2014) writes, "Be sure to check that the reference list is formatted as a hanging indent in both MLA and APA, but be cautious of the differences in the formatting of authors' names as well as the capitalization of book and article titles" (40).

Summary

Experienced writers understand the importance of selecting credible resources, documenting references, and applying the exact reference style required in the report. Learning to document your references accurately is an important step toward becoming an experienced writer.

Lesson 24R Review

Warmup *Lesson 24Ra Warmup*

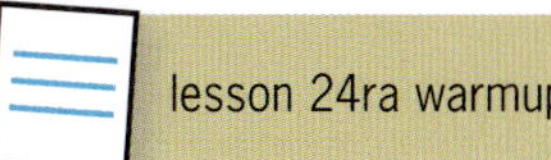

Skill Building

24Rb Master Numbers and Symbols

Key each line once; work for fluency.

1 E-mail invoice #397 to gmeathe@skd.org; the $7 will be paid.
2 Jane and Ken may go to town to handle the pale and sick dog.
3 The answers to pop quiz #12 are: (1) a, (2) c, (3) b, (4) c.
4 Uncle Jeff rented a burgundy minivan for three days a month.
5 Check #42 was sent on 6/15 for the amount of $89 as payment.
6 Zale played amazing pop jazz on a saxophone and a xylophone.
7 L & D Bank pays 7% interest on savings accounts, 10% on CDs.

24Rc Timed Writing

1. Key a 1' timing on each paragraph; work to increase speed.
2. Key a 3' timing on all paragraphs.

	gwam 1'	3'
Do you find yourself forgetting the names of people that	12	4
you have known for quite some time? Did you put something down	25	8
and a few minutes later were not able to find it again? Memory	37	12
lapses like these are normal, and there are things you can do	50	17
to prevent them from happening as often. Just a few simple	62	21
lifestyle changes can easily help improve your memory.	72	24
Everyone can take steps to better their memory; it will	12	28
take both time and practice. It is important to get enough	24	32
sleep and to eat properly. Exercise both the mind and the	36	36
body. Read, write, and do puzzles each day to help develop	47	44
your memory. Make time for family and friends and have a good	60	48
time with them.	63	49

24Rd Enrichment

1. Key the paragraphs, making revisions as you key.
2. Key your name and 24Rd below the paragraph.
3. Save as *xx-24Rd*.

Any one who expects some day to find an ~~excellent~~ job should learn the value of accuracy. To be worth any thing ~~completed~~ work must ~~accurate~~, without ~~any~~ question. ~~Naturally~~ we realize that the aspect of the work equation raises always the chance of errors; we should ~~know~~ that those same ~~mistakes~~ can be found and fixed. Every job completed should carry at least 1 stamp; the stamp of ~~approval~~ in work that is ~~outstanding~~.

DRILL 2 SAVE AS TEMPLATE

chart

File/Save As

1. Open *chart* from the data files. Replace (*Student's name*) with **Sophia Johnson.**

2 Select to save as Word Template. Close the document. (*46-drill2 keyboarding progress template*)

HANGING INDENT

Hanging indent places the first line of a paragraph at the left margin and indents all other lines to the first tab. It is commonly used to format bibliography entries, glossaries, and lists. Hanging indent can be applied before or after text is keyed.

SHORTCUT

CTRL + T; then key the paragraph; or select the paragraphs to be formatted as hanging indents and press CTRL + T.

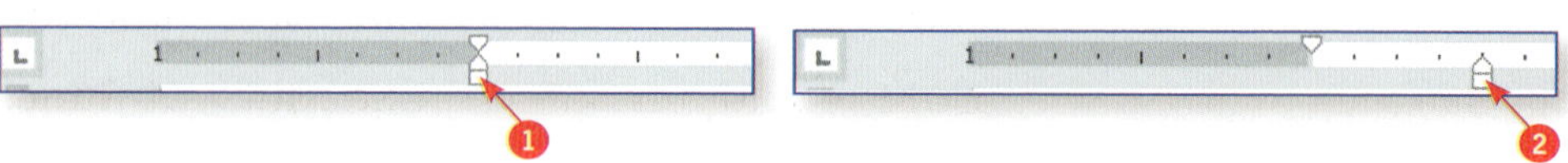

To create a hanging indent:

1. From the Horizontal Ruler, click on the Hanging Indent marker 1.
2. Drag the Hanging Indent marker 2 to the position where the indent is to begin.
3. Key the paragraph. Note that the second and subsequent lines are indented beginning at the marker.

DRILL 3 HANGING INDENT

glossary

1. Open *glossary* from the data files. Select all the glossary entries and format them with a hanging indent. **Hint:** Use the shortcut CTRL + T.

2. Save and close. (*46-drill3*)

Lesson 25 Assessment

Warmup *Lesson 25a Warmup* 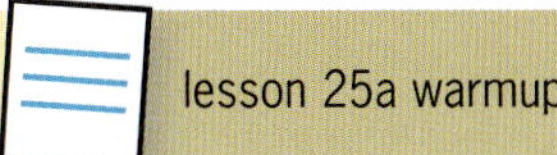 lesson 25a warmup

Skill Building

25b Improve Keystroking

n/y
1 deny many canny tiny nymph puny any puny zany penny pony yen
2 Jenny Nyles saw many, many tiny nymphs flying near her pony.

b/r
3 bran barb brim curb brat garb bray verb brag garb bribe herb
4 Barb Barber can bring a bit of bran and herbs for her bread.

c/e
5 cede neck nice deck dice heck rice peck vice erect mice echo
6 Can Cedric erect a decent cedar deck? He erects nice condos.

n/u
7 nun gnu bun nut pun numb sun nude tuna nub fun null unit gun
8 Eunice had enough ground nuts at lunch; Uncle Launce is fun.

25c Improve Fluency

Key each line once.

9 is if he do rub ant go and am pan do rut us aid ox ape by is
10 it is | an end | it may | to pay | and so | aid us | he got | or own | to go
11 Did the girl make the ornament with fur, duck down, or hair?

12 us owl rug box bob to man so bit or big pen of jay me age it
13 it | it is | time to go | show them how | plan to go | one of the aims
14 It is a shame they use the autobus for a visit to the field.

25d Timed Writing

Key two 3' writings. Strive for accuracy. Save the timings as *xx-25d-t1* and *xx-25d-t2*. Use wordwrap.

Goal: 3', 19–27 *gwam.*

Build confidence—trust your reach instincts.

gwam 3'

The term career can mean many different things to 4
different people. As you know, a career is more than just an 8
occupation. It includes the jobs an individual has over time. 12
It also involves how the work life affects the other parts of 16
our life. There are as many types of careers as there are 20
people. 20

Almost every person has a career of some kind. A career 24
can help us attain unique goals, such as having a stable 28
livelihood or a rewarding vocation. The kind of career you 32
have will affect your life in many ways. For example, it can 36
determine where you live, the money you make, and how you feel 40
about yourself. A good choice can thus help you realize the 44
life you want. 45

3' | 1 | 2 | 3 | 4 |

SAVE AS TEMPLATE

A template is a set of predefined styles for a particular type of document. The purpose of a template is to reuse a document's formatting while easily changing the content. Templates are available for numerous types of documents and others can be downloaded from the Microsoft website. However, when existing documents are unique, it is useful to save them as a template.

By default, templates are saved to the Templates folder within the program. In a classroom environment, you will want to save templates you create to a USB memory device (flash drive) or another location.

To save a document as a template:

File/Save As

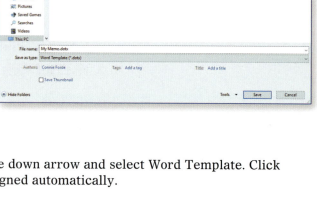

1. Click the File tab and then Save As. Click Browse. The Save As dialog box displays.
2. *Save to a hard drive:* By default the software will save to the Custom Office Templates folder.

   -or-

   Save to a USB memory device (flash drive): Browse to the flash drive.
3. In the File name box, key an appropriate template name such as **my memo**.

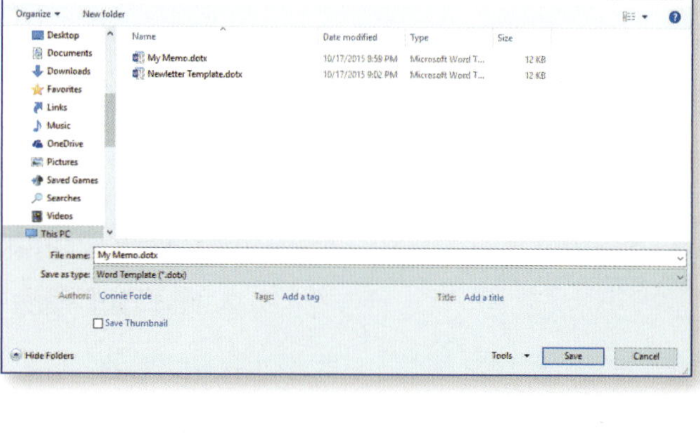

4. In the Save as type box, click the down arrow and select Word Template. Click Save. The extension *.dotx* is assigned automatically.

To use the template:

File/New

From a hard drive: Click the File tab and select New. From the Available Templates pane, click Personal and browse to locate the desired template. Click OK.

-or-

From a flash drive: Click the File tab and select Open and browse to locate the desired template. Click OK.

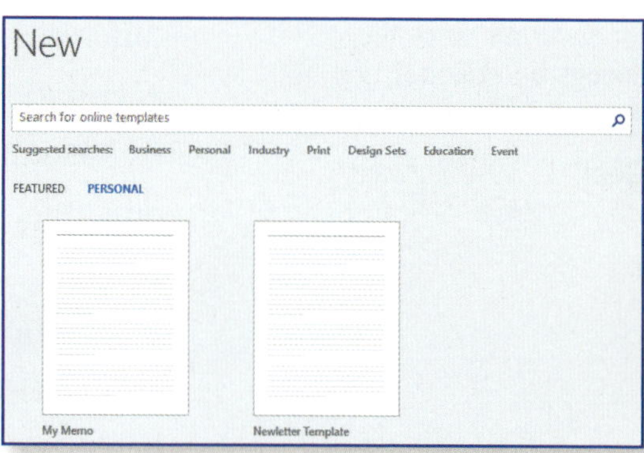

25e Figure Check

Key two 3' writings at a controlled rate. Save the timings as *xx-25e-t1* and *xx-25e-t2*. Use wordwrap.

Goal: 3', 14–16 *gwam*.

gwam 3'

Do people read the stock market pages in the news? Yes; 4
at approximately 9 or 10 a.m. each morning, I know lots of 8
excited people who do that. Some people still like to have the 12
paper delivered to their home each morning. Others like the 16
convenience of reading the news on their computer or their 20
cell phone. Nevertheless, we can't wait to obtain the first 24
stock report each day. 26

Some people take the stock market very seriously. They 30
watch their stocks carefully and note the rise and fall of 34
each stock. Most investors like to be able to "buy at 52 and 38
sell at 60." Some would like to receive a dividend of 7 or 8 42
percent on their stocks. Regardless, each morning we zip 45
immediately to the stock report to see how the market is 49
doing. When the stock is down, we quickly purchase more shares 53
and keep them until they increase in value. The stock market 58
is an important and vital part of our life. 60

3' | 1 | 2 | 3 | 4 |

Communication

25f Edit Copy

1. Key your name, class, and date at the left margin.
2. Key the paragraphs and make the corrections marked with proofreaders' marks. Use the Backspace key to correct errors.
3. Save as *xx-25f*.

Last week the healthy heart foundation relased the findings of a study that showed exercise diet and if individuals don't smoke are the major controllable factors that led to a healthy heart. Factors such as heredity can not be controlled. The study included 25 to 65 year old males as well as females.

The study also showed that just taking a walk benefits our health. Those who walked an average of 2 to 3 hours a week were more then 30 percent less likely to have problems than those who did no exercise.

25g Proofread and Edit

1. Open *xx-24Rd*.
2. Turn to page 1-68 and proofread your document with Writing 11.
3. Make corrections as needed. Save as *xx-25g*.

Lesson 46 Reports in MLA Style

New Commands

- Header
- Save As Template
- Hanging Indent

Warmup *Lesson 46a Warmup*

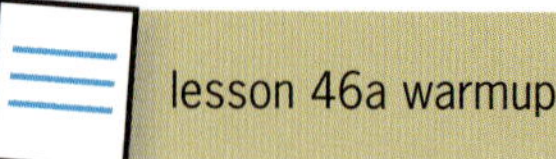

New Commands

46b

HEADER

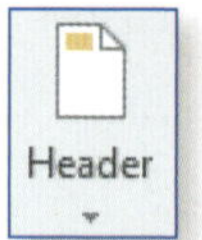

A header contains text that is keyed in the top margin of the page. In this lesson you will create a header for an MLA report that displays on all pages.

To insert a header with text and page number:

Insert/Header & Footer/Header

1. Display the Built-in gallery of Header styles. Click the Blank style.
2. Tap the TAB key twice to place the insertion point at the far-right position. Key the desired text followed by a space.
3. From the Header & Footer group, click the Page Number drop-list arrow and choose Current Position. Choose the Plain Number style.

To edit a header:

Insert/Header & Footer/Header

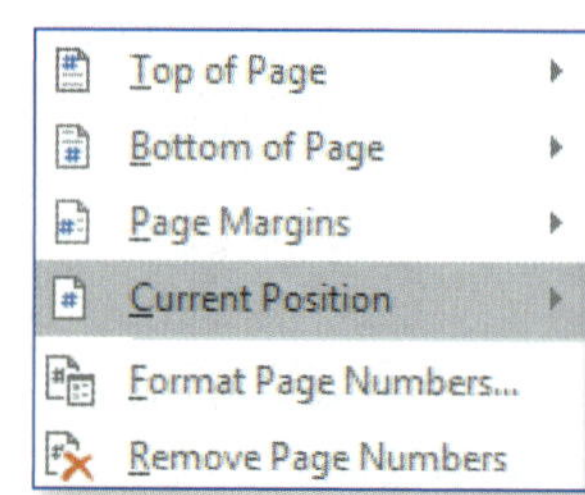

To edit a header, click Edit Header. An alternate method is to double-click in the header section of the document. To move to the text of the document, double-click in the document—not the header.

To remove a header, click Remove Header.

DRILL 1 HEADER

1. In a new document, double-click in the header section. Change to 12-point Times New Roman font.
2. Click the Align Right command and key **LNAME**. Tap the Space Bar and insert the Page Number command as shown above.
3. Save and close. (*46-drill1*)

Skill Builder 2

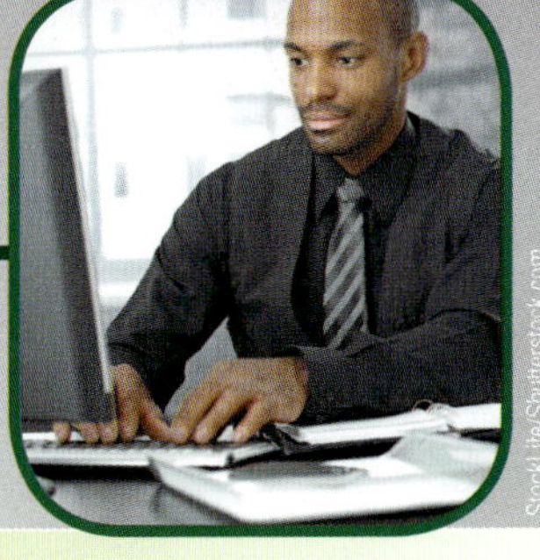

Skill Building *Emphasis on Improving Techniques*

DRILL 8

Opposite Hand Reaches

Key each line once and double space (DS) between groups of lines. Key at a controlled rate; concentrate on the reaches.

i/e

1 ik is fit it sit laid site like insist still wise coil light
2 ed he ear the fed egg led elf lake jade heat feet hear where
3 lie kite item five aide either quite linear imagine brighter
4 Imagine the aide eating the pears before the grieving tiger.

w/o

5 ws we way was few went wit law with weed were week gnaw when
6 ol on go hot old lot joy odd comb open tool upon money union
7 bow owl word wood worm worse tower brown toward wrote weapon
8 The workers lowered the brown swords toward the wood weapon.

DRILL 9

Proofreaders' Marks

Key each line once and DS after each sentence. Correct the sentence as edited, making all handwritten corrections. Do not key the numbers.

- Capitalize
- Change letter
- Close up space
- Delete
- Insert
- Lowercase
- Space
- Transpose

1. When a writer create the preliminary version of a document, they are concentrating on conveying the intended ideas.
2. This ver sion of a preleminary document is called a rough.
3. After the draft is created the Writer edits refines the copy.
4. Sometimes proofreader's marks are used to edit the draft.
5. The changes will them be make to the original.
6. After the changes have been made then the Writer reads the copy.
7. Edit ing and proofreading requires alot of time and effort.
8. An attitute of excellance is reqiured to produce error free message.

DRILL 10

Proofreading

Compare your sentences in Drill 9 with Drill 10. How did you do? Now key the paragraph for fluency. Concentrate on keying as accurately as possible.

When a writer creates the preliminary version of a document, he or she is concentrating on conveying ideas. This preliminary version is called a rough draft. After the draft is created, the writer edits or refines the copy. Proofreaders' marks are used to edit the rough draft. The editing changes will be made to the original. Then the writer reads the copy again. Editing requires a lot of time and effort. An attitude of excellence is required to produce an error-free message.

Top right 0.5"

- Invoke the Widow/Orphan control feature to ensure that no lines display alone at the bottom or top of a page. Use the Keep with next command to keep side headings from appearing alone at the bottom of the page.
- Take advantage of automatic features, such as a table of contents and citations.
- Use styles to format tables and charts.
- Be sure to use the online thesaurus, spelling, and grammar features of the word processing software.
- Bookmark widely accepted online desk references and style manuals for easy use.
- Use the Show/Hide command to show the ¶ marks and other hidden formatting symbols.

1.5" These simple steps will assist you in your goal to create well-written and attractive reports. The next step is to practice, practice, and practice. 1"

Multiple-Page Report

Assess Skill Growth

1. Select the writing number such as Writing 8.
2. Key 1' writings on each paragraph of a timing. Note that paragraphs within a timing increase by two words.
   Goal: to complete each paragraph
3. Key a 3' timing on the entire writing.

Writing 8

	gwam 1'	3'
Any of us whose target is to have success in our professional	12	4
work will understand that we must learn how to work in harmony	25	8
with others whose paths may cross ours daily.	34	11
We will, unquestionably, work for, with, and beside people, just	13	15
as they will work for, with, and beside us. We will judge them,	25	20
as most certainly they are going to be judging us.	35	23
A lot of people realize the need for solid working relations and	13	27
have a rule that treats others as they, themselves, expect to be	26	32
treated. This seems to be a sound, practical idea for them.	37	35

Writing 9

	1'	3'
I spoke with one company visitor recently; and she was very much	13	4
impressed, she said, with the large amount of work she had noted	26	9
being finished by one of our front office workers.	36	12
I told her how we had just last week recognized this very person	13	16
for what he had done, for output, naturally, but also because of	26	21
its excellence. We know this person has that "magic touch."	38	25
This "magic touch" is the ability to do a fair amount of work in	13	29
a fair amount of time. It involves a desire to become ever more	26	34
efficient without losing quality--the "touch" all workers should	39	38
have.	40	38

Writing 10

	1'	3'
Isn't it great just to untangle and relax after you have keyed a	13	4
completed document? Complete, or just done? No document is	25	8
quite complete until it has left you and passed to the next step.	38	13
There are desirable things that must happen to a document before	13	17
you surrender it. It must be read carefully, first of all, for	26	22
meaning to find words that look right but aren't. Read word for	39	26
word.	40	26
Check all figures and exact data, like a date or time, with your	13	31
principal copy. Make sure format details are right. Only then,	26	35
print or remove the work and scrutinize to see how it might look	39	39
to a recipient.	42	40

1' | 1 | 2 | 3 | 4 | 5 | 6 | 7 | 8 | 9 | 10 | 11 | 12 | 13
3' | 1 | 2 | 3 | 4

Tap ENTER three times (about 2")

Title → # Essentials for Writing Success: Revise, Revise, Revise and Use Technology to Create Attractive and Correct Style ↓2

Being able to communicate effectively in a clear, concise, and logical manner continues to be one of the most demanded work skills. Employees who practice effective revision skills are far ahead of their counterparts who have had the mind-set that the first draft is the final draft. This report details excellent procedures for revising a report draft, explaining effective technology tools that make the process easier. The result is a more professional and accurate final product.

Heading 1

Revising the Draft ↓1

After a first draft of a report is completed, the writer is ready to refine or polish the report. The writer must be objective when revising the report draft and cultivate an attitude for improving the report by always considering the draft as a process.

1.5" First, read the draft for content. This might mean rewriting sections of the report or adding information to areas that appear weak in this review. In this evaluative review, the writer may realize that one section would fit more logically after another section. 1"

When the writer is satisfied with the content, it is time to verity that all style rules have been followed. For example, check all headings to ensure they are "talking" headings. Do the headings describe the content of the section? Also, be sure all headings are parallel. If the writer chooses the side heading Know Your Audience, other side headings must also begin with a verb. Note that the side headings in this report are parallel, with both beginning with a gerund.

Ensuring Correct and Attractive Formats

The effective writer understands the importance of using technology to create an attractive document that adheres to correct style rules. Here are a few examples of how to use technology to create a professional final document. ↓1

- Select attractive headers and footers from the built-in design galleries to provide page numbers and other helpful information to the reader.
- Suppress headers, footers, and page numbering on the title page and on the first page of the report.

Multiple-Page Report

Writing 11

gwam 1' | 3'

Anyone who expects some day to find a great job should 11 4
begin now to learn the value of accuracy. To be worth anything, 23 8
final work must be correct, without question. Of course, we 35 12
realize that the human aspect of the work equation always raises 48 16
the chance of errors; but we should understand that those same 60 20
errors can be found and fixed. Every completed job should carry 73 24
at least one stamp; the stamp of true pride in work that is exemplary. 87 29

Writing 12

gwam 1' | 3'

No question about it: Many of the personal problems we face 12 4
today arise from the fact that we have never been very wise 24 8
consumers. We have not used our natural resources well; as a result, 38 13
we have jeopardized much of our environment. We excused our 50 17
actions because we thought that our stock of most resources had no 63 21
limit at all. So, at last, we are beginning to realize just how indiscreet 78 26
we were; and we are taking steps to rebuild our world. 89 30

Writing 13

gwam 1' | 3'

When I see people in top jobs, I know I am seeing people who 12 4
sell. I am not just referring to employees who work in a retail outlet; I 27 9
mean all people who put extra effort into convincing others to 39 13
recognize their best qualities. They, themselves, are what they sell; 53 18
and the major tools they use are their appearance, their language, and 67 22
their personality. They look great, they talk and write well; and, with 82 27
much self-confidence, they meet you eye to eye. 91 30

1' | 1 | 2 | 3 | 4 | 5 | 6 | 7 | 8 | 9 | 10 | 11 | 12 | 13 |
3' | 1 | 2 | 3 | 4 |

Apply It

45-d1

Multiple-Page Report

writing

Discover

Insert a File

Insert/Text/Object

1. Click the arrow next to Object.
2. Click Text from File.
3. Select the desired file and click Insert.

1. In a new document, apply Parallax theme. Key the first paragraph of the leftbound two-page report shown on the next two pages. Apply the appropriate style for the title of the report. Tap ENTER two times after title.
2. Insert the data file *writing* below the first PARAGRAPH. **Note:** Be sure to position the insertion point where you want the text to appear before inserting the file.
3. Apply the appropriate style for the side headings.
4. In the last bulleted item, delete the word *paragraph* and insert the ¶ mark from the Special Characters tab of the Symbol dialog box.
5. Use the Page Number command to number the pages at the top right. Select the Plain Number 3 number style. Click Different First Page to suppress the page number on the first page.
6. Preview the document to verify page numbers and that side headings are not left alone at the bottom of the page.
7. Save and close. (*45-d1*)

45-d2

Edit Report

1. Open the file (*45-d1*) that you created in the previous exercise. Change the leftbound report to an unbound report. Apply the Slate document theme.
2. Position the insertion point on page 2 of the report. Change the page number style to Accent Bar 2.
3. Key the following as the last item in the bulleted list. Insert the symbols from the Wingdings font or the Special Characters tab.
   - **Use a wide array of symbols to provide a fresh and up-to-date appearance, such as ❶, ☑, ©, or ®.**
4. Save and close. (*45-d2*)

wavebreakmedia/Shutterstock.com

WORKPLACE SUCCESS

Integrity

Integrity is synonymous with the word *honesty* and is confronted by employees in the workplace daily. Think about these rather common situations where integrity is clearly a choice:

- Arriving at work ten minutes late and then drinking coffee and chatting with coworkers for ten more minutes
- Talking with relatives and friends throughout the day
- Leaving work early regularly for personal reasons
- Presenting a report to the supervisor as original work without crediting the proper individuals for thoughts and ideas in the report
- Presenting a report that was completed at the last minute and that includes facts and figures that have not been verified as accurate

In all situations, ask the question, "Am I being honest?"

gwam 1' | 3'

Writing 14

What do you expect when you have the opportunity to travel 12 | 4
to a foreign country? Quite a few people realize that one of the real 26 | 9
joys of traveling is to get a brief, but revealing glimpse of how 39 | 13
foreigners think, work, and live. 45 | 15

The best way to enjoy a different culture is to learn as much 12 | 19
about the country being visited and its culture as you can before you 26 | 24
leave home. Then you can concentrate on being an informed guest 39 | 28
rather than trying to find local people who can meet your needs. 52 | 32

gwam 1' | 3'

Writing 15

What do you enjoy doing in your free time? Health experts tell us 13 | 4
that far too many people choose to be lazy rather than to be 25 | 8
active. The unpleasant result of that misguided decision shows up in 39 | 13
our weight. 41 | 14

Working to control what we weigh is difficult, and seldom can 12 | 18
it be accomplished quickly. However, it is extremely important if our 26 | 22
weight exceeds what it should be. Part of the problem results from 39 | 27
the amount and type of food we eat. 46 | 29

If we desire to appear fit, we should include exercise as a 12 | 33
substantial component of our weight loss program. Walking at least 25 | 37
thirty minutes each day at a very fast rate can make a major 37 | 41
difference in our appearance and in the way we feel. 48 | 45

gwam 1' | 3'

Writing 16

Doing what we enjoy doing is quite important; however, 11 | 4
enjoying what we have to do is equally important. As you ponder 23 | 8
both of these concepts, you may feel that they are the same, but they 37 | 12
are quite different. 41 | 14

If we could do only those things that we prefer to do, the 12 | 18
chances are that we would do them exceptionally well. Generally, we will 26 | 22
take more pride in doing those things we thoroughly enjoy 37 | 26
doing, and we will not stop until we get them done correctly. 50 | 30

We realize, though, that we cannot restrict the tasks and 11 | 34
responsibilities that we must do just to those that we prefer to do. 25 | 39
Therefore, we need to build an interest in and an appreciation of all 39 | 43
the tasks that we must do in our positions. 48 | 46

1' | 1 | 2 | 3 | 4 | 5 | 6 | 7 | 8 | 9 | 10 | 11 | 12
3' | 1 | 2 | 3 | 4

45c

MULTIPLE-PAGE REPORT

Because reports are often longer than one page, page numbers are required for ease in reading the report. Remember when formatting a multiple-page document, insert page numbers on all pages except the first page.

Traditionally, page numbers are positioned at the top right of the page. However, in lengthy and more formal documents such as annual reports or manuals, attractive headers and footers are designed. The applications that follow will include the Simple gallery of page number designs. Advanced headers and footers will be presented later.

Study the illustration below, noting specifically the position of page numbers. Review the callouts to reinforce your understanding of report formats.

To format a multiple-page report with page numbers at the top right:

1. Insert page numbers at the upper-right corner in the header position (0.5").
2. Suppress the page number on the first page.
3. Protect side headings that may be separated from the related paragraph with the Keep with next command. **Note:** When styles are applied to side headings, Keep with next is automatically applied, and side headings will not display alone at the bottom of a page.

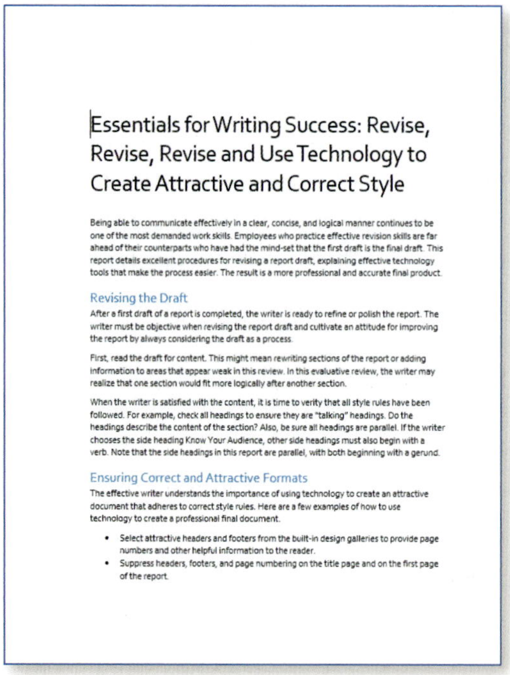

Essentials for Writing Success: Revise, Revise, Revise and Use Technology to Create Attractive and Correct Style

Being able to communicate effectively in a clear, concise, and logical manner continues to be one of the most demanded work skills. Employees who practice effective revision skills are far ahead of their counterparts who have had the mind-set that the first draft is the final draft. This report details excellent procedures for revising a report draft, explaining effective technology tools that make the process easier. The result is a more professional and accurate final product.

Revising the Draft

After a first draft of a report is completed, the writer is ready to refine or polish the report. The writer must be objective when revising the report draft and cultivate an attitude for improving the report by always considering the draft as a process.

First, read the draft for content. This might mean rewriting sections of the report or adding information to areas that appear weak in this review. In this evaluative review, the writer may realize that one section would fit more logically after another section.

When the writer is satisfied with the content, it is time to verity that all style rules have been followed. For example, check all headings to ensure they are "talking" headings. Do the headings describe the content of the section? Also, be sure all headings are parallel. If the writer chooses the side heading Know Your Audience, other side headings must also begin with a verb. Note that the side headings in this report are parallel, with both beginning with a gerund.

Ensuring Correct and Attractive Formats

The effective writer understands the importance of using technology to create an attractive document that adheres to correct style rules. Here are a few examples of how to use technology to create a professional final document.

- Select attractive headers and footers from the built-in design galleries to provide page numbers and other helpful information to the reader.
- Suppress headers, footers, and page numbering on the title page and on the first page of the report.

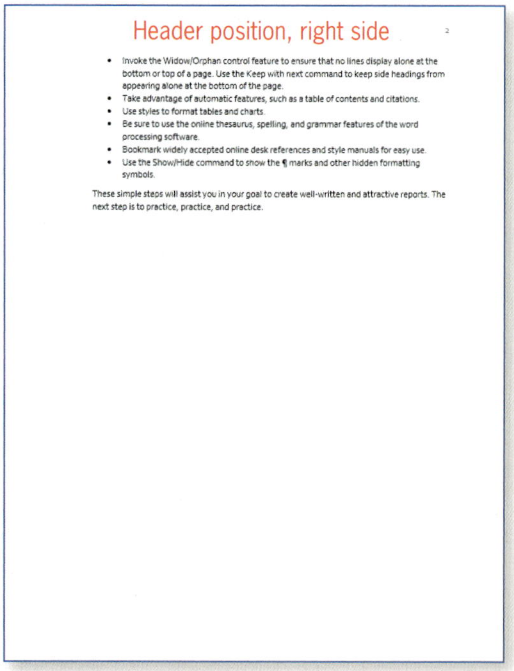

Header position, right side

2

- Invoke the Widow/Orphan control feature to ensure that no lines display alone at the bottom or top of a page. Use the Keep with next command to keep side headings from appearing alone at the bottom of the page.
- Take advantage of automatic features, such as a table of contents and citations.
- Use styles to format tables and charts.
- Be sure to use the online thesaurus, spelling, and grammar features of the word processing software.
- Bookmark widely accepted online desk references and style manuals for easy use.
- Use the Show/Hide command to show the ¶ marks and other hidden formatting symbols.

These simple steps will assist you in your goal to create well-written and attractive reports. The next step is to practice, practice, and practice.

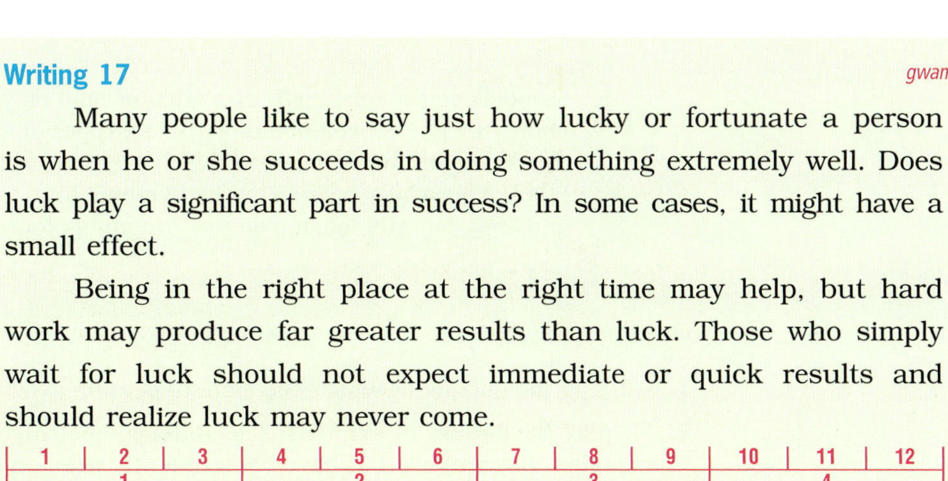

Writing 17

	gwam 1'	3'
Many people like to say just how lucky or fortunate a person	13	4
is when he or she succeeds in doing something extremely well. Does	26	9
luck play a significant part in success? In some cases, it might have a	40	13
small effect.	43	14
Being in the right place at the right time may help, but hard	13	19
work may produce far greater results than luck. Those who simply	26	23
wait for luck should not expect immediate or quick results and	39	27
should realize luck may never come.	46	30

1' | 1 | 2 | 3 | 4 | 5 | 6 | 7 | 8 | 9 | 10 | 11 | 12
3' | 1 | 2 | 3 | 4

Writing 18

	gwam 1'	3'
New golfers must learn to zero in on several social rules. Do	12	4
not engage in conversation, stand close, or move around when	24	8
another person is hitting. Be prepared to play when it is your turn.	38	13
Always take practice swings in an area away from other	11	16
people. Do not rest on your club on the green when waiting your turn.	25	21
Proper etiquette requires you to let the group behind you play through	39	25
if your group is slow.	43	27
Set your other clubs down off the green. Leave the green	11	31
quickly when you have finished; update your card on the next tee.	24	35
Always leave the course in good condition for others to enjoy.	37	39
Good sportsmanship is just as important as having a good time.	49	43

1' | 1 | 2 | 3 | 4 | 5 | 6 | 7 | 8 | 9 | 10 | 11 | 12
3' | 1 | 2 | 3 | 4

Writing 19

	gwam 1'	3'
Do you know how to utilize time wisely? If you do, then its	12	4
appropriate use can help you organize and run a business better. If	25	8
you find that your daily problems tend to keep you from planning	38	13
properly, then perhaps you are not utilizing time well. You may find	52	17
that you spend too much time on tasks that are not important. Plan	65	22
your work to save valuable time.	71	24
A firm that does not plan is liable to experience trouble. A	12	28
small firm may have difficulty planning. It is important to know just	26	32
where the firm is headed. A firm may have a fear of learning things it	40	37
would rather not know. To say that planning is easy would be absurd.	54	42
It requires a significant amount of thinking and planning to meet the	67	46
expectations of the firm.	72	48

1' | 1 | 2 | 3 | 4 | 5 | 6 | 7 | 8 | 9 | 10 | 11 | 12
3' | 1 | 2 | 3 | 4

SYMBOLS AND SPECIAL CHARACTERS

Symbols and special characters that are not on your keyboard can be inserted using the Symbol command. Different types of symbols can be inserted depending on the font selected. Some symbols are scientific or mathematical and are generally located on the Symbols font. Other symbols are decorative and are generally located on the Wingdings font.

To insert symbols:

Insert/Symbols/Symbol

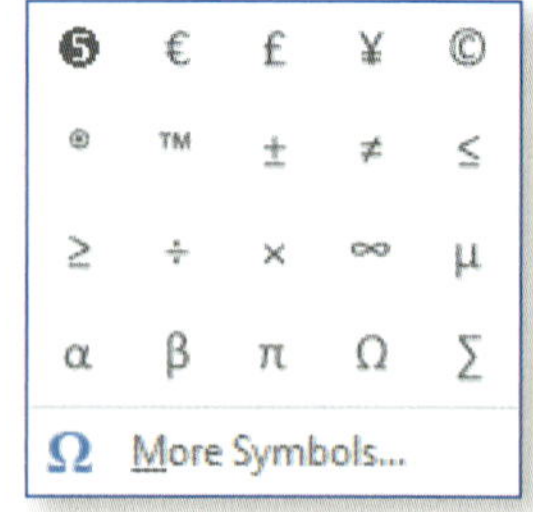

1. Click in the document where the symbol is to be inserted.
2. Display the gallery of symbols. The gallery generally contains the symbols that have been recently used on that computer. If the symbol you want to insert is not among the options, click More Symbols to display the Symbol dialog box.
3. Make sure the Symbols tab is selected and then check the Font box for the appropriate font. If Symbol (or the font you want to use) is not displayed, click the drop-list arrow and scroll to the desired font and select it.
4. Scroll down to locate the desired symbol and select it.
5. Click Insert and Close.

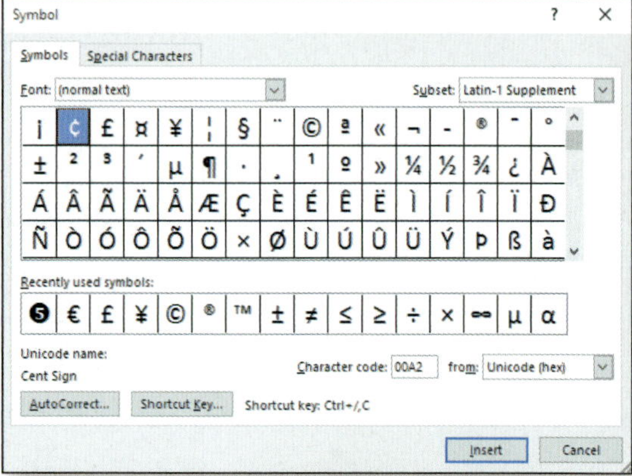

Special characters not located on the keyboard are located on the Special Characters tab. Examples include the em dash, nonbreaking hyphen, registered, trademark, and paragraph characters.

To insert special characters:

Insert/Symbols/Symbol

1. Click in the document where the special character is to be inserted.
2. Click the Special Characters tab in the Symbol dialog box.
3. Select the special character desired; click Insert and then click Close.

DRILL 2 SYMBOLS AND SPECIAL CHARACTERS

1. In a new document, apply Verdana 16-point font.
2. Insert these symbols; do not key the description or the parentheses. Tap ENTER after each symbol.

   Plus or minus symbol (±) from the Symbol font

   Smiley face (☺) from the Wingdings font

   Checkbox (☑) from the Wingdings 2 font

3. Key the text below and insert the special characters; do not key the description of the character in parenthesis. Tap ENTER after each character.

   Farbe Microfiber™ (Trademark)
   § (Section)
   ¶ (Paragraph)

4. Save and close. (*45-drill2*)

Writing 20

1' | 3'

If asked, most people will agree that some people have far 13 | 4
more creative skills than others, and they will also say that 25 | 8
these skills are in great demand by most organizations. A follow-up 38 | 13
question is in order. Are you born with creative skills or can you 52 | 17
develop them? There is no easy answer to that question, but 64 | 21
it is worth spending a good bit of time pondering. 74 | 25

If creative skills can be developed, then the next issue is 13 | 29
how can you develop these skills. One way is to approach each 25 | 33
task with a determination to solve the problem and a refusal to 38 | 37
accept failure. If the normal way of doing a job does not work, 50 | 41
just keep trying things never tried before until you reach a good 63 | 46
solution. This is called thinking outside the box. 73 | 49

Writing 21

1' | 3'

Figures are not as easy to key as many of the words we use. 12 | 4
Balanced-hand figures such as 16, 27, 38, 49, and 50, although 24 | 8
fairly easy, are slower to key because each one requires longer 37 | 12
reaches and uses more time per stroke. 44 | 15

Figures such as 12, 45, 67, and 90 are even more difficult 12 | 19
because they are next to one another and each uses just a single 24 | 23
hand to key. Because of their size, bigger numbers such as 178, 37 | 27
349, and 1,220 create extra speed losses. 45 | 30

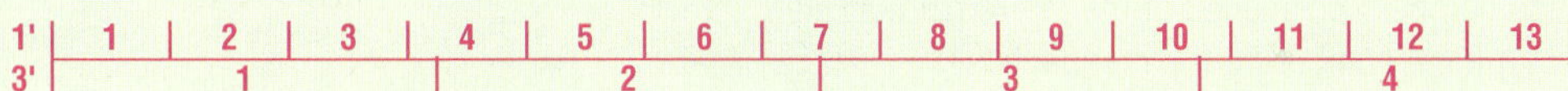

Skill Transfer

1. Take a 2' writing on paragraph 1.
2. Take a 2' writing on paragraph 2.
3. Take 2 or more 2' writings on the slower paragraph.

Writing 22

1' | 2'

Few people are able to attain financial success without some kind 13 | 7
of planning. People who realize the value of wise spending and 25 | 13
saving are those who set up a budget. A budget will help them to 38 | 19
determine just how much they can spend and how much they 49 | 25
can save so that they will not squander their money recklessly. 62 | 31

Keeping records is a crucial part of a budget. Complete 11 | 37
records of income and expenses over a period of a number of 23 | 42
months can help to determine what bills, as water or rent, are 35 | 49
static and which are flexible. To get the most out of your 47 | 54
income, pay attention to the items that you can modify. 58 | 60

1' 1 2 3 4 5 6 7 8 9 10 11 12
2' 1 2 3 4 5 6

LINE AND PAGE BREAKS

Pagination or breaking pages at the appropriate location can easily be controlled using two features: Widow/Orphan control and Keep with next.

Widow/Orphan control prevents a single line of a paragraph from printing at the bottom or top of a page. A check mark displays in this option box indicating that Widow/Orphan control is "on" (the default).

Keep with next prevents a page break from occurring between two paragraphs. Use this feature to keep a side heading from being left alone at the bottom of a page.

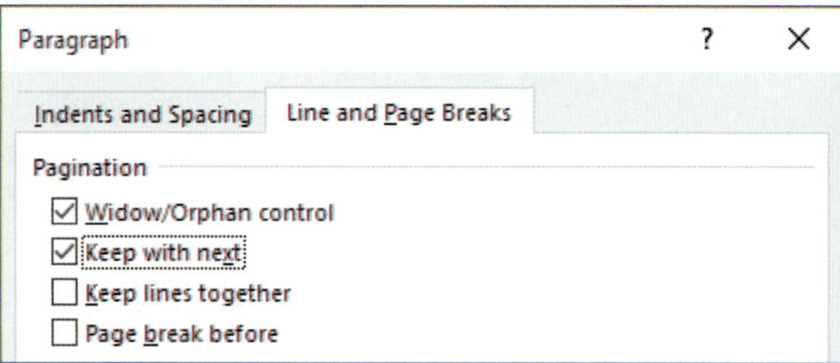

To use Keep with next:

Home/Paragraph/Dialog Box Launcher

1. Select the side heading and at least two lines of the paragraph that follow it.
2. Display the Paragraph dialog box.
3. From the Line and Page Breaks tab, select Keep with next.

DRILL 1 PAGE NUMBERS

keep with next

Insert/Header & Footer/Page Number

1. Open *keep with next* from the data files.
2. Add page numbers positioned at the top of page at the right. Do not print a page number on the first page.
3. Select the side heading at the bottom of the page along with the entire address and the 9:00 entry. Apply Keep with next so the side heading moves to page 2.
4. Preview to verify that the page number appears on page 2 only and that the side heading appears on page 2.
5. Save and close. (*45-drill1*)

QUICK ✓

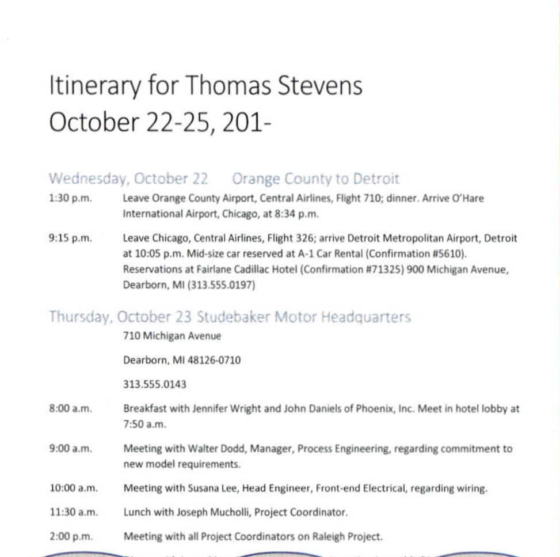

Itinerary for Thomas Stevens
October 22-25, 201-

Wednesday, October 22 Orange County to Detroit

1:30 p.m.	Leave Orange County Airport, Central Airlines, Flight 710; dinner. Arrive O'Hare International Airport, Chicago, at 8:34 p.m.
9:15 p.m.	Leave Chicago, Central Airlines, Flight 326; arrive Detroit Metropolitan Airport, Detroit at 10:05 p.m. Mid-size car reserved at A-1 Car Rental (Confirmation #5610). Reservations at Fairlane Cadillac Hotel (Confirmation #71325) 900 Michigan Avenue, Dearborn, MI (313.555.0197)

Thursday, October 23 Studebaker Motor Headquarters

710 Michigan Avenue

Dearborn, MI 48126-0710

313.555.0143

8:00 a.m.	Breakfast with Jennifer Wright and John Daniels of Phoenix, Inc. Meet in hotel lobby at 7:50 a.m.
9:00 a.m.	Meeting with Walter Dodd, Manager, Process Engineering, regarding commitment to new model requirements.
10:00 a.m.	Meeting with Susana Lee, Head Engineer, Front-end Electrical, regarding wiring.
11:30 a.m.	Lunch with Joseph Mucholli, Project Coordinator.
2:00 p.m.	Meeting with all Project Coordinators on Raleigh Project.

2

Friday, October 24 Flint Assembly Plant

42 Roland Avenue

Flint, MI 48532-0042

313.555.0125

9:00 a.m.	Drive to Flint Assembly plant.
11:00 a.m.	Lunch with Russ Nguyen, Plant Manager.
1:00 p.m.	Plant tour
2:30 p.m.	Meet with Jon Tallaski, Plant Facilities Engineer, regarding retooling.
3:30 p.m.	Meet with Janice Schmidt, Quality Control Specialist, about testing requirements for meeting federal environmental regulations.

Saturday, October 25 Detroit to Orange County

9:00 a.m.	Leave Detroit Metropolitan Airport, Central Airlines, Flight 318; breakfast. Arrive Orange County Airport at 1:08 p.m.

Skill Builder 3

StockLite/Shutterstock.com

LESSON A

Skill Building

Tips for Building Speed

- Setting individual goals and striving to reach your goal is your most effective speed building strategy.
- Practice drill lines to gain confidence and fluency. Drills in Skill Builders 1, 2, and 3 are designed to build keystroking skill.
- Drills with balance-hand combinations like those on the next two pages are designed to help you key faster.
- Take short timings; then repeat them with the goal of keying two or three more words more the second time.
- After you build speed on short timings, gradually move to longer timings.

Tips for Improving Accuracy

- Relax and focus on using good techniques rather than worrying about errors.
- Make sure your arms, fingers, and feet are in the proper position.
- Strive to stroke keys fluently.
- Work for speed for short intervals and then drop back to a comfortable pace.
- At the slower speed, concentrate on one technique at a time such as keeping your eyes on the copy or minimizing hand movement.

Timed Writings

1. Key a 1' writing on each paragraph, focusing on good techniques. Compare your *gwam* on the two paragraphs.
2. Take a 1' writing on the slower paragraph, striving to exceed your speed on the faster paragraph.
3. Key both paragraphs at a comfortable pace.

Writing 23

	gwam 1'	3'
The most valuable employees stand a greater chance of	11	4
maintaining their job in hard economic times. There are many	23	8
qualities which distinguish an excellent employee from other workers.	37	12
In the first place, they remain focused and keep their minds on the	51	17
tasks at hand. Good employees think about the work they perform and	64	21
how it relates to the total success of the project. They act as team	78	26
leaders and guide the project to completion.	87	29
Second, good workers have the ability to work consistently and	14	33
fully realize every goal. Many people in the workplace perform just	27	38
bits and pieces of a job. They begin one thing, but allow themselves	41	42
to be quickly distracted from the work at hand. Many people are good	55	47
starters, but fewer are also good finishers.	64	50

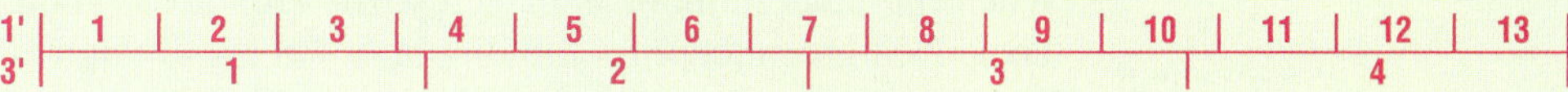

Lesson 45 Multiple-Page Reports

New Commands

- Page Number
- Line/Page Breaks
- Insert File
- Symbols
- Special Characters

Warmup *Lesson 45a Warmup* — lesson 45a warmup

New Commands

45b

PAGE NUMBERS

Multiple-page documents, such as reports, require page numbers. The Page Number command automatically inserts the correct page number on each page. Page numbers may be positioned in the header position (0.5" from top of page) or in the footer position (bottom of page). To prevent the number from printing on the first page, you can modify the page layout on the first page.

To insert page numbers:

Insert/Header & Footer/Page Number

1. Display a list of page number positions and formatting options.
2. Click an option such as Top of Page ❶ to display a gallery of page number styles.
3. Click the down scroll arrow to browse the various styles ❷. **Note:** To remove page numbers, click Remove Page Numbers ❸ .

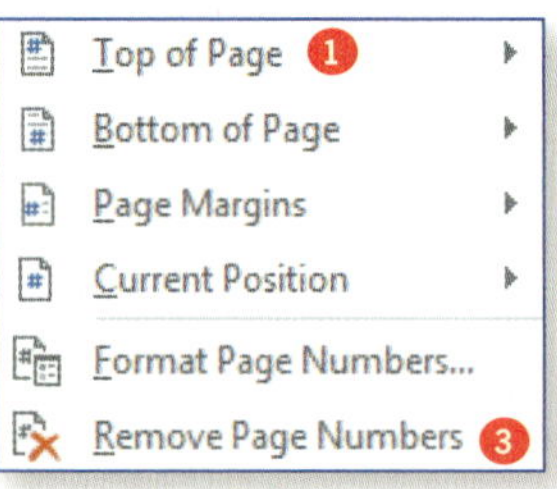

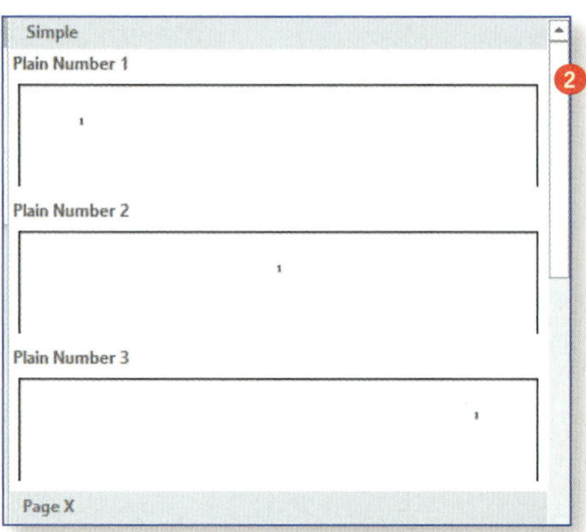

Double-click in the body of the document to close the header. Double-click in the header area to open the header.

To remove the page number from the first page:

Header & Footer Tools/Design/Options/Different First Page

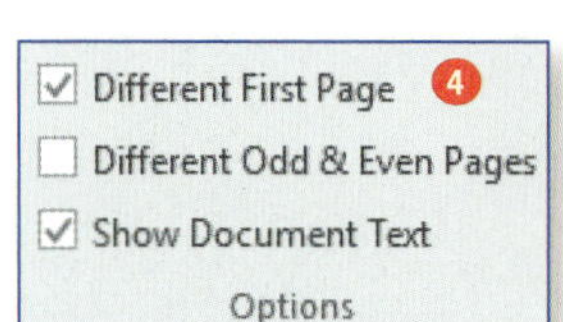

When the page number is inserted, the Header & Footer Tools Design conceptual tab displays. On the Design tab from the Options group, click Different First Page ❹. The page number does not display on the first page.

Option: Select Different First Page from the Layout tab of the Page Setup dialog box (Layout/Page Setup/Dialog Box Launcher).

LESSON B

Skill Building

Key balanced-hand words quickly and as phrases to increase speed.

DRILL 11

Balanced-Hand

Key each line once, working for fluency.

1 to today stocks into ti times sitting until ur urges further tour
2 en entire trend dozen or order support editor nd and mandate land
3 he healthy check ache th these brother both an annual change plan
4 nt into continue want of office softer roof is issue poison basis

5 Did Pamela sign the title to the big lake mansion by Lamb Island?
6 Rick is to pay the eight men and women if they do the work right.
7 My time for a land bus tour will not change until further notice.
8 I am to blame for the big problem with the maid; I can handle it.

Timed Writings

1. Key a 1' writing on each paragraph. Compare your *gwam*.
2. Key an additional 1' writing on the slower paragraph.
3. Then key both paragraphs at a comfortable pace.

Writing 24

gwam 1' | 3'

Most of us have, at some time or another, recognized an annoying 14 5
problem and had valid reasons to complain. The complaint may have 27 9
been because of a defective product, poor customer services, or 40 13
perhaps growing tired of talking to voice mail. However, many of us 54 18
feel that complaining to a business firm is an exercise in futility 67 22
so we do not bother. Instead, we just remain quiet, write it off as a 81 27
bad experience and continue to be taken advantage of. 92 31

Today more than at any time in the past consumers are taking some 13 35
steps to let their feelings be known—and with a great amount of 26 39
success. As a result, firms are becoming more responsive to 38 43
the needs of the consumer. complaints from customers alert firms 51 48
to produce or service defect and there by cause action to be taken 64 52
for their benefit. 68 53

1' | 1 | 2 | 3 | 4 | 5 | 6 | 7 | 8 | 9 | 10 | 11 | 12 | 13
3' | 1 | 2 | 3 | 4

Apply It

44-d1

Leftbound Report

1. In a new document, key the model leftbound report shown on the previous page. Change the left margin to 1.5". Tap ENTER three times to position the title at about 2". Tap ENTER twice.
2. Apply appropriate styles to the title and side headings. Click Decrease font size to make the report title fit on one line.
3. Key the table and apply the List Table 5 Dark – Accent 1 style. Size the columns attractively and center the table horizontally. Click in the paragraph below the table and apply Add Space Before Paragraph to adjust the spacing after the table.
4. Save and close. (*44-d1*)

Add Space Before Paragraph

Home/Paragraph/Line and Paragraph Spacing/Add Space Before Paragraph

44-d2

Edit Report

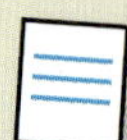

brochure

1. Open *brochure* from the data files. Format as a leftbound report. Apply the Retrospect document theme.
2. Key the paragraph shown below as the last paragraph. Apply Heading 1 style to the side heading.
3. Search for the word *photos* and replace with **photographs**.
4. Search for all occurrences of italics and replace them with no italic.
5. Search for all occurrences of bold and replace them with no bold except the side headings. **Hint:** Click the No Formatting button in the Find and Replace dialog box before you begin the new search. Click Find Next to review each replacement.
6. Click Pages in the Navigation pane. Search for the word *readability*. Which page displays as a result of your search?
7. Click Headings (*readability* is displayed in the search box). Which heading is displayed in yellow to indicate readability is discussed under that heading in the document?
8. Save and close. (*44-d2*)

Replace Font Attribute (Italic)

Find what:

1. Click Format and then Font.
2. Under Font style, click Italic.

Replace with:

1. Click Format and then Font.
2. Under Font style, click Not Italic.

Summary Apply Heading 1 style

Remember to plan your page layout with the three basic elements of effective page design. Always include sufficient white space to give an uncluttered appearance. Learn to add bold when emphasis is needed, and do consider your audience when choosing typestyles. Finally, use typestyles to add variety to your layout, but remember, no more than two typestyles in a document.

LESSON C

Skill Building

Work for fluency as you key these balanced-hand words.

DRILL 12

Balanced-Hand

Key each line once for fluency.

1 an anyone brand spans th their father eighth he head sheets niche
2 en enters depends been nd end handle fund or original sport color
3 ur urban turns assure to took factory photo ti titles satin still
4 ic ice bicycle chic it item position profit ng angle danger doing

5 I want the info in the file on the profits from the chic bicycle.
6 Hang the sign by the lake not by an island by six or eight today.
7 Did Vivian, the widow, pay for eight flair pens, and eight gowns?
8 When did Viviana go to the firm to sign the title to the emblems?

Timed Writings

1. Take a 1' writing on each paragraph at a fast pace.
2. Take a 3' writing on both paragraphs at a comfortable pace.

Writing 25

	gwam 1'	3'
Practicing basic health rules will result in good body condition.	14	5
Proper diet is a way to achieve good health. Eat a variety of foods each	29	10
day, including some fruit, vegetables, cereal products, and foods rich	43	14
in protein, to be sure that you keep a balance. Another part of a good	57	19
health plan is physical activity, such as running.	67	22
Running has become quite popular in this country. Some people	13	27
run for the joy of running, others run because they want to maximize	27	31
the benefits that can be gained by running on a regular basis. Some	41	36
of the benefits include weight loss, improved heart health, improved	55	41
bone health, and improved mood. Running is one of the most effective	68	45
forms of exercise that will help achieve ideal body weight.	80	49

1' | 1 | 2 | 3 | 4 | 5 | 6 | 7 | 8 | 9 | 10 | 11 | 12 | 13
3' | 1 | 2 | 3 | 4

Tap ENTER three times (about 2")

Title style

Title → # Audience Analysis and Strategic Purpose ↓ 2

Effective presenters realize the need to prepare for a successful presentation. Two areas of extensive preparation are the development of a thorough audience analysis and identification of a well-defined presentation purpose. ↓ 1

Side heading → ## Audience Analysis Heading 1 style

The presenter must conduct a thorough audience analysis before developing the presentation. A listing of common audience demographics is shown in the table below. ↓ 1

Audience Profile	
Age	Gender
Education	Ethnic group
Marital status	Geographic location
Group membership	Vested interest in topic

1.5" Given sufficient time, the presenter will research each of these areas carefully. Additionally, interviews with program planners and organization leaders will provide insight into the needs, desires, and expectations of the specific audience. ↓ 1 1"

Many successful presenters find it useful to arrive early to the presentation and greet participants as they enter the meeting room. Often presenters may begin the presentation with one or two directed questions to understand the profile and demeanor of the audience. Knowing the audience is an important first step in preparing a successful presentation. ↓ 1

Purpose of the Presentation

After initially analyzing the audience profile well in advance, the presenter has a clear focus on the needs of the audience and then writes a well-defined purpose of the presentation. With a clear focus, the presenter confidently conducts research and organizes a presentation that is on target. The presenter remembers to state the purpose in the introduction of the presentation to assist the audience in understanding the well-defined direction of the presentation.

Leftbound Report

LESSON D

Skill Building

Keep your eyes on the copy as you key each line.

DRILL 13

Adjacent Key Review

Key each line once; at a comfortable pace.

1 nm many enmity solemn kl inkling weekly pickle oi oil invoice join
2 iu stadium medium genius lk milk talk walks uy buy buyer soliloquy
3 mn alumni hymn number column sd Thursday wisdom df mindful handful
4 me mention comment same fo found perform info le letter flew files

5 The buyer sent his weekly invoices for oil to the group on Thursday.
6 Mindful of the alumni, the choirs sang a hymn prior to my soliloquy.
7 An inmate, a fogger, and a genius joined the weekly talks on Monday.
8 They were to join in the talk shows to assess regions of the Yukon.

Timed Writings

1. Take a 1' writing on each paragraph.
2. Take a 3' writing on both paragraphs at a comfortable pace.

Writing 26

gwam 1' | 3'

All people, in spite of their eating habits, have two major needs 13 | 4
that must be met by their food. They need food that provides a 26 | 9
source of energy, and they need food that will fill the skeletal and 40 | 13
operating needs of their bodies. Carbohydrates, fats, and protein 53 | 18
form a major portion of the diet. Vitamins and minerals are also 66 | 22
necessary for excellent health. 72 | 24

Carbohydrates make up a major source of our energy needs. 12 | 28
Fats also serve as a source of energy and act as defense against 25 | 32
cold and trauma. Proteins are changed to amino acids, which are 38 | 37
the building units of the body. These, in turn, are utilized to make 52 | 41
most body tissue. Minerals are required to control many body 64 | 45
functions, and vitamins are used for normal growth and aid against 77 | 50
disease. 84 | 52

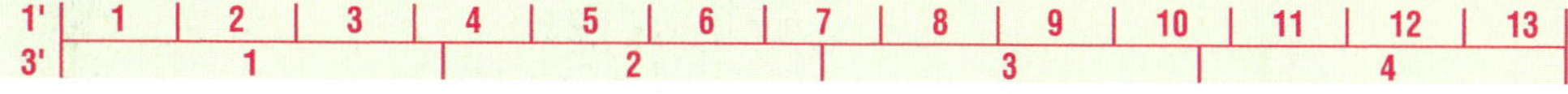

DRILL 2 NAVIGATION

speeches

Home/Editing/Find

1. Open *speeches* from the data files.
2. Display all occurrences of the word *speeches* and replace with **presentations**.
3. Display all occurrences of the word *objective*. Click on the last occurrence and replace with **goal**.
4. Display all occurrences of the word *confident*. Click Options and select Find whole words only. Replace the one occurrence with **assured**.
5. Find *audience* and highlight each occurrence in yellow.
   Hint: Be sure to set the Highlight button in the Font group on the Home tab to yellow.
6. Key **discussion** in the Search box. Click Pages to browse the pages where this word occurs.
7. Click Headings to display the headings where the word *discussion* occurs. Click on the second heading and then the third heading to move in the report.
8. Click the Magnifying Glass button and click Tables to go to the table in the report.
9. Save and close. (*44-drill2*)

Document Design

44e

LEFTBOUND REPORT

Reports prepared with binders are called leftbound reports. The binding takes 0.5" of space. Study the illustration below and the full model on page 2-101 and note the 1.5" left margin required for leftbound reports. Review the other report formats that are the same for unbound and leftbound reports.

Theme: Use the default Office theme.

Left margin: 1.5"

Right margin: 1"

Bottom margin: Approximately 1"; last page may be deeper

Font: 11 point for body of report

Title: 1

- Position at about 2".
- Capitalize the first letter of all main words and apply Title style. Tap ENTER two times.

Side headings: 2

- Capitalize the first letter of all main words and apply Heading 1 style.

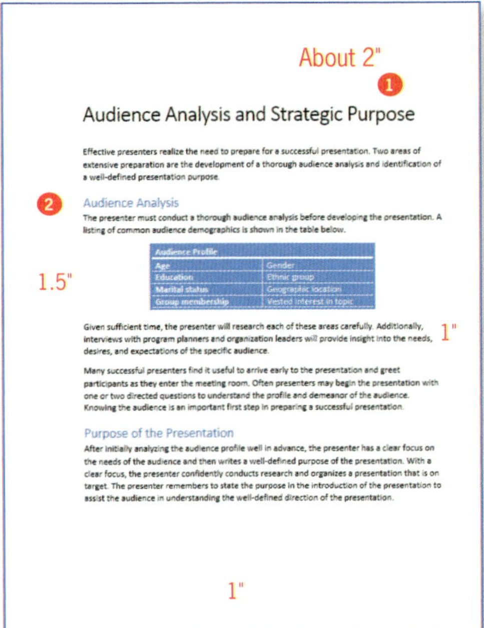

Audience Analysis and Strategic Purpose

Effective presenters realize the need to prepare for a successful presentation. Two areas of extensive preparation are the development of a thorough audience analysis and identification of a well-defined presentation purpose.

Audience Analysis

The presenter must conduct a thorough audience analysis before developing the presentation. A listing of common audience demographics is shown in the table below.

Audience Profile	
Age	Gender
Education	Ethnic group
Marital status	Geographic location
Group membership	Vested interest in topic

Given sufficient time, the presenter will research each of these areas carefully. Additionally, interviews with program planners and organization leaders will provide insight into the needs, desires, and expectations of the specific audience.

Many successful presenters find it useful to arrive early to the presentation and greet participants as they enter the meeting room. Often presenters may begin the presentation with one or two directed questions to understand the profile and demeanor of the audience. Knowing the audience is an important first step in preparing a successful presentation.

Purpose of the Presentation

After initially analyzing the audience profile well in advance, the presenter has a clear focus on the needs of the audience and then writes a well-defined purpose of the presentation. With a clear focus, the presenter confidently conducts research and organizes a presentation that is on target. The presenter remembers to state the purpose in the introduction of the presentation to assist the audience in understanding the well-defined direction of the presentation.

LESSON E

Skill Building

Keep your eyes on the copy as you key each line.

DRILL 14

Letter Combinations

Key each line once, concentrating on techniques.

br
1 bright brown bramble bread breath breezes brought brother broiler
2 In February my brother brought brown bread and beans from Boston.

exe
3 exercises exert executives exemplify exemption executed exemplary
4 They exert extreme effort executing exercises in exemplary style.

bt
5 doubt subtle obtains obtrusion subtracts indebtedness undoubtedly
6 Extreme debt will cause more than subtle doubt among my creditors.

ny
7 tiny funny company nymph penny nylon many anyone phony any brainy
8 Anyone as brainy and funny as Penny is an asset to their company.

Timed Writings

1. Take a 1' writing on each paragraph.
2. Take a 3' writing on both paragraphs at a comfortable pace.

Writing 27

	gwam 1'	3'
Many people believe that an ounce of prevention is worth a pound	14	5
of cure. Care of your heart can help you prevent serious physical	27	9
problems. The human heart is the most important pump ever	39	13
developed. It constantly pushes blood through the body tissues. But	52	17
the layers of muscle that make up the heart must be kept in proper	66	22
working order. Exercise can help this muscle to remain in good	78	26
condition.	80	27
Another important way to maintain a healthy heart is just by	13	31
avoiding habits which are considered to be greatly detrimental to the	27	36
body. Food that is high in cholesterol is not a good choice. Also,	41	40
use of tobacco has quite a negative effect on the function of the	54	49
heart. You can minimize your chances of heart problems by avoiding	67	54
these bad health habits.	72	55

1' | 1 | 2 | 3 | 4 | 5 | 6 | 7 | 8 | 9 | 10 | 11 | 12 | 13
3' | 1 | 2 | 3 | 4

To group search results by pages:

1. Click Pages below the Search document box ❶. Only pages that contain results will display.
2. Click the desired page ❷ to go to that heading in the document.
3. Click x ❸ to end your search and display all your pages.

Note: For other searches, click the Magnifying Glass button to search for Graphics, Tables, Equations, Footnotes/Endnotes, or Reviewers.

To replace text:

Home/Editing/Replace

1. Display the Find and Replace dialog box.
2. Key the text you wish to locate in the Find what box.
3. Key the replacement text in the Replace with box.
4. Click Find Next to find the next occurrence of the text. Click Replace to replace one occurrence or Replace All to replace all occurrences of the text.

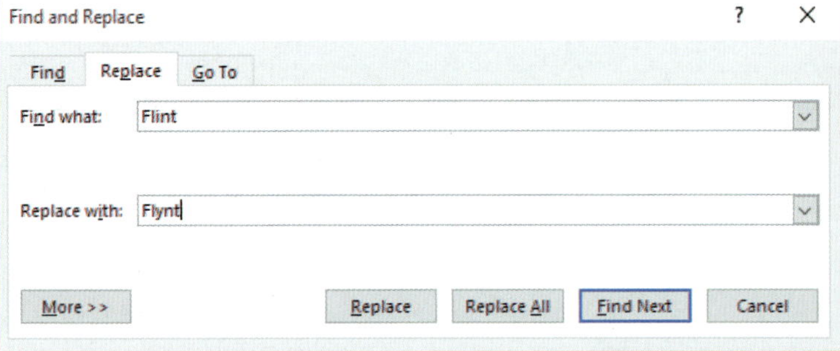

To find text and apply a format such as highlight:

Home/Editing/Replace

1. Display the Find and Replace dialog box.
2. Key the text you wish to locate in the Find what box.
3. Click More to display additional options.
4. Click in Replace with and then click Format ❹ and select the desired format. ❺

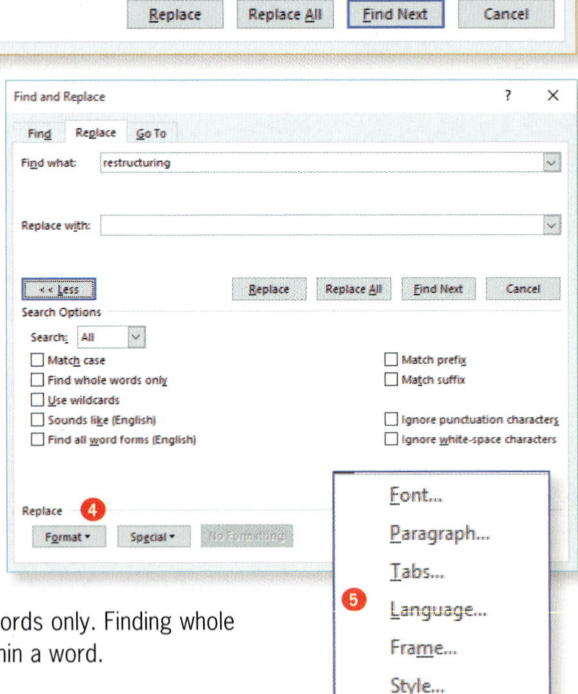

Note the search options available when you click More, such as Match case or Find whole words only. Finding whole words only prevents you from finding letters within a word.

Numeric Keypad

Overview

In the lessons you completed in this text, you learned to key numbers on the 4th row of the keyboard. Many jobs require extensive use of numeric data. Using the numeric keypad on your keyboard or as a separate device is more efficient and effective than making the reaches to the 4th row to key numbers.

In this section, you will learn to use the touch system on the numeric keypad to key numbers rapidly and accurately. The most important thing to remember in using a touch system is that position—especially correct finger placement and keeping your arm parallel to the keypad–is the best way to improve speed and accuracy.

Standard Plan for Numeric Drills

Review these these steps and use them to key each drill:

1. Open the numeric keypad data file nk-drill + the drill number (nk-drill1, nk-drill2, etc.) and save it in a new folder named Numeric Keypad.
2. Read the instructions in the left column of the drill carefully.
3. Review the Numeric Keypad Layout below on the left and in the left column of the drills. The numbers at the bottom indicate the correct fingers of the right hand for each number.
4. Review the Finger Position illustration below on the right. It illustrates the correct finger position for 4, 5, and 6, which is the home row. Each drill will have an illustration showing the proper finger position.
5. Look at the numeric keypad and place your fingers over the 4, 5, and 6 keys to locate home position. All reaches are made from the home row. Move the appropriate finger up or down from home position to key a number.
6. Open the data file and key the numbers as shown in the textbook below the heading beginning with column **a**; tap the TAB key after each number is keyed to move to the next column.
7. Tap ENTER after you key the number in the last column (**f**).
8. Tap ENTER twice at the end of each group of numbers.
9. Proofread the numbers checking each against the source copy in the textbook.
10. Save and close. (nk-drill+number).

Note: Drill 4 focuses on numbers with decimals, and Drill 5 is a review to improve your mastery of keying numbers.

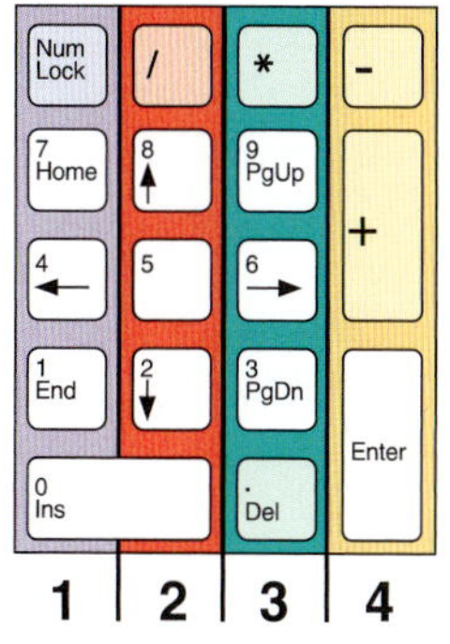

Numeric Keypad Layout

Correct Finger Position

FIND AND REPLACE

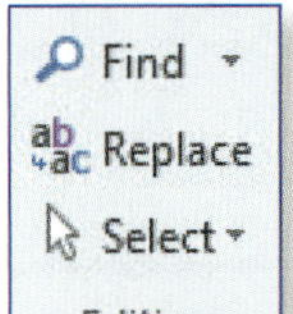

Locating text, headings, footnotes, graphics, page breaks, comments, formatting, and other items within a document quickly is an essential skill when working with long documents such as reports.

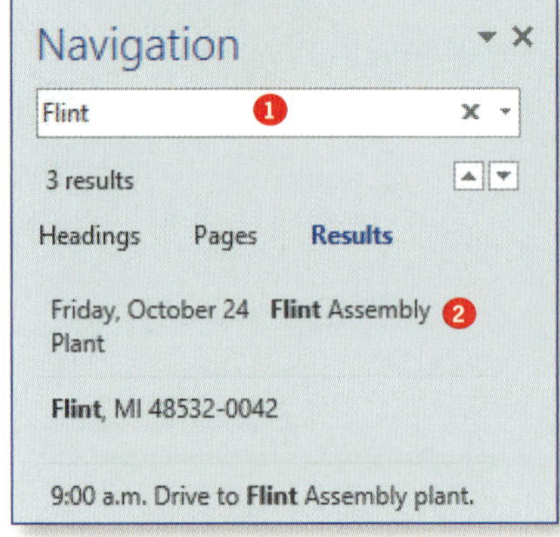

To find text:

Home/Editing/Find

1. Display the Navigation pane on the left side of the screen.

2. Key the text to be located in the search box 1. The matches display below the search box. Click each match 2 to go to the location in the document.

To display other find options:

Click the Magnifying Glass button 3. Click Options. The Find Options dialog box displays. Review the various find options to determine its usefulness in a search.

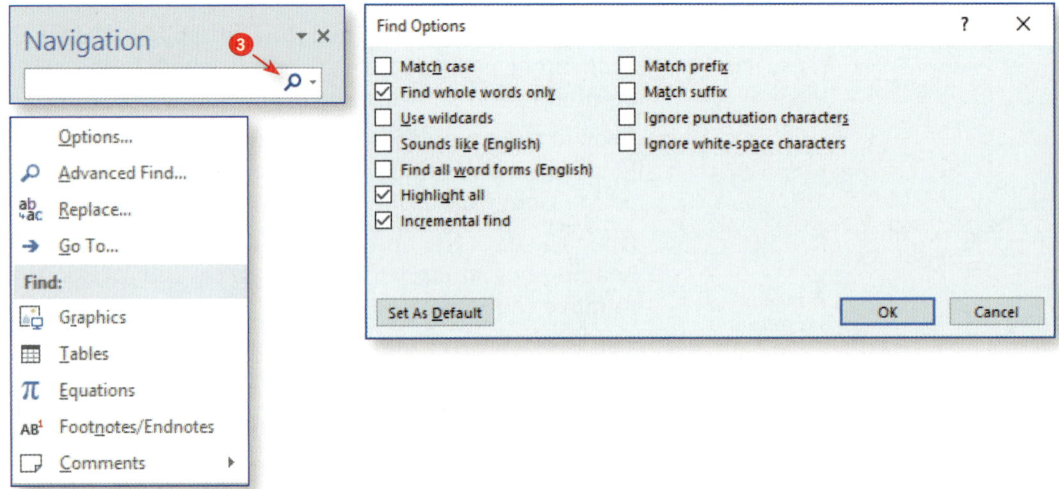

To group search results by headings:

1. Click Headings below the Search document box 4. Headings that contain text with the search results display in yellow.

2. Click the desired heading 5 to go to that heading in the document.

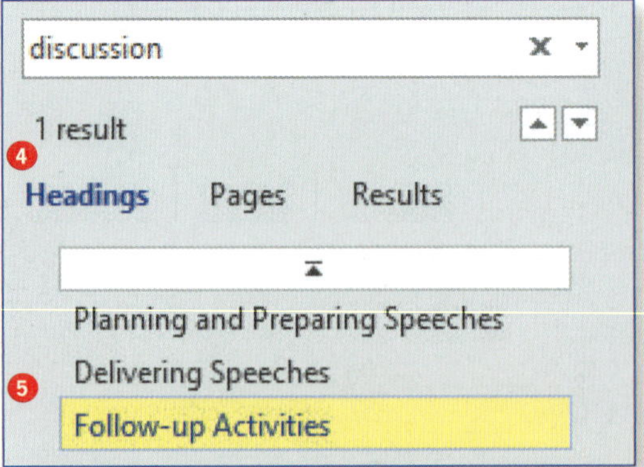

DRILL 1

nk-drill1

4, 5, 6, 0, and ENTER

1. Turn on NUMLOCK. Open the data file and save to the Numeric Keypad folder.
2. Learn the reaches for this drill. As you practice each reach, tap the key with a quick, sharp stroke and return to the home-key position. Keep the other fingers in the home key position.
   a. To key the number 4, tap the key with the index finger.
   b. To type the number 5, tap the 5 key with the middle finger.
   c. To key the number 6, tap the 6 key with the ring finger.
   d. To key the number 0, reach down with the index finger, tap the 0 key and return to the home-key position.
   e. To move to the next line, reach down with the fourth finger, tap the ENTER key and return to the home-key position.
3. Remember to tap TAB after each number and tap ENTER after keying the number in the f column. Tap ENTER twice at the end of each group of numbers.
4. Save and close. (*nk-drill1*)

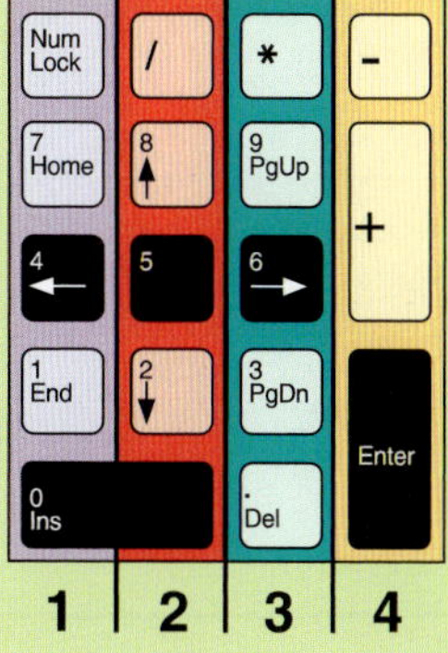

a	b	c	d	e	f
46	55	56	46	55	56
45	64	45	45	64	45
66	56	64	66	56	64
56	44	65	56	44	65
54	65	45	54	65	45
65	54	44	65	54	44
466	445	546	654	465	665
564	654	465	545	446	645
456	464	546	545	564	456
556	544	644	466	644	646
644	455	464	654	464	554
454	546	565	554	456	656
400	404	505	606	500	600
404	505	606	500	600	400
500	600	400	404	505	606
650	506	404	550	440	550
506	460	605	460	604	640
406	500	640	504	460	560
504	640	550	440	660	406
560	450	650	450	505	550
640	504	440	640	450	660
400	600	500	500	600	400
650	505	404	606	540	560
504	404	640	404	406	606

New Commands

44d

MARGINS

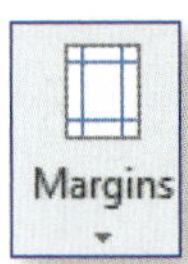

Margins are the distance between the edge of the paper and the text of a document. The default margins referred to as "Normal" are 1" top, bottom, right, and left. To fit more information on a page, select Narrow margins or select Wide margins to increase the white space.

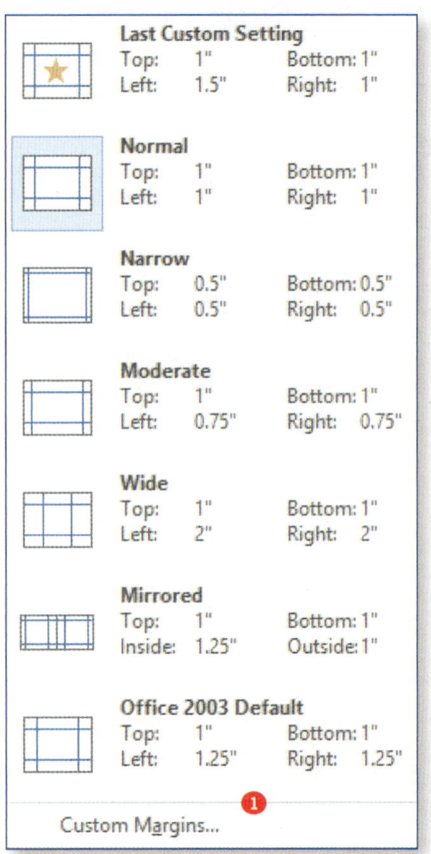

To change margin settings:

Layout/Page Setup/Margins

1. Click on the down arrow to display the gallery of margins options.
2. Click the desired margins option.

To set custom margins not listed in the gallery:

3. Click Custom Margins ❶. From the Margins tab, click the up or down arrows to increase or decrease the default settings ❷.
4. Apply margins to the Whole document ❸ unless directed otherwise. Click OK.

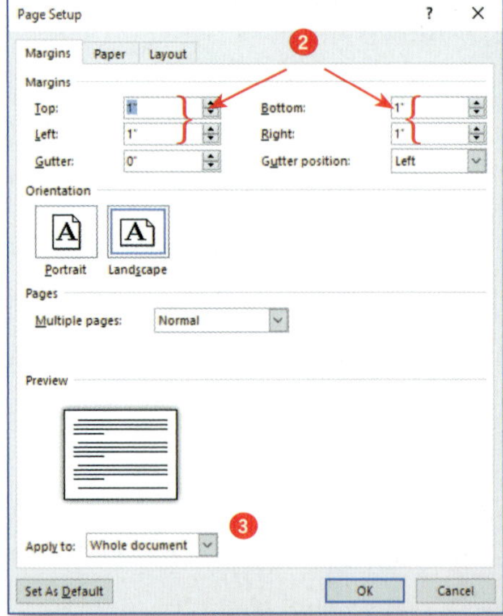

DRILL 1 MARGINS

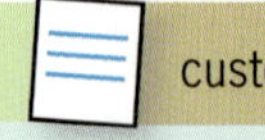

custom margins

Layout/Page Setup/Margins/Custom Margins

1. Open *custom margins* from the data files. Apply Wide margins.
2. Apply Narrow margins.
3. Change the left, right, and top margins to 1.5". Apply margin settings to the whole document.
4. Save and close. (*44-drill1*)

DRILL 2

nk-drill2

7, 8, 9

1. Turn on NUMLOCK and open the data file and save in Numeric Keypad folder.
2. Learn the key reaches for this drill. As you practice each reach, tap the key with a quick, sharp stroke and return to the home-key position. Keep the other fingers in the home key position.
   a. To key the number 7, reach up with the index finger.
   b. To key the number 8, reach up with the middle finger.
   c. To key the number 9, reach up with the ring finger.
3. Remember to tap the TAB key after keying each number, and tap ENTER after keying the number in the f column.
4. Tap ENTER after each group of numbers.
5. Save and close. (*nk-drill2*)

© Cengage Learning

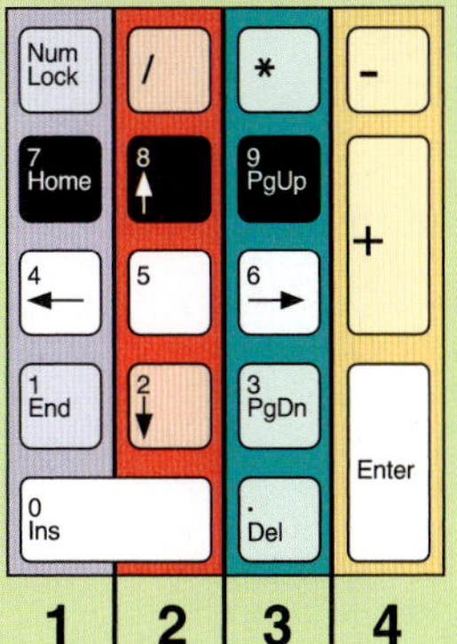

a	b	c	d	e	f
74	85	96	70	80	90
47	58	96	87	78	98
90	70	80	90	90	70
89	98	78	89	77	87
86	67	57	48	68	57
59	47	48	67	58	69
470	580	690	770	707	407
999	969	888	858	474	777
777	474	888	585	999	696
858	969	747	770	880	990
757	858	959	857	747	678
579	849	879	697	854	796
857	967	864	749	864	795
609	507	607	889	990	448
597	847	449	457	684	599
85	74	96	98	78	88
957	478	857	994	677	579
657	947	479	76	94	795
887	965	789	577	649	849
90	80	70	806	709	407
407	567	494	97	80	70
50	790	807	90	75	968
408	97	66	480	857	57
87	479	567	947	808	970
690	85	798	587	907	89
94	754	879	67	594	847
489	880	97	907	69	579

Lesson 44 Leftbound Reports

New Commands

- Margins
- Find and Replace

Warmup *Lesson 44a Warmup*

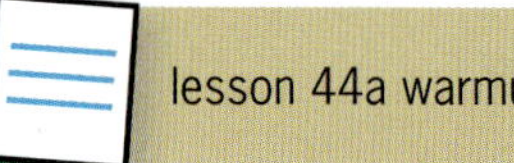

lesson 44a warmup

Skill Building

44b Improve Keystroking

first row

1 Take the Paz exit; make a right turn; then the street veers left.
2 Stop by and see the amateur videos of Zoe at six o'clock tonight.
3 I made an excellent pizza with leftover bread, cheese, and beef.

home row

4 Dallas shall ask Sal to sell fake flash fads; Sal sells all fads.
5 A small fast salad is all Kallas had; Dallas adds a dash of salt.
6 Dallas saw all flasks fall; alas Dad adds a fast fake hall flask.

third row

7 We used thirty pails of yellow powder; Wesley threw the rest out.
8 I should go to the store with Paul to get eggs for the apple pie.
9 Did you see the request for Sy to take the test with your sister?

Communication

44c

1. Review the "Number Expression" section of Appendix C.
2. Key the numbered list at the right single-spaced; correct any number expression errors as you key.
3. Save and close. (44c)

NUMBER EXPRESSION

1. Address the letter to 1 Elm Street and postmark by April 15th.
2. The retirement reception will be held on the 1st of May in Room Twelve at 5 o'clock.
3. Program participants included fifteen supervisors, five managers, and two vice presidents.
4. 12 boxes arrived damaged and about 2/3 of the contents were crushed.
5. The manager reported that 85% of the project was complete, with 9 days remaining until the March 15th due date.
6. The presiding officer called the meeting to order at two p.m. and requested that the 2 50-page reports be distributed.
7. Nearly 10 million people visited the virtual museum this year.
8. Jim lives at 1 21st Street and works on 6th Avenue.

DRILL 3

nk-drill3

1, 2, 3

1. Turn NUMLOCK on. Open data file and save to Numeric Keypad folder.
2. Learn the key reaches for this drill. As you practice each reach, tap the key with a quick, sharp stroke and return to the home-key position. Keep the other fingers in the home key position.
   a. To key the number 1, reach down with the index finger.
   b. To key the number 2, reach down with the middle finger.
   c. To key the number 3, reach down with the ring finger.
3. Key the numbers for this drill. Remember to tap TAB afrer each number and tap ENTER after keying the number in the f column.
4. Tap ENTER twice after each group of numbers.
5. Save and close. (*nk-drill3*)

1 | 2 | 3 | 4

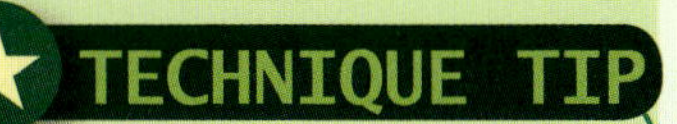

Keep fingers curved and upright over home keys. Keep right thumb tucked under palm.

a	b	c	d	e	f
11	22	33	14	15	16
41	52	63	36	34	35
24	26	25	22	42	62
27	18	39	30	20	10
30	30	10	19	61	43
32	31	21	53	83	71
414	141	525	252	636	363
141	111	252	222	363	333
111	414	222	525	333	636
111	141	222	252	366	336
152	342	624	141	243	121
330	502	331	302	110	432
913	823	721	633	523	511
702	612	513	712	802	823
213	293	821	813	422	722
24	36	15	12	32	34
115	334	226	254	346	246
20	140	300	240	105	304
187	278	347	159	357	158
852	741	963	654	321	987
303	505	819	37	92	10
28	91	37	22	13	23
524	631	423	821	922	733
15	221	209	371	300	25
823	421	24	31	19	107
652	813	211	354	231	187
50	31	352	16	210	30

Apply It

43-d1

Unbound Report

1. In a new document, key the model report on the previous page. Apply the Droplet theme. Tap ENTER three times to position the title at about 2". Use default side margins. Key a dash in line two of the report after *13.02*.
2. Capitalize the first letter of all main words in the title; tap ENTER twice after the title. Then select the title and apply Title style.
3. Select the side headings and apply Heading 1 style. Tap ENTER once after the side heading.
4. Insert the footnote in the first paragraph.
5. Apply square bullets to the list.
6. Save and close. (*43-d1*)

43-d2

Edit Report

1. Open the file (*43-d1*) that you created in the previous exercise and apply Frame theme.
2. Change the word *appropriate* in the first paragraph to *effective*.
3. Key the word **Communication** before the word *Preferences* in the second heading.
4. In the footnote, change the revision date to 9/2/2018.
5. Delete the last paragraph and replace with the following text:

   Contact the General Administration Office with questions.
6. Insert a footnote after the word *Office* in the last sentence just added. Key the footnote text below:

Anne Holifield, Information Officer, extension 6932, AHolifield@sa.com

7. Select the bulleted list and change to numbers. Reorder the items as shown below and make the one correction shown.
8. Save and close. (*43-d2*)

1. Write clear, concise sentences, avoiding clichés, slang, redundancies, and wordiness.
2. Avoid emoticons and text message jargon or acronyms.
3. Break the message into logical paragraphs, sequencing in an appropriate order. ~~White space is important in email messages as well as printed documents, so be sure to add extra space between paragraphs.~~
4. Limit email messages to one idea per message, and preferably limit to one screen.
5. Always include a subject line that clearly defines the email message.
6. Consider carefully the recipients of the email; do not waste your colleagues' valuable time by sending or copying unnecessary emails.
7. Spell-check email messages carefully; verify punctuation and content accuracy.
8. Check the tone of the message carefully. If angry, wait at least one hour before clicking the Send button. Review the message, modify if needed, and then send the message.

DRILL 4

nk-drill4

Decimal

1. Turn NUMLOCK on. Open data file and save in Numeric Keypad folder.
2. Locate the decimal (.) key. It is usually located at the bottom right of the keypad.
3. Use the third finger to reach down to tap the decimal key with a quick, sharp stroke, and return to the home-key position. Keep the other fingers in the home-key position.
4. Key the drills. Remember to tap the TAB key after each number and the ENTER key after keying the number in the f column. Tap ENTER twice after each group of numbers.
5. Save and close. (*nk-drill4*)

TECHNIQUE TIP

Tap each key with a quick, sharp stroke. Release the key quickly. Keep the fingers curved and upright, the wrist low and relaxed.

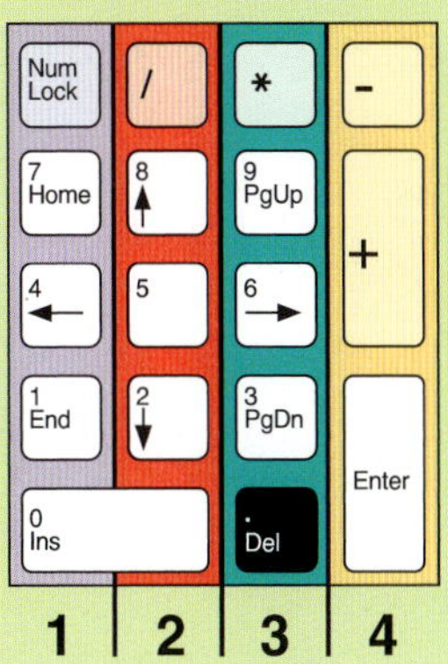

a	b	c	d	e	f
.28	.19	.37	.42	.81	.96
.51	.67	.81	.27	.55	.80
.64	.50	.60	.50	.62	.43
7.10	8.91	5.64	3.12	6.04	5.01
5.32	4.27	9.21	6.47	5.28	3.24
8.94	3.06	7.38	5.89	1.37	6.78
3.62	36.94	86.73	.60	8.21	4.02
8.06	10.31	537.34	5.21	100.89	6.51
321.04	10.55	687.52	164.84	.85	207.65
.75	.26	10.85	627.98	2.57	46.51
687.46	357.95	159.46	85.21	654.32	753.15
20.46	220.48	6.10	3.04	123.54	315.47
761.64	2.82	627.25	196.25	82.99	4.02
285.46	34.60	.29	89.24	512.69	99.80
33.99	739.45	290.23	563.21	701.21	546.78
60.41	52.79	105.87	951.32	357.02	123.94
108.97	211.00	46.24	82.47	61.28	75.61
3.54	5.79	5.41	1.32	8.54	.27
.05	1.19	77.54	112.96	33.68	2.75
112.54	561.34	114.85	.24	647.21	432.89
35.67	22.01	67.90	41.08	71.28	11.00
579.21	105.24	731.98	258.96	741.21	546.21
.34	1.68	.24	.87	.63	.54
21.87	54.89	2.34	5.89	4.68	10.72

Tap ENTER three times (about 2")

Title Style

Title → # Email Communication Policy Update ↓2

To encourage acceptable, consistent, and appropriate use of email, Sudduth and Associates has adopted AUP 13.02—Email Acceptable Use Policy.[1] To reap full benefit of this means of communication, follow the basic guidelines regarding message content and communication preferences. ↓1

Side Heading →

Message Content

Heading 1 Style

1"

Although perceived as informal documents, email messages are business records and archived as a part of the official records of Sudduth and Associates. Follow these effective communication guidelines: ↓1

Bulleted list →

- Write clear, concise sentences, avoiding clichés, slang, redundancies, and wordiness.
- Avoid emoticons and text message jargon or acronyms.
- Break the message into logical paragraphs, sequencing in an appropriate order. White space is important in email messages as well as printed documents, so be sure to add extra space between paragraphs.
- Limit email messages to one idea per message, and preferably limit to one screen.
- Always include a subject line that clearly defines the email message.
- Consider carefully the recipients of the email; do not waste your colleagues' valuable time by sending or copying unnecessary emails.
- Spell-check email messages carefully; verify punctuation and content accuracy.
- Check the tone of the message carefully. If angry, wait at least one hour before clicking the Send button. Review the message, modify if needed, and then send the message. ↓1

Preferences

Although email is a common means of communication, other methods include face-to-face communication, telephone, voice mail, and instant messaging. It is important to realize that each person has preferred methods of communication, and the method will vary depending upon the message content. To accomplish tasks more effectively, be aware of individuals' preferred channels of communication and use those channels if appropriate for the business purpose.

Remember that effective communication is essential to be successful in reaching the goals of Sudduth and Associates. Apply these important email acceptable use guidelines as directed in AUP 13.02.

[1] Adopted 1/15/2009; revised 6/30/2014

Unbound Report

DRILL 5

nk-drill5

Review

1. Turn NUMLOCK on. Open the data file and save in Numeric Keypad folder.
2. Key drills. Remember to tap the TAB key after each number, and tap ENTER after keying the number in the f column. Tap ENTER twice after each group of numbers.
3. Save and close. (*nk-drill5*)

TECHNIQUE TIP

Keep fingers curved and upright over home keys. Keep right thumb tucked under palm.

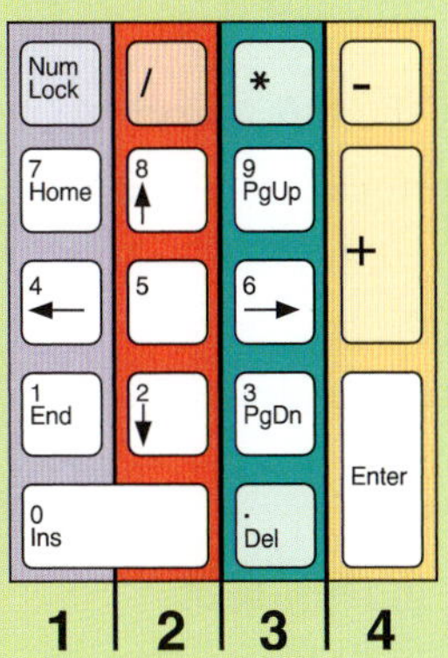

a	b	c	d	e	f
349	854	961	789	631	80
64	97	164	64	972	167
108	326	207	207	803	549
25	40	83	153	54	23
51	467	825	347	901	208
873	54	258	540	467	375
106	208	504	45	95	34
24	13	13	126	238	160
94	648	21	52	178	341
157	72	341	412	57	89
687	645	32	87	461	541
21	58	647	281	38	1,923
2,753	1,002	549	105	20	567
3,054	25	4,008	2,194	3,079	2,089
369	4,770	158	3,066	657	478
1,004	123	2,560	38	2,098	3,257
71.64	2.72	27.59	89.24	4.02	.57
285.36	118.50	438.96	102.46	55.71	6.37
3.79	24.73	4.71	527.90	.64	1.27
42.08	63.87	91.47	159.34	28.47	1.25
31.07	128.46	1.50	.28	374.95	116.00
365.87	.24	163.48	22.84	24.96	514.38
.25	394.28	452.87	349.51	852.43	234.94
147.25	32.54	821.47	164.87	.08	3.54
183.12	20.80	.60	5.07	121.07	.97

UNBOUND REPORT FORMAT

43d

Reports prepared without binders are called unbound reports. Unbound reports may be attached with a staple or paper clip in the upper-left corner. Often reports are attached to an email. Study the illustration below to learn to format a one-page unbound report. A full-page model is shown on page 2-94. In this module you will generally use the default Office theme.

Email Communication Policy Update 

To encourage acceptable, consistent, and appropriate use of email, Sudduth and Associates has adopted AUP 13.02—Email Acceptable Use Policy.[1] To reap full benefit of this means of communication, follow the basic guidelines regarding message content and communication preferences.

Message Content 

Although perceived as informal documents, email messages are business records and archived as a part of the official records of Sudduth and Associates. Follow these effective communication guidelines:

- Write clear, concise sentences, avoiding clichés, slang, redundancies, and wordiness.
- Avoid emoticons and text message jargon or acronyms.
- Break the message into logical paragraphs, sequencing in an appropriate order. White space is important in email messages as well as printed documents, so be sure to add extra space between paragraphs.
- 3 Limit email messages to one idea per message, and preferably limit to one screen.
- Always include a subject line that clearly defines the email message.
- Consider carefully the recipients of the email; do not waste your colleagues' valuable time by sending or copying unnecessary emails.
- Spell-check email messages carefully; verify punctuation and content accuracy.
- Check the tone of the message carefully. If angry, wait at least one hour before clicking the Send button. Review the message, modify if needed, and then send the message.

Preferences

Although email is a common means of communication, other methods include face-to-face communication, telephone, voice mail, and instant messaging. It is important to realize that each person has preferred methods of communication, and the method will vary depending upon the message content. To accomplish tasks more effectively, be aware of individuals' preferred channels of communication and use those channels if appropriate for the business purpose.

Remember that effective communication is essential to be successful in reaching the goals of Sudduth and Associates. Apply these important email acceptable use guidelines as directed in AUP 13.02.

Margins: Use the default 1" top, side, and bottom margins.

Font size: Use the 11-point default font size.

Spacing: Use the default line spacing for all reports.

Title: 1

- Position at about 2". (Tap ENTER three times.)
- Capitalize the first letter of all main words.
- Tap ENTER twice after the title.
- Apply Title style. If the title is long, shrink the font so the title fits on one line.

Side heading: 2

- Key side headings at the left margin.
- Capitalize the first letter of all main words.
- Apply Heading 1 style.
- Tap ENTER once after heading.

Enumerated or bulleted items: 3

- Use the default 0.25" indention of bulleted and numbered items.
- Tap ENTER once after each item.

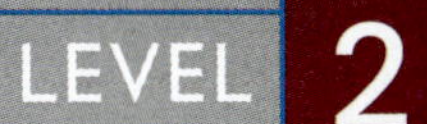

Formatting and Word Processing Essentials

Learning Outcomes

Keyboarding

- Key fluently using good keying techniques.
- Key about 40 words a minute with good accuracy.

Document Design Skills

- Format memos, letters, tables, and reports appropriately.
- Apply basic design skills to announcements, invitations, and newsletters.
- Enhance documents with basic graphics.

Word Processing Skills

- Learn essential word processing commands.
- Apply word processing commands to create, edit, and format documents effectively.

Communication Skills

- Review and improve basic communication skills.
- Compose simple documents.
- Use proofing tools effectively.
- Proofread and edit text effectively.

FOOTNOTES

References cited in a report are often indicated within the text by a superscript number (. . . story.[1]) and a corresponding footnote with full information at the bottom of the same page where the reference is cited. Additionally, content footnotes supplement the information included in the body of the report.

Word automatically numbers footnotes sequentially with Arabic numerals (1, 2, 3), positions them at the left margin, and applies 10-point type.

A footnote is positioned with the same margin widths as the body of the report. Do not indent the footnotes.

To insert and edit footnotes:

References/Footnotes/Insert Footnote

1. From Print Layout view, position the insertion point in the document where the footnote reference is to be inserted.
2. Click the Insert Footnote button. The reference number and the insertion point appear at the bottom of the page. Key the footnote ❶.

   A footnote divider line ❷ is automatically added above the first footnote on each page. Tap ENTER once to add one blank line between footnotes.
3. Click anywhere above the footnote divider line to return to the document.
4. To edit a footnote, click in the footnote at the bottom of the page and make the revision.
5. To delete a footnote, select the reference number in the text and tap DELETE.

❶ [1] All computers are installed with the *Windows 10* operating system and *Office 2016*.

[2] Instructors must pick up the gift certificate from Mary Katherine Morgan, Office 208.

DRILL 3 FOOTNOTES

1. Open *checklist* from the data files.
2. Insert the following content footnotes to the administration checklist. Add a blank line between footnotes.

   18 computers[1]

   [1] All computers are installed with the *Windows 10* operating system and *Office 2016*.

   Door prize—Joey's Steak House Gift Certificate[2]

   [2] Instructors must pick up the gift certificate from Mary Katherine Morgan, Office 208.
3. Save and close. (*43-drill3*)

DRILL 4 DELETE FOOTNOTES

1. Open the file (*43-drill3*) that you created in the previous drill and delete the second footnote.
2. Save and close. (*43-drill4*)

MODULE 3

Word 2016 Essentials

LEARNING OUTCOMES

- Learn and apply essential *Word 2016* commands.
- Create, save, and print documents.
- Apply text, paragraph, and page formats.
- Navigate, review, and edit documents.
- Build keyboarding skills.

Lesson 26 Getting Started with Word

New Commands

- Launch *Word*
- Blank Document
- New Folder
- Save As
- Close
- Open
- New
- Print
- Exit

New Commands

26a Getting Started with Word

LEARNING THE BASICS

In Module 3, you will to learn how to use the basic commands in *Word 2016* software. In this lesson, you will create, format, and print *Word* documents. Learning these basic skills will enhance your use of *Word* in your other classes, in a part-time job, or in your personal business activities. You will also learn to manage your own files effectively.

LAUNCH WORD

Word can be launched in several different ways. The first time you launch *Word*, you will probably have to click the Word icon on the Start screen or the Start button on the taskbar at the bottom on your desktop screen. If you are new to *Windows 10*, review the information in Appendix A.

If your computer is using other versions of *Windows*, your screen may look slightly different. Your instructor will provide information on how to launch *Word* with the version of *Windows* that is on your computer.

Remember to proofread and preview each document SOP. You will not be reminded to do this.

STYLES

The Styles feature enables you to apply a group of formats automatically to text, which saves time and ensures a consistent and professional format. When a new document is opened, the Office theme and the Normal style are the default settings. Text keyed using these defaults is 11-point Calibri, left-aligned, 1.08 spacing, 8-point spacing after a paragraph, and no indent. Other styles available include Heading 1, Heading 2, Heading 3, Heading 4, and Title. Each style has its own specific formatting associated with it.

Styles include both character and paragraph styles. The attributes listed in the Font group on the Home tab and in the Font dialog box make up the character styles.

Character styles apply to a single character or characters that are selected. You have already learned how to apply character styles using the Font group.

Paragraph styles include both the character style and other formats that affect paragraph appearance such as line spacing, bullets, numbering, and tab stops.

Apply the document theme and desired formatting before applying styles.

To apply paragraph styles:

Home/Styles

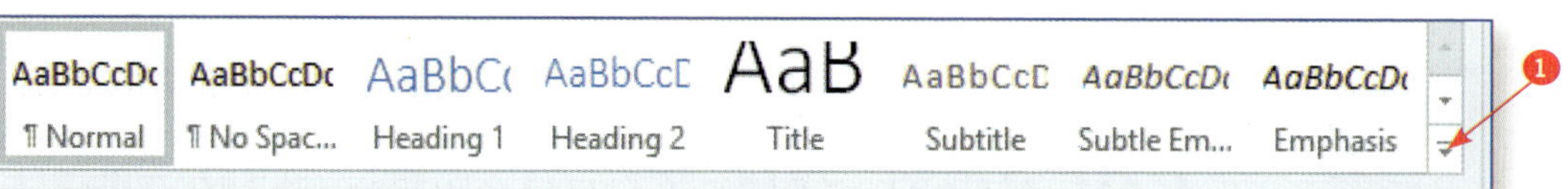

1. Select the text to which you wish to apply a style.
2. Choose a desired style from the Quick Styles gallery.
3. If the desired style does not display, click the More button ❶ to expand the Quick Styles gallery.
4. Select the desired style from the expanded list of styles.

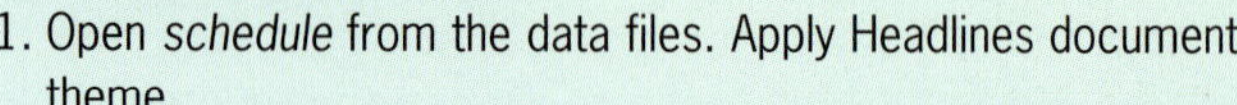

DRILL 2 STYLES

schedule

1. Open *schedule* from the data files. Apply Headlines document theme.
2. Select the title on the first line. Apply Title style. Click the More button to select this style if it is not visible.
3. Select the subtitle on the second line. Apply Subtitle style.
4. Select *Monday;* apply Heading 1 style. **Hint:** Click the scroll buttons to the right of the Styles button to move in the Styles list.
5. Select *Monday* and use Format Painter to copy the Heading 1 style to the remaining days of the week and the heading *Extracurricular Activities.*
6. Save and close. (*43-drill2*)

Taskbar

The taskbar is located at the bottom of your screen. It contains the Start button, the Search box, and several applications on the left side. The right side of the taskbar contains the date, time, and system information and is called the Notification panel.

To launch Word from taskbar:

1. Check the taskbar to locate the Word icon.
2. Click the icon to launch *Word*.

If the *Word* icon is not on the taskbar, then check the Start screen.

Start Screen

The Start screen consists of a number of tiles that enable you to access applications from your computer and from the Internet. If you are connected to the Internet, the tiles are dynamic—that is, the information may change. The *Word* icon and icons of other Office apps may have been added to the Start screen during the installation.

To launch Word from the Start Screen:

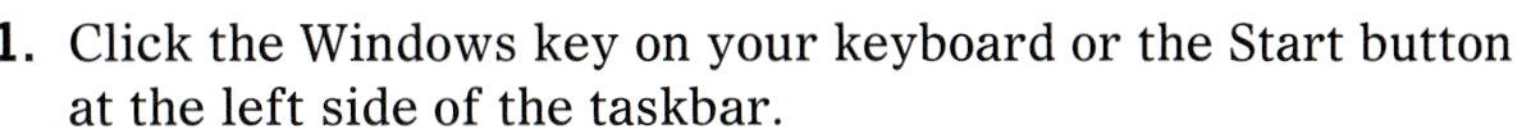

1. Click the Windows key on your keyboard or the Start button at the left side of the taskbar.

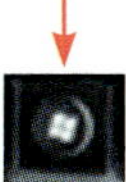

2. Check to see if applications are listed on your Start screen. If so, click the *Word* icon to launch it.

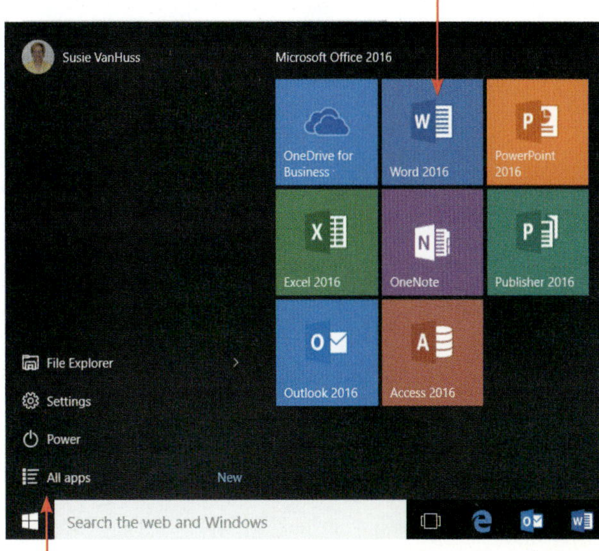

3. If the icon is not on the Start screen, you may have to scroll down to find the applications or click the All apps icon on the left side of the Start screen.
4. Click *Word*.

Discover

Once *Word* is open, the *Word* icon displays on the taskbar. Pin it to the taskbar so that it will remain on the taskbar when *Word* is closed.

To pin Word to the taskbar:

1. Right-click the icon.
2. Click Pin to taskbar.

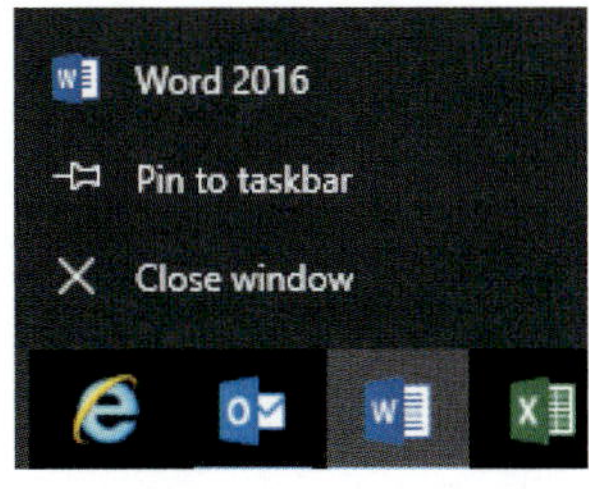

New Commands

43c

DOCUMENT THEMES

Built-in document themes incorporate colors, fonts, and effects that can be applied to a *Word* document or to documents in other *Microsoft Office* applications. The default theme is Office Theme.

To apply a document theme:

Design/Document Formatting/Themes

1. Click the down arrow to display the gallery of Built-in themes. The default theme is Office.
2. Click the document theme you wish to use.

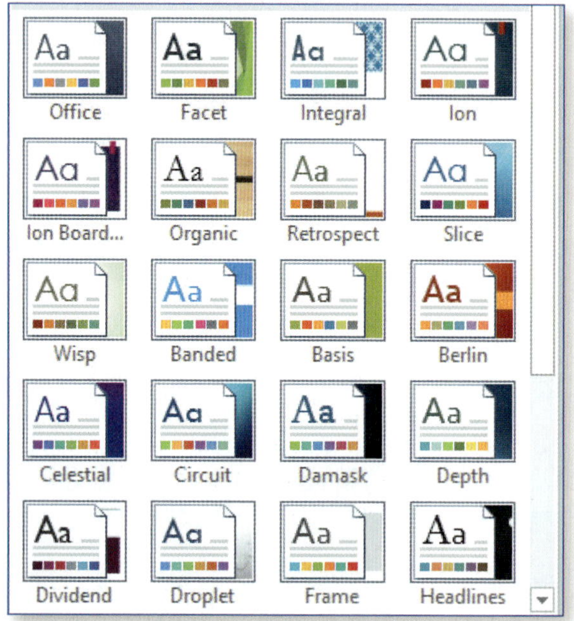

DRILL 1 THEMES

document themes

1. Open *document themes* from the data files.
2. Apply Depth document theme.
3. Save and close. (*43-drill1*)

OPENING WORD SCREEN

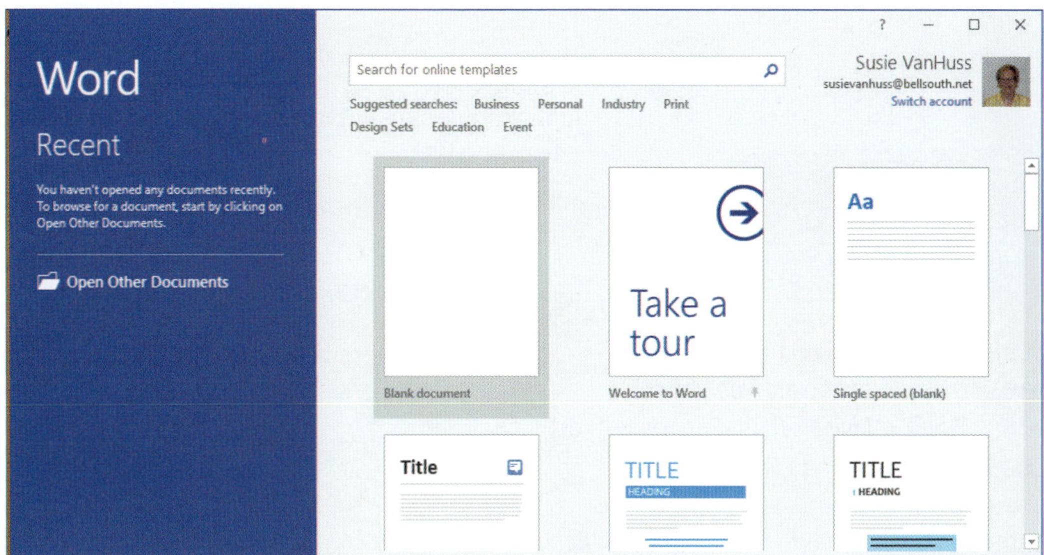

Note the following parts of the screen:

Left pane—contains a list of recently created documents and an option to open other documents that you may have created. If this is the first time you have opened *Word*, no documents may be listed.

Main pane—provides the option to create a new blank document or create a document using one of the templates. At the top right side of this pane, your name will appear with either a picture or blank icon. If your Microsoft account has a picture, it will automatically appear at the top of your documents. Click the Blank document icon to begin working in *Word*.

Status bar—appears at the bottom of the screen. On the left side, the Start button, the Search box, and the Start icons for any open applications display. On the right side, the Notification panel provides the time, the date, and information about your system.

BLANK DOCUMENT

The opening screen displays when you launch *Word*. To display the document screen, click the Blank document icon in the main pane. This screen is also referred to as the New document screen because you use it to create new documents.

MODULE 6

Reports

Lesson 43 *Unbound Reports*
Lesson 44 *Leftbound Reports*
Lesson 45 *Multiple-Page Reports*
Lesson 46 *Reports in MLA Style*
Lesson 47 *Reports in APA Style*
Lesson 48 *Palmetto Event Solutions, Inc.*
Lesson 49 *Assessment Modules 5 and 6*

LEARNING OUTCOMES

- Format two-page reports with document themes and styles.
- Insert footnotes.
- Insert file.
- Format academic reports in MLA and APA style.
- Find and replace text and formatting in a document.
- Build keyboarding skills.

Lesson 43 Unbound Reports

New Commands

- Themes
- Styles
- Footnotes

Warmup *Lesson 43a Warmup*

lesson 43a warmup

Skill Building

43b Timed Writing

1. Key a 1' timing on each paragraph; work to increase speed.
2. Key a 3' timing on all paragraphs.

	gwam 1'	3'	
The most vital element of a business is its clientele. It is for	13	4	60
this reason that most organizations adopt the slogan that the	25	8	64
customer is always right. The saying should not be taken literally,	38	13	68
but in spirit.	41	14	69
Patrons will continuously use your business if you provide an	12	18	73
exceptional product and service. The product you sell must be high	25	22	78
quality and last a long time. The product must perform just as you	39	27	82
claim. The environment and surroundings must be safe and clean.	51	31	86
Customers expect you to be well groomed and neatly dressed.	12	35	90
They expect you to know your products and services and to be	24	39	94
dependable. When you tell a customer you will do something, you	36	43	99
must perform. Patrons expect you to help them willingly and	48	47	103
quickly. Add a personal touch by greeting clientele by name, but	61	51	107
be cautious about conducting business on a first-name basis.	73	55	111

1' | 1 | 2 | 3 | 4 | 5 | 6 | 7 | 8 | 9 | 10 | 11 | 12 | 13 |
3' | 1 | 2 | 3 | 4 |

BLANK DOCUMENT SCREEN

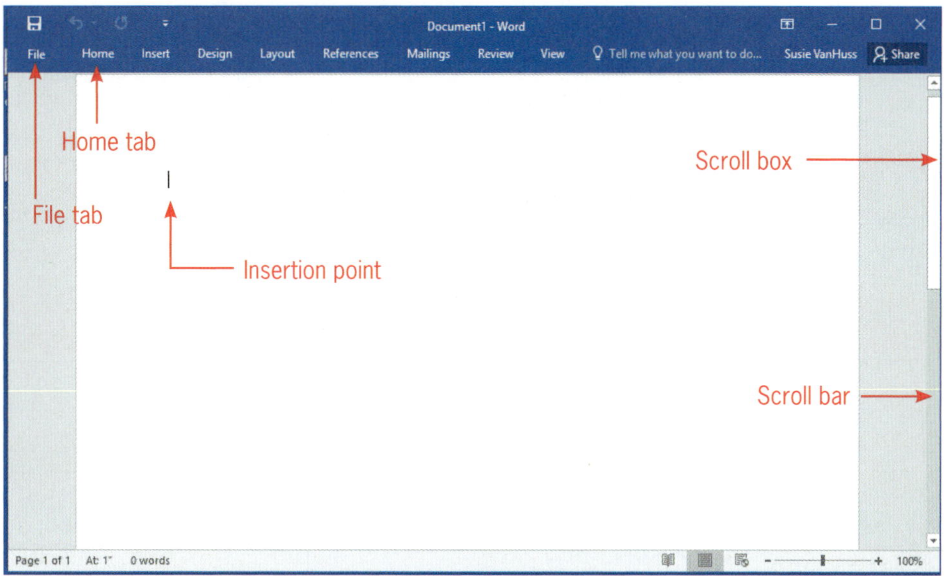

1. The document title, *Document1*, displays at the top center. When you save the document, you will give it a new name.
2. The Ribbon Display options and the Minimize, Maximize, and Close buttons appear in the top upper-right corner of the screen. If your *Word* screen does not open large enough to fill the computer screen, enlarge it by clicking the Maximize button.

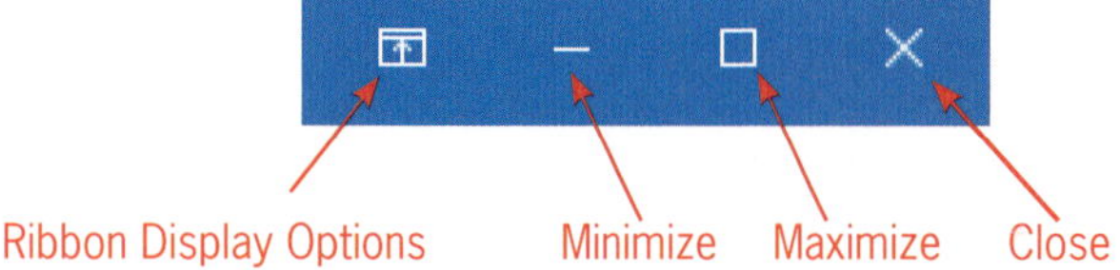

3. A row of tabs displays beginning in the upper-left corner beginning with the File tab and then the Home tab. These tabs are part of the Ribbon.
4. The center portion is the document screen on which you will key your documents. It resembles a blank sheet of paper. The insertion point indicates the position at which you will begin to key.
5. The Status bar appears at the bottom of the page. The page number and the word count are listed on the left side. The right side provides different ways to view the document on the screen.

6. The scroll bar on the right side of the screen provides options for moving through a document.

42-d3

Table with Table Style

1. Key the table below. Arrange the speakers in alphabetical order according to the speaker's last name.
2. Apply Grid Table 5 Dark—Accent 4 table style. Adjust column widths to display the address information correctly on three lines without wrapping.
3. Change the height of row 1 to 0.5". Change the font to 16-point and Align Center the text in row 1.
4. Change the height of row 2 to 0.3". Bold the column headings in columns B and C. Align Center all the columns headings in row 2.
5. Apply Align Center Left alignment to the names in cells A3–A6.
6. Apply Align Center Left alignment to the topics in cells B3–B6.
7. Save and close. (*42-d3*)

WEALTH PROTECTION STRATEGIES SPEAKERS		
Speaker	Topic	Address
James M. Kohn	Estate Protection The Probate Process	Kohn and Crane, Attorneys at Law 325 Munras Avenue Carmel, CA 93923
Lindsey Cunningham, CPA	Estate Taxes Trust Accounts	Certified Public Accounting Services 100 North Main, Suite 300 Memphis, TN 38103
William L. Nelson	Wealth Preservation	Gottrocks Financial Planners 6590 Madison Avenue New York, NY 10022
Maria C. Hernandez	Risk Management	Ortega Risk Management Consultants 100 Redwood Avenue, Suite 200 Palo Alto, CA 94304

42-d4

Compose Letter

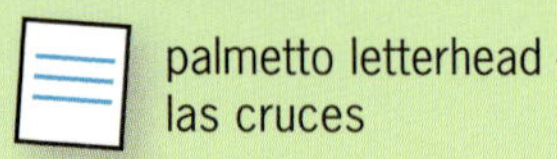

palmetto letterhead – las cruces

1. Compose a letter to William Nelson telling him that Carlos Torres would like to meet with him to discuss his speech at the opening session. Mr. Torres will be picking him up at the airport and taking him to the hotel. Request the date, time, airline, and flight number of his arriving flight to Orange County airport so that Carlos can schedule the meeting.
2. Save and close. (*42-d4*)

MANAGING FILES IN WORD

File management refers to saving documents in an organized manner so that they can be easily located and used again. Name files logically so that you will be able to find them easily, such as *business plan*. Use the file name in parentheses at the end of each drill (*26-drill1*) or document in the Apply It section (*28-d1*).

FILE TAB

File/command

TIP

OneDrive may appear slightly different than the illustration depending on whether you have a personal or business account.

The File tab located in the upper-left corner of the document screen provides you with all of the commands that you need to work with files. When you click the File tab, the options for things you can do to a document display, such as open, close, save, or print.

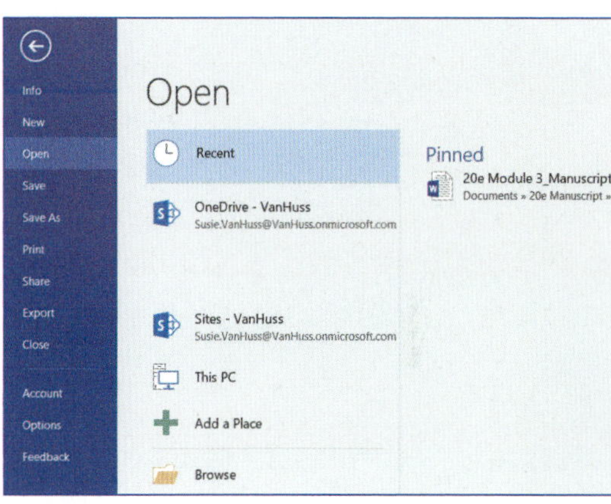

- Commands are on the left pane. The left arrow in the circle at the top takes you back to your open document.
- Places for storing documents are shown in the middle pane.
- Recent documents are shown in the right pane. Documents that are pinned remain at the top of the list.
- Click the File tab any time you want to use a command to work with files.

The default in *Word 2016* with *Windows 10* is to save documents to your OneDrive. Therefore, you have to select the appropriate place on your computer or your flash drive when you save folders or documents.

SAVE AND CREATE NEW FOLDER

The Save and Save As commands on the File menu preserve documents for future use.

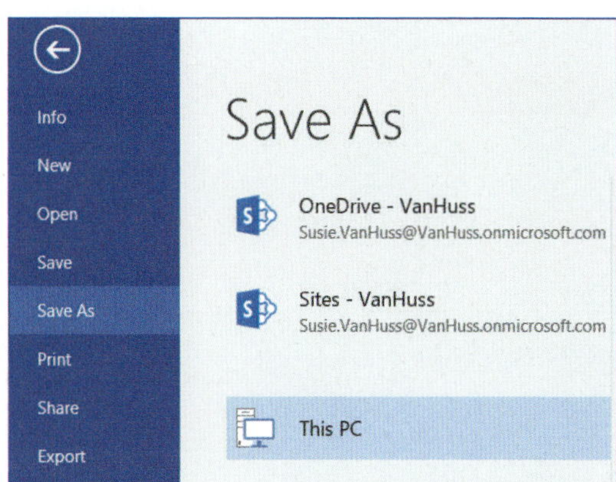

- Save is used to save a document with the same name.
- Save As is used to save a document with a name for the first time, with a different name, or to a different place.
- New folders can be created from the Save As dialog box.

42-d2

Memo with table

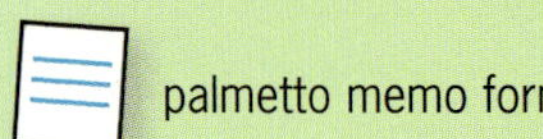

palmetto memo form

1. Key the memo to **Wealth Protection Strategies Seminar Attendees**, from *Carlos Torres, Regional Manager*. The subject is **Appointment with Seminar Speaker**.
2. Create the table. Change the width of column A to 0.3". Change the width of column B to 3.5" and the width of column C to 2".
3. Apply Grid Table 4—Accent 5 table style. Center the table horizontally.
4. Change the row height to 0.4" for the entire table.
5. Change the font size in row 1 to 12 points. Align Center the text in row 1.
6. Save and close. (*42-d2*)

Your seminar speakers are renowned practitioners in their respective career fields. One of the benefits your participation in the seminar provides you is the opportunity to meet on a one-on-one basis with these noted speakers.

Please indicate the speaker(s) with whom you would like to meet. If you would like to meet with more than one speaker, indicate your first, second, and third choices. We will attempt to honor all requests. Individual sessions will be scheduled for 20 minutes each.

X	**Name**	**Indicate 1st, 2nd, or 3rd Choice**

Complete the form above and return to me no later than September 1, 2018. A list of the speakers, their contact information, and the topics they will be addressing is attached.

A path similar to the one shown under the heading at the right will be shown each time you use a command on the File tab.

Double-click—click the left mouse button twice quickly.

Discover

To save a document to a flash drive, use the same steps shown in this activity except for step 2.

In step 2, scroll down and click the name of your flash drive (or Removable Disk if the specific name is not listed). Note the Kingston flash drive listed below.

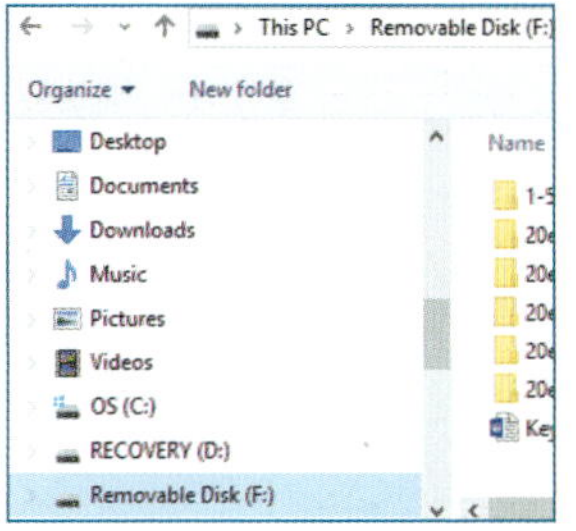

To save a document in a new folder:

File/Save or Save As

1. Click File and then Save As. A shortcut known as a path (File/Save or Save As) lists the File tab and the command to select for this activity.
2. Double-click the place in which to store the document, such as Computer, to display the Save As dialog box.
3. Click the New folder button to create a new folder in which to store the document. The new folder name box displays in blue.
4. Click in the New folder name box and key the name, such as *Module 3*.
5. Click Open or double-click the new folder (*Module 3*) to open it.

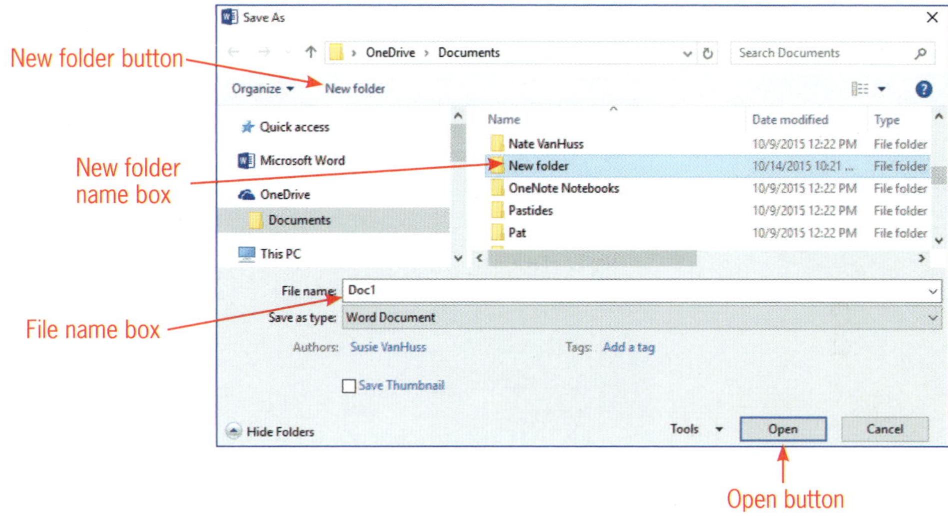

6. In the File name box, select *Doc1* and key the name of the file, such as *26-drill1*.
7. Click Save.

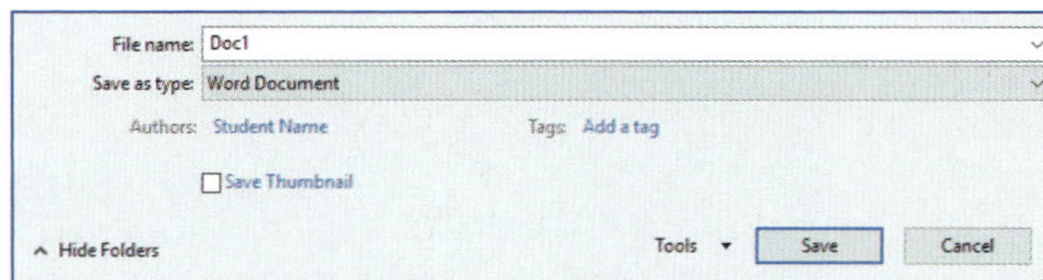

Note: You will always be given the drill and application name in parentheses at the end of the last line instructing you to save and close the document.

DRILL 1 SAVE DOCUMENT IN NEW FOLDER

1. Launch *Word* and open a blank document.
2. In the new document, key your name; then tap ENTER, and key the text below.
3. Save the document on your flash drive or computer in a new folder named *Module 3*; name it *26-drill1*.
4. Leave the document open.

An effective way to manage files is to create folders to store related documents. Always name folders and files logically. Typically, folder names are formatted using initial caps, and file names using lowercase.

42-d1

Seminar Schedule Table

1. Create a four-column, 12-row table. Key the table below. Merge the cells as needed for Row 1 and Column A.
2. Apply Grid Table 5 Dark—Accent 6 style. Adjust column widths to display the information attractively.
3. Change the height of row 1 to 0.6. Change the title to 16-point font. Align Center the title.
4. Change the height of row 2 to 0.3". Apply bold to the column heads in columns B, C, and D. Align Center the column headings in row 2.
5. Change the text in cells A3–A5 to 12-point font; change the text to Align Center.
6. Align Center Right to the time of the breakout sessions in column B. Align Center Left to the room names in column C.
7. Save and close. (*42-d1*)

WEALTH PROTECTION STRATEGIES			
Day	**Time**	**Room**	**Breakout Session**
Monday **To Tax or Not to Tax the Estate**	9:30 a.m.	Harvard	Protect your estate for the family.
	10:30 a.m.	Princeton	The why, what, and how of a Revocable Living Trust.
	1:30 p.m.	Harvard	Resolve probate and conservatorship problems.
	3:30 p.m.	Yale	Solutions to eliminate 37%–45% estate taxes.
Tuesday **Using Trust Accounts to Minimize Estate Taxes**	9:30 a.m.	Princeton	Dynasty Trusts are used to protect family wealth, real estate, and business interests.
	10:30 a.m.	Duke	Use Irrevocable Life Insurance Trusts to protect life insurance from estate taxes.
	1:30 p.m.	Harvard	Wealth Accumulation Trusts and Income Savings Trusts can be used to minimize federal and state taxes.
	3:30 p.m.	Yale	Qualified Personal Residence Trusts can be used to safely transfer your home.
Wednesday **Wealth Preservation**	9:30 a.m.	Duke	Protect your family, business, and assets from the risks of lawsuits.
	10:30 a.m.	Yale	Use limited partnerships and limited liability companies to held real estate and other investments.

CLOSE DOCUMENT

If you have only one document open and you click the Close button at the upper-right side of the screen, you will close the document and exit *Word*. If you have more than one document open, only the document will close.

Clicking the Close command on the File menu closes the document and keeps *Word* open.

To close a document and leave *Word* open:

File/Close

1. Click the File tab.
2. Click the Close command on the File menu.

OPEN EXISTING DOCUMENT

Existing documents can be opened in two ways. When you launch *Word*, recent documents will display in the left pane of the opening screen.

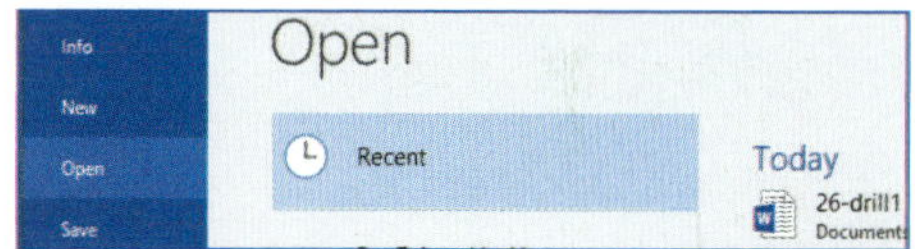

If you are working in *Word*, you can open existing documents not listed as recent documents by using the Open command on the File menu.

To open an existing document:

File/Open

1. Click File, Open, and then Computer in the Places pane.
2. Click the Browse icon and select the folder in which you have stored the document.
3. Double-click the document name or select it and click Open.

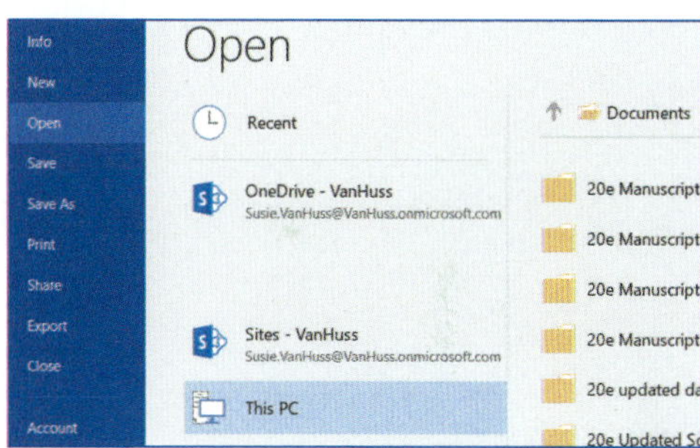

TIP

Note the way the drill name is shown in parentheses at the end of step 3 below.

In future lessons, the following directions will be used to save a document with a specific name, such as *26-drill2*:

Save and close. (*26-drill2*)

DRILL 2 OPEN AND CLOSE

1. Close the open document. (*26-drill1*)
2. Open *26-drill1* and on the line below your name, key **26-drill2**. (Note: Text to be keyed is set off in bold; do not apply bold.)
3. Save as **26-drill2** and close. (*26-drill2*)

Lesson 42 Palmetto Event Solutions Inc.—Wealth Protection Strategies Seminar

Learning Outcomes

- Apply keying, formatting, and word processing skills.
- Work independently with few specific instructions.

Warmup *Lesson 42a Warmup*

lesson 42a warmup

Skill Building

42b Timed Writing

Key two 3' timed writings.

gwam 3'

Whether your company can succeed depends on how well it fits 4
into the economic system. Success rests on certain key factors that 8
are put in line by your management team that has set goals for the 13
company and has enough good judgment to recognize how best to reach 17
these goals. Because of competition, only those companies that are 22
very well organized get to the top. 24

A commercial enterprise is formed for a specific purpose; that 28
purpose is usually to equip others, or consumers, with whatever 32
they cannot equip themselves. Unless there is only one provider, a 37
consumer will search for a company that returns the most value in 41
terms of price, and a relationship with such a company, once set 45
up, can endure for many years. 47

Thus our system ensures that the businesses that manage to survive 52
are those that have been able to combine successfully an excellent 56
product with a low price and the best service—all in a place that 61
is convenient for the buyers. With no intrusion from outside forces, 65
the buyer and the seller benefit both themselves and each other. 69

| 1 | 2 | 3 | 4 |

Project Setting

WEALTH PROTECTION STRATEGIES SEMINAR

The Southwest office of Palmetto Event Solutions accepted a contract to promote, set up, and direct the Wealth Protection Strategies Seminar to be held in Newport Beach, California. Renowned speakers from around the country will be presenting at the seminar. The three-day seminar will be held at the Thirty-nine Palms Hotel and Resort.

You will assist Ellen Miller, the executive assistant to the president and CEO of Palmetto Event Solutions, Inc., with preparing promotional material, creating the agenda, and scheduling appointments for the speakers.

Shortcut: To go directly to a new *Word* document when you launch *Word*, press the ESC key or tap ENTER.

NEW DOCUMENT

You have already opened a new blank document when you launched *Word*. If you are already working in *Word*, you can create a new document by using the New command.

To create a new *Word* document:

File/New

1. On the File menu, click New to display the new document options.
2. Click the Blank document icon to open a new document.

PRINT

Print displays the printing options next to the File menu and provides a preview of the document on the right side of the screen.

TIP

Reminder: Save the document using the name of the drill and the application provided in parentheses after the last direction. If you will not key another document, then exit Word.

To print a document:

File/Print

1. On the File menu, click Print to display the Print options. Note the settings that are available.
2. Preview the document.
3. Select the printing options desired.
4. Click Print.

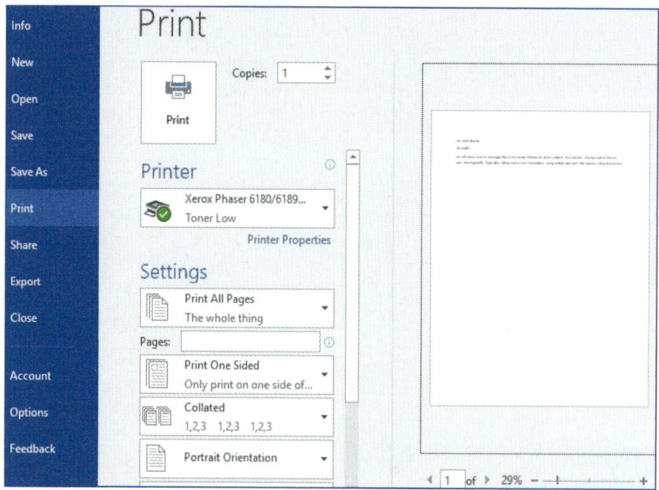

DRILL 3 PRINT AND CREATE A NEW DOCUMENT

1. Open *26-drill2*.
2. Preview and print one copy of the document.
3. Close the document.
4. Open a new document.
5. Key your name on the first line and **26-drill3** on the line below it.
6. Save and close. (*26-drill3*)

Apply It

26-d1

Create, Save, and Print Document

1. In a new document, key your name on the first line, and then key **26-d1** on the next line. (Note: Text to be keyed is set off in bold; do not apply bold.)
2. Save the document as **26-d1** in a new folder named *Applications*.
3. Preview and print the document.
4. Save and close. (*26-d1*)

Check your document against the illustration below.

REGENTS MEMORIAL MEDICAL CENTER February Seminars		
Seminar Title	**Description**	**Registration**
Surgical Weight Loss	Methods of losing weight, including healthy diet, exercise, and medication, will be discussed in detail. Surgical weight loss is an option for those who are motivated and willing to commit to lifestyle changes.	Classes will be held at the Outpatient Surgery Center 75 Pacific Crest Laguna Niguel, CA 92677-5773. Call 949.555.0111 to register.
Life in Motion with Osteoarthritis	Osteoarthritis no longer means that you need to live with a painful disability. Modern medicine, diet, exercise, and surgery can help you enjoy life more fully. Intricate surgical procedures including joint replacement and spinal fusion will be covered.	Register online at www.regents.org/calendar. Materials fee $10.00.
Experts' Cancer Updates	The cancer experts of Regents Medical Center will unveil the results of the latest cancer studies. New breakthrough treatments will be discussed. They will explain what you should know about cancer screenings. Tips on preventing various types of cancers will be provided.	Call 949.555.0100 or register online at www.regents.org/calendar.

41-d4

Composition

1. Key a memo to your instructor. In the first paragraph, request a meeting to discuss the agenda for the next Business Club meeting. Tell your instructor that you are available to meet at any time that you are not scheduled to be in class.
2. Key your class schedule in a table, the table will be the second paragraph.
3. In the third paragraph, ask your instructor to email you with a couple of dates and times that will be convenient to meet. Include your email address.
4. Save and close. (*41-d4*)

Power and Versatility of Tables

Communicating Today ▶

Tables have traditionally been used to present data in documents. Today, the table feature is one of the most widely used tools in *Microsoft Word*. A table can be used to create a page layout, forms, newsletters, brochures, flyers, resumes, certificates, and more. Tables often provide the structure for web pages.

The table feature is one of the most powerful and flexible features available in *Word*. You can use a table to organize a complex page layout. A table can hold text, graphics, or contain a nested table. You can remove the borders so that the table structure is not visible. If you are keying a table that contains numbers, you can perform basic calculations without having to use a calculator. *Word* also allows you to convert regular text to table format and vice versa.

You can always dress up a document by displaying text or data in a table and applying an attractive table style. The colorful table will attract the reader's attention and add some pizzazz to your document.

Lesson 27 Text Formats

New Commands

- Font Group commands
- Mini Toolbar

Warmup *Lesson 27a Warmup*

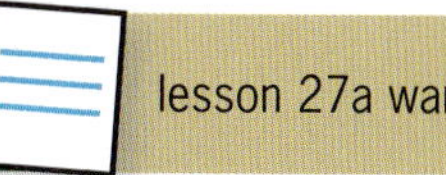

lesson 27a warmup

Skill Building

27b Timed Writing

1. Key a 1' timed writing on each paragraph; work to increase speed. Use wordwrap.
2. Key a 3' timed writing on all paragraphs.

gwam 1' | 3'

Many students and young professionals find it quite 10 | 3
difficult to juggle the things they prefer to do with the things 23 | 8
they ought to do. Too often the most tempting and desirable things 36 | 12
are just distractions from doing the things that should be given 49 | 16
priority. 51 | 17

The key is to set priorities and stick with them. 10 | 20
Individuals who organize their work effectively and do the most 22 | 24
critical things first not only accomplish more, they are the most 35 | 29
likely to have sufficient time to do those things they enjoy doing 49 | 33
as well. 50 | 34

Choosing friends wisely can help you to stay on target. 11 | 37
Individuals who have similar expectations help each other to meet 24 | 42
their goals. They know how important goals are to success, and they 37 | 46
value their time and try to use it appropriately. 47 | 49

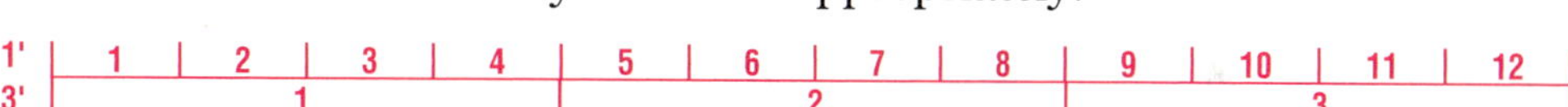

New Commands

27c

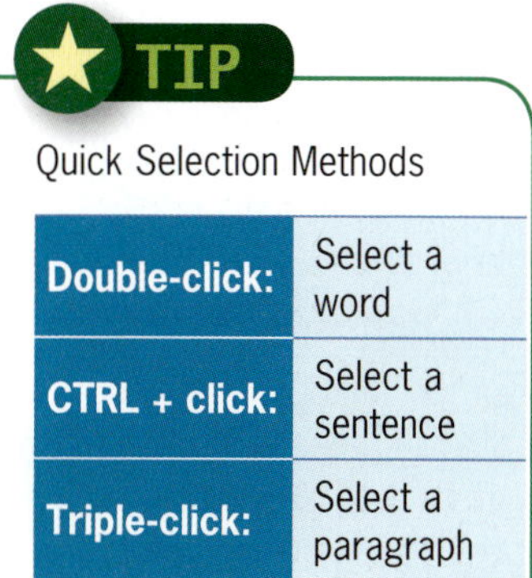

Quick Selection Methods

Double-click:	Select a word
CTRL + click:	Select a sentence
Triple-click:	Select a paragraph

FORMAT TEXT WITH FONT COMMANDS

Text must be selected in order to format it using font commands. To access the text you wish to select, move the insertion point with the mouse or the arrow keys on the keyboard.

To select text:

- Move the I-beam pointer to the beginning of the text you wish to select and click the left mouse button.
- Drag the mouse over the text to highlight it. The selected text is highlighted in blue.

Home

To format text, you will use commands on the Home tab on the ribbon. Note that when you click the Home tab, the Ribbon displays with a number of commands clustered in groups.

41-d2

Memo with Table

REVIEW

Don't forget to insert space before the paragraph that follows the table.

Home/Paragraph/Line and Paragraph Spacing/Add Space Before Paragraph

1. Key the memo below to **Roberto Perez** from **Marcia Lewis**. The subject is **Purchase Order 5122**. Insert the current date.
2. Apply the List Table 6 Colorful—Accent 1 table style. (Hint: List table styles are located toward the bottom of the list.) Center columns A and C. Adjust column width to remove extra space in each column; center the table horizontally.
3. Save and close. (*41–d2*)

The items you requested on Purchase Order 5122 are in stock and will be shipped from our warehouse today. The shipment will be transported via Romulus Delivery System and is expected to arrive at your location in five days.

Item Number	Description	Unit Price
329-8741	Lordusky locking cabinet	$265.00
336-1285	Anchorage heavy duty locking cabinet	$465.00
387-6509	Lordusky locking cabinet (unassembled)	$195.00

Please call us if we can assist you any further.

41-d3

Block Letter with Table

TIP

Remember to remove the spacing before paragraph when keying the complimentary closing.

1. Key the block letter below with open punctuation. The letter is from **Veejah Patel, Collections Manager**. Supply necessary letter parts.
2. Apply the table style Grid Table 1 Light—Accent 2. Change the row height to 0.25; vertically center data in columns. Center and bold column headings. Center the data in column A; right-align the amounts in column D.
3. Adjust column width to fit the data and center table horizontally on the page.
4. Save and close. (*41–d3*)

Ms. Beatrice Snow | Collections Manager | Precision Office Products | 2679 Orchard Lake Road | Farmington Hills, MI 48333-5534

Thank you for allowing International Financial Systems to assist you in managing your delinquent accounts. We provide you with the fastest interface to International Systems Collection Services. The activity report for last month is shown below.

Client Number	Last Name	First Name	Current Balance
1487	Rodriguez	Delia	$1,567.00
1679	Kim	Lisa	$954.35
1822	Batavia	Kirsten	$1,034.21
1905	Vokavich	Kramer	$832.09

Please verify the accuracy of the names transmitted by your billing office. If you find any transmission errors, please contact Joseph Kerning at 888.555.0134 immediately. | Sincerely

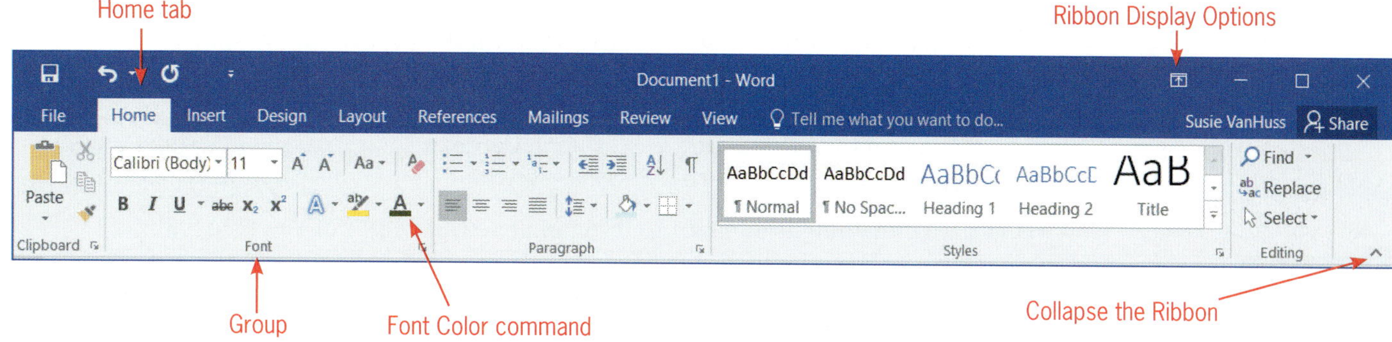

Tabs—located at the top of the ribbon. The Home tab is selected as shown by the blue text color. The other tabs also have commands that display as a ribbon when the tab is selected. If the commands do not display below the tabs on the ribbon, click the Ribbon Display Options button on the upper-right side and select Show Tabs and Commands.

Groups—contain a number of related commands. Logical names are positioned at the bottom of the ribbon below each group of commands. See the Font group.

Commands—the icons, the boxes for entering information, and the drop-down lists that provide a variety of options. The Font Color command identifies changes the color of text—in this case to Red. The small drop-down arrow next to the Font Color command displays the colors available.

Ribbon—remains open with the commands displayed unless you click the Collapse the ribbon icon to display only the tabs. To display commands again, click the Ribbon Display Options button again and select Show Tabs and Commands.

Syda Productions/Shutterstock.com

WORKPLACE SUCCESS

Social Networks

Social networks are websites designed to foster social interaction among a group of people with common interests. *Facebook* and *MySpace* popularized the idea of social networks and initially appealed to teenagers and college students. Today, many other networks and social media tools have been created, and the profiles of those who use them have changed significantly. Millions of adults of all ages are active users of *Facebook*, *LinkedIn*, *Twitter*, *YouTube*, *Flickr*, and a host of other social media tools. Businesses as well as nonprofit organizations actively use social media tools to promote their organizations and enhance their businesses. Although using social media is extremely popular and offers many advantages, care needs to be taken to protect against the abuse of the media that is also rampant.

Apply It

41-d1

Table with Table Style

Grid table styles are displayed in the second group.

Key the text in cell C3 so that the name and address of the Surgery Center is easily readable. Adjust column width so that the ZIP Code fits on the same line as the city and state.

1. Key the table; double-space between paragraphs beginning in row 3.
2. Format the main heading using 14-point font, uppercase, and bold, and the secondary heading in 12-point bold, capitalizing each word. Align Center both lines of the headings in row 1. Key the table, double-spacing between paragraphs as shown below.
3. Change the height of row 1 to 0.75"; change the height of row 2 to 0.3".
4. Apply Grid Table 4—Accent 5 table style. Adjust column widths for column B to 3.0 and column C to 2.25.
5. Use the Quick Check on page 2-84 to compare your table.
6. Save and close. (*41–d1*)

REGENTS MEMORIAL MEDICAL CENTER **February Seminars**		
Seminar Title	**Description**	**Registration**
Surgical Weight Loss	Methods of losing weight, including healthy diet, exercise, and medication, will be discussed in detail. Surgical weight loss is an option for those who are motivated and willing to commit to lifestyle changes.	Classes will be held at the Outpatient Surgery Center 75 Pacific Crest Laguna Niguel, CA 92677-5773. Call 949.555.0111 to register.
Life in Motion with Osteoarthritis	Osteoarthritis no longer means that you need to live with a painful disability. Modern medicine, diet, exercise, and surgery can help you enjoy life more fully. Intricate surgical procedures including joint replacement and spinal fusion will be covered.	Register online at www.regents.org/calendar. Materials fee $10.00.
Experts' Cancer Updates	The cancer experts of Regents Medical Center will unveil the results of the latest cancer studies. New breakthrough treatments will be discussed. They will explain what you should know about cancer screenings. Tips on preventing various types of cancers will be provided.	Call 949.555.0100 or register online at www.regents.org/calendar.

FONT COMMANDS

Home tab/Font group/Font commands

Note that the path shown above (Home tab/Font group/Font commands) guides you in the location of commands. To follow the path, click on the tab (Home); then look for the group label (Font) at the bottom of the ribbon, and finally select the desired command (such as Font Size or Bold). The path will be provided for most commands throughout this textbook to assist you in locating commands quickly and easily. In this lesson, you will apply the format commands from the Font group to text that you have selected.

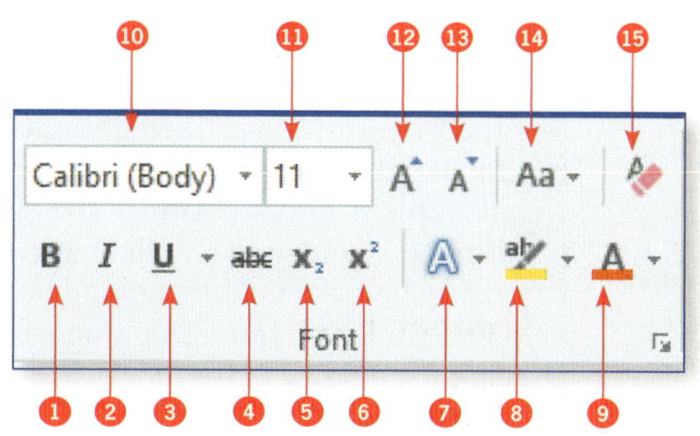

1 Bold 2 Italic 3 Underline 4 Strikethrough 5 Subscript 6 Superscript

7 Text Effects and Typography 8 Text Highlight Color 9 Font Color

10 Font 11 Font Size 12 Increase Font Size 13 Decrease Font Size

14 Change Case 15 Clear Formatting

Position the mouse pointer over each of the 15 commands in the Font group to identify the commands and note the short description of each. Also note that some of the commands have drop-down arrows on the side of the command. Click each to see the options that can be selected.

The primary purpose of illustrating all of the font commands at one time is to stress the concept that all font commands can be applied simply by selecting the desired text and clicking the desired command. You will apply some of the most frequently used font formats in Drill 1. They will be reinforced many times in this textbook. Remember that the Home tab and the Font group are the primary places for formatting text.

DRILL 1 FORMAT TEXT WITH FONT COMMANDS

1. In a new document, key the names of the following numbered commands in sequential order: 1, 2, 3, 8, 9, 10, 11, 12, and 13. Tap ENTER after each command. Do not key the numbers.
2. Select each of the first three commands you keyed and apply the format to the name of the command.
3. Select *Text Highlight Color* and apply yellow highlight.
4. Select *Font Color* and change the color to Blue from the Standard Colors palette.
5. Select *Font* and change to Cambria; select *Font Size* and change to 14 point.
6. Select *Increase Font Size* and click the Increase Font Size command twice.
7. Select *Decrease Font Size* and click the Decrease Font Size command once.
8. Save and close. (*27-drill1*)

Application Review

POSITION A TABLE IN A DOCUMENT

In previous lessons, you worked with stand-alone tables, or tables that are introduced by a simple heading and/or subheading. In the business world, however, tables are frequently inserted within documents. A table showing sales by quarter may be inserted in a memo on annual sales, for example, or a table showing items ordered may be included with a purchase confirmation.

When inserting a table into a document, care must be taken to provide the same amount of space below the table as above the table. *Word*'s default Normal style inserts an 8-point space after a paragraph and uses 1.08 line spacing. However, *Word* defaults to single spacing in a table with no spacing after a paragraph. Therefore, when a table is keyed within a document, extra spacing needs to be inserted below the table. The extra space can easily be inserted by clicking on the paragraph below the table, clicking the Line and Paragraph Spacing drop-down arrow, and choosing Add Space Before Paragraph.

1.0
1.15
1.5
2.0
2.5
3.0
Line Spacing Options...
Add Space Before Paragraph
Remove Space After Paragraph

Tables in documents may be formatted with the same design and layout options as stand-alone tables. A table that is less than the full-page width should be centered horizontally.

Default paragraph formats with 1.08 line spacing and 8 points after ¶

The items you requested on Purchase Order 7051 are in stock and will be shipped from our warehouse today.

Item Number	**Description**	**Unit Price**
531-8741	Base cabinet	$365.00
596-1285	Hutch	$765.00
542-6509	Shelf unit	$275.00

Click in this paragraph and select Add Space Before Paragraph

Please call us if we can assist you any further.

DRILL 2 POSITION A TABLE IN A DOCUMENT

1. Key the text as shown in the illustration above.
2. Turn on Show/Hide.
3. Click the Line and Paragraph Spacing drop-down arrow and choose Add Space Before Paragraph. Add 12 points of spacing before.
4. Change column width as follows: A to 1.25; B to 1.5, and C to 1.0. Center the table horizontally on the page.
5. Center and bold column headings. Center the data in column 1 and right-align column 3.
6. Save and close. (*41-drill2*)

MINI TOOLBAR

The Mini toolbar simplifies editing text by positioning frequently used commands at the point they are needed. It appears when you select text.

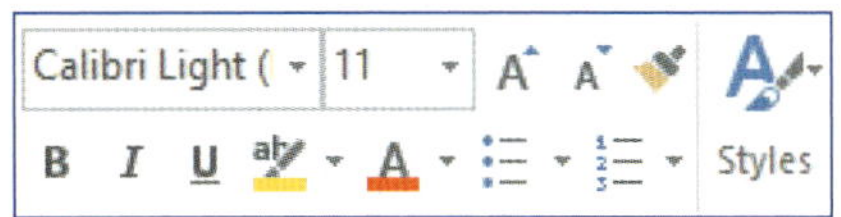

To use the Mini toolbar:

1. Select text to which you want to apply a commonly used format.
2. Move the mouse pointer toward the Mini toolbar when it appears in a faded view.
3. Click the command (s) that you want to apply when the Mini toolbar darkens.

DRILL 2 EDIT USING MINI TOOLBAR

1. In a new document, key **Keyboarding Class** at the top of the page and tap ENTER; then key the document name **27-drill2** at the top of the document; do not apply bold to any text.
2. Key the sentences shown below; do not format them; Then use the Mini toolbar to edit all sentences following the remaining directions in this drill.
3. Select the document name; use the Mini toolbar to change the font to Calibri Light and the font size to 14 point.
4. Select *Keyboarding Class* and click Increase Font Size twice; then apply Blue font color.
5. Select *new document* in the sentence and highlight both words in Bright Green color.
6. Select *single underline* in the second sentence; apply Underline to both words. Then select the entire sentence and click Decrease Font Size once.
7. Select *Standard Operating Procedures* and apply Italic and Bold format.
8. Proofread and ensure that you followed directions carefully.
9. Save and close. (*27-drill2*)

This is a new document I have created.

Use a single underline below numbers in a column.

Read and follow the Standard Operating Procedures below.

STANDARD OPERATING PROCEDURES

Be sure to follow these directions for every drill and document. You will not be reminded to take these steps at the end of each activity.

1. Key and format documents as directed in the textbook.
2. Save the document using the file name shown in parentheses at the end of the drill or Apply It document.
3. Proofread for keying or formatting errors.
4. Check your document against the directions in the textbook.

Table styles are located in the Table Styles group on the Design tab. As you move the mouse over each style, you will also see your table formatted in that style. A ToolTip also displays with the name of the style. Click the More button to display the entire list of styles.

The styles are arranged in three groups: Plain Tables display at the top, Grid Tables follow, and List Table styles display at the bottom.

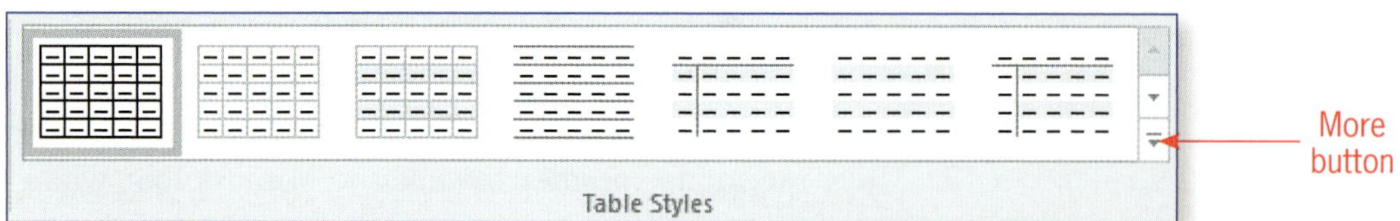

Table styles can be modified by selecting and deselecting options in the Table Style Options group of the Table Tools Design tab. For example, if you choose a table style that places extra emphasis on the header row and you do not want the first row emphasized, you can deselect Header Row to remove the formatting.

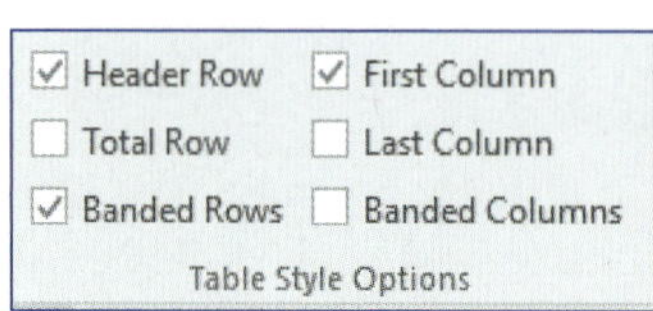

To apply table styles:

Table Tools Design/Table Styles

1. Click in the table to display the Table Tools tabs.
2. Click the More button to display the Table Styles gallery.
3. Move the mouse pointer over each table style until you find the desired one. Use the scroll bar, if needed, to view all available styles.
4. Click a style to apply it to the table.
5. Adjust Table Style options, if necessary.
6. Recenter the table horizontally after applying a style.

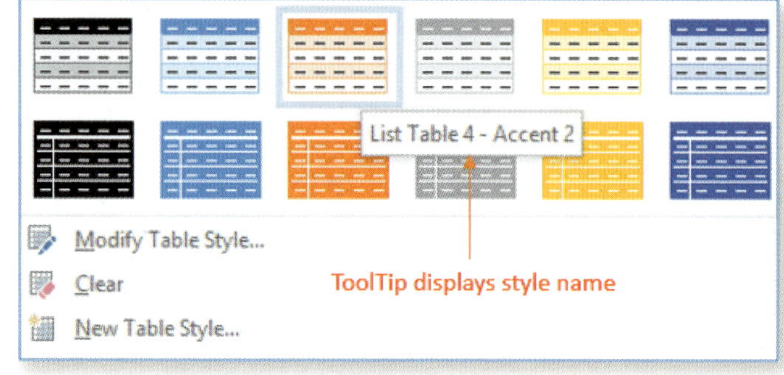

DRILL 1 TABLE STYLES AND STYLE OPTIONS

styles

1. Open the *styles* document from the data files. Click in the table and display the Table Styles gallery.
2. Apply Grid Table 2—Accent 1 style.
3. Insert a row at the end of the table. Key **Total** in cell A8. Key **$581,700** in cell C8.
4. Click the Total Row checkbox in the Table Styles Options group so that additional formatting will be applied to the total row.
5. Remove the check mark from the First Column checkbox to change the look of the first column.
6. Center the table horizontally on the page.
7. Save and close. (*41–drill1*)

Apply It

27-d1

Create a New Document

1. In a new document, key **Keyboarding Class** on the first line; tap ENTER and key **27-d1** on the next line. Do not format using bold.
2. Key the following sentences. Do not key the letters used to identify the sentences. Tap ENTER after each sentence. Use the Mini toolbar to make the edits listed below the sentences. Remember to select the text that you want to edit and then apply the edits specified below the sentences.

   a. The default for Heading 1 is Calibri Light 16-point font.

   b. I use red font color, yellow highlighting, or bold for emphasis.

   c. This sentence illustrates bold text, italic text, and underline format.

   d. We plan to use a script font for our invitation.

   e. Use text formats to emphasize text in documents, but do not overuse them.

   f. The default Theme is Office, and the font color is Blue, Accent 1, Darker 25%.

3. In sentence a, apply Calibri Light 16-point font size to *Heading 1*.
4. In sentence b, apply Red font color to the word *red*, Yellow highlight to the word *yellow*, and bold to the word *bold*.
5. In sentence c, apply bold format to the word *bold*, italic format to the word *italic*, and underline format to the word *underline*.
6. In sentence d, select the sentence and apply Lucida Calligraphy font. Increase the font size to 14 point.
7. In sentence e, select the entire sentence and apply Dark Red highlight and then apply White font color.
8. In sentence f, select *Theme* and apply bold; select *Office* and apply italic format; and then select Blue, Accent 1, Darker 25% from the Theme color palette that displays.
9. Save and close. (*27-d1*)

TIP

Look at the Blue, Accent 1 column (column 5)—the Darker 25% color is the second to the last color in the column. Position the mouse over the color to display its name.

Lesson 41 Table Tools—Design and Tables Within Documents

New Commands

- Table Styles
- Memos with Tables
- Letters with Tables

Warmup *Lesson 41a Warmup*

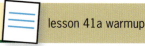

lesson 41a warmup

Skill Building

41b Timed Writing

Key two 3' timed writings.

gwam 3'

I have an interesting story or two that will transport you to 4
faraway places, to meet people you have never known, to see things 8
you have only fantasized, to experience things that you thought 13
would only be a figment of everyone's imagination. 16
I can help you master appropriate skills you desire and need. I 20
can inspire, excite, instruct, challenge, and entertain you. I 24
answer your questions. I work with you to realize a talent, to 28
express a thought, and to determine who you really are and desire 33
to become. 33
I am your online library. My digital format provides easy and 38
fast access from most places in the world as long as you have a 42
computer and an Internet connection. You can use the library any 46
hour of the day or evening; I do not close. You will never have 50
a problem with a book being checked out, as books in an online 54
library are available to many users simultaneously. You can quickly 59
search for information in my vast collection using my information 63
retrieval software. Use any search term, such as a word, phrase, 67
title, name, or subject, to quickly find needed information. 71

| 1 | 2 | 3 | 4 |

New Commands

41c

DESIGN TAB

After a table is created, it needs to be formatted to make it more attractive and enhance its readability. Table design features can be accessed by clicking in the table and then clicking the Design tab. The Design tab is divided into three groups: Table Style Options, Table Styles, and Borders.

TABLE STYLES

Microsoft Word has preformatted table styles that you can use to make your tables more attractive. The styles contain a combination of font attributes, colors, shading, and borders to enhance the appearance of a table.

Lesson 28 Paragraph Formats

New Commands

- Alignment
- Show/Hide
- Line Spacing
- Quick Access Toolbar

Warmup *Lesson 28a Warmup*

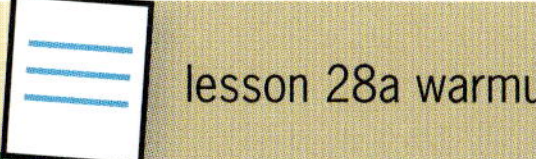

Skill Building

28b Technique Improvement

1. Key each line once, concentrating on using good keying techniques.
2. Repeat the drill if time permits.

one-hand

1 A few treats were served as reserve seats were set up on a stage.
2 In my opinion, a few trees on a hilly acre created a vast estate.

balanced hand

3 Pam and Jake did go to visit the big island and may fish for cod.
4 Ken and six men may go to visit an island with an ancient chapel.

1st/2nd fingers

5 Kimberly tried to grab the bar, but she missed and hurt her hand.
6 My name is Frankie, but I prefer to be called Fran by my friends.

3rd/4th fingers

7 Zola and Polly saw us play polo at Maxwell Plaza; we won a prize.
8 Zack quickly swam past all six boys at a zoo pool on Saxony Land.

New Commands

28c

PARAGRAPH FORMATS

Home/Paragraph/Command

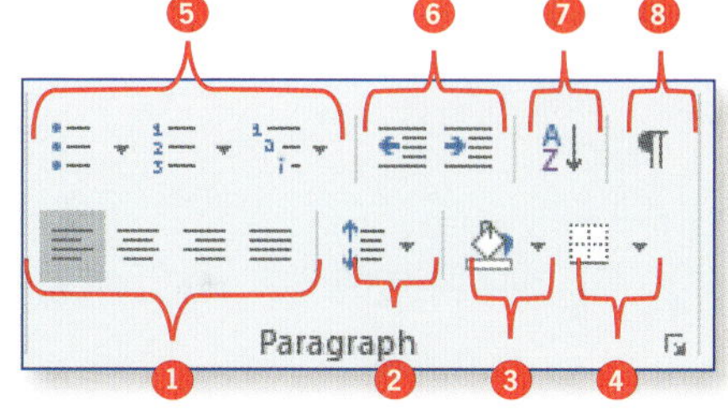

Some paragraph commands are positioned together in subgroups separated from one another by divider bars. The following overview presents the commands by the subgroups.

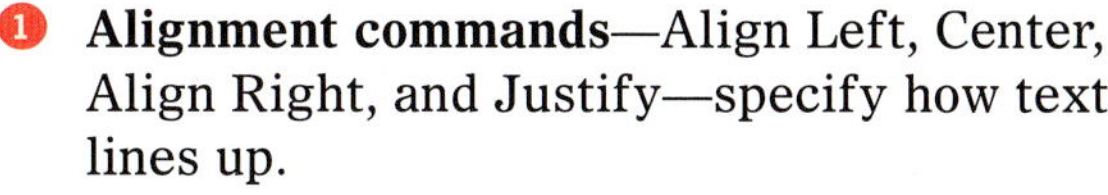

1. **Alignment commands**—Align Left, Center, Align Right, and Justify—specify how text lines up.
2. **Line and Paragraph Spacing**—determines the amount of space between lines of text and before and after paragraphs.
3. **Shading**—applies color as a background for text and paragraphs.
4. **Borders**—apply and remove inside and outside borders and horizontal lines.
5. **Bullets, Numbering, and Multilevel List**—apply formats to lists of information. Bullets and Numbering present information on one level, whereas Multilevel List presents information in a hierarchy.
6. **Decrease and Increase Indent**—move all lines of a paragraph to the right or left.
7. **Sort**—alphabetizes selected text or arranges numerical data in ascending or descending order.
8. **Show/Hide**—displays paragraph markings and other nonprinting characters.

40-d3

Insert and Delete Columns and Rows

1. Open *39–d2*. Delete column D (*Unit Price*).
2. Insert a new column between columns A and B.
3. Key the text below in the new column. Align Center the column heading and align the remainder of the column with Align Center Left.

   Publisher
   Bodwin
   American
   TWSS
   Bodwin
   TWSS

4. Insert a new row above *Law and Ethics in Computer Crimes* and add the following information:

   Digital Data Analysis Tools | American | 2016 | $9,675.95

5. Insert a blank row above row 1; merge the cells in the new row. Key **OXFORD LEARNING SYSTEMS** in 14-point font and apply bold. Change the row height to 0.4" and center the text vertically and horizontally in the cell.
6. Save and close. (*40–d3*)

Communication

ABBREVIATIONS

40d

1. Review the "Abbreviations" section of Appendix C.
2. Open the *abbreviations* data file.
3. In the *Corrected* column, apply the abbreviation guidelines to key a corrected copy of the text in the *Original* column view.
4. Add a row above row 1 of the Application table and merge the cells. Key the main heading, **USING ABBREVIATIONS CORRECTLY**, in 14-point bold font. Change the height of row 1 to 0.4". Center the main heading vertically and horizontally in the row.
5. Change the height of row 2 to 0.25" and boldface the headings. Center the text vertically and horizontally in the row.
6. Save and close. (*40–d*)

Discover

Enhanced ScreenTips—Position the mouse pointer over a command to display its name, a description of it, and the keyboard shortcut to apply (if available).

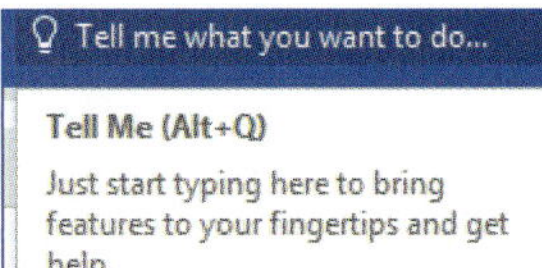

ALIGNMENT

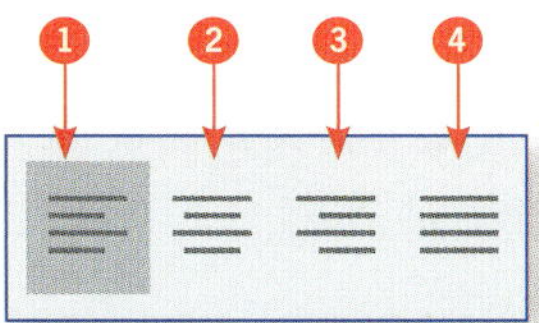

1. **Align Left**—all lines begin at left margin.
2. **Center**—all lines are centered.
3. **Align Right**—all lines are aligned at the right margin.
4. **Justify**—all lines are aligned at both the left and right margins.

To apply alignment formats:

Home/Paragraph/Align Left, Center, Align Right, or Justify

1. Click in a single paragraph or select multiple paragraphs to which a format is to be applied.
2. Click the format to be applied.

Right-aligned text

Centered Text

Left-aligned text is the most frequently used alignment. All lines begin at the left margin. The right margin is uneven when text is aligned at the left side.

Justify aligns text at both the left and the right margins. All lines are even on both sides except that the last line of a paragraph may be shorter and will not end at the right margin. The system allocates additional space as needed to force the right margin to align evenly.

Position the mouse over each alignment command to learn more about the alignment.

DRILL 1 ALIGNMENT

1. Key the document shown above; do not format as you key.
2. Apply the alignment formats shown above.
3. Save and close. (*28-drill1*)

DRILL 3 MERGE AND SPLIT CELLS

1. Create a two-column, five-row table.
2. Merge the cells in row 1; key the main heading in uppercase 14-point bold font. Change the height of row 1 to 0.4".
3. Key **Course Name** in cell A2 and **Enrollment Figures** in cell B2.
4. Select cells B3–B5; split these cells into two columns and three rows. Key **Undergraduates** in cell B3 and **Graduates** in cell C3. Key the rest of the table as shown.
5. Select cells A2 and A3; merge the cells. Select all the headings and apply Align Center. Bold all column headings.
6. Right-align all numbers.
7. Adjust column width and center table horizontally.
8. Save and close. (*40-drill3*)

FINAL SEAT COUNT		
Course Name	**Enrollment Figures**	
	Undergraduates	**Graduates**
English Reading and Composition	12,875	97
Medical Microbiology	782	1,052

Apply It

40-d1

Insert Column/Row and Merge

1. Open *39-d1*. Insert the following column between columns B and C.

   Division
   Commercial
   Space Shuttle
   Military
   Commercial

2. Left-align the new data in column C. (You will center the heading in step 3 below).
3. Insert a blank row above row 1. Merge the cells in row 1. Key **SAFETY AWARDS** in 14-point font and apply bold.
4. Change the height of row 1 to 0.4". Use Align Center to center the text in rows 1 and 2.
5. Save and close. (*40–d1*)

40-d2

Insert and Delete Rows

1. Open *40-d1*. Insert a row after *Lorianna Mendez* and add the following information:

   Robert Ruiz | Research | Military | $2,250

2. Insert a row at the end of the table and add the following information:

   Frank Cousins | Security | Space Shuttle | $500

3. Delete the row for William Mohammed.
4. Save and close. (*40–d2*)

SHOW/HIDE

Home/Paragraph/Show/Hide

¶ Paragraph formats apply to an entire paragraph. Each time you tap ENTER, *Word* inserts a paragraph mark and starts a new paragraph. Thus, a paragraph may consist of a partial line or of several lines. You must be able to see where paragraphs begin and end to format them. Turning on the Show/Hide button displays all nonprinting characters such as paragraph markers (¶) or spaces (..). The Show/Hide button appears highlighted when it is active. Nonprinting characters can be turned off by clicking the Show/Hide button again.

DRILL 2 SHOW/HIDE

1. In a new document, turn on Show/Hide. Tap ENTER three times.
2. Key the text shown below; then apply both the text formats and the alignment formats listed in the following steps.
3. Apply bold format to *My Personal Assistant*; right-align it.
4. Apply Cambria 14-point font and bold to the centered text.
5. Add italic in the last line to *personal assistant*.
6. Save and close. (*28-drill2*)

My Personal Assistant

Why Use Show/Hide?

Using Show/Hide will help you format your documents correctly. It can also help you earn better scores on your work as it will display symbols to indicate spacing and other errors that you may miss in proofreading.

Think of Show/Hide as a personal assistant when you key documents!

LINE AND PARAGRAPH SPACING

Line and paragraph spacing enable you to choose the amount of space between lines and between paragraphs. The illustration at the right shows the options that display when you click the drop-down arrow. To view the default line and paragraph spacing, click Line Spacing Options.

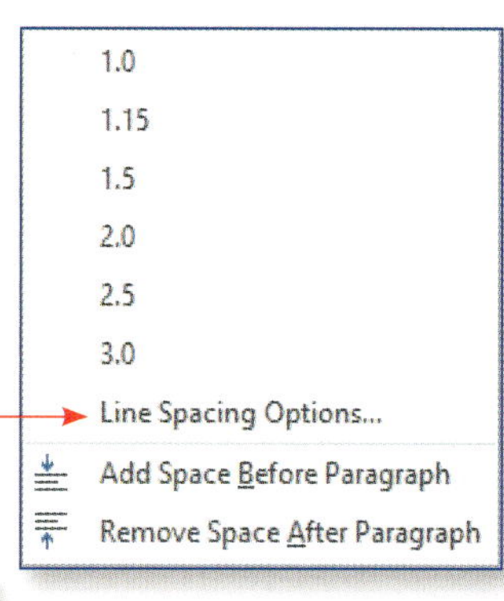

The 1.08 line spacing and 8 points after paragraph defaults are shown in the illustration below.

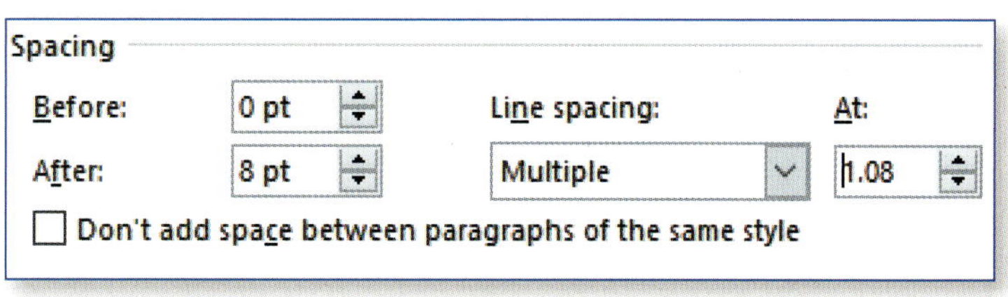

DRILL 2 INSERT ROWS AND COLUMNS

insert

1. Open the Insert document from the data file. Insert the following rows so that the items are in correct alphabetical order.

Connors, Margaret	**South**	**$87,560**
Roberts, George	**East**	**$97,850**
Zales, Laura	**West**	**$93,500**

2. Delete the row containing Hoang, Thomas.
3. Insert a column between columns B and C and key the following entries in the column.

Office
Wilshire
Toledo
Atlanta
Tampa
Las Vegas
Boston
Chicago
San Francisco

4. Left-align cells C2–C9. Click in column C and change the column width to 1.3" so that *San Francisco* does not wrap.
5. Save and close. (*40-drill2*)

MERGE AND SPLIT CELLS

Merging is the process of combining two or more table cells located in the same row or column into a single cell. Cells can be joined horizontally or vertically. For example, you can merge several cells horizontally to create a table heading row that spans several columns. A cell or several selected cells can be divided into multiple cells and columns by using the Split Cells feature.

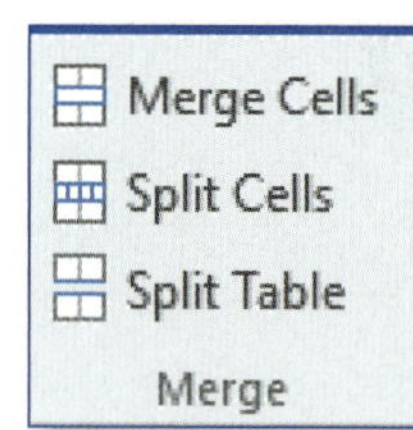

To merge cells:

Table Tools Layout/Merge/Merge Cells

1. Select the cells that are to be merged.
2. Follow the path to merge the selected cells.

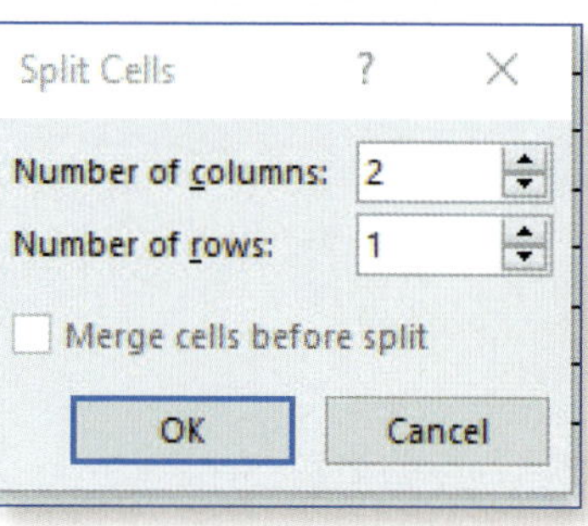

To split cells:

Table Tools Layout/Merge/Split Cells

1. Click in the cell that is to be divided into multiple cells. If multiple cells are to be split, select them.
2. Follow the path to display Split Cells dialog box.
3. Key the number of columns or rows that the selected cells are to be split into.

To change line spacing:

Home/Paragraph/Line and Paragraph Spacing

1. Position the insertion point in the paragraph whose spacing you wish to change.
2. Click the Line and Paragraph Spacing button and select the desired spacing.

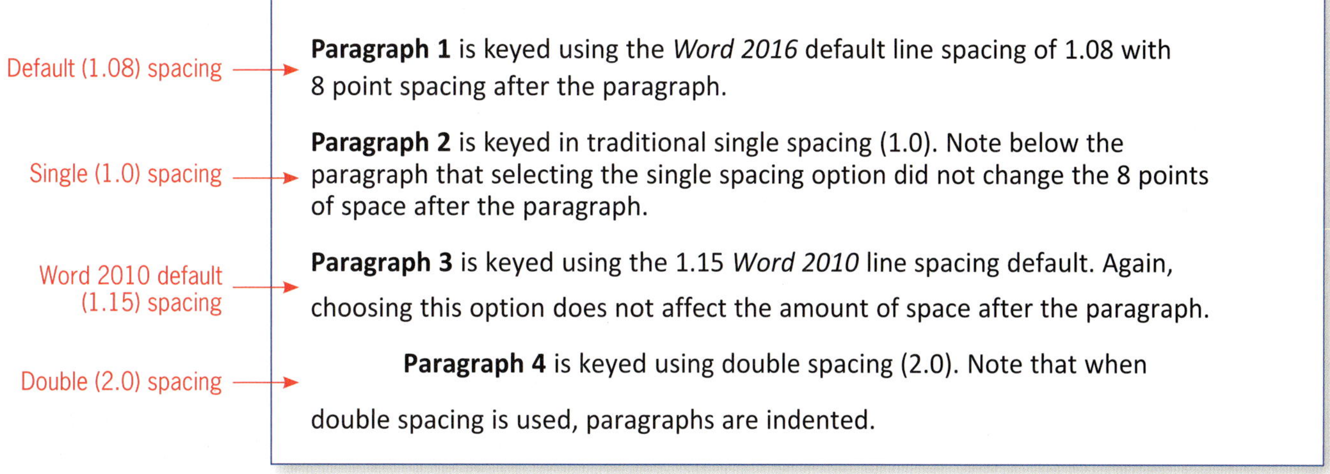

Paragraph 1 is keyed using the *Word 2016* default line spacing of 1.08 with 8 point spacing after the paragraph.

Paragraph 2 is keyed in traditional single spacing (1.0). Note below the paragraph that selecting the single spacing option did not change the 8 points of space after the paragraph.

Paragraph 3 is keyed using the 1.15 *Word 2010* line spacing default. Again, choosing this option does not affect the amount of space after the paragraph.

Paragraph 4 is keyed using double spacing (2.0). Note that when double spacing is used, paragraphs are indented.

DRILL 3 LINE SPACING

1. In a new document, key the four paragraphs above; then apply the formatting shown in each paragraph. Remember to apply bold and italics.
2. Save and close. (*28-drill3*)

Note: The amount of space (8 points) between paragraphs does not change when you change the line spacing. It is 8 points after each paragraph. Also note the differences between 1.08 spacing, 1.15 spacing, 1.0 spacing, and 2.0 spacing shown above.

TIP

The Quick Access Toolbar is available from all tabs on the ribbon.

QUICK ACCESS TOOLBAR

The Quick Access Toolbar (QAT) is located in the upper-left corner of the screen above the File and Home tabs. It contains icons for three frequently used commands: Save, Undo, and Redo. The QAT provides a shortcut or one-click option for these frequently used commands.

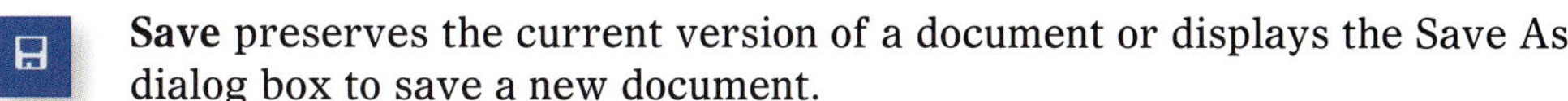

Save preserves the current version of a document or displays the Save As dialog box to save a new document.

Undo reverses the most recent action taken (such as inserting or removing formats). The drop-down arrow displays a list of the commands that you can undo. Selecting an item on the list will undo all items above it.

Redo reverses the last undo; it can be used several times to redo the past several actions. You can also select new text and click Redo to repeat the past Undo.

A column can be inserted using the same process. Move the mouse pointer above the table and point to the border where the new column is to be inserted, then click the plus symbol.

Award Winners	Department	Amount
Lorianna Mendez	Accounting	$2,000
William Mohammed	Marketing	$800
Cynthia Khek	Engineering	$1,500
Charles Pham	Purchasing	$1,000

DRILL 1 INSERT ROW AND COLUMN

1. Open *38-drill2* and insert a row following *Ms. Man Jin Callentonni.*
2. Key **Mr. Frederick Douglas, Compliance Committee Chair** in the blank row.
3. Insert a column between columns A and B.
4. Key: **Extension | 5278 | 4902 | 2561 | 9302 | 3715.**
5. Center the text in column B.
6. Align center the column headings in row 1.
7. Apply bold to the column headings.
8. Adjust column width to fit the contents, and center the table horizontally on the page.
9. Save and close. (*40-drill1*)

INSERT AND DELETE ROWS AND COLUMNS USING TABLE TOOLS

Rows and columns can also be inserted or deleted by using commands on the Table Tools Layout tab.

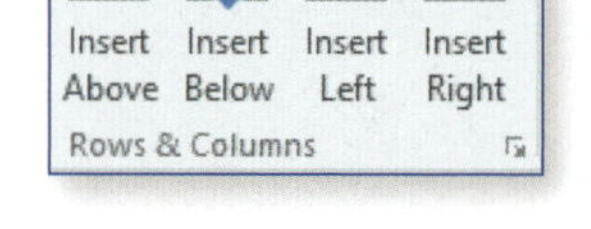

To insert rows or columns in a table:

Table Tools Layout/Rows & Columns

1. Position the insertion point where the new row or column is to be inserted. If several rows or columns are to be inserted, select the number you want to insert.
2. Follow the path to the Rows & Columns group. Click the appropriate command.

To delete rows or columns in a table:

Table Tools Layout/Rows & Columns/Delete

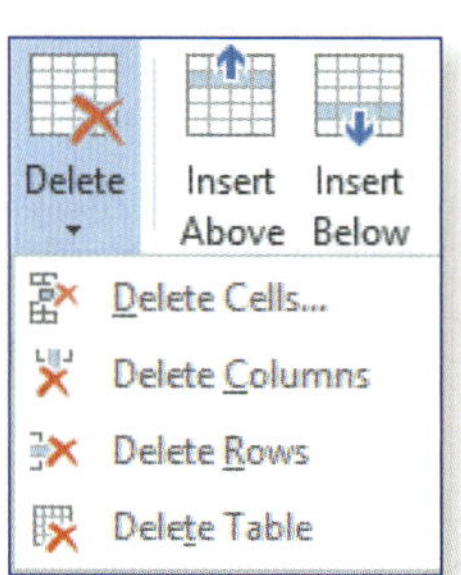

1. Position the insertion point in the row or column that is to be deleted. If more than one row or column is to be deleted, select them first.
2. Follow the path to display the Delete options. Select the appropriate command.

QUICK ACCESS TOOLBAR, CONTINUED

Customize Quick Access Toolbar down arrow provides access to additional commands that can be added to the QAT as shown at the right.

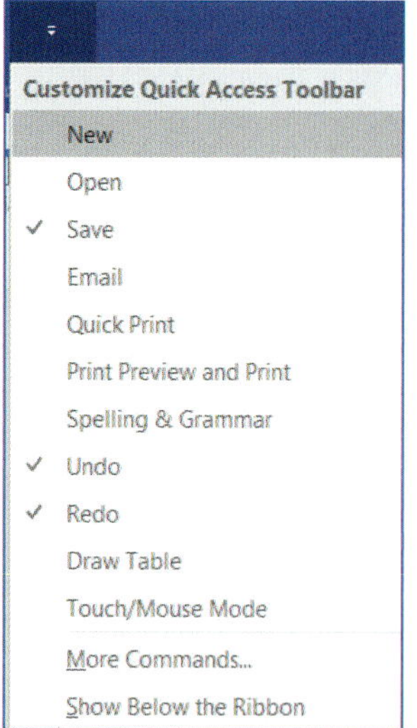

Commands can be added one at a time by clicking the desired commands. Click the Customize Quick Access Toolbar down arrow; then click New to add it to the QAT. Repeat the process and click Open, to add it to the QAT as shown below.

New Blank Document opens a new document.

Open is used to open an existing file from the Recent list or the Document list.

DRILL 4 QUICK ACCESS TOOLBAR

1. Use the QAT to open a new document.
2. Key the four sentences shown below.
3. In sentence 1, apply bold and underline to *Undo/Redo*.
4. Undo the underline on Undo in sentence 1.
5. Apply bold to Undo in sentence 2 and to Redo in sentence 3.
6. In sentence 4, apply bold to *use*.
7. Select *You can* and then click Redo to repeat the bold command.
8. Save and close. (*28-drill4*)
9. Use QAT to open *28-drill4*. Tap ENTER at the beginning of the first sentence and key Quick Access Toolbar; then right-align it.
10. Use Undo to remove the right-align; then align it at the center.
11. Save and close. (*28-drill4a*)

Keying and formatting changes can be reversed easily by using the Undo/Redo commands.

If you make a change, one click of the Undo command can reverse the change.

If you undo a change and decide that you want to keep the change as it was originally made, you can go back to the original change by clicking the Redo command.

You can use the Redo command as a Repeat command.

Lesson 40 Table Tools—Change Table Structure

New Commands

- Insert and Delete Columns and Rows
- Merge and Split Cells

Warmup *Lesson 40a Warmup*

lesson 40a warmup

Skill Building

40b Textbook Keying

1. Key each line concentrating on good keying techniques.
2. Repeat the drill if time permits.

d 1 do did dad sad faded daddy madder diddle deduced hydrated dredged
k 2 keys sake kicked karat kayak karate knock knuckle knick kilometer
d/k 3 The ten tired and dizzy kids thought the doorknob was the donkey.
w 4 we were who away whew snow windward waterway window webworm award
o 5 on to too onto solo oleo soil cook looked location emotion hollow
w/o 6 Those who know their own power and are committed will follow through.
b 7 be bib sub bear book bribe fiber bombard blueberry babble baboons
v 8 vet vat van viva have over avoid vapor valve seven vanish vanilla
b/v 9 Bo gave a very big beverage and seven coins to everybody bowling.
r 10 or rear rare roar saturate reassure rather northern surge quarrel
u 11 yours undue unity useful unique unusual value wound youth succumb
r/u 12 The truth of the matter is that only Ruth can run a rummage sale.

| 1 | 2 | 3 | 4 | 5 | 6 | 7 | 8 | 9 | 10 | 11 | 12 | 13 |

New Commands

40c

INSERT A COLUMN OR ROW

A row can be inserted in a table by placing the mouse pointer at the left edge of the table and pointing to the position where the new row is to be inserted. If you need to add a row below Lorianna Mendez in the illustration below, place the insertion on the border between Lorianna Mendez and William Mohammed. Click the plus symbol to insert a new row. If more than one row is to be inserted, first select the number of rows, place the insertion point where the new rows will be inserted, then click the plus symbol.

Award Winners	Department	Amount
Lorianna Mendez	Accounting	$2,000
William Mohammed	Marketing	$800
Cynthia Khek	Engineering	$1,500
Charles Pham	Purchasing	$1,000

Apply It

28-d1

Announcement

1. In a new document, key all paragraphs below using default font, size, and spacing. Turn on Show/Hide.
2. Position the insertion point at the beginning of the title, *Standard Operating Procedures*, and tap ENTER three times; apply bold, 16-point Arial font to the title, and center it.
3. Apply bold and 14-point Arial font to the three side headings.
4. Save and close. *(28-d1)*

Standard Operating Procedures

Many companies develop standard operating procedures (SOPs) for virtually every phase of their business. When standard operating procedures are mentioned, most people think of a manufacturing or service business and are surprised to learn that standard operating procedures apply to management and office administration as well. Most companies have SOPs for producing documents in their offices for several reasons.

Quality Control

SOPs ensure that company image is consistent throughout the organization. Guides are presented for using and protecting the company logo, standard colors may be specified, and document formats are standardized.

Training Tools

New and experienced employees both want to do a good job. SOPs provide an excellent training tool to ensure that all employees do their work accurately and meet company expectations consistently. Most employees do not like to be told repeatedly what to do. Having a set of guides to follow enables them to work independently and still meet quality standards.

Productivity Enhancement and Cost Reduction

Documents are very expensive to produce. SOPs are designed to be efficient, and efficiency translates to cost savings.

28-d2

Apply Font and Paragraph Formats

1. Open *28-d1*; turn on Show/Hide. Select the three side headings and decrease font size to 12 point.
2. Click in the paragraph below the centered title and change the line spacing to double spacing. Tap TAB to indent the first line of the paragraph. Select the entire paragraph and change the font to Times New Roman 11 point.
3. Click in the paragraph below each side heading, and change the line spacing to double spacing. Then tap TAB to indent the first line of the paragraphs. Triple-click to select the entire paragraph and change the font to Times New Roman 11 point.
4. Turn off Show/Hide.
5. Save and close. *(28-d2)*

Apply It

39-d1

Create table, adjust cell height and width, and center horizontally

1. Key the table below.
2. Adjust the width of column A to 1.95". Adjust the width of column B to 1.5". Adjust the width of column C to 1.15". Right-align column C.
3. Center the table horizontally on the page.
4. Adjust the height of row 1 to 0.3". Align Center and bold the column headings.
5. Save and close. (*39-d1*)

Award Winners	Department	Amount
Lorianna Mendez	Accounting	$2,000
William Mohammed	Marketing	$800
Cynthia Khek	Engineering	$1,500
Charles Pham	Purchasing	$1,000

39-d2

Create Table, Adjust Cell Sizes

1. Key the table; adjust column width so that the text does not wrap to a second line.
2. Adjust Cell Size height to 0.3 for the entire table. Center the text vertically in the cells. Align Center and bold the column headings.
3. Center columns B and D. Right-align the values in column C. Center the table horizontally.
4. Save and close. (*39–d2*)

Book Title	Publication	Sales	Unit Price
Computer Crimes	2015	$478,769.00	$69.50
Digital Data Forensics	2015	$91,236.00	$63.00
Computer Criminology	2015	$89,412.50	$75.50
Law and Ethics in Computer Crimes	2016	$104,511.00	$93.50
Role of Operating Systems in Computer Forensics	2016	$194,137.50	$83.50

Lesson 29 Format Paragraphs/Navigate Documents

New Commands

- Bullets and Numbering
- Scroll Bars
- Slider Zoom
- View
- Spelling and Grammar
- Thesaurus
- Define
- Word Count

Warmup *Lesson 29a Warmup*

lesson 29a warmup

Skill Building

29b Improve Speed

Key each line once, concentrating on using good keying techniques.

balanced-hand words, phrases, and sentences

1 if me to so he is us do go or sod fir for pen may big dig got fix
2 dog jam sit men lap pay cut nap tug lake worn make torn turn dock

3 he is | it is | of it | is it | go to | to go | is he | he is it | for it | she can
4 did he | pay them | she may | is it torn | it is worn | he may go | the lake

5 He may also go with them to the dock or down to the lake with us.
6 Did she go with Keith to the lake, or can she go to town with us?

29c Timed Writing

1. Key a 1' timed writing on each paragraph; work to increase speed. Use wordwrap.
2. Key a 3' timed writing on all paragraphs.

gwam 1' | 3'

Learning new software applications can be exciting, but it 12 4
often requires much hard work. However, if you are willing to work 25 8
hard and to work smart, in a relatively short period of time you 38 13
can learn very important skills. 44 15

If you accept change easily and willingly, you are more 11 18
likely to learn new things quickly. A person who avoids change has 24 23
just about the same chance of learning new software applications as 38 27
a lazy person. 40 28

Working smart might be just as important as working hard. 11 32
Help is easy to use if you will take the time to explore the 23 36
resources that are provided in your software. Valuable information 37 40
is also available on the provider's website. 45 43

CHANGE CELL SIZE

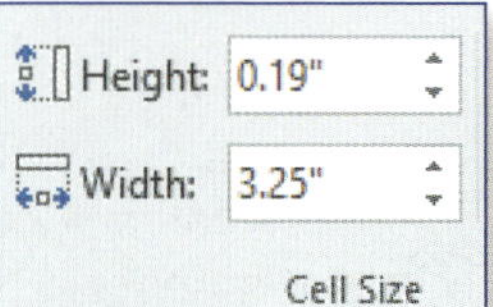

The Cell Size group on the Layout tab allows you to set cell height and width to exact dimensions. The height of a row is often increased to provide some blank space above and below the text to make the contents in the cell easier to read.

To change cell height or width:

Table Tools Layout/Cell Size

- Click in the cell or column and then key the dimension in the Height box or use the spin arrows to set the height dimension.
- Select the cell or row and then key the dimension in the Width box or use the spin arrows to set the width dimension.

CHANGE TEXT ALIGNMENT IN CELL

Table Tools Layout/Alignment

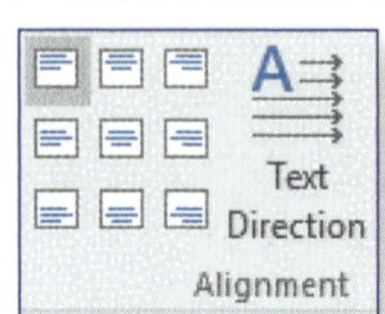

By default, text displays left aligned at the top of the cell. When cell height is increased, text may need to be centered vertically in the cell to make the table more attractive.

Commands in the Alignment group allow text to be aligned at the top, middle, or bottom of the cell. You can also align text at the left, middle, or right of the cell. Select the button that provides the best combination of vertical and horizontal alignment.

To change the alignment of the text in the cell, select the cell(s) and click the appropriate alignment command.

DRILL 3 ADJUST CELL HEIGHT AND WIDTH

1. Open *38-d1* and select column A. Change the width of the column to 2.2".
2. Select column B. Change the width of column B to 1.4".
3. Select column C. Change the width of column C 1.5".
4. Select row 1. Change the height of row 1 to 0.3".
5. Align center the column headings in row 1.
6. Apply bold to the column headings.
7. Center the table horizontally on the page.
8. Save and close. (*39-drill3*)

New Commands

29d

BULLETS AND NUMBERING

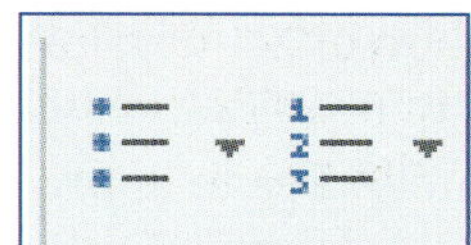

Bullets are used for lists of unordered items, whereas numbering is used for items that are in a sequence. Bullets can be converted to numbers, and numbers can be converted to bullets. The drop-list arrow on bullets and numbering displays a library of styles for each command. If you have recently used bullets or numbering, the style used will display at the top of the library. Bullets and numbering are easier to apply after text has been keyed.

To apply bullets and numbering:

Home/Paragraph/Bullets or Numbering

1. Key the list.
2. Select the list and click either the Bullets or the Numbering command.

To select a different format for bullets and numbering:

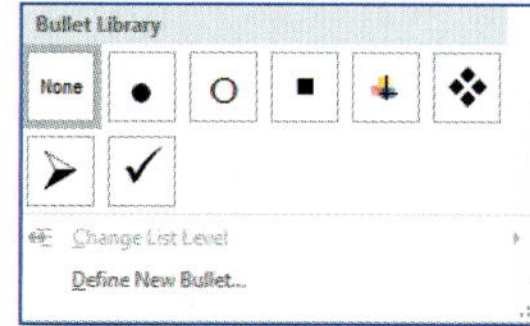

1. Click the drop-down arrow on either the Bullets or the Numbering button to display the library of styles.
2. Select the desired style.

Note: The gallery that displays on your computer may have different bullet styles than the one shown at the right.

DRILL 1 BULLETS AND NUMBERING

1. In a new document, key the two lists below.
2. Bold the headings. Apply bullets to the first list below the heading *Procedures for Completing an Activity*.
3. Apply numbering to the second list, *Things to Do This Weekend*.
4. Convert the first list with bullets to numbering using the number format with right parentheses (Left alignment).
5. Convert the second list with numbering to square bullets.
6. Save and close. (*29-drill1*)

Procedures for Completing an Activity

Preview and proofread the document.

Print the document.

Save document with appropriate name and close it.

Things to Do This Weekend

Complete library research.

Pick up office supplies.

Install new software.

To View the Ruler, go to the View tab and click the Ruler checkbox under the Show Group.

To adjust column widths using the mouse:

1. Point to the column border that needs adjusting.
2. When the pointer changes to +||+, hold down the left mouse button and drag the border to the left to make the column narrower or to the right to make it wider.
3. Adjust the column widths appropriately. Leave approximately 0.5" to 0.75" between the longest line and the border. Use the Horizontal Ruler as a guide.
4. The widths of the columns can be displayed by pointing to the column marker on the Ruler, holding down the ALT key, and clicking the left mouse button.

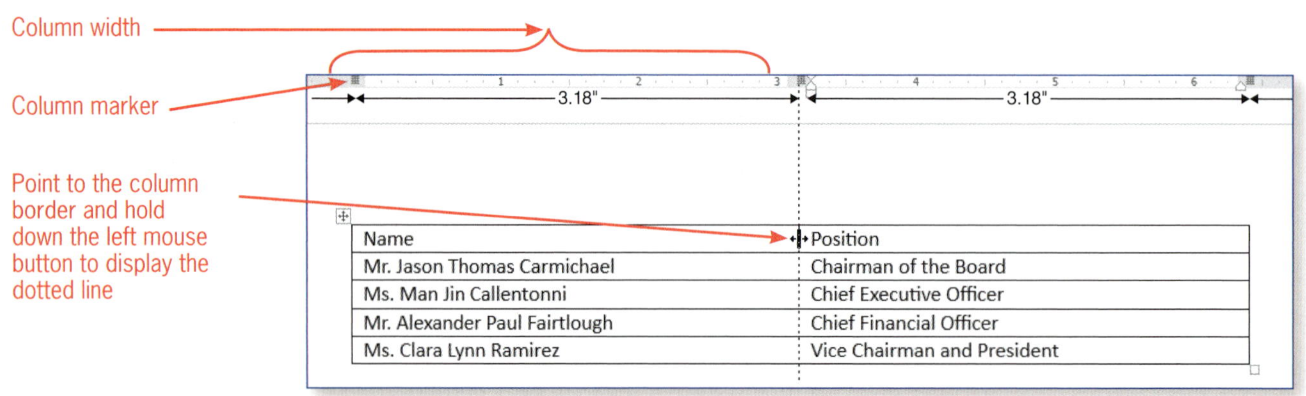

Name	Position
Mr. Jason Thomas Carmichael	Chairman of the Board
Ms. Man Jin Callentonni	Chief Executive Officer
Mr. Alexander Paul Fairtlough	Chief Financial Officer
Ms. Clara Lynn Ramirez	Vice Chairman and President

Another method of centering a table horizontally is to click the Table Move handle to select the table and then click the Center button on the Home tab.

CENTER TABLE HORIZONTALLY

Once column widths have been adjusted, a table will no longer be full-page width. Use the Table Properties dialog box to center the table horizontally on the page.

To center table horizontally on page:

Table Tools Layout/Table/Properties

1. Click in a table cell.
2. Follow the path to open the Table Properties dialog box.
3. On the Table tab, select Center.

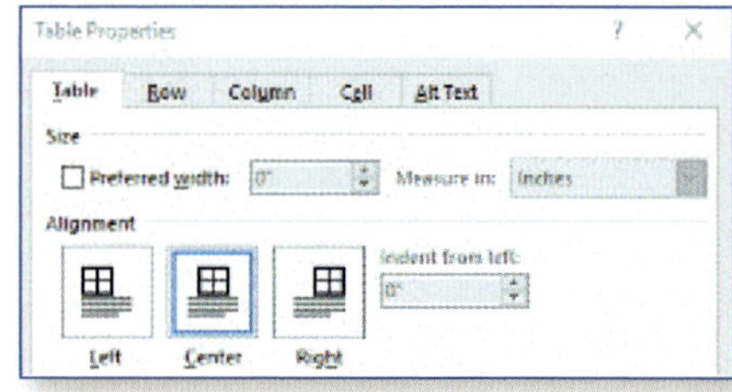

DRILL 2 ADJUST COLUMN WIDTH AND CENTER TABLE

1. Open *39-drill1* and click in the table.
2. Use the mouse to adjust column borders. Leave approximately 0.5" between the longest line and the right border.
3. Center the table horizontally on the page.
4. Save and close. (*39-drill2*)

NAVIGATE AND VIEW A DOCUMENT

The document window displays only a portion of a page at one time. The keyboard, mouse, and scroll bars can be used to move quickly through a document to view it.

Keyboard options—press CTRL + HOME to go to the beginning of a document and CTRL + END to move to the end of the document. The Page Up and Page Down keys can also be used to move through a document.

Mouse and scroll bar—use the scroll bar located on the right side of the screen to move through the document. Scrolling does not change the position of the insertion point; it only changes your view of the document. You must click in the text to change the position of the insertion point.

Zoom—enables users to view the document with enlarged or reduced text. Zoom is located on the status bar and the View menu.

View tab—provides additional options for viewing documents.

SCROLL BAR

The scroll bar on the right side of the screen provides options to move through the document. The scroll bar at the bottom of the screen allows you to move to the left or right to see the entire line of writing.

To move through a document:

- Click the up and down arrows. -or-
- Click above or below the scroll box. -or-
- Click the scroll box and drag it to the desired position.

Note the position displays when you drag the scroll box.

ZOOM

Zoom, located on the status bar at the lower right side of the *Word* window, controls the magnification of your document. Zoom is positioned in the center of the slider bar, which displays text at 100% of its actual size. The Zoom slides to the right or left to increase or decrease text size. Clicking the plus or minus sign of the end of the bar changes the settings in increments of 10 percent.

You can also select an entire table, a row, or a column by moving the mouse pointer to different locations on or near the table.

To select	Move the insertion point:
Entire table	Over the table and click the Table Move handle at the upper-left corner of the table. To move the table, drag the Table Move handle to a new location.
Column	To the top of the column until a solid down arrow (⬇) appears; click the left mouse button.
Row	To the left area just outside the table until the pointer turns to an open diagonal arrow (⇗); then click the left mouse button.

Cells can also be selected by clicking in the cell, holding down the mouse button, and dragging across or down.

ADJUST COLUMN WIDTH

A new *Word* table extends from margin to margin when first created, with all columns the same width regardless of the width of the data in the columns. Some tables, however, would be more attractive and easier to read if the columns were narrower or adjusted to fit the data in the cells.

Use the AutoFit option on the Layout tab to adjust the width of a column to fit the widest entry in each column.

Height: 0.19"
Width: 1.62"
AutoFit
AutoFit Contents
AutoFit Window
Fixed Column Width

To adjust column width using AutoFit:

Table Tools Layout/Cell Size/AutoFit

1. Click a table cell.
2. Follow the path to display the AutoFit options.
3. Select the desired option.

You can also change column width manually using the mouse. Using the mouse enables you to adjust the widths as you like. Columns look best when approximately 0.5" of blank space is left between the longest line and the column border.

DRILL 1 ADJUST COLUMN WIDTH USING AUTOFIT

Table Tools Layout/Cell Size/AutoFit

1. Open *38-drill2* and click in the table.
2. Click AutoFit Contents. The columns adjust to fit the data.
3. Click AutoFit Window to restore the table to full size.
4. Place the insertion point in the last cell and tap TAB.
5. Key **Ms. Judy Jones** and **Administrative Assistant** in the last row.
6. Save and close. (*39-drill1*)

To view smaller or larger versions of text:

1. To view a larger version of a segment of text, move Zoom toward the right or positive (+) side. The text will be larger, but you see a smaller segment of it.
2. To see more of the document, move Zoom toward the left or the negative (–) side. To view two full pages, move the Zoom to about 50 percent. Clicking the plus or minus signs increases or decreases size in increments of 10 percent.

VIEW

Document views display a document in different formats. The view that is selected when you save and close a document will be the view that displays when that document is opened again.

Document views can be accessed by clicking the view on the status bar or the View tab. With Outline view, the Close option must be clicked to exit it.

To access document views from the status bar:

1. Click the desired view. Print Layout is the default view.
2. To close the view, click Print Layout.

To view documents using Views:

View/Views/Read Mode or other views

1. Click the desired view.

   Hover the mouse over each view and review the Enhanced ScreenTip that describes the view and when it is best used. Two additional views—Outline and Draft—are added to those on the status bar.

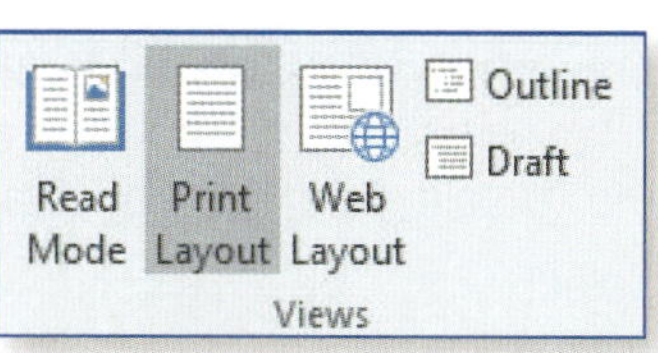

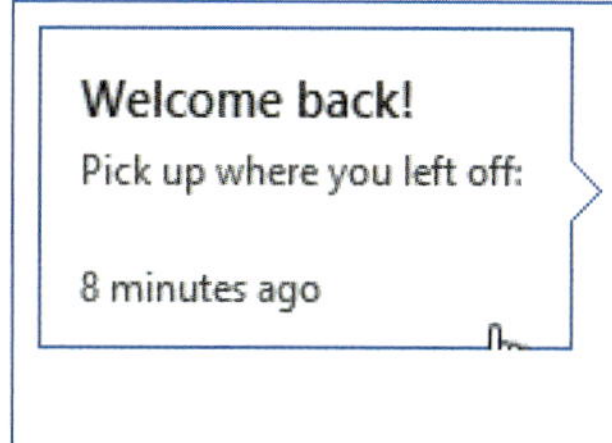

2. Click the Close Outline view button to exit that view.

The Read Mode has additional tools designed to enhance reading. When you close a document and later return to finish reading it, the bookmark shown at the right brings you back to the page you were reading.

Lesson 39 Table Tools—Layout

New Commands

- Adjust Column Width
- Center Table on Page
- Change Cell Size
- Text Alignment in Cells

Warmup *Lesson 39a Warmup*

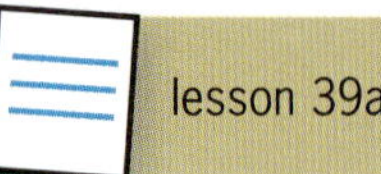

lesson 39a warmup

Skill Building

39b Textbook Keying

1. Key each line, concentrating on good keying techniques.
2. Repeat the drill if time permits.

t 1 it cat pat to top thin at tilt jolt tuft mitt flat test tent felt
r 2 fur bur try roar soar ram trap rare ripe true rear tort corral
t/r 3 The track star was triumphant in both the third and fourth heats.
m 4 me mine memo mimic named clam month maximum mummy summer remember
n 5 no snow ton none nine ninety noun mini mind minnow kennel evening
m/n 6 Men and women in management roles maximize time during commuting.

New Commands

39b

LAYOUT TAB

When you click in a table, the Table Tools tab displays with two tabs—the Design tab and the Layout tab. The Design tab contains commands for changing the appearance of the table. The Layout tab contains commands for altering the table structure.

SELECT PORTIONS OF A TABLE

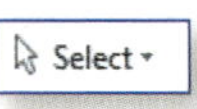

To alter the table structure, select the cells, column, or row that will be altered. Use the mouse to select the cells or the Select command on the Table Tools Layout tab to select parts of the table or the entire table.

To use the Select command to select portions of a table:

Table Tools Layout/Table/Select

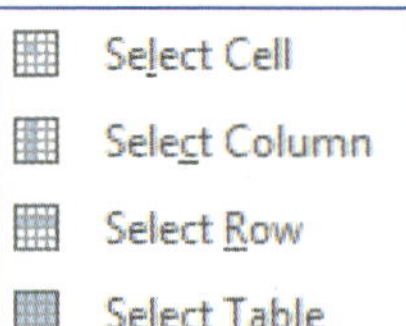

1. Click the insertion point in a table cell; then follow the path to display the Select options.
   a. Choose Select Cell to select only the cell the insertion point is in.
   b. Choose Select Column or Select Row to highlight the entire column or row that contains the cell.
   c. Choose Select Table to highlight the entire table.

To view documents using Zoom options:

View/Zoom/Zoom or Page Options

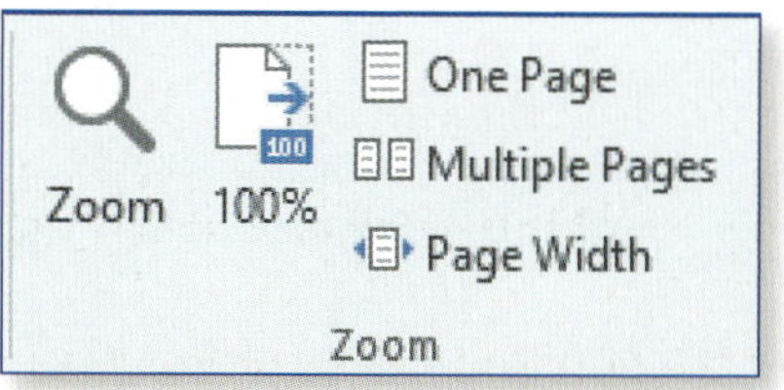

1. To view smaller or larger portions of text, click Zoom and select a percentage.
2. To view a full page, two pages, or page width, click the appropriate alternative.

DRILL 2 NAVIGATION AND VIEW

1. In the open document (*28-d2*), move to the end of the document (CTRL + END). Tap ENTER and key **29-drill2**; right-align the document name.
2. Use the keyboard to move up and down through the document. Press CTRL + HOME to go to the beginning of the document, then CTRL + END to move to the end.
3. Use the mouse, the scroll box, and the up and down arrows to move in the document.
4. Move the Zoom to the left to 50% and view the document; then move it to 200% and view the document.
5. Move the Zoom back to the center at 100%.
6. Use the View tab to change the document view to Page Width.
7. From the View tab, hover the mouse over each document view to display the ScreenTip.
8. Click each view on the View tab. To exit Read Mode, click Print Layout view on the status bar. To exit Outline view, click the Close Outline View button.
9. Return to Print Layout view from the status bar.
10. Save and close. (*29-drill2*)

Communicating Today ▶

Proofing Tools: Technology Assisted Communication

Many errors made while you key are corrected automatically by a feature called AutoCorrect. In addition, *Word 2016* provides three enhanced proofing tools that are designed to help you compose, edit, and proofread documents. It also provides an Insights tool and language tools.

Spelling and Grammar. In addition to marking errors, this feature provides the correct alternative and explains the rule that applies.

Thesaurus. An online thesaurus helps you to select the best word to express a particular thought and provides synonyms for words that you tend to overuse.

Word Count. In many situations, documents such as articles and resumes are limited to a specific number of pages or words. Document statistics are readily available.

Smart Lookup. This new feature provides insights, such as definitions, syllables, images and other information, about words selected.

Language Tools. The translate feature translates words to many different languages and helps in the selection of the proper word to use. The language feature assists those working with a second language.

38-d3

Create Table

1. Key the three-column, eight-row table below. Your columns will be wider, so your text will not wrap as shown below.
2. Select cells C1–C8 and click Center. When all the items in a column are the same length, the column will look better centered.
3. Select cells A1 and B1 and click Center.
4. Save and close. (*38-d3*)

Movie Title	Time of Showing	Location
The Amazing Bionic Woman	1:15, 4:10, 7:10	Theatre 1
Global Warming: 3D	1:20, 6:25, 9:10	Theatre 2
The Hourglass	12:00, 2:30, 5:10, 7:45, 10:25	Theatre 3
The Circus Comes to Town: 3D	12:25, 2:40, 5:00, 7:40, 10:10	Theatre 4
Time Marches On	12:30, 3:30, 6:30, 9:30	Theatre 5
Humpty Dumpty's Great Fall	11:00, 1:40, 4:20, 7:10	Theatre 6
The Silver Knight: The IMAX	12:00, 3:30, 7:00, 10:30	Theatre 7

StockLite/Shutterstock.com

WORKPLACE SUCCESS

High-Tech Etiquette

In today's day and age, high-tech manners can be just as critical as dining etiquette in developing your professional image. Knowing the difference between Bluetooth and houndstooth is just as important as knowing how to host a business luncheon.

Improper or ill-timed use of new high-tech devices can destroy your professional image rather than enhance it. Using a smartphone may make you appear technically savvy; however, continually glancing at your device during a meeting is like checking your watch. It is considered rude and inappropriate behavior.

Cell phone usage should be limited during work hours. Some companies require that employees keep their cell phones in their car. If your company allows you to bring your cell phone to your desk, set it on vibrate. Do not walk around the office building talking on a cell phone; it annoys others and is not professional. If you work in a cubicle environment, be mindful that others can hear your conversation and that what you say may not be appropriate for coworkers to hear.

SPELLING AND GRAMMAR

Review/Proofing/Spelling & Grammar

Errors that are not corrected automatically are marked in the text as you key. Although this feature is helpful, it is not totally accurate. Careful proofreading is still required. See the example below:

> We plan too interview a mail athlete and a female athletes tomorow.

Errors are detected in three ways.

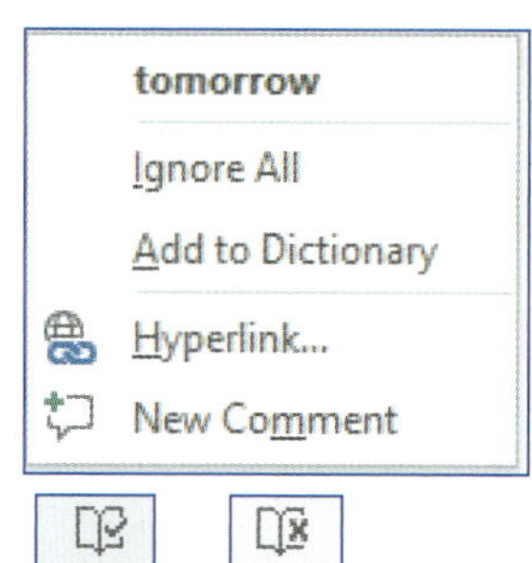

1. Color-coded squiggly lines appear in your text as you key.
   - Red indicates spelling or keying errors.
   - Blue indicates grammar or contextual errors. Right-click the errors while you are keying. An option box displays and provides the correct version as shown at the lower-right side.
2. The error detection button with an X displays in the status bar when an error is detected. Click the button to display the Grammar or Spelling pane and correct the error. When the document is error free, the button displays a check (✓).
3. The Spelling & Grammar command in the proofing group is generally used to check the entire document at once. Click the command and the Spelling or Grammar pane displays to correct each error. Even if you have corrected errors as they were marked, it is important to run the check after you have completed the document. The illustration below shows the error that was missed early was detected when the final check was run after the document was completed. Note the explanation that is provided in the Grammar pane on the right.

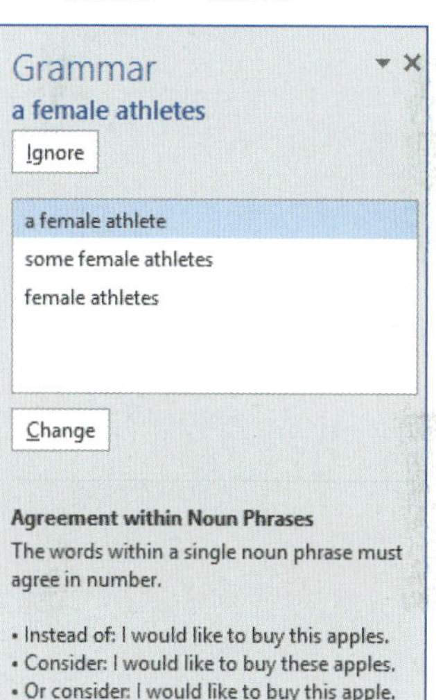

We plan to interview a male athlete and a female athletes tomorrow.

DRILL 3 SPELLING AND GRAMMAR

1. Key the paragraph on the right exactly as shown.
2. Correct the three errors.
3. Save and close. (*29-drill3*)

Spelling errors are ofen corrected automatically. If an error are not detected by the software, you should proofread and correct it. To often writers skip the proofreading step.

Apply It

38-d1

Create Table

TIP

Text is keyed left-aligned. Numerical amounts are right-aligned.

1. Create and key the table below.
2. Select cells C2–C5 and click Align Right (Home/Paragraph/Align Right) to right-align the numbers in column C. Select row 1 and click Center.
3. Place the insertion point in the last cell and tap TAB to add a row.
4. Key the following copy in row 6:

   Lawrence Jose Gonzalez **East** **$83,479**
5. Save and close. (*38-d1*)

Sales Representative	Region	Amount of Sale
Stephanie Acosta	Northwest	$1,157,829
Mitzi Fujitsu	Central	$99,016
Joanna B. Breckenridge	Southwest	$6,301,625
Jack M. Harrigan	Midwest	$4,245,073

38-d2

Create Table

1. Use the Insert Table command to create the table below. Create a three-column, four-row table using AutoFit to contents.
2. Your columns will adjust as you key. Your columns will be wider, so your text will not wrap at the same position as shown.
3. Save and close. (*38-d2*)

The Golden Mile	Boutique Shops	The Golden Mile is one square mile of boutique shops located between Beverly Boulevard and Pacific Coast Highway. You will find many designer-label retail outlets, high-end jewelry stores, and charming sidewalk cafes.
Birds of Paradise	Floral District	The Floral District offers exceptional values on fresh flowers, plants, and floral arrangements. Flowers and plants are locally grown.
Wellington Gardens	Mall	The Wellington Gardens Mall provides a luxury shopping experience with over 200 retail shops and 12 department stores. This mall is noted for its extraordinary boutiques, personal service, and upscale amenities.
Sew and Sew Fabrics	Textile District	Sew and Sew Fabrics houses over 150 vendors of fabrics and notions from around the world. Shoppers will find fabrics for apparel, crafts, and home décor.

THESAURUS

The Thesaurus command displays the Thesaurus pane, which provides synonyms and in some cases antonyms.

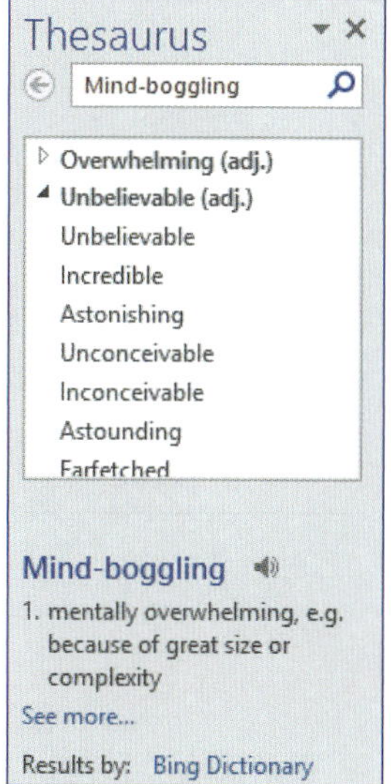

To find the synonym of a word:

Review/Proofing/Thesaurus

1. Click in the word for which you want to locate a synonym.
2. Select the appropriate synonym.
3. Click the Close (X) button at the top of the pane.

TIP

Word 2016 eliminates the Define command and incorporates definitions with the Thesaurus command and with Smart Lookup. If you are not signed in to your *Microsoft Live* account, you may be asked to do so to get results from the Bing Dictionary

WORD COUNT

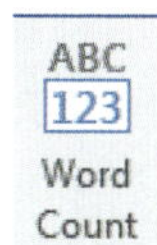

The word count displays by default in the status bar. However, additional statistics can be accessed with the Word Count command.

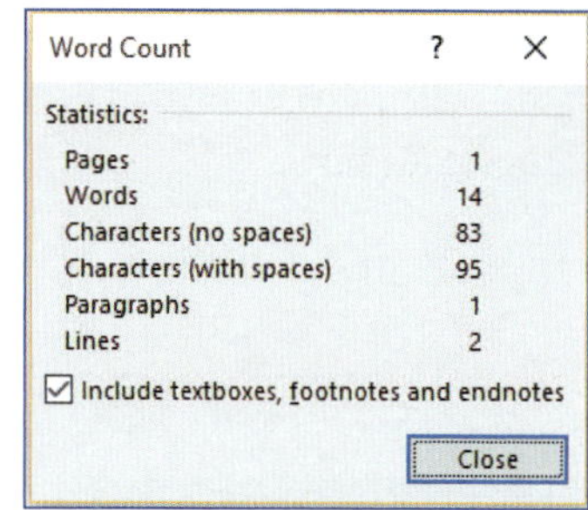

To find document statistics:

Review/Proofing/Word Count

1. Click Word Count to display the Word Count statistics.
2. Click Close (X) at the bottom of the dialog box.

DRILL 4 THESAURUS AND WORD COUNT

1. Key the sentence shown at the lower right. Look up the definition and synonyms of the last three words.
2. On the next line, key a new sentence substituting the following synonyms:
   a. mind-boggling—second under *unbelievable*
   b. albeit—first option
   c. extravagant—fourth under *exaggerated*
3. Determine the number of characters with spaces in the two sentences. Key the answer on the next line.
4. Save and close. (*29-drill4*)

My Smart TV is mind-boggling, albeit extravagant.

USE THE INSERT TABLE COMMAND

The Insert Table dialog box lets you specify the number of columns and rows for the table. This option can be easier to use than dragging over the table grid if you need a large number of rows or columns.

To create a table using the Insert Table command:

Insert/Tables/Table

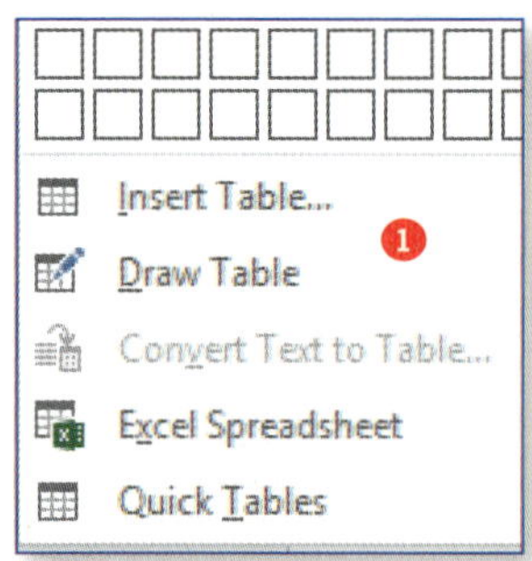

1. Click the insertion point where the table is to be inserted.
2. Follow the path to display the Insert Table menu.
3. Click Insert Table (1) to display the Insert Table dialog box.
4. Insert the number of columns by keying the number or using the spin arrows (2).
5. Insert the number of rows by keying the number or using the spin arrows (3).

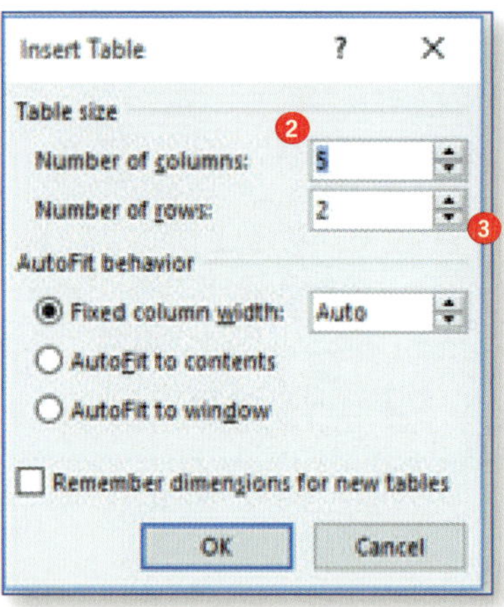

Word automatically creates a table with fixed column widths. You can adjust the column widths in the Insert Table dialog box or choose an AutoFit option to fit column widths to the longest line or to the current window size.

DRILL 2 CREATE AND FORMAT TABLE

1. Use the Insert Table command to create a two-column, four-row table.
2. Key **Name** in cell A1 and **Position** in cell B1. Row 1 contains the column headings and is often called the header row. Key the rest of the table below (your columns will be wider).
3. Place the insertion point in the last cell and tap TAB to add a row at the bottom of the table.
4. Key the following text in cell A5.

   Ms. Clara Lynn Ramirez
5. Key the following text in cell B5.

   Vice Chairman and President
6. Save and close. (*38-drill2*)

Name	Position
Mr. Jason Thomas Carmichael	Chairman of the Board
Ms. Man Jin Callentonni	Chief Executive Officer
Mr. Alexander Paul Fairlough	Chief Financial Officer

Header row

Apply It

29-d1

Edit and Proofread

1. In a new document, key the 10 sentences; tap ENTER after each sentence.
2. Proofread and correct errors.
3. Use proofing tools as needed.
4. Save and close. (*29-d1*)

TIP

Review proofreaders' marks in Lesson 23, page 1-60.

Do you assess you writing skills as average, great, or mediocre?

You should also ask your instructor about your writing skills.

Your instructor will know how to greatly improve your writing skills.

Do you always edit and proofread carefully things that you write?

few people who donot bother to edit there work are good writers.

Learning to edit effective may be just as important as writing well.

Another question to ask is: how important are writing skills?

Good writing skills are needed to be successful in most careers.

You can improve your writing skills by making it a priority.

Judge your writing only if you have proofread and edited your work.

Discover

Insert/Delete—To insert text, click in the document at the point you wish to insert text and key the text.

To delete text, select the text and tap DELETE.

29-d2

Compose and Edit

1. In a new document, compose a document by filling in the information indicated. Use the information in *29-d1* to help you with your composition. Use Undo and Redo as well as proofing tools as you compose and edit.
2. Edit and proofread your document carefully.
3. Recheck the document using proofing tools.
4. Save and close. (*29-d2*)

Improving my writing skills during my career preparation is important to me because (*complete the sentence*). Proofreading and editing skills are especially important because (*complete the sentence*).

(*In a new paragraph, complete the following introductory sentence using three numbered sentences.*) Three things that I can do to improve my writing skills are:

To create a table using the Table grid:

Insert/Tables/Table

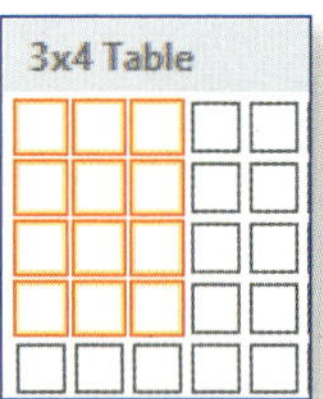

1. Click the insertion point at the position where the table is to be inserted. Follow the path to display the Insert Table menu.
2. Drag on the grid to select the number of columns and rows needed for the table.
3. Click the left mouse button to display the table in the document.
4. Click in the first cell (A1); key your text. The cell widens as you key to accommodate the length of your text. Tap TAB to move to the next cell, and then key the text. Continue to tap TAB and key until all text has been keyed.

MOVE WITHIN A TABLE

The insertion point displays in cell A1 when a table is created. Tap TAB to move to the next cell, or simply use the mouse to click in a cell. Refer to the table below as you learn to key text in a table.

Press or Tap	Movement
TAB	To move to the next cell. If the insertion point is in the last cell, tapping TAB will add a new row.
SHIFT + TAB	To move to the previous cell.
ENTER	To increase the height of the row. If you tap ENTER by mistake, tap BACKSPACE to delete the line.

DRILL 1 CREATE TABLE USING THE TABLE GRID

1. Create a three-column, four-row table using the table grid. Turn on Show/Hide.
2. The insertion point is in cell A1. Press TAB to move to cell B1. Press TAB to move to cell C1.
3. Tap ENTER. Notice the increase in the row height. Delete the ¶ symbol by tapping the BACKSPACE key.
4. Position the mouse pointer on the table to display the Table Move handle and the Sizing handle. Notice the markers at the end of each cell and each row.
5. Drag the Table Move handle down the page. This moves the table. Drag the handle back to the original position.
6. Click in the last cell (C4). Tap TAB to insert an additional row at the bottom of the table.
7. Save and close. (*38-drill1*)

Lesson 30 Clipboard Commands and Center Page

New Commands

- Page Orientation
- Clipboard
- Cut
- Paste
- Format Painter
- Center Page

Warmup *Lesson 30a Warmup*

lesson 30a warmup

Skill Building

30b Improve Techniques

1. Key each line once; concentrate on using good keying techniques.
2. Repeat the drill if time permits.

direct reach words, phrases, and sentences

1 hung deck jump cent slope decide hunt serve polo brave cedar pump

2 no way | in tune | many times | jump in | funny times | gold plated | in sync

3 June and Cecil browsed in craft shops and found many funny gifts.

adjacent reach words, phrases, and sentences

4 were pop safe sad quick column tree drew opinion excite guy point

5 we are | boil over | are we | few rewards | short trek | where are we going

6 Bert said he tries to shop where we can buy gas, oil, and treats.

New Commands

ORIENTATION

Layout/Page Setup/Orientation

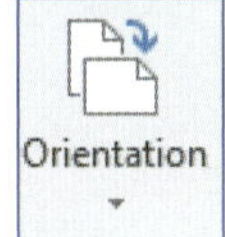

Orientation provides a choice of Portrait (8½" × 11") or Landscape (11" × 8½").

1. Click Orientation to display options.
2. Select either Portrait or Landscape.

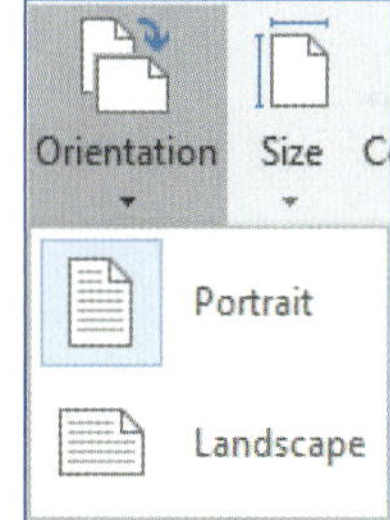

DRILL 1 ORIENTATION

1. Open *28-d2*.
2. Click Orientation and select Landscape.
3. Key **30-drill1** below the last line and align right.
4. Save and close. (*30-drill1*)

Communicating Today ▶ Clipboard Commands: Editing Reminder

Cut, copy, and paste are excellent editing tools; however, they can create editing challenges. Always check to determine if the addition or deletion of text had any effect on surrounding paragraphs or on the whole document. Read the document carefully to ensure that necessary information is included. Check the flow of information to ensure that the transition between paragraphs is smooth. Also ensure that the new information does not duplicate or conflict with existing content.

New Commands

38c

TABLE OVERVIEW

The Table commands make it easy to present data and graphics in a *Word* document. A table helps you easily align columns and rows of text and numbers.

Table: Columns and rows of data—either alphabetic, numeric, or both.

Column: Vertical list of information labeled alphabetically from left to right.

Row: Horizontal list of information labeled numerically from top to bottom.

Cell: An intersection of a column and a row. Each cell has its own address consisting of the column letter and the row number (cell A1).

The table displays with end-of-cell and end-of-row markers. These markers are useful when editing tables. Place the mouse pointer on the table to see the Table Move handle in the upper-left corner of the table. Drag the Table Move handle to move the table to a different location in the document. Use the Sizing handle at the lower-right corner of the table to make the table larger or smaller.

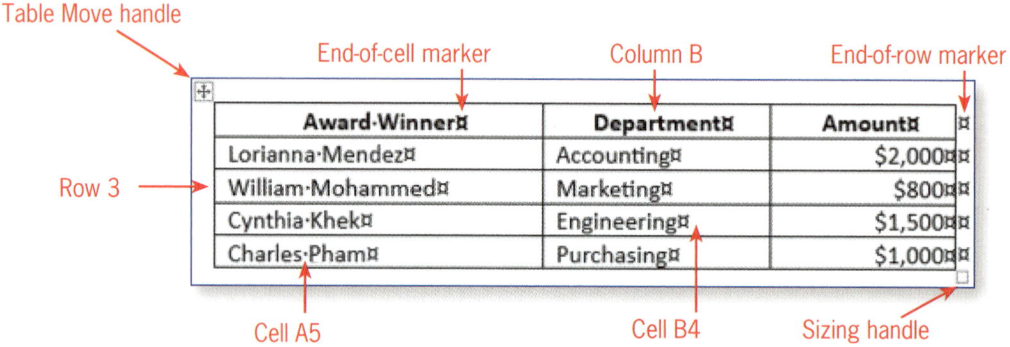

Award·Winner¤	Department¤	Amount¤
Lorianna·Mendez¤	Accounting¤	$2,000¤
William·Mohammed¤	Marketing¤	$800¤
Cynthia·Khek¤	Engineering¤	$1,500¤
Charles·Pham¤	Purchasing¤	$1,000¤

USE THE TABLE GRID

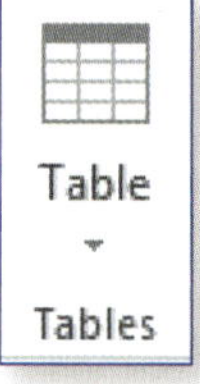

Tables are inserted into existing documents or new documents. Begin creating a table by locating the Tables group on the Insert tab. The Table button contains options for creating various types of tables; you will use two of the options in this module.

Tables are created by using the grid or the Insert Table command. Click the Table button to display the Insert Table menu, which provides several methods for creating tables. The table grid ❶ is often used to create tables with a few columns and rows. Larger tables can be created by using the Insert Table command ❷.

Insert Table
❶
Insert Table... ❷
Draw Table
Convert Text to Table...
Excel Spreadsheet
Quick Tables

New Commands

CLIPBOARD GROUP

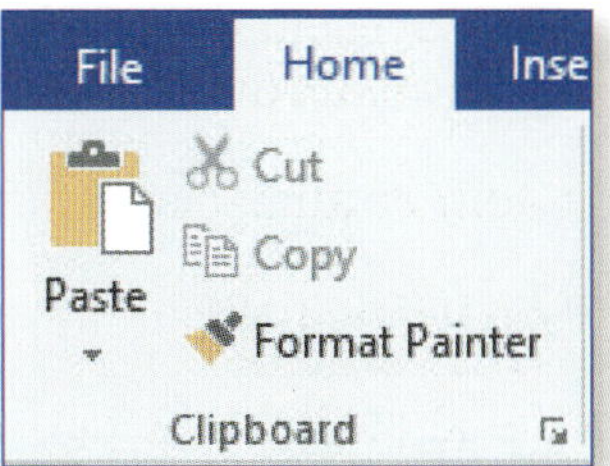

The commands in the Clipboard group, located on the Home tab, enable you to store text or graphics temporarily until you need them.

Cut—removes the selected text from its current location and saves it on the Clipboard.

Paste—positions text that was cut or copied in another location.

Copy—makes a copy of the selected text.

Format Painter—copies formatting from one place to another.

Clipboard pane—displays up to 24 items cut or copied to the Clipboard. The Clipboard pane is opened by clicking the Dialog Box Launcher (the small arrow in the lower-right corner of the Clipboard group).

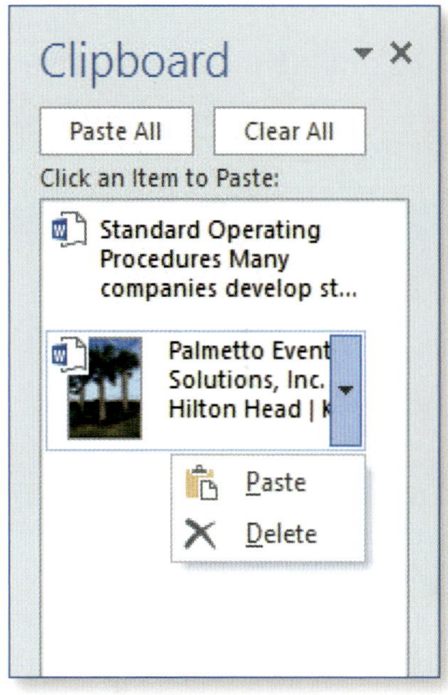

CUT, COPY, AND PASTE

Home/Clipboard/Cut, Copy, or Paste

1. Select the text or graphics to be cut or copied.
2. To remove the text or graphics, click Cut; to copy the text or graphics, click Copy.
3. To paste the text or graphics, position the insertion point in the desired location and click Paste.

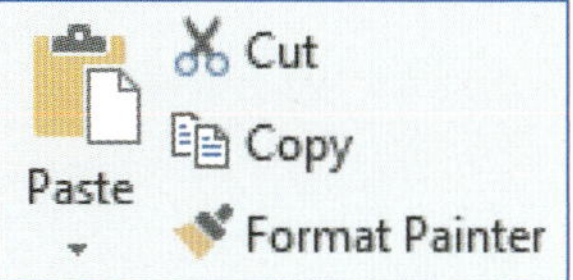

To use the following Clipboard shortcuts, select the text and then apply the shortcut:

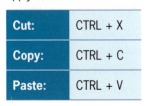

Cut:	CTRL + X
Copy:	CTRL + C
Paste:	CTRL + V

MODULE 5

Tables

LEARNING OUTCOMES

- Create tables.
- Change table structure.
- Format tables.
- Create tables within documents.
- Build keying speed and accuracy.

Lesson 38 Create Tables

New Commands

- Table Grid
- Insert Table

Warmup *Lesson 38a Warmup*

lesson 38a warmup

Skill Building

38b Timed Writing

1. Key two 3' timings on all paragraphs; work for control.

A ALL LETTERS

gwam 3'

Your perception of yourself has a strong impact on how others 4
perceive you. The more confidence you have, the more likely it is 8
you will succeed. Having confidence in yourself and your abilities 13
helps you when you are making a difficult decision or adapting 17
to a new situation. A great number of factors that affect self- 21
confidence are beyond your control, but there are many things 25
that you can do to build confidence. 28

People with confidence are just full of energy and have established 32
goals; they have places to go, people to see, and important work 36
to do. Confident people make a positive impression on others and 41
empower others. They stand up straight, walk quickly, hold their 45
head up high, and make eye contact. They present themselves well by 49
having a good personal appearance and are cognizant of the new styles. 54

Educating yourself and being prepared are some of the keys to 58
being a confident person. If you are asked to give a speech, for 62
example, research the topic ahead of time. Use the research as 67
supporting evidence in your speech. Finally, practice your speech 71
over and over to make it a polished presentation. So prepare and 75
you will feel more comfortable and confident. 78

3' | 1 | 2 | 3 | 4 |

Paste Options

Paste options determine how the text will look once it is inserted at the target location. Paste options are accessed in two ways: the drop-down arrow at the bottom of the Paste button or the Paste Options button that displays when text is pasted.

To apply options from the Paste button:

1. Click the drop-down arrow on the Paste button to display the paste options.

1. Use Destination Theme
2. Keep Source Formatting
3. Merge Formatting
4. Keep Text Only

2. Click the desired option.

TIP

The Keep Text Only option does not display when a graphic or object is pasted.

To apply options from the Paste Options button:

1. When the Paste command is clicked to paste text, the Paste Options button displays at the end of the pasted text.
2. Click the drop-down arrow to display the options, and select the desired option.

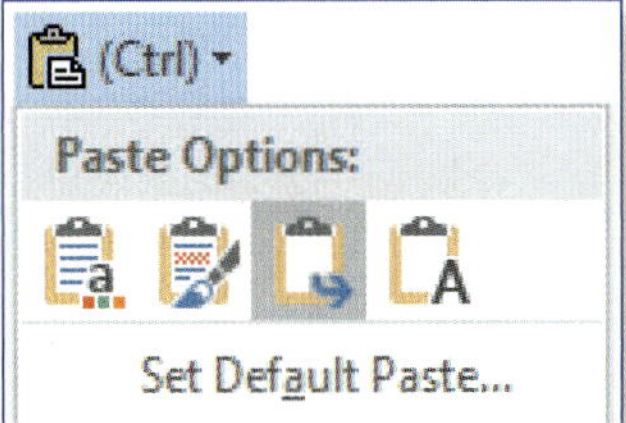

Note that the results occur whether you use the Paste button drop list options or those from the Paste Options button.

DRILL 2 CUT, COPY, AND PASTE

1. In a new document, key only the first two sentences below.
2. Select *carefully* in the first sentence, cut it, and paste it after *packing*. Use the Merge Formatting option.
3. Select *enclosed* in the second sentence; cut and paste it before *diagram*. Use the Keep Text Only option.
4. Copy the second sentence. Paste it below the second sentence and then key the additional text shown in the third sentence below. Use the Keep Source Formatting option.
5. Use Show/Hide and delete paragraph symbols at the end of the document if any exist.
6. Save and close. (*30-drill2*)

Please try to carefully remove the packing before taking the computer out of the box.

The diagram enclosed provides step-by-step instructions for assembling the computer.

The enclosed diagram provides step-by-step instructions for assembling the computer. A Help number to call for assistance is provided on the diagram.

37-d3

Modified Block Letter

1. In a new document, key the following letter in the modified block format with mixed punctuation. Insert the current date. Remove extra spacing as necessary.
2. Supply the correct salutation, a complimentary closing, your reference initials, and an enclosure notation.
3. Create an envelope and add it to the letter.
4. Preview for letter placement, save, and close. (*37-d3*)

Ms. Mukta Bhakta
9845 Buckingham Road
Annapolis, MD 21403-0314

Thank you for your recent inquiry about our wireless pet fence. The Hilton Pet Fence was developed to assist many pet owners like you who desire the safety of their pets without the barrier of a traditional fence.

Hilton Pet Fence also provides a customer support service to assist you in training your pet and a technical support team for providing technical assistance. For additional information, please call:

Customer and Technical Support
Telephone: 410.555.0112
9:00 a.m.-5:30 p.m. EST, Monday-Friday

Please look over the enclosed brochure. I will call you within the next two weeks to discuss any additional questions you may have.

Alexander Zampich | Marketing Manager

37-d4

Memo

1. In a new document, key the following memo in correct format.
2. Save and close. (*37-d4*)

TO: All Sunwood Employees

FROM: Julie Patel, Human Resources Director

DATE: Current date

SUBJECT: Eric Kershaw Hospitalized

We were notified by Eric Kershaw's family that he was admitted into the hospital this past weekend. They expect that he will be hospitalized for another ten days. Visits and phone calls are limited, but cards and notes are welcome.

A plant is being sent to Eric from the Sunwood staff. Stop by my office before Wednesday if you wish to sign the card. If you would like to send your own "Get Well Wishes" to Eric, send them to Eric Kershaw, County General Hospital, Room 401, P.O. Box 13947, Atlanta, GA 38209-4751.

FORMAT PAINTER

Format Painter copies a format from one paragraph to another or to multiple paragraphs.

TIP

1. To copy both text and paragraph formats, select the paragraph including the paragraph marker.
2. Apply to the text you want to format.

To copy a paragraph format to a single paragraph:

Home/Clipboard/Format Painter

1. Click in the paragraph that has the desired format.
2. Click the Format Painter.
3. Drag Format Painter across the paragraph to copy the desired format.

To copy a paragraph format to multiple paragraphs:

1. Click in the paragraph that has the desired format.
2. Double-click the Format Painter to keep it turned on.
3. Drag Format Painter across the paragraphs to copy the desired format.
4. Click Format Painter to turn it off or tap ESC.

DRILL 3 FORMAT PAINTER

Home/Paragraph/Show/Hide

1. In a new document, turn on Show/Hide, tap ENTER three times, and key the document below. Be sure to read the tip below.
2. Apply 14-point Arial font and bold to the title, **HOW MUCH IS TOO MUCH?**, and center it.
3. Use the Format Painter to copy the title format to the subtitle directly below the title.
4. Format the paragraph below the subtitle using 12-point Times New Roman font, and justify.
5. Double-click Format Painter to copy the same format to the last two paragraphs.
6. Save and close. (*30-drill3*)

TIP

When you key two hyphens with no spaces before or after, *Word* automatically converts them to an em dash.

HOW MUCH IS TOO MUCH?

Executive Compensation—A Hot Topic!

Many people question the huge salaries paid to top executives. Employees earning less than $50,000 a year do not understand how their company can pay one person millions of dollars each year. The gap between executive pay and employee pay creates problems.

Shareholders clearly want to reward and retain executives who increase shareholder value, but they expect pay to be linked to performance. In many cases, executive compensation has increased at the same time that performance has decreased significantly.

Media coverage about mega-bonuses has caused an outrage among investors. In response, the SEC now requires public companies to disclose the amount and source of all compensation paid to their top executives. This information is readily available to the public and to employees.

Lesson 37 Assessment Modules 3 and 4

Warmup *Lesson 37a Warmup*

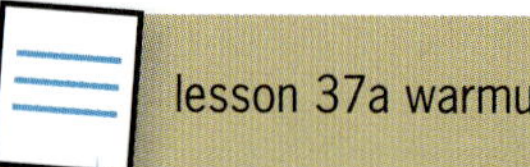

Apply It

37-d1

Announcement

1. In a new document, key the title and paragraph first. For the title, center and apply Calibri Light 72-point font, and apply Fill - Black, Text 1, Shadow text effect.
2. Format the remainder of the text; apply Calibri Light 36-point font and bold.
3. Center the page vertically.
4. Save and close. (*37-d1*)

Center Page

Layout/Page Setup dialog box launcher/Layout tab/ Vertical alignment

Room Change Notice

All classes and laboratories held in Room 250 of Westbrook Hall have been moved to Room 102 of Eastbrook Hall. This change will be in effect from October 10 until October 25.

37-d2

Block Letter

1. In a new document, key the letter below in the block letter style with open punctuation. Add an appropriate salutation. Send a copy of the letter to **Olivia Cavenaugh.**
2. Add an envelope to the document.
3. Save and close. (*37-d2*)

Current date | Mr. John Long, Manager | Durrington Electronics Store | 9822 Trevor Avenue | Anaheim, CA 92805-5885

With your letter came our turn to be perplexed, and we apologize. When we had our refund coupons printed, we had just completed a total redesign program for our product boxes. We had detachable logos put on the outside of the boxes, which could be peeled off and placed on a coupon.

We had not anticipated that our distributors would use back inventories with our promotion. The e-book readers you sold were not packaged in our new boxes; therefore, there were no logos on them.

We are sorry you or your customers were inconvenienced. In the future, simply ask your customers to send us their sales slips, and we will honor them with refunds until your supply of older e-book readers is depleted.

Sincerely | Cynthia Wertz | Sales and Promotions Department | xx

CENTER PAGE

The Center Page command centers a document vertically on the page. Should extra hard returns (¶) appear at the beginning or end of a document, these blank lines are also considered to be part of the document. Therefore, it is important to turn on Show/Hide and delete extra hard returns at the beginning and end of the document before centering a page.

To center a page vertically:

Layout/Page Setup/Dialog Box Launcher

1. Position the insertion point on the page to be centered.
2. Turn on Show/Hide and remove any extra hard returns.
3. Display the Page Setup dialog box.
4. Click the Layout tab.
5. Click the Vertical alignment drop-down arrow and select Center.

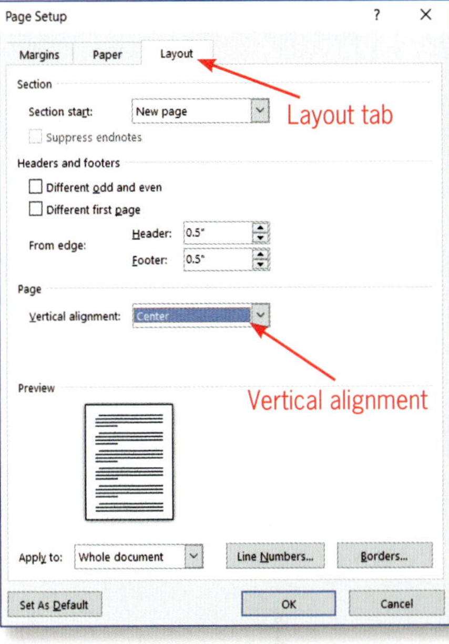

DRILL 4 CENTER PAGE

1. Open *30-drill3* and remove the three hard returns at the top of the page.
2. After the last line, key **30-drill4** and right-align it.
3. Center the page.
4. Save and close. (*30-drill4*)

Communication

1. Review the "Proofreading" section of Appendix C.
2. Proofread each sentence on the right and then key the sentence, correcting the error in it. Do not key the number.
3. Save and close. (*30d*)

PROOFREADING

1. The only way to proofread numbers effectively is too compare the keyed copy to the original source.
2. Concentration is an important proofreading skill, especially it you proofread on screen.
3. May people skip over the small words when they proofread; yet the small words often contain errors.
4. They sole 15 baskets at $30 each for a total of $450. Always check the math when you proofread.
5. Names are often spelled in different ways; there fore, you must verify the spelling to ensure that you use the correct version.
6. Reading copy on a word-bye-word basis is necessary to locate all errors.
7. Checking for words that my have been left out is also important.
8. Of course, you should also check to make sure the content in correct.

36-d3

Letter

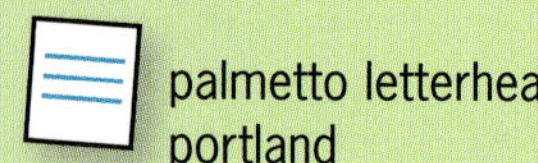

palmetto letterhead
portland

1. Key the letter below in 11-point Calibri font; do not create an envelope as it will be attached to an email.
2. Send a copy to Garrett Russell, President (of Palmetto Event Solutions, Inc.).
3. Save and close. (*36-d3*)

Mr. Jacob Burch | Tri-City Partnership | 760 Rockdale Street | Portland, OR 97204-0760 | Dear Mr. Burch

We are pleased to have been chosen as your event planner for the upcoming City Center Centennial Gala. Planning for this event is progressing as projected, and listed below are major activities at this point:

- Neil Ferguson with Ferguson Caterers has agreed to cater the food for the event. Ten caterers submitted bids, and five finalists were interviewed. Ferguson Caterers was selected based on five criteria deemed essential for this prestigious event. His creative menu complementing the farm-to-table philosophy and his budget projection were very impressive in the final decision.
- Bids have been solicited from 12 local florists. We are expecting to make this selection in two weeks.
- The entertainment committee is busy scouting available talent and will report their top three choices to me on Friday.

An initial meeting with Neil Ferguson of Ferguson Caterers, Jean Blake, convention center manager, and Tyler Crockett, account associate, is scheduled for September 23, at 10 a.m. at the convention center offices. You are invited to attend this meeting to meet these key players and to tour the venue. Please let me know if your schedule permits you to attend.

36-d4

Compose Email

1. Compose an email to your instructor, who is posing as Jennifer Anderson. You have been asked to draft an email that Ms. Anderson will send to the nine caterers who were not selected for the event. Key **Draft of Email to Caterers Not Selected for the City Center Centennial Gala** as the subject line.
2. The first paragraph should tell Ms. Anderson that the draft of the email to the nine caterers not selected for the event follows in the email.
3. The remaining paragraphs should be the draft email to the nine caterers. First, thank the caterers for submitting a bid and let them know that the submissions were very competitive. Using a kind tone, state that the bid was not chosen. In a new paragraph, build goodwill by sharing that other events are scheduled in the coming months and encourage the caterer to submit future bids. End with how important excellent caterers are to the success of Palmetto Event Solutions.
4. Save and close. (*36-d4*)

Apply It

30-d1

Invitation

1. In a new document, key the text shown below. Apply Lucida Calligraphy 14-point font. Center all lines except the last one, which should be left-aligned. Decrease the font size on the last line to 11 point. Replace *201-* with the current year.
2. Apply 3.0 line spacing and Landscape Orientation.
3. Center the page. Verify the page is centered.
4. Save and close. (*30-d1*)

You are cordially invited to attend a reception
Honoring Dr. Fritz H. Schmohe
Honorary Degree Recipient
September 28, 201- at 7:30 in the evening
Koger International Center
Black Tie Optional
RSVP by September 20, 803-555-0174

30-d2

Heading, Indent, Format Painter

1. In a new document, tap ENTER three times, and then key the document below.
2. Apply Verdana 16-point font and bold to the title, *Weekly Report*, and center it.
3. Use the Format Painter to copy the title format to the date shown below the title.
4. In the first sentence, cut *with reporters* and paste it after *spoke*. The sentence should read: *The head football coach spoke with reporters at his weekly news conference.*
5. Apply Verdana 12-point font to the first paragraph below the date. Justify the text.
6. Use Format Painter to copy the first paragraph's format to the last two paragraphs.
7. Save and close. (*30-d2*)

WEEKLY REPORT

June 20, 201-

The head football coach spoke at his weekly news conference with reporters. He was asked about the summer workout program and seemed to be very frustrated with some of his student-athletes.

The coach pointed out that summer workouts are voluntary programs, and it is against the rules to require student-athletes to participate. However, the workouts are a good way to judge the commitment level of your players. He indicated that some of our players are very committed and are very likely to get playing time. Others are lazy, and it is doubtful they will be ready to play when the season begins.

In response to a reporter's question, he indicated only about a dozen of the 95 scholarship players did not show up regularly. The goal of the program is to improve conditioning and lessen the likelihood of injuries.

36-d1

Memo

palmetto memo

1. Prepare the following memo to Susan Walker, Executive Chef. Key the subject line **Menu for City Center Centennial Gala Due Tomorrow**.
2. Save and close. (*36-d1*)

Please send the menu for the City Center Centennial Gala by close of day tomorrow. As always, include all details required for caterers submitting bids.

Bids to the top ten caterers that you recommended will be mailed on Monday with a response required in ten days. You will be called upon to evaluate the bids.

Thank you for your excellent work on the catering needs of this project.

36-d2

Letter

palmetto letterhead
portland

1. Key the letter below. Create an envelope and add to the letter.
2. Key the writer's name and title on separate lines.
3. Save and close. (*36-d2*)

Current date | Mr. Neil Ferguson | Ferguson Catering | 4535 Lakeview Street | Portland, OR 97204-4535 | Dear Mr. Ferguson

Congratulations! I am pleased to inform you that Ferguson Catering was selected as the caterer for the City Center Centennial Gala. Your bid for $20,000 was well within the budget set by our client, Tri-City Partnership. Your creative menu complements perfectly the farm-to-table philosophy of our organizers.

A contract outlining your responsibilities is enclosed for your review and signature. Please sign both copies and return to me by the end of next week.

I have tentatively scheduled our initial meeting for Thursday, September 23, at 10 a.m. at the convention center offices. Other participants include Jacob Burch of the Tri-City Partnership, Jean Blake, convention center manager, and Tyler Crockett, one of our event planners.

Please contact me if you have any questions about the contract or if we need to plan a different date and time for the meeting.

Lesson 31 Palmetto Event Solutions, Inc.

Learning Outcomes

- Apply keying, formatting, and word processing skills.
- Work independently with few specific instructions.

Warmup *Lesson 31a Warmup*

lesson 31a warmup

Skill Building

31b Timed Writing

Key two 3' timed writings.

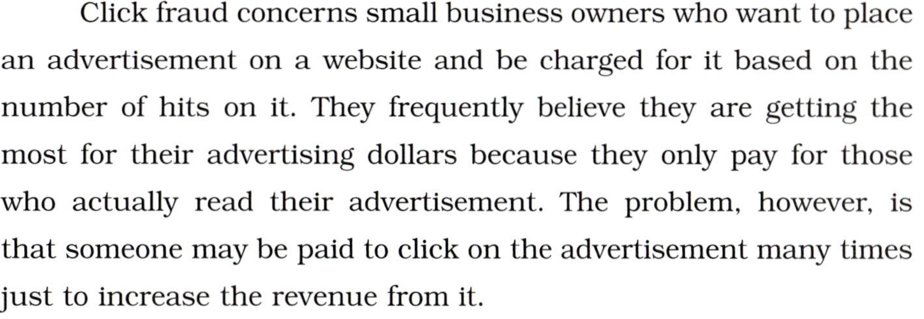

gwam 3'

Click fraud concerns small business owners who want to place 4 | 61
an advertisement on a website and be charged for it based on the 8 | 65
number of hits on it. They frequently believe they are getting the 13 | 70
most for their advertising dollars because they only pay for those 17 | 74
who actually read their advertisement. The problem, however, is 21 | 78
that someone may be paid to click on the advertisement many times 26 | 83
just to increase the revenue from it. 28 | 85

This problem is not a very easy one to resolve, but a few 32 | 89
things can be done to minimize the risk. Research shows that late- 37 | 94
night advertisements and advertisements in certain countries are 40 | 97
the most likely to be targeted. By choosing not to run 44 | 101
advertisements at those times and in those locations, you can lower 48 | 105
your risk. In addition, a number of very sophisticated and very 53 | 110
effective technical tools can be used to help detect click fraud. 57 | 114

3' | 1 | 2 | 3 | 4 |

Project Setting

Palmetto Event Solutions prefers to use periods rather than hyphens and parentheses to separate units in telephone numbers, which is the current trend in industry.

PALMETTO EVENT SOLUTIONS, INC.

At the end of each module in this book, you will work as an assistant preparing documents for various executives of Palmetto Event Solutions, an international company that specializes in managing corporate events for businesses and organizations. You will apply the formatting and word processing skills that you have developed in the module. The logo and contact information for the headquarters office are shown below.

Palmetto Event Solutions, Inc.

24 Palmetto Bay Road, Hilton Head, SC 29928-3220 | 864.555.0124

www.palmettoeventsolutions.com

Lesson 36 Palmetto Event Solutions, Inc.

Warmup *Lesson 36a Warmup*  lesson 36a warmup

Skill Building

36b Timed Writing

1. Key a 1' timing on each paragraph; work to increase speed.
2. Key a 3' timing on all paragraphs.

	gwam 1'	3'	
Have simple things such as saying please, may I help you, and	12	4	55
thank you gone out of style? We begin to wonder when we observe	25	8	59
front-line workers interact with customers today. Frequently their	38	13	64
careless attitudes indicate that the customer is a bother and not	51	17	68
important. But we realize there would be no business without the	64	21	72
customer. So what can be done to prove to consumers that they	76	25	76
really are king?	79	26	77
First, require that all workers train in good customer service.	13	31	81
They must recognize that their jobs exist for the customer.	24	35	85
Also, explain why they should talk to their supervisors about	37	39	89
any problem. You do not want workers to talk about lack of	48	42	93
breaks or schedules in front of customers. Remember customers	60	47	97
must always feel that they are king and should never be ignored.	73	51	102

Project Setting

Read the *About Us* section on page 2-37 to review information about Palmetto Event Solutions. Read the Standard Operating Procedures for the project carefully. You will not be reminded to do these steps. Refer to them as needed during the project.

In this project, you are assigned to the regional office of Palmetto Event Solutions, Inc., located in Portland, Oregon. You report to Jennifer Anderson, Senior Account Executive, who is charged with planning the City Center Centennial Gala, a major fundraising event sponsored by the Tri-City Partnership.

Standard operating procedures for the project:

1. Use block letter style with open punctuation and the Palmetto letterhead from the data files. Use appropriate opening and closing lines. Use the Date command to add the current date and begin the date at approximately 2".
2. Create envelopes for letters only when directed, as many letters are attached to an email.
3. The data files also contain a Palmetto memo form. Use appropriate subject lines if a subject line is not provided.
4. Add your reference initials, enclosure notations, and copy notations as appropriate.
5. Proofread carefully; save and close the document.

DATA FILES

Data files are extra documents you will need to complete an assignment. When a data file is required, an icon and filename are listed after the drill name or document name.

Download the data files from the student companion website to your hard drive or flash drive. You can find the student companion website by searching for this textbook on www.cengage.com. The files are organized by module.

31-d1

Standard Operating Procedures

Your first assignment is to work with Ellen Miller, the executive assistant to the president and CEO of Palmetto Event Solutions, Inc. Ellen has been working on revising the standard operating procedures (SOPs) that are used in the main office and the four regional offices. This document will be sent to the regional offices for review and will continually be updated.

Pay particular attention to the SOPs and the documents you prepare in this lesson because they will provide you with information that you will use each time you work with Palmetto Event Solutions. You will be directed to review these procedures periodically.

1. Tap ENTER three times, and key the document below; apply the following formats.
2. Center the heading, and apply Calibri Light 14-point heading bold font to both lines.
3. Change the bullets to numbering using Number Alignment Left style and periods.
4. Add **Procedures revised** and the current date using 00/00/0000 format after the last numbered item and apply Align Right format.
5. Save and close. (*31-d1*)

Standard Operating Procedures

For Document Formatting

These procedures are designed to enhance our image and to ensure that our brand is used consistently and appropriately.

- Use the letterhead and memo form provided digitally for all letters and memos. Letterhead is provided with addresses for each of the five office locations. Use block-letter format with open punctuation.
- Ensure that all documents are error-free. Use proofing tools and then edit, proofread, and correct errors. Verify dates and all numerical data against the source copy.
- Use email for brief communications, which do not contain information needed to work with clients or as a delivery vehicle. Any information that will become a part of our records should be prepared in memo, letter, table, or report format and attached to the email for distribution.
- Additional procedures may be provided by each of the regional offices.

Apply It

35-d1

Modified Block Letter

1. In a new document, key the model letter on page 2-56 in modified block format with mixed punctuation.
2. Set a left tab at 3.25". Tap ENTER three times to position the date at about 2". Do not key the letterhead.
3. Press SHIFT + ENTER to remove the added space in the letter address and between the writer's name and title. Use Show/Hide to view paragraph markers to confirm correct spacing between letter parts.
4. Add an envelope to the letter. Omit a return address.
5. Save and close. *(35-d1)*

35-d2

Modified Block Letter

1. In a new document, key the following letter in modified block letter style with mixed punctuation. Add all required letter parts. ❊ Remove the hyperlink in the second paragraph. **Note:** Remove the hyperlink if the document is not read on screen.
2. Add an envelope to the letter.
3. Save and close. (*35-d2*)

❊ Discover

Remove Hyperlink

Insert/Links/Hyperlink

Click the hyperlink and follow the path above. Then click Remove Link.

Shortcut: Right-click and click Remove Hyperlink.

Current date | Mr. Ricardo Delgado | Wildwood Sports Goods | 1525 South Ash Street | Gainesville, FL 32601-1525 | Dear Mr. Delgado:

Thank you for your generous donation of 100 golf caps for the players in our upcoming Carter Alverston Scholarship Golf Tournament. Your kind contribution will allow us to attract more players, thereby increasing funding for our scholarship program. Last year's tournament raised over $10,000 to assist our students in pursuing distant internships. This year's goal is to attract 100 players and 20 sponsors.

As one of our key sponsors, you are invited to participate with a team in the tournament. All participant fees are waived for sponsors. We also ask you to encourage your business colleagues and personal contacts to join us either as sponsors or players. Sponsor and player forms can be downloaded at www.sw-de.edu/tournament.pdf.

Once again, thank you for your generous support of this important scholarship program.

Sincerely, | Leslie Gregory | Director of Public Relations | xx

35-d3

Edit Letter

1. Open *35-d2* and edit to change to a block letter style with open punctuation. *Hint:* Select the entire letter (CTRL + A) and remove the tabs. If necessary, tap Backspace to return date and closing lines to the left margin.
2. In the company name in the letter address, change *Sports* to **Sporting**. Change the house address to **323 Second Street**.
3. Select the letter address, and create a new envelope. Click Change Document to accept the change on the previously created envelope.
4. Save and close. (*35-d3*)

 REVIEW

Clear Tabs

Home/Paragraph Settings dialog box launcher/Line and Page Breaks Tab/Tabs/Clear All

31-d2

About Us

Read the information below about Palmetto Event Solutions carefully. This information will become the first webpage of the About Us section of the company website. It will help you understand the type of company you will work for in each module.

1. Tap ENTER three times and key the document as shown.
2. Change the case of the title to uppercase, apply 18-point bold Verdana font, and center.
3. Select paragraph 1; apply double-spacing (2.0), Verdana 12 point. Indent the first line of the first paragraph as recommended by the web developer for draft copy.
4. Then use Format Painter to copy the formats to the remaining paragraphs.
5. Save and close. (*31-d2*)

About Us

Palmetto Event Solutions was founded by Mrs. Roberta Russell in 1992 in Hilton Head, South Carolina. The initial emphasis was on catered dinners, weddings, and other social events. Many corporate executives attended impressive functions managed by Mrs. Russell and requested her services for corporate events. By 2000, corporate events represented more than 75 percent of the business. Mrs. Russell retired, and her son Garrett Russell became president and CEO.

Many events we managed were corporate reward trips, trade shows, and professional meetings in various locations. Our management team determined that clients could be served better if we focused on corporate events and established offices in other regions of the United States and Canada. In 2002, four regional offices were established in the Midwest, Northwest, Canada, and Southwest to complement the Hilton Head office.

Today, our company has more than quadrupled its size and has established key partnerships with service providers in all regions who can provide full services for virtually any type of corporate event requested.

31-d3

Compose and Format an Invitation

1. Ellen Miller asked you to compose, edit, and format a draft of an invitation. Review the instructions for *30-d1* on page 2-34. Use this same style and format for this invitation.
2. Use the notes below to compose the invitation. (Do not key these notes.) Remember to format the phone number with periods.
   - Ask clients to please join us for a tour of our new reception center, followed by a client appreciation reception.
   - The event will be on Friday, September 10, at 5:30 p.m. in the Palmetto Event Solutions Reception Center. Include an RSVP by September 6 and our telephone number. Tip: The number is contained in the contact information on page 2-35.
   - The attire for the event is business attire.
3. Save and close. (*31-d3*)

Tap ENTER three times (about 2").

E-Market Firm
10 East Rivercenter Boulevard
Covington, KY 41016-8765
Telephone: 513.555.0139

Set tab at 3.25" → January 14, 2018

Ms. Kathryn Vanderford
Professional Document Designs, Inc.
P.O. Box 3891
Weatherford, TX 76086-3891

} Press SHIFT + ENTER to remove extra space

Dear Ms. Vanderford: ← Mixed punctuation

Your inquiry concerning a comparison of the modified block letter format and the block letter format is one often answered by our document designers. The modified block format differs from block format in that the date, complimentary close, and the writer's name and title are keyed at the center point. For production efficiency, we recommend block paragraphs.

Although modified block format is an accepted letter style, we do recommend the block letter style. The block letter style is more efficient for a standard letter style, requires no additional settings by the user, and is attractive.

For additional formats, please refer to the enclosed report related to formatting with the latest version of *Word* and the *Model Documents Reference Guide*. Our designers are available at 666.555.0197 to assist you with your design needs.

Sincerely, ← Mixed punctuation

Jeremy Gillespie } Press SHIFT + ENTER
Communication Consultant ↓ 2

xx

Enclosures

Modified Block Letter with Mixed Punctuation

MODULE 4

Memos and Letters

LEARNING OUTCOMES

- Format memo.
- Format block and modified block business letters.
- Create envelopes.
- Edit letters.
- Build keyboarding skills.

Lesson 32 Memos and Email

New Commands

- Date/Time
- Vertical Page Position

Warmup *Lesson 32a Warmup*

lesson 32a warmup

Skill Building

32b Timed Writing

1. Key a 1' timing on each paragraph; work to increase speed.
2. Key a 3' timing on all paragraphs.

gwam 1' | 3'

Congratulations, you have just learned to key with very little 12 | 4
visual help and are moving quickly from one key to the next. As 25 | 8
you continue to build speed and become productive, it is always 38 | 13
important to continue keying with proper techniques. Because it 50 | 17
is easy to become lazy, take a quick check of correct techniques. 63 | 21

Sit up straight with both feet on the floor with back against the 13 | 25
chair. Drop hands to your side and allow your fingers to curve 25 | 30
naturally; maintain this curve as you key. If hands are in correct 39 | 34
position, you can balance a penny on your wrists. Keep your eyes 51 | 38
on the copy or screen, and key continuously without any breaks. 64 | 42
An excellent method to monitor progress is to record yourself for 77 | 47
several minutes. Evaluate your techniques carefully, and make 89 | 51
needed changes. 92 | 52

1' | 1 | 2 | 3 | 4 | 5 | 6 | 7 | 8 | 9 | 10 | 11 | 12
3' | 1 | 2 | 3 | 4

Document Design

35c

MODIFIED BLOCK LETTER

In the modified block format, the date line and the closing lines (complimentary close and writer's name and title) begin at the center point of the page. All other guidelines for the block letter style are applied to the modified block letter. Remember to remove the extra spacing between the letter address and other short lines. Review the model modified block letter on the next page.

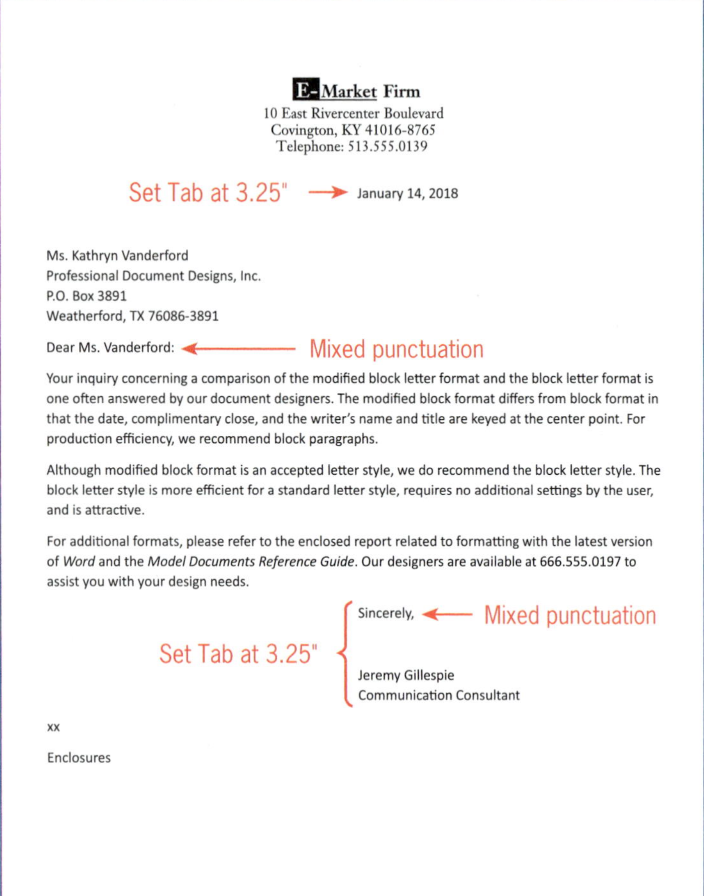

E-Market Firm
10 East Rivercenter Boulevard
Covington, KY 41016-8765
Telephone: 513.555.0139

January 14, 2018

Ms. Kathryn Vanderford
Professional Document Designs, Inc.
P.O. Box 3891
Weatherford, TX 76086-3891

Dear Ms. Vanderford:

Your inquiry concerning a comparison of the modified block letter format and the block letter format is one often answered by our document designers. The modified block format differs from block format in that the date, complimentary close, and the writer's name and title are keyed at the center point. For production efficiency, we recommend block paragraphs.

Although modified block format is an accepted letter style, we do recommend the block letter style. The block letter style is more efficient for a standard letter style, requires no additional settings by the user, and is attractive.

For additional formats, please refer to the enclosed report related to formatting with the latest version of *Word* and the *Model Documents Reference Guide*. Our designers are available at 666.555.0197 to assist you with your design needs.

Sincerely,

Jeremy Gillespie
Communication Consultant

xx

Enclosures

Dateline:

- Tap ENTER three times (about 2").
- Begin at least 0.5" below the letterhead.
- Set a left tab at 3.25". Determine the position of the tab by subtracting the side margin from the center of the paper.

4.25" Center of the paper
–1.00" Margin
3.25" Tab setting

Complimentary closing: Begin keying at 3.25".

Writer's name and title: Begin keying at 3.25".

MIXED PUNCTUATION

Although most letters are formatted with open punctuation, some businesses prefer mixed punctuation. To format a letter using mixed punctuation, key a colon after the salutation and a comma after the complimentary close.

Dear Mr. Hathorn:

Sincerely,

New Commands

32c

DATE AND TIME

Date & Time The Date and Time command allows the selection of the desired format. Often the month/day/year format is used for letters, and the numerical format (00/00/0000) for documents with statistics.

To insert the date and/or time:

Insert/Text/Date and Time

1. Click at the point the date is to be inserted.
2. Select the desired date format 1 (October 6, 2015) or time format 2 (18:16).
3. Leave Update automatically 3 blank unless you want the date/time to update each time the document is opened. Click OK.

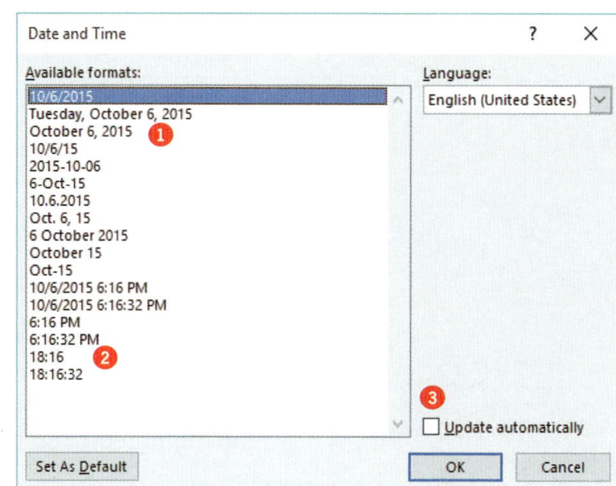

Discover

Automatic Current Date

Key the first four characters of the current month and tap ENTER to accept the date. Tap Space Bar to display the remainder of the current date.

VERTICAL PAGE POSITION

Although the default top margin is 1", not all documents are attractive beginning at the top of the page. To move the insertion point lower on the page, simply tap ENTER.

The status line is located at the bottom left of the screen and displays important information about the page, including the vertical page position when turned on.

To display the vertical page position on the status line:

1. Right-click on the status line located at the bottom of the screen.
2. Click Vertical Page Position. The vertical page position now displays at the bottom left of the status line, showing the default top margin at 1".

Page 1 of 1 At: 1"

TIP

Remember to proofread and preview each document as standard operating procedure (SOP). You will not be reminded to do this.

DRILL 1 DATE AND TIME

1. In a new document, display the vertical page position on the status line.
2. Tap ENTER three times to position the insertion point at about 2". Key the first four characters of the current date, e.g., Octo for October. Tap ENTER and then the Space Bar to display the current day. Tap ENTER to begin a new line.
3. Insert the date and time in the numerical format 10/6/2015 3:35 PM, and tap ENTER.
4. Save and close. (*32-drill1*)

Lesson 35 Modified Block Letter

New Commands • Tabs

Warmup *Lesson 35a Warmup* — lesson 35a warmup

New Commands

35b

TABS

Tabs are used to indent paragraphs and to align text vertically. The default tab stops are set every half inch. *Hint:* If the ruler is not displayed, go to View/Show and click Ruler.

To set a left tab:

1. Check the tab selector to be sure the left tab is selected.
2. Click the Horizontal Ruler where you want to set the left tab.

When a new tab stop has been set, all default tabs to the left of the newly set tab are automatically cleared. Therefore, if other tabs are needed, simply choose the desired tab alignment, and then click the Horizontal Ruler where the desired tab is to be set.

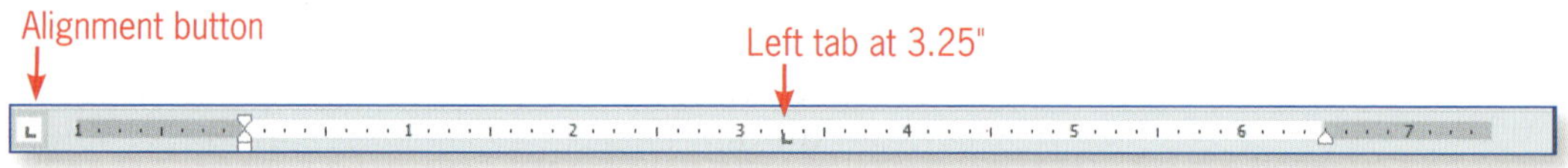

To move a tab:

Select all of the text that will be affected, and drag the tab to be moved to the new desired location. *Note:* If you do not select all of the text, only the tab that your cursor is on will be moved.

To clear a tab:

Select all of the text that will be affected and drag the tab off the Horizontal Ruler bar.

DRILL 1 SET TABS

1. In a new document, set a left tab at 3.25". Insert the current date at 3.25", and tap ENTER twice.
2. Set a left tab at 1". Key the following lines and tap ENTER once. Press SHIFT + ENTER to remove the added space between the items.

   Enclosures: Promissory Note
   Amortization Schedule

3. Set a left tab at 0.5". Key the following lines. Press SHIFT + ENTER to remove the added space between the lines. Be sure to undo automatic capitalization so the *c* in copy notation is not capitalized.

   c Ashley Nobles
   Ethan Vilella

4. Save and close. (*35-drill1*)

Document Design

32d

ELECTRONIC MAIL AND MEMOS

Informal communications shared among individuals in a company are prepared as emails, instant messages, text messages, or memos. In a business setting, correct grammar, spelling, capitalization, and professional tone are required in all messages to portray professionalism and to gain/maintain respect among supervisors and peers.

The memo is the most formal type of informal message and may be preferred when a somewhat formal communication with company employees is demanded, such as the announcement of a new policy or participation in a mandatory training program. Often this formal memo is attached to an email as a method of distribution to all employees. *Word*'s Share option allows the user to email the memo as a *Word* attachment or a PDF without even opening the email system.

An email is commonly used to convey casual internal messages that do not demand a more formal tone and presentation. Examples would include an email transmitting a memo or letter, providing the location and time of a meeting, or requesting routine information.

To format a memo:

1. Tap ENTER three times to position the first line of the heading at about 2".
2. Key the memo headings and format them in bold and uppercase. Tap TAB once or twice after each heading to align the information. Generally, courtesy titles (Mr., Ms., etc.) are not used; however, the receiver's name may include a title depending on rank in the company.
3. Single-space (1.08 default spacing) the body of the memo. Tap ENTER once after each paragraph.

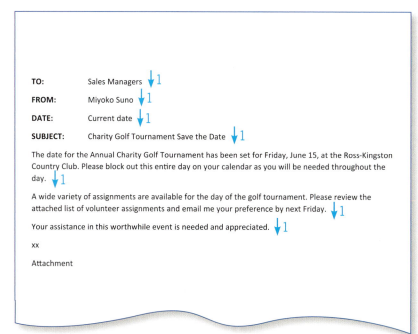

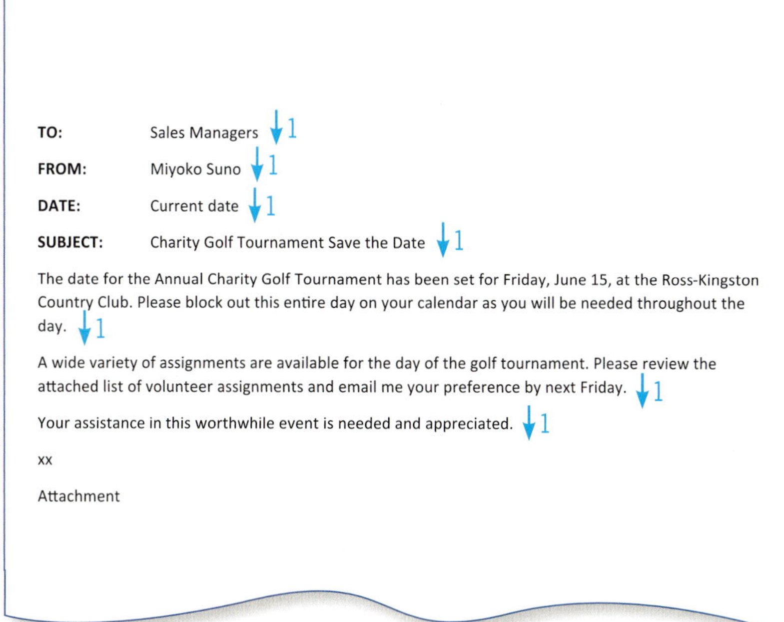
TO: Sales Managers ↓1

FROM: Miyoko Suno ↓1

DATE: Current date ↓1

SUBJECT: Charity Golf Tournament Save the Date ↓1

The date for the Annual Charity Golf Tournament has been set for Friday, June 15, at the Ross-Kingston Country Club. Please block out this entire day on your calendar as you will be needed throughout the day. ↓1

A wide variety of assignments are available for the day of the golf tournament. Please review the attached list of volunteer assignments and email me your preference by next Friday. ↓1

Your assistance in this worthwhile event is needed and appreciated. ↓1

xx

Attachment

4. Add reference initials one line below the body if the memo is keyed by someone other than the sender. Do not include initials when keying your own memo.
5. Items clipped or stapled to the hard-copy memo and electronic files attached to an email are noted as attachments. Items included in an envelope with a memo are noted as enclosures.

   Key enclosure or attachment notations one line below the reference initials.

Apply It

34-d1

Block Letter

1. In a new document, key the letter below in block style with open punctuation. Tap ENTER three times to begin the date at about 2". Press SHIFT + ENTER to remove the extra space in the letter address, signature line, and enclosures.
2. Add an envelope to the letter.
3. Save and close. (*34-d1*)

May 19, 2018 | Ms. Coralia Lopez | Chief Financial Officer | Midland Corporation | 1001 North Tenth Avenue | Chicago, IL 60290-1001 | Dear Ms. Lopez

Thank you for your continuing business with Henderson, Blakney, Hardin, Mayfield CPA Firm. We appreciate the long-term partnership between our organizations.

The audit for Midland Corporation is scheduled for September 1-5, 2018. Ken Smith and Jill Matthews, the on-site auditors, will arrive at 9 a.m. on September 1. They will meet with you for approximately one hour before beginning the audit. Please review the enclosed audit questionnaire prior to this meeting. Also, to ensure security of sensitive financial records, they will require a private office with Internet access.

Ms. Lopez, if you have questions concerning the audit, please call me at 312.555.0138.

Sincerely | John D. Henderson, Partner | xx | Enclosure | c Ms. Lynda Maxwell, President

34-d2

Edit Letter

1. Open *34-d1*. Make the following edits.
2. Change the ZIP Code to 60291-1001; update the envelope.
3. Change the dates of the audit to October 1–5; auditors will arrive on October 1.
4. Ken Smith will not be assigned to this audit. Change to Rory Jones.
5. Move the third sentence of the second paragraph to the end of the paragraph.
6. Send a copy also to Mr. Wendell Havard, Controller. Remember to press SHIFT + ENTER to remove the extra space between the names; tap TAB and key Mr. Havard's name.
7. Save and close. (*34-d2*)

34-d3

Envelope

1. In a new document, key an envelope to the following address and add to the document.
2. Save and close. (*34-d3*).

Mr. Jacob Gillespie
1783 West Rockhill Road
Bartlett, TN 38133-1783

To prepare an email:

1. Prepare the email header:

   To: Key the email address of the receiver accurately.

   Cc: Key the email address of individuals who are to receive a copy of the message.

   Bcc: Key the email address of individuals designated to receive a blind copy (meaning the recipient is not aware of the message being sent to the blind recipient/s).

   Subject: Key a specific subject line that is helpful to the busy recipient sorting through important email to read and act upon.

   Attachment: Follow the steps to attach any electronic files referred to in the body of the memo.

2. Prepare the email body:

   a. Single-space (SS) the body of an email and tap ENTER twice between paragraphs. Do not indent paragraphs.

   b. Do not add bold or italic or vary the fonts. Do not use uppercase letters for emphasis. Avoid using emoticons or email abbreviations in business email (e.g., ;- for wink or BTW for by the way).

   c. Write a clear, concise message about one topic. State the purpose in the first paragraph, and then provide the needed details. End with a courteous closing that states the required action, if any.

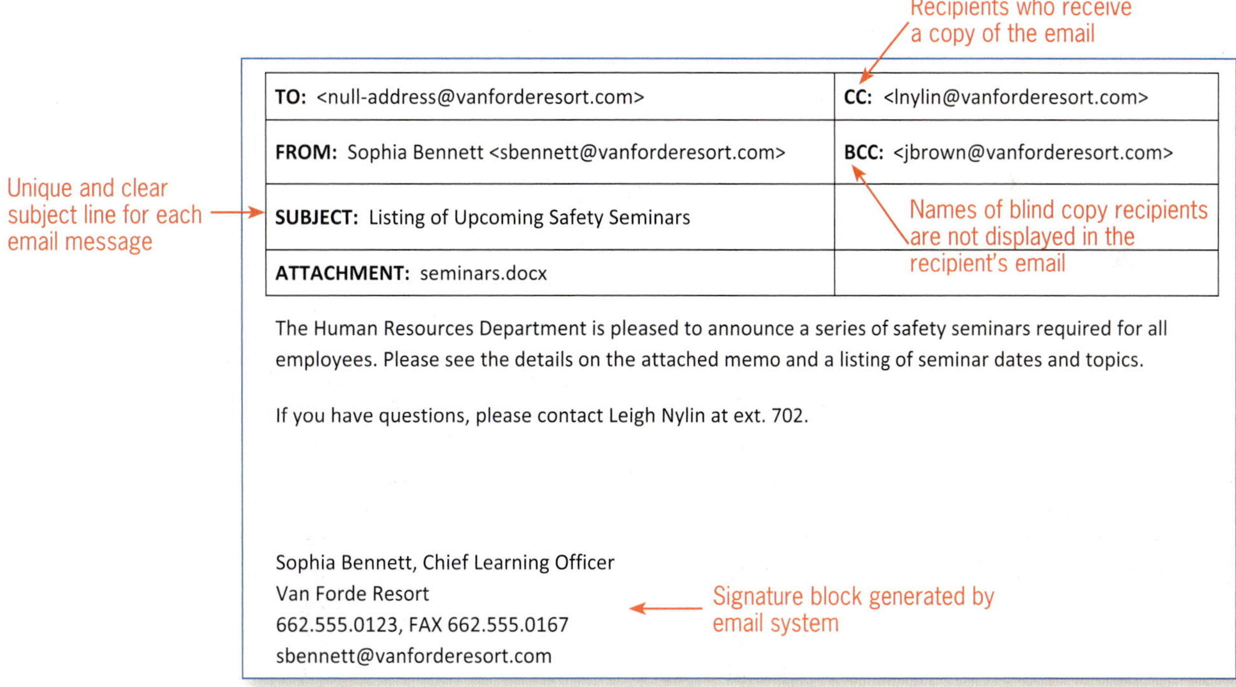

TO: <null-address@vanforderesort.com>	**CC:** <lnylin@vanforderesort.com>
FROM: Sophia Bennett <sbennett@vanforderesort.com>	**BCC:** <jbrown@vanforderesort.com>
SUBJECT: Listing of Upcoming Safety Seminars	
ATTACHMENT: seminars.docx	

The Human Resources Department is pleased to announce a series of safety seminars required for all employees. Please see the details on the attached memo and a listing of seminar dates and topics.

If you have questions, please contact Leigh Nylin at ext. 702.

Sophia Bennett, Chief Learning Officer
Van Forde Resort
662.555.0123, FAX 662.555.0167
sbennett@vanforderesort.com

Document Design

34e

ADDITIONAL LETTER PARTS

In Lesson 33, you learned the standard letter parts. Listed below are several optional letter parts.

Enclosure notation/Attachment notation: If an item is included with a letter, key an enclosure notation/attachment notation one blank line below the reference initials. If enclosures/attachments are itemized, tap TAB to align the enclosures at 1" using default tabs.

Left tab at 1"

Enclosures: Certificate of Completion
Receipt

Enclosures: 2

Copy notation: A copy notation (c) indicates that a copy of the document has been sent to the person(s) listed. Key the copy notation one line below the reference initials or enclosure notation (if used). Tap TAB to align the names. If necessary, click Undo Automatic Capitalization after keying the copy notation to lowercase the letter *c*.

Left tab at 0.5"

c Francine Milam
Janet Bevill

When two lines are keyed for either the enclosure notation or the copy notation, press SHIFT + ENTER to remove the extra space after the paragraph.

xx

Enclosures: Certificate of Completion
Receipt

c Francine Milam
Janet Bevill

Attachment: Commonly used when emailing a letter or memo that references other documents to be included in the mailing.

Enclosure: Used when mailing in an envelope a letter or memo that references other documents to be included in the mailing.

Communicating Today

Business Letters: Then and Now

The delivery of business letters has changed dramatically since the origin of the U.S. Post Office in 1775 and the Internet Protocol Suite (TCP/IP) introduced in 1982. Documents that once took two to three days or longer to deliver are now delivered instantaneously with a reply supplied in the same speed.

Reading a business letter on the computer screen has become the new normal. Default fonts designed for online reading and increased spacing in word processing software address these new approaches to accomplishing our work. Reading online also makes accessing links seamless. When the letter is read and action taken, the recipient can easily store the letter electronically, which also supports today's focus to protect the environment. However, the increased focus on speed of delivery can lead to challenges.

Do remember that sending letters quickly does not change the need for factual accuracy, completeness, appropriate format, correct spelling, proper grammar, and precise punctuation. Write clearly and proofread all documents carefully before sending them by any means of distribution. Your reputation is on the line.

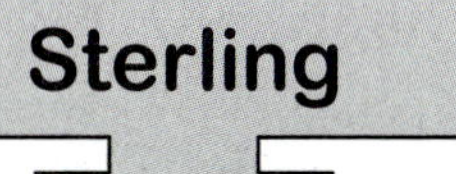

1195 Singing Cactus Avenue
Tucson, AZ 85701-0947

Tap ENTER 3 times (About 2")

TO: All Employees ↓ 1

FROM: Sophia Bennett, Human Resources Director ↓ 1

DATE: Current date ↓ 1

SUBJECT: Safety Seminars Offered for Certification ↓ 1

The Human Resource Department is pleased to announce a series of safety seminars for all employees. The purpose of the seminars is to provide safety knowledge and procedures included in the certification examination administered at the end of the seminar. ↓ 1

The seminars are offered in two formats to meet the needs of all employees. Face-to-face seminars are scheduled in room 310 on Wednesday afternoons from 1 to 5 p.m. and Thursday mornings from 8 a.m. until noon. Online seminars are also available which can be completed at times that meet your specific schedule.

Please meet with your supervisor to determine the seminars needed for your position. Thank you for your participation in these important seminars. ↓ 1

xx ← Student's first and last initials

Memo

New Commands

34d

ENVELOPES

The Envelopes command can insert the delivery address automatically if a letter is displayed. The default is a size 10 envelope (4⅛" by 9½"); other sizes are available by clicking the Options button on the Envelopes tab.

TIP

To create an envelope without a letter, follow the same steps, but key the address in the Delivery address box.

To generate an envelope:

Mailings/Create/Envelopes

1. Select the letter address and click Envelopes; the mailing address automatically displays in the Delivery address box.
2. Click the Return address Omit box if using business envelopes with a preprinted return address (assume you are).

   To include a return address, do not check the Omit box; click in the Return address box and key the return address.
3. Click Print to print the envelope or click Add to Document to add the envelope to the top of the document containing the letter.

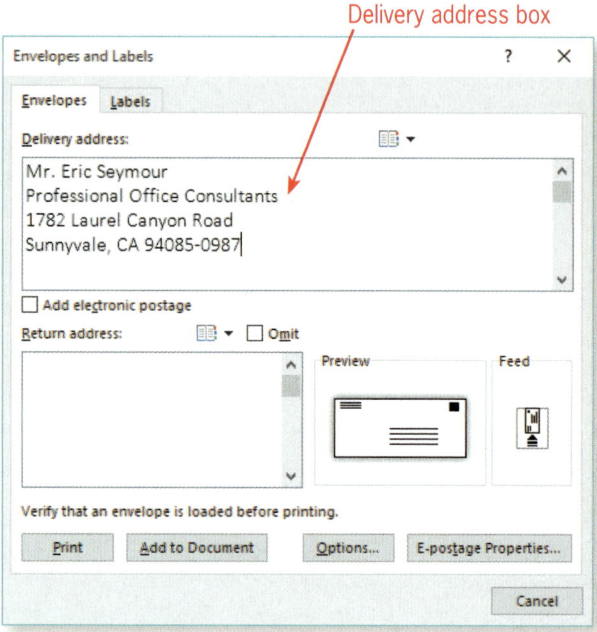

DRILL 1 CREATE ENVELOPE

1. Open *33-d1*. Select the letter address. Create an envelope. Omit the return address.
2. Add the envelope to the document.
3. Save and close. (*34-drill1*)

Note: Your instructor may have you print envelopes on plain paper.

DRILL 2 CREATE ENVELOPE

1. In a new document, go to the Envelopes and Labels dialog box without keying a letter address.
2. Key the following letter address in the Delivery address box.

   Mr. Andrew Callais
   993 North Carpenter Lane
   Shreveport, LA 71106-0993
3. Add the envelope to the document.
4. Save and close. (*34-drill2*)

Apply It

32-d1

Memo

Discover

1. In a new document, tap ENTER three times and key the memo illustrated on page 2-42. Do not key the memo letterhead. *Hint:* Select *TO:* and then apply bold; bold the colon. Remember to turn off bold and uppercase. Repeat for remaining heading items. Be sure to insert the date.
2. If the first letter of your reference initials is automatically capitalized, point to the initial until the AutoCorrect Options button appears. Click the button, then choose Undo Automatic Capitalization.
3. Save and close. (*32-d1*)

32-d2

Memo

1. In a new document, key the memo below.
2. Save and close. (*32-d2*)

TIP

Numbering

Home/Paragraph/Numbering

TO: Emily Welch, Brian McKenzie, Olivia von Staden

FROM: Michael Holcomb

DATE: July 18, 2018

SUBJECT: Video Conference Call Scheduled Friday, July 26

The final video conference call to select the contractor for the Keystone Community Project will be held on Friday, July 26, from 3:30 to 5:00 p.m. EST. To join the video conference, follow these steps:

1. Call 601.555.0168 and enter the passcode 8103622 when prompted.
2. Go to www.conferences.com/holcomb/PDS/ and join the meeting.

Please review the proposals carefully and be prepared to make a recommendation at the meeting. If you have questions about the proposals, please call me at 601.555.0193 or email me at mholcomb@svdco.com.

xx

32-d3

Compose Email

1. In a new document, compose an email to your instructor from you. Key **Email Etiquette** as the subject of the email. Send a copy to one of your classmates.
2. In the body of the email, share three specific email etiquette rules that are important but often abused. Number the three items. Refer to the discussion on email on page 2-41.
3. Save and close. (*32-d3*)

Lesson 34 Block Letter with Envelope

New Commands

- Envelopes

Warmup *Lesson 34a Warmup*

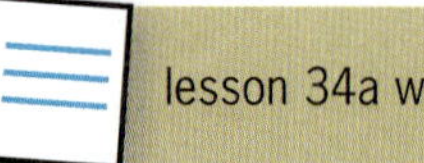

lesson 34a warmup

Skill Building

34b Timed Writing

1. Key a 1' timing on each paragraph; work to increase speed.
2. Key a 3' timing on all paragraphs.

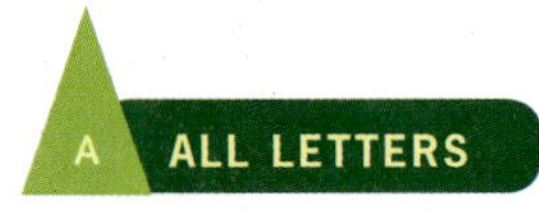

	gwam 1'	3'	
Many people are sometimes quite surprised to learn that either	12	4	56
lunch or dinner is included as part of a job interview. Most of	25	8	60
them think of this component of the interview as a friendly gesture	38	13	65
from the organization.	43	14	66
The meal is not provided to be thoughtful to the person	11	18	70
interviewing. The organization expects to use that function to	23	22	74
observe the social skills of the person and to determine if he	36	26	79
or she might be effective doing business in that type of setting.	49	31	83
What does this mean as you prepare for a job interview?	11	34	87
Spend time reading and practicing social etiquette just as you	23	38	91
would on how to answer questions or about what to wear. The time	36	43	95
committed to reading about and learning to apply excellent social	49	47	99
skills pays off during the interview and also after you accept	62	51	103
the job.	63	52	104

34c Improve Keystroking

1. Key each drill, concentrating on using good keying techniques.
2. Repeat the drill if time permits.
3. Save and close. (*34c*)

adjacent reach

1 The people were sad as the poor relish was opened and poured out.

2 Sophia moved west with her new silk dress and poor walking shoes.

direct reach

3 Freddy stated that hurricanes are much greater in number in June.

4 Many juniors decide to work free to add experience to the resume.

balanced hand

5 The eight ducks lay down at the end of right field for cozy naps.

6 Kala is to go to the formal town social with Henry and the girls.

Lesson 33 Block Letter

New Commands

- Remove Space after Paragraph

Warmup *Lesson 33a Warmup*

lesson 33a warmup

New Commands

33b

REMOVE SPACE AFTER PARAGRAPH

Word automatically adds extra white space after ENTER is tapped to make text easier to read and to save the user time in only tapping ENTER once between paragraphs.

To remove space after a paragraph when the extra space is not needed, press SHIFT + ENTER to begin a new line.

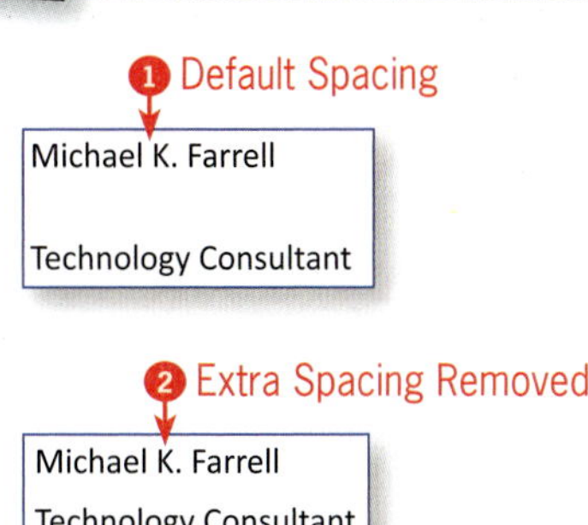

DRILL 1 REMOVE SPACE

1. In a new document, key the following letter address; press SHIFT + ENTER at the end of each line.

   Mr. Grayson T. Winston
   Winston & Smith Law Firm, LLC
   389 Main Street
   San Antonio, TX 78229-0389

2. Save and close. (*33-drill1*)

Communication

33c

1. Review the "Spelling Rules" section of Appendix C.
2. Key each sentence correcting the one planted spelling error.
3. Save and close. (*33c*)

SPELLING

1. Turkeyes are in the meat department.
2. The locker room for gentlemens is being remodeled.
3. Companys with more than 50 employees have different requirements.
4. Managers are asked to investigate reoccuring tardiness.
5. Only cash or checkes are accepted at the ice cream store.
6. Do you beleive the time is right for you to invest in higher risk investments?
7. Mr. Jones closes his letters with Yours truley or Sincerely yours.
8. The theives were apprehended, and the stolen property was returned.
9. Give the reciept to the accounting manager.
10. Are you refering to Purchase Order #2051?

33-d3

Block Letter

1. In a new document, key the following letter in block style with open punctuation. Begin the date at about 2". Remember to remove the extra space by using SHIFT + ENTER.
2. Save and close. (*33-d3*)

April 4, 2018 | Ms. Rose Shikamuru | 55 Lawrence Street | Topeka, KS 66607-6657 | Dear Ms. Shikamuru

Thank you for your recent inquiry about employment opportunities with our company. We are happy to inform you that Mr. Edward Ybarra, our recruiting representative, will be on your campus on April 23–25 to interview students who are interested in our company.

We suggest that you talk soon with your student placement office, as all appointments with Mr. Ybarra will be made through that office. Please bring with you the application questionnaire the office provides.

You will want to visit our website at www.skylermotors.com to find facts about our company mission and accomplishments as well as learn about the beautiful community in which we are located. We believe a close study of this information will convince you, as it has many others, that our company builds futures as well as small motors.

If there is any way we can help you, please email me at mbragg@skylermotors.com.

Sincerely | Margaret K. Bragg | Human Services Director | xx

WORKPLACE SUCCESS

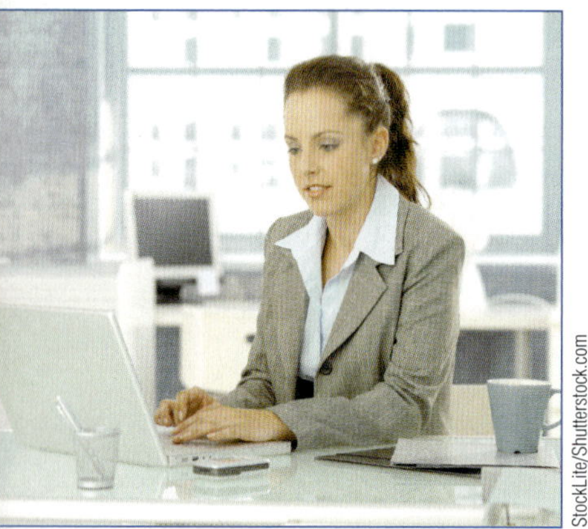

StockLite/Shutterstock.com

Organizational Skills

Well-organized employees accomplish daily tasks in a timely manner, avoid stress, and impress their employers and coworkers. Following simple daily time management practices reaps benefits and often even a promotion. How would you rate yourself on the following time management practices?

1. Set designated times to handle email, social media updates, and other routine tasks.
2. Use instant messaging to ensure understanding and to avoid multiple email threads.
3. Prioritize tasks to be done each day and the amount of time needed to complete each task. Assign tasks to a specific time on the calendar.
4. Break projects into smaller chunks to make less overwhelming.
5. Use checklists for detailed projects to ensure accuracy.
6. Use technology tools such as a digital notebook to help you become organized and keep you organized.

Document Design

33d

BUSINESS LETTERS

Business letters are used to communicate with persons outside of the business. Business letters carry two messages: the first is the tone and content; the second is the appearance of the document. Appearance is important because it creates the critical first impression. Stationery, use of standard letter parts, and placement should convey that the writer is intelligent, informed, and detail minded.

P P I Park Place International
300 Park Place
Atlanta, GA 30303-1142
404.555.0131 • 404.555.0132

April 9, 2018

Ms. Pamela FoxMeyer
Human Resources Director
Letter Beams, Inc.
2112 Smythe Road, North
Arlington, VA 22201-1201

Dear Ms. FoxMeyer

Mr. Terry Beckett, an employee of Letter Beams, Inc., from 2017-2018, has applied for a position with our company as a computer analyst. He has given us your name and his permission to ask about his work history with Letter Beams, Inc.

Therefore, will you please verify Terry's employment with you and respond as you desire about his performance with your organization? Thank you, Ms. FoxMeyer.

Sincerely

A. Alonzo Cruz
Human Resources Director

xx

Stationery

Letters should be printed on high-quality (about 24-pound) letterhead stationery. Standard size for letterhead is 8½" × 11". Envelopes should match the letterhead in quality and color.

P P I Park Place International
300 Park Place
Atlanta, GA 30303-1142
404.555.0131 • 404.555.0132

Ms. Pamela FoxMeyer
Human Resources Director
Letter Beams, Inc.
2112 Smythe Way, North
Arlington, VA 22201-1201

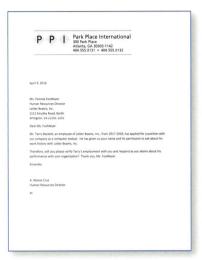

SALUTATIONS AND COMPLIMENTARY CLOSINGS

The salutation, or greeting, consists of the individual's personal title (*Mr., Ms.,* or *Mrs.*) or professional title (*Dr., Professor, Senator, Honorable*), and his or her last name. Do not use a first name unless you have a personal relationship. The salutation should agree in number with the addressee. If the letter is addressed to more than one person, the salutation is plural.

	Receiver	Salutation
To individuals	Dr. Alexander Gray	Dear Dr. Gray
	Dr. and Mrs. Thompson	Dear Dr. and Mrs. Thompson
To organizations	TMP Electronics, Inc.	Ladies and Gentlemen
Name unknown	Advertising Manager	Dear Advertising Manager

Choose a complimentary closing that reflects the relationship with the receiver. Use *Sincerely* to show a neutral relationship, *Cordially* for a friendly relationship, and *Respectfully* when requesting approval.

PROOFREAD AND FINALIZE A DOCUMENT

Apply these procedures when processing all documents:

1. Use Spelling and Grammar to check spelling when you have completed the document.
2. Proofread the document on screen to be sure that it makes sense.
3. Preview the document, and check the overall appearance.
4. Save the document and compare it to the source copy.
5. Revise, save, and print if necessary.

Apply It

33-d1

Block Letter

1. In a new document, tap ENTER three times to position the date at about 2". Key the model block letter on page 2-47. Do not key the letterhead.
2. Press SHIFT + ENTER to remove the added space in the letter address and between the writer's name and title.
3. Replace the reference initials *xx* with your initials. Be sure to undo automatic capitalization of the first letter of your initials.
4. Save and close. (*33-d1*)

33-d2

Block Letter

1. In a new document, key the letter below in block format with open punctuation. Insert the current date. Add your reference initials in lowercase letters. Remove added space in the letter address and the writer's name and title.
2. Save and close. (*33-d2*)

Current date

Ms. Ramona Vilella
Wicker Hotel and Resort
89 Airport Road
Omaha, NE 68105-0089

Dear Ms. Vilella

Certainly having a web presence is essential, but have you updated your hotel's website recently? Advances in technology and the increased sophistication of your clients are both good reasons for you to meet with our designers at Internet Solutions to discuss advanced hotel web design that will improve your marketing efforts.

Our online reservation system is designed for today's clients; it is easy to navigate and provides many extras such as 360-degree panoramic pictures of the hotel lobby, guest rooms, restaurants, spa, and pool, as well as maps to your beautiful hotel. Two-way communication is also important today as clients are eager to provide review ratings and valuable comments to others desiring a pleasant hotel experience. Our design offers seamless means of valuable dialog between you and your clients.

Call today for a consultation with one of our designers and discuss our many innovative website marketing strategies. Give your clients the best when they are shopping for hotel reservations.

Sincerely

Daniel Jankoski
Marketing Manager
xx

LETTER PARTS AND BLOCK LETTER STYLE

Businesspeople expect to see standard letter parts arranged in the proper sequence. Letters consist of three main parts: the opening lines to the receiver (letter address and salutation), the body or message, and the writer's closing lines. Standard letter parts and the required spacing using the defaults of *Word* are explained below and illustrated on the following page.

Block letter style is a typical business letter format in which all letter parts are keyed at the left margin. For most letters, use open punctuation, which requires no punctuation after the salutation or the complimentary closing.

Letterhead: Preprinted stationery that includes the company name, logo, address, and other optional information such as telephone number and fax number.

Dateline: Date the letter is prepared. Position at about 2" (tap ENTER three times). Be sure to begin at least 0.5" below the letterhead.

Letter address: Complete address of the letter recipient. Begin two lines below the date (tap ENTER twice).

Generally includes receiver's name, company name, street address, city, state (one space after state), and ZIP Code. Include a personal title, e.g., Mr., Ms., Dr. Press SHIFT + ENTER after each line of the letter address to remove the added space.

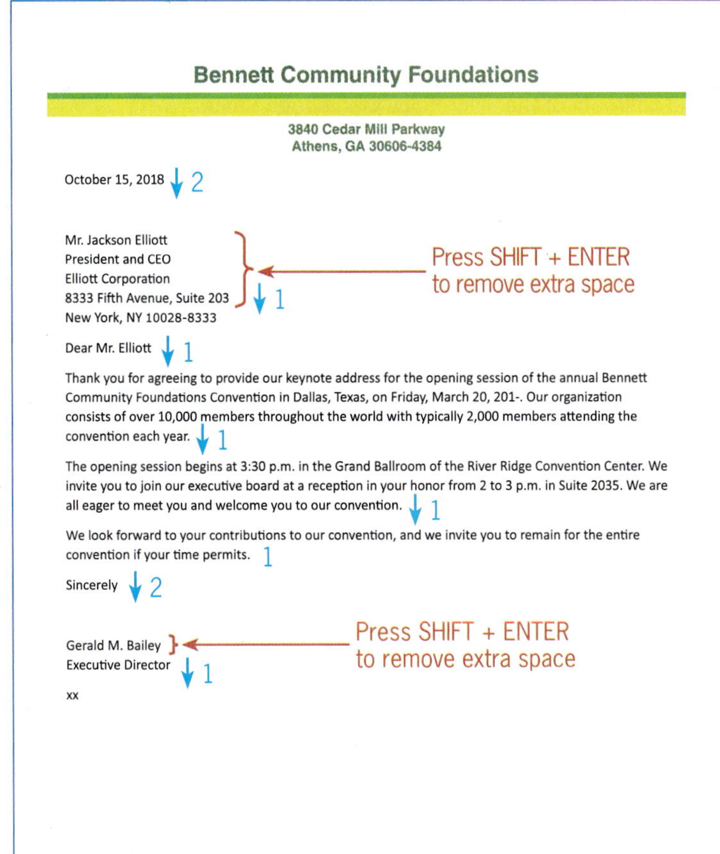

Bennett Community Foundations

3840 Cedar Mill Parkway
Athens, GA 30606-4384

October 15, 2018

Mr. Jackson Elliott
President and CEO
Elliott Corporation
8333 Fifth Avenue, Suite 203
New York, NY 10028-8333

Dear Mr. Elliott

Thank you for agreeing to provide our keynote address for the opening session of the annual Bennett Community Foundations Convention in Dallas, Texas, on Friday, March 20, 201-. Our organization consists of over 10,000 members throughout the world with typically 2,000 members attending the convention each year.

The opening session begins at 3:30 p.m. in the Grand Ballroom of the River Ridge Convention Center. We invite you to join our executive board at a reception in your honor from 2 to 3 p.m. in Suite 2035. We are all eager to meet you and welcome you to our convention.

We look forward to your contributions to our convention, and we invite you to remain for the entire convention if your time permits.

Sincerely

Gerald M. Bailey
Executive Director

xx

Salutation (or greeting): Begin one line below the letter address (tap ENTER once). Include courtesy title with person's name, e.g., Dear Mr. Smith.

Body: Begin one line below the salutation. Use the default line spacing; tap ENTER once between paragraphs.

Complimentary closing: Begin one line below the body. Capitalize only the first letter of the closing.

Writer's name and title: Begin two lines below the complimentary closing (tap ENTER twice). Include a personal title to designate gender only when the writer's name is not gender specific, such as Pat or Chris, or when initials are used, such as J. A. Moe.

Key the name and title on either one or two lines, whichever gives better balance. Use a comma to separate name and title if on one line. If two lines are used, press SHIFT + ENTER to remove the added space between the two lines.

Reference initials: Begin one line below the writer's name and title. Key reference initials, e.g., **xx** in lowercase. Replace *xx* with your initials.

Bennett Community Foundations

3840 Cedar Mill Parkway
Athens, GA 30606-4384

Tap ENTER three times (About 2")

Date line October 15, 2018 ↓ 2

Letter address
Mr. Jackson Elliott
President and CEO
Elliott Corporation
8333 Fifth Avenue, Suite 203
New York, NY 10028-8333 ↓ 1

Press SHIFT + ENTER to remove extra space

Salutation Dear Mr. Elliott ↓ 1

Body Thank you for agreeing to provide our keynote address for the opening session of the annual Bennett Community Foundations Convention in Dallas, Texas, on Friday, March 20, 201-. Our organization consists of over 10,000 members throughout the world with typically 2,000 members attending the convention each year.

The opening session begins at 3:30 p.m. in the Grand Ballroom of the River Ridge Convention Center. We invite you to join our executive board at a reception in your honor from 2 to 3 p.m. in Suite 2035. We are all eager to meet you and welcome you to our convention.

We look forward to your contributions to our convention, and we invite you to remain for the entire convention if your time permits.

Complimentary close Sincerely ↓ 2

Writer's name & title
Gerald M. Bailey
Executive Director

Press SHIFT + ENTER to remove extra space

Reference initials xx

Block Letter with Open Punctuation

Appendices

Appendix A Windows 10

START WINDOWS 10

Windows 10 is the newest operating system software released by Microsoft. The operating system software controls the operations of the computer and works with the application software. *Windows 10* works with *Word* in opening, printing, deleting, and saving files. It also allows you to work with photos, play music and videos, and access the Internet.

Some new features in *Windows 10* includes Cortana, a personal assistant. Cortana can assist you with finding files on your computer, manage your calendar, or chat with you. *Microsoft* introduced a new web browser, *Microsoft Edge*. This new default browser is faster and more secure than *Internet Explorer*. *OneDrive*, formerly called *Sky Drive*, is the online storage service that is easily accessible from *Windows 10*.

When you turn on your computer, the *Windows 10* Lock screen displays. Tap any key to display the *Windows 10* Sign-in screen. Key your password and tap ENTER to display the *Windows 10* Desktop.

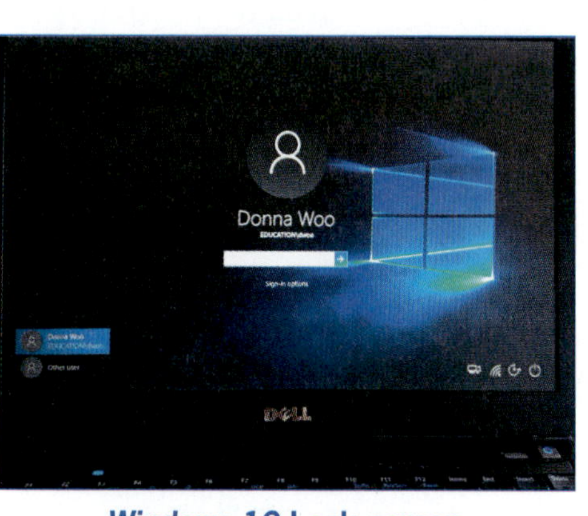

Windows 10 **Lock screen**

Windows 10 **Sign-in screen**

WINDOWS 10 DESKTOP

The *Windows 10* desktop displays once the sign-in procedure is competed. The *Windows* desktop, similar to the actual top of a desk, will be the surface on which you work. You can open files and folders and place them on the desktop. When you open *Microsoft Word*, it will display on the desktop. To display the desktop from any location, press ⊞ + D. The Windows key (⊞) is located to the left of the Space Bar; it is often referred to as the WinKey. *Microsoft* provides keyboard shortcuts that make it easy for you to interface with *Windows 10*. Pressing WinKey + D is a shortcut because it quickly displays the *Windows* desktop. WinKey + E is another shortcut that opens *File Explorer*.

Refer to the illustration on the following page to familiarize yourself with the basic screen elements.

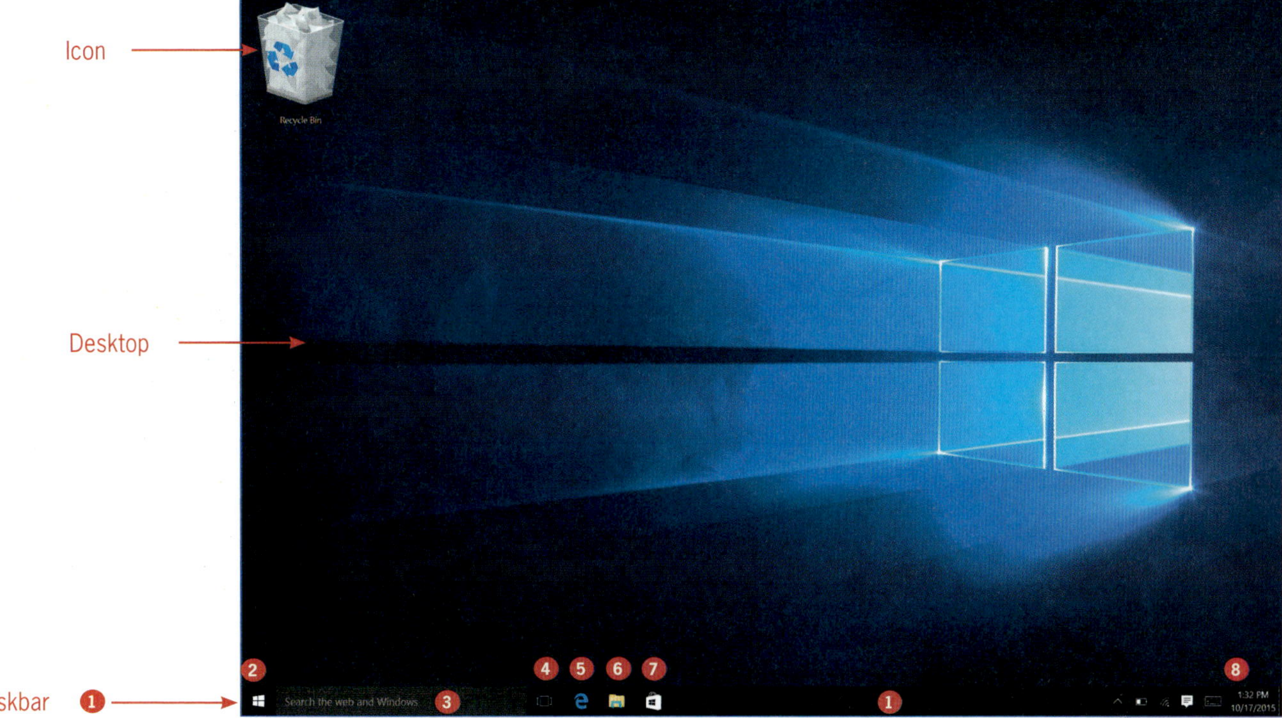

Windows 10 Desktop

- *Taskbar* ❶. The taskbar displays across the bottom of the window. Use the mouse to point to each item in the taskbar. Look for the ScreenTip that displays identifying each element.
  - *Start button* ❷. Click the Start button to display the Start menu. The Start menu provides access to the recently used apps, commonly used settings, and live tiles.
  - *Search box* ❸. The search box allows searches of files and folders on the computer and online.
  - *Apps and file buttons*. Buttons display for the apps that are open or pinned to the taskbar and allow you to switch between them easily. The *Task View* ❹ icon shows all open applications. The *Microsoft Edge* ❺ icon is displayed to provide quick access to the Internet. The *File Explorer* ❻ icon provides quick access to your files. The *App Store* ❼ leads to the Windows Store and access to purchase digital content including apps, games, and media.
  - *Notification Area* ❽. The notification area provides helpful information, such as the date and time and the status of the computer. When you plug in a USB drive, Windows displays an icon in the notification area letting you know that the hardware is connected.
- *Icons and Shortcuts*. Icons, small pictures representing certain items, may be displayed on the desktop. The Recycle Bin, shown as a wastepaper basket, displays when Windows is installed. Other icons and shortcuts may be added.
- *Desktop*. This is the work area where you will be working on your documents and apps.

SHUT DOWN COMPUTER

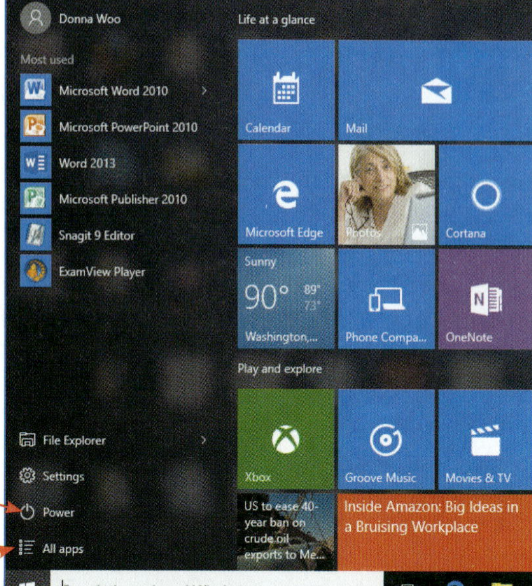

Start menu

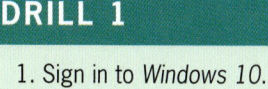

Shut down menu

1. Move your mouse pointer to the lower left of the Desktop and click Start, or tap the WinKey on your keyboard to open the Start menu. The right side of the Start menu displays application tiles. The left side of the menu displays the recently accessed apps and programs, as well as frequently accessed places on the PC. Your Start menu probably does not look identical to the illustration.
2. Click Power to display the Power options.
3. Click Shut down.

DRILL 1 START WINDOWS

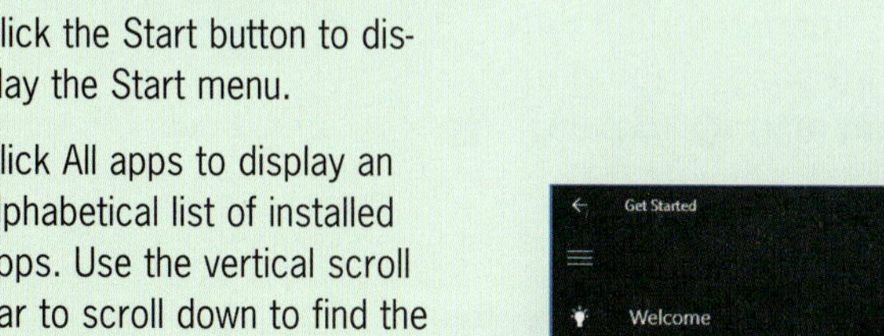

1. Sign in to *Windows 10.*
2. Click the Start button to display the Start menu.
3. Click All apps to display an alphabetical list of installed apps. Use the vertical scroll bar to scroll down to find the Get Started tile.
4. Click Get Started; the *Get Started* app opens.
5. Click *Cortana* from the list on the left, then click What is *Cortana?* Read about *Cortana*, using the scroll bar to view all the information.
6. Click *Microsoft Edge* from the list on the left, then click Get to know *Microsoft Edge*. Use the scroll bar to view all the information. Close the window.
7. Click the WinKey to display the Start menu.
8. Click Power, then Shut down.

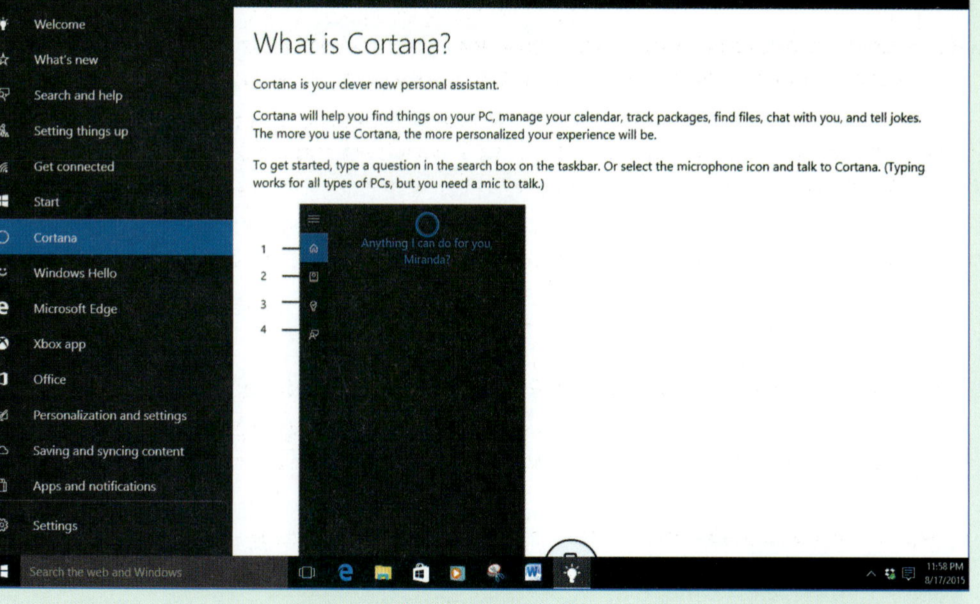

What is *Cortana?*

WINDOWS 10 HELP

The *Windows 10 Help and Support* feature contains documentation on how to use *Windows 10*; this feature is stored online. You must be connected to the Internet to access online help.

You can access Help by keying your question in the Search box located in the taskbar area. You can also access Help by tapping F1 from within Windows or any desktop program. A list of topics will display; click the link to display the information.

Windows 10 Search box

Windows 10 Getting Started Tutorials

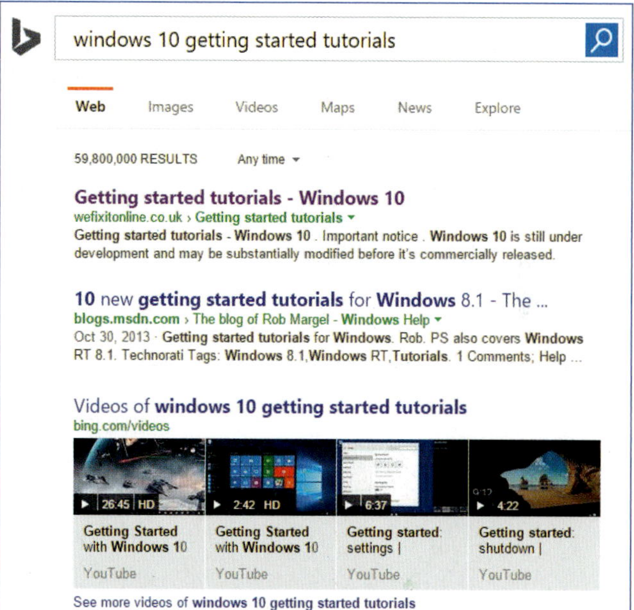

Windows search results

DRILL 2 USING WINDOWS HELP AND SEARCH

1. Sign in to *Windows 10.*
2. Key **Windows 10 getting started tutorials** in the *Windows 10* Search box, then tap ENTER.
3. A list of related topics displays. Click on one of the icons below **Videos of windows 10 getting started tutorials** to view the video.
4. When you finish viewing the video, click the close button ☒ in the upper right to close the window, then return to the Desktop.
5. Click the *File Explorer* icon in the Taskbar.
6. With the application open, tap the F1 key to display the help topics relating to *File Explorer*.
7. After viewing, close the window and return to your desktop.

Appendix B File Management

FILE EXPLORER

Expand and collapse icons may not display until the mouse moves into the left Navigation page.

Data is stored in files on the computer. To use the files, you need to know the name of the file and the location in which it is saved. *Windows 10* stores related files in folders. Folders can also be stored within folders, called subfolders. *File Explorer* provides the interface for you to manage the file system. Click the File Explorer icon on the taskbar to display the *File Explorer* window.

The left pane is the Navigation pane, which shows the drives on the computer and the files stored on each drive. If an expand icon > displays to the left of the folder or drive, that means the folder or drive contains subfolders. You can expand the list to view the subfolders by clicking the > icon. Once the list is expanded, the expand icon changes to a collapse icon; clicking the collapse icon V will hide the subfolders.

The Contents pane lists the contents of the folders. Click on a folder in the Navigation pane to display the contents of the folder in the Contents pane. If you want to get a preview of what a file looks like, click the View tab; then in the Panes group, click Preview pane to display an additional pane that shows a preview of your file.

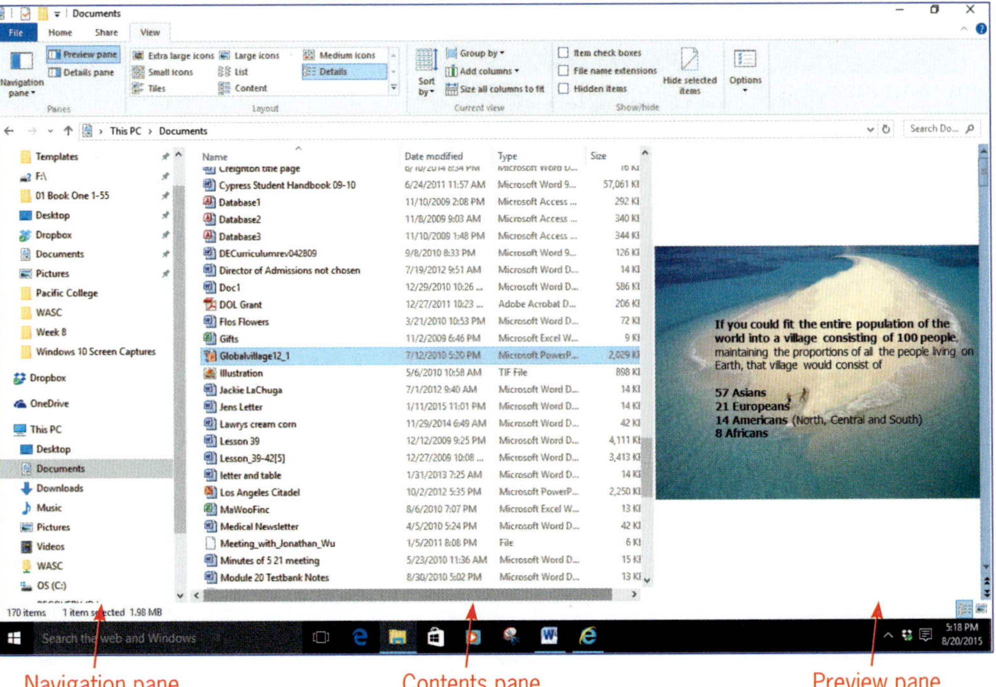

File Explorer Window

When you open *File Explorer*, it displays six Quick Access areas—Desktop, Downloads, Documents, Music, Pictures, and Videos. Documents, by default, save in the Documents folder. To view the Documents folder, move the mouse over Documents in the left pane, then click the expand icon. Click the expand icon to the left of the Documents folder to display its contents.

Files can be stored in various locations or drives on the computer. To view the drives on your computer, click This PC in the Navigation pane. The drives display in the right pane. They are labeled with letters followed by a colon (C:, D:, E:). The local disk, which stores the software, is usually labeled as drive (C:). If you are using a USB drive to save your files, it is often designated as drive E: or F:.

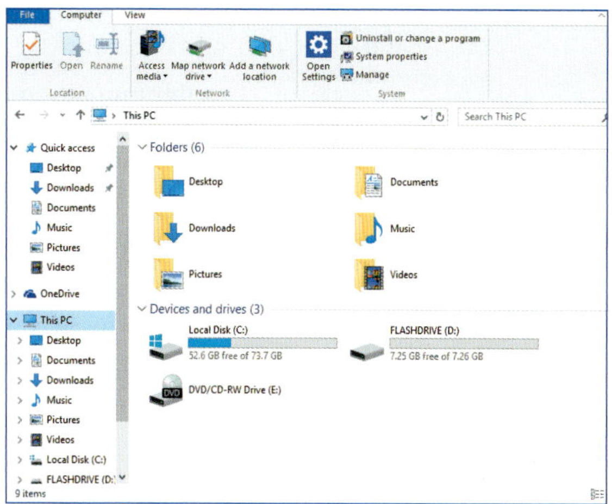

This PC

FILE ADDRESSES

The address bar, located above the Navigation and Contents pane, shows the location or address of the file. Each level of the file hierarchy is separated with a > symbol; the highest level displays at the left of the address bar. The > symbol indicates the next lower level. The illustration below shows that the selected file, How To Earn A's ❶, is located in the Success subfolder ❷, which is located in the Documents folder ❸.

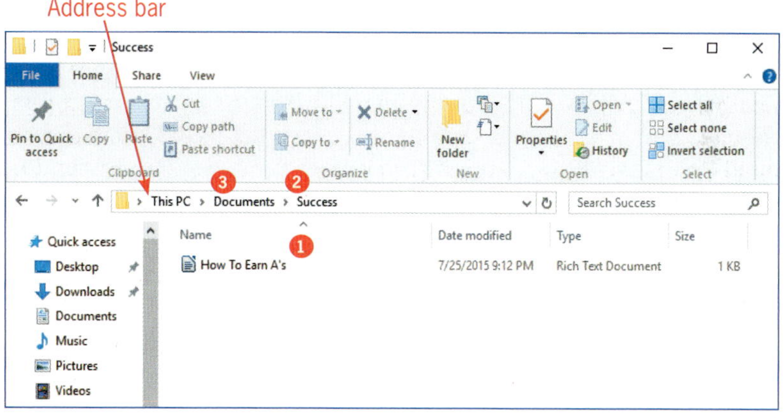

Address Bar Path

You can move up the hierarchy by clicking on the higher level in the address bar or by clicking on a higher level in the Navigation pane. You can also display the contents of the folder by clicking on the folder name in the address bar.

WORK WITH FILES AND FOLDERS

Folders are extremely important in organizing files. You will create and manage folders and the files within them so that you can easily locate them. A folder can store files, or it may contain subfolders that store files. The use of folders and subfolders helps to reduce clutter so that you can find, navigate, and manage your files, folders, and disks with greater speed.

NAMING FILES

Good file organization begins with giving your folders and files names that are logical and easy to understand. A filename should be meaningful and reflect the contents of the file. Filenames can be up to 255 characters long, but in practice you will not use filenames that long. In addition, the following symbols cannot be used in a filename: \ / : * ? " , . The descriptive name is followed by a period (.), which is used to separate the descriptive name from the file extension. The file extension is three or four letters that follow the period. When renaming a file, do not delete or change file extensions as this may cause problems opening the file.

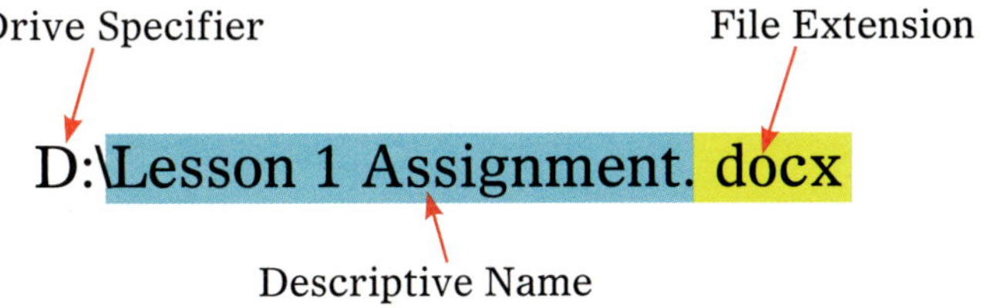

FILE EXPLORER HOME TAB

Commands that are commonly used are located on the Home tab. The Ribbon is divided into groups, similar to those of other *Microsoft Office* products. The commands to create new folders and to rename files and folders are located on the Home tab.

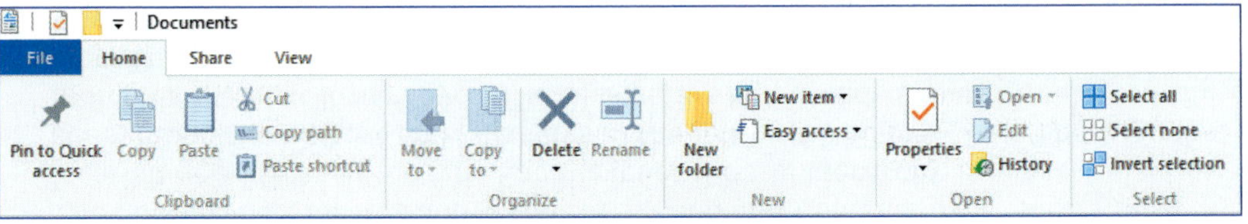

Home tab on the Ribbon

To create a file folder:

Home/New/New folder

1. In the left pane of *File Explorer*, double-click the drive or folder that is to contain the new folder ❶.
2. Click the New folder command. A yellow folder icon displays in the right pane with the words *New folder* highlighted ❷.
3. Key the new folder name and tap ENTER.

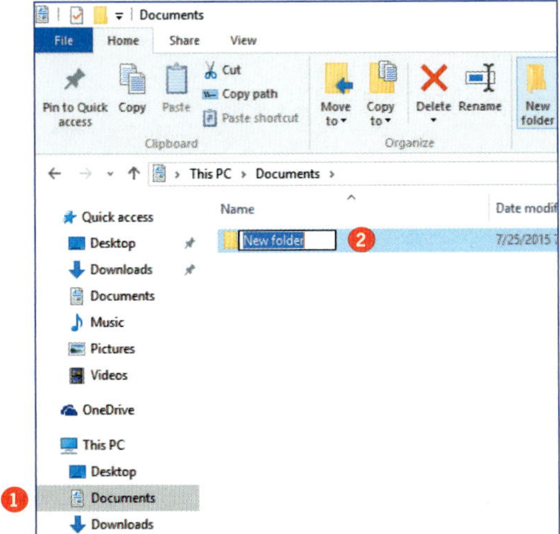

New Folder Creation

To rename a file or folder:

Home/Organize/Rename

1. Access *File Explorer* and display the contents of your removable storage drive (or the location where you have been instructed to save your document files or folders).
2. Click the file or folder icon to be renamed.
3. Click Rename on the Ribbon.
4. Key the new name and tap ENTER.

The names of the files need to be selected from the Contents pane in order to use the commands in the Home tab on the ribbon.

COPY, MOVE, OR DELETE FILES OR FOLDERS

You can use the commands in the Organize group on the Home tab to move, copy, or delete files and folders.

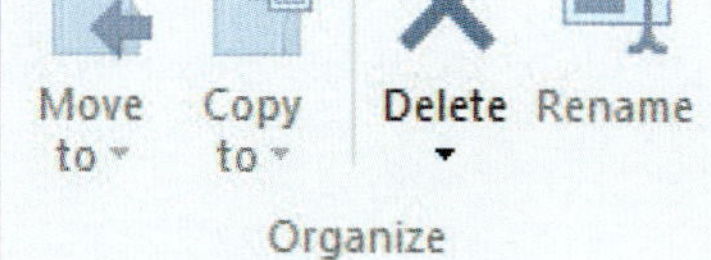

Organize Group

To move a file or folder:

Home/Organize/Move to

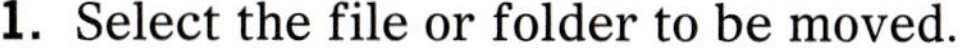

1. Select the file or folder to be moved.
2. Click the Move to drop-down arrow; a list of folders on your computer displays.
3. Select a location from the Move to drop-down list, *or*
4. Click Choose location to display the Move items dialog box. Select the destination and click Move.

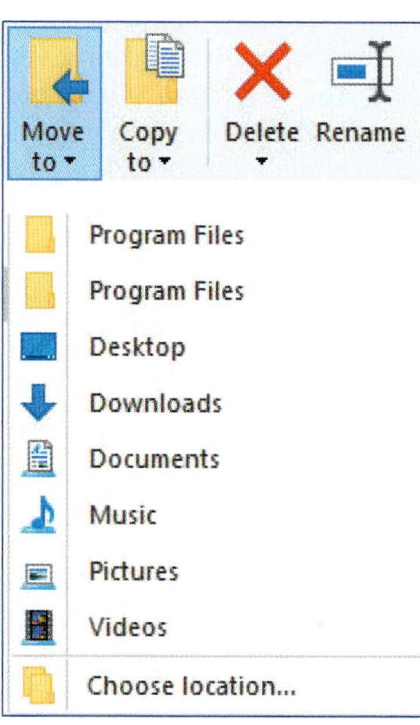

Move to drop list

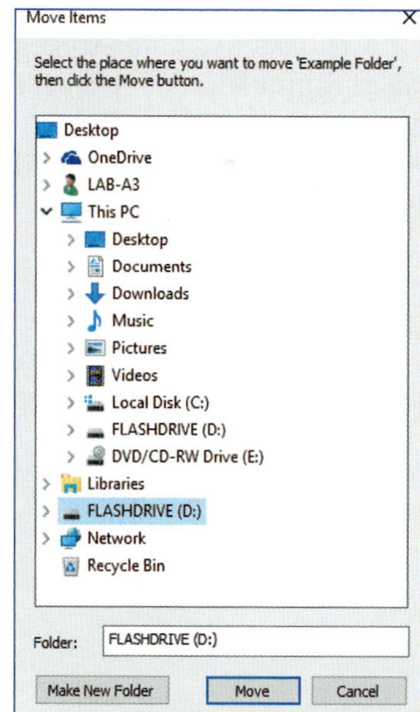

Move Items dialog box

To copy a file or folder:
Home/Organize/Copy to

1. Select the file or folder to be copied.
2. Click the Copy to drop-down arrow to display the Copy to drop-down list.
3. Select a location from the Copy to drop-down list or click Choose location to display the Copy items dialog box. Select the location for the copy to be placed and click Copy.

To delete a file or folder:
Home/Organize/Delete

1. Select the file or folder to be deleted.
2. Click Delete.

When you delete a file or folder from the hard drive, it is not removed from storage immediately. It moves to the Recycle Bin and remains there until the Recycle Bin is emptied. This gives you the opportunity to restore the file to its original location if you discover that it should not have been deleted.

ONEDRIVE APP

Microsoft made OneDrive an integral part of the *Windows 10* operating system by including the *OneDrive* app as part of the *File Explorer* navigation. OneDrive is a service that allows you to store documents, photos, videos, and audio files on the Microsoft servers. A benefit of storing files on OneDrive is the ability to access the files from any computer or *Windows* phone. The files can be shared with family and friends. Coworkers can collaboratively work on *Microsoft Office* documents. You need to have a Microsoft account to access OneDrive.

Updates are continually made to OneDrive. Read your screen carefully as its appearance and steps may vary over time.

To access OneDrive: *(Internet connection and a Microsoft account needed.)*

1. From the *Windows 10* Desktop, open the Start menu, click All apps, and find the *OneDrive* app. Alternatively, you may access OneDrive using the navigation menu of *File Explorer*.
2. If this is the first use of OneDrive on the computer, you may be prompted to sign in with your Microsoft account. Folders and files located on OneDrive will display; you may use these files as if they were on your computer, and changes made will synchronize to OneDrive.
3. OneDrive can be used in the same way a file or folder on your computer is used.

Welcome to OneDrive

Appendix C Reference Guide

Pronoun Case Agreement

1. Use the nominative case when the pronoun is the subject of a verb.

   She enjoys reading before going to sleep.

2. Use the nominative case for a predicate pronoun following a linking verb.

   It is **she** who made the motion to adjourn.

3. Use the objective case when the pronoun is the object of a preposition.

   This information must be kept between you and **me**.

4. Use the objective case when the pronoun is a direct or an indirect object.

   He told **her** to take the subway.(direct object)
   Please send **me** Joe's address. (indirect object)

5. Use *who* in the nominative form as a subject of the sentence; use *whom* in the objective form as a direct object

   Who is knocking at the door?
   To **whom** do I write my check?

6. Use the possessive case to show ownership.

   My sister is moving to Paris for **her** internship.

Pronoun Agreement (Person, Gender, Number)

1. A personal pronoun agrees in person, gender, and number with the noun or pronoun it represents.

   The **students** worked to pay **their** tuition.
   You worked in the summer to pay **your** tuition.

2. Indefinite pronouns such as *each, every, everyone, everything, somebody, anybody, either,* and *neither* are singular. The indefinite pronouns such as *many, both, few,* and *several* are plural.

   Each of the honorees worked to pay **his/her** tuition.
   All of the honorees had guests for **their** banquet.

3. A personal pronoun that represents a collective noun may be singular or plural, depending on the meaning of the collective noun.

   The **team** voted unanimously to keep Coach Johnson as **its** head coach. (individual action)
   The **family** are debating on **their** vacation destination this summer. (separate actions)

Subject/Verb Agreement

1. Use a singular verb with a singular subject. Use a plural verb with a plural subject.

   The **granddaughter is** loved by her grandparents.
   The **honorees are** seated at the head table.

2. Use a singular verb with singular indefinite pronouns. Use a plural verb with plural pronouns.

   Each of the honorees **works** to pay his/her tuition.
   All of the winners **work** to pay their bills. (plural)

3. Use a plural verb with a compound subject joined by *and.*

   The **students** and the **faculty attend** the meeting.

4. For subjects joined by words like *or* or *nor* use a singular verb if the subject closer to the verb is singular and plural if the subject closer to the verb is plural.

   Neither Susie nor **I is** available today.
   Either Pat or his team **members are** available.

5. Use a singular verb with a collective noun when the group acts as a unit. Use a plural verb when the members act individually.

   The **team votes** unanimously today. (singular)
   The **family are** debating their vacation. (plural)

Abbreviations

1. With a few exceptions, do not use abbreviations in general writing.

2. Spell out an abbreviation for the first use and key the abbreviation in parenthesis. For future use of the word, use the abbreviation.

   First time: National Science Foundation (NSF)
   Second and subsequent times: NSF

3. Abbreviate the names of well-known organizations and agencies with capitals and no periods.

   NSF NATO

4. Abbreviate professional designations and academic degrees after a name.

   CPA PhD

5. Add *s* to make most abbreviations plural. Generally to make them plural possessive, add an apostrophe.

   CPAs

6. Spell out standard units of measure in general writing; elsewhere, use abbreviations for space or readability.

   He weighs 200 pounds and is 5 feet 10 inches tall.

Punctuation

Use an apostrophe

1. To make most singular nouns and indefinite pronouns possessive (add **apostrophe** and **s**).

   computer + 's = computer's   Jess + 's = Jess's
   anyone's   one's   somebody's

2. To make a plural noun that does not end in s possessive (add **apostrophe** and **s**).

   women + 's = women's   men + 's = men's
   deer + 's = deer's   children + 's = children's

3. To make a plural noun that ends in s possessive. Add only the **apostrophe**.

   boys + ' = boys'   managers + ' = managers'

4. To make a compound noun possessive or to show joint possession. Add **apostrophe** and **s** to the last part of the hyphenated noun.

   son-in-law's   Rob and Gen's game

5. To form the plural of numbers and isolated lowercase letters and the capital letters A, I, M, and U, add **apostrophe** and **s**. To show omission of letters or figures, add an **apostrophe** in place of the missing items.

   7's   A's   p's and q's   It's   '70s

Use a colon

1. To introduce a listing.

   The candidate's strengths were obvious: experience, community involvement, and forthrightness.

2. To introduce an explanatory statement.

   Then I knew we were in trouble: The item had not been scheduled.

Use a comma

1. After an introductory phrase or dependent clause.

   After much deliberation, the jury reached its decision.
   If you have good skills, you will find a job.

2. After words or phrases in a series.

   Mike is taking Greek, Latin III, and Chemistry II.

3. To set off nonessential or interrupting elements.

   Troy, the new man in MIS, will install the hard drive.
   He cannot get to the job, however, until next Friday.

4. To set off the date from the year and the city from the state.

   John, will you please reserve the center in Billings, Montana, for January 10, 2018.

5. To separate two or more parallel adjectives (adjectives could be separated by *and* instead of a comma).

   The loud, whining guitar could be heard above the rest.

6. Before the conjunction in a compound sentence. The comma may be omitted in a very short sentence.

   You must leave immediately, or you will miss your flight. We tested the software and they loved it.

7. Set off appositives and words of direct address.

   Karen, our team leader, represented us at the conference.
   Paul, have you ordered the ten dozen red roses?

Use a hyphen

1. In two-word adjectives before a noun

   two-car family

2. In compound numbers between twenty-one and ninety-nine.
3. In fractions and some proper nouns with prefixes/suffixes.

   two-thirds   ex-Governor   all-American

Use italic

1. With titles of complete literary works.

   College Keyboarding   *Hunt for Red October*

2. To emphasize special words or phrases.

   What does *professional* mean?

Use a semicolon

1. To separate independent clauses in a compound sentence when the conjunction is omitted.

   Please review the information; give me a report by Tuesday.

2. To separate independent clauses when they are joined by conjunctive adverbs (*however, nevertheless, consequently,* etc.).

   The traffic was heavy; consequently, I was late.

3. To separate a series of elements that contain commas.

   The new officers are Fran Pena, president; Harry Wong, treasurer; and Muriel Williams, secretary.

Use a dash

1. To show an abrupt change of thought.

   Invoice 76A—which is 10 days overdue—is for $670.

2. After a series to indicate a summarizing statement.

   Noisy fuel pump, worn rods, and failing brakes—for all these reasons I'm trading the car.

Use an exclamation point

After emphatic interjections or exclamatory sentences.

Terrific! Hold it! You bet! What a great surprise!

Capitalization

Capitalize:

1. First word of a sentence and of a direct quotation.

   We were tolerating instead of managing diversity. The speaker said, "We must value diversity, not merely recognize it."

2. Names of proper nouns—specific persons, places, or things.

   Common nouns: continent, river, car, street
   Proper nouns: Asia, Ohio, Buick, State Street

3. Derivatives of proper nouns and geographical names.

   American history English accent
   German food Ohio Valley
   Tampa, Florida Mount Rushmore

4. A personal or professional title when it precedes the name or a title of high distinction without a name.

   Lieutenant Kahn Mayor Walsh
   Doctor Welby Mr. Ty Brooks
   Dr. Frank Collins Miss Tate
   the President of the United States

5. Days of the week, months of the year, holidays, periods of history, and historic events.

   Monday, June 8 Labor Day Renaissance

6. Specific parts of the country but not compass points that show direction.

   Midwest the South northwest of town

7. Family relationships when used with a person's name.

   Aunt Helen my dad Uncle John

8. Noun preceding a figure except for common nouns such as *line, page,* and *sentence.*

   Unit 1 Section 2 page 2 line 2

9. First and main words of side headings, titles of books, and works of art. Do not capitalize words of four or fewer letters that are conjunctions, prepositions, or articles.

   Computers in the News *Raiders of the Lost Ark*

10. Names of organizations and specific departments within the writer's organization.

    Girl Scouts our Sales Department

Number Expression

General guidelines

1. Use **words** for numbers *one* through *ten* unless the numbers are in a category with related larger numbers that are expressed as figures.

   He bought three acres of land. She took two acres. She wrote 12 stories and 2 plays in 13 years.

2. Use **words** for approximate numbers or large round numbers that can be expressed as one or two words. Use **numbers** for round numbers in millions or higher with their word modifier.

   We sent out about three hundred invitations. She contributed $3 million dollars.

3. Use **words** for numbers that begin a sentence.

   Six players were cut from the ten-member team.

4. Use **figures** for the larger of two adjacent numbers.

   We shipped six 24-ton engines.

Times and dates

5. Use **words** for numbers that precede o'clock (stated or implied).

   We shall meet from two until five o'clock.

6. Use **figures** for times with *a.m.* or *p.m.* and days when they follow the month.

   Her appointment is for 2:15 p.m. on July 26.

7. Use **ordinals** for the day when it precedes the month.

   The 10th of October is my anniversary.

Money, percentages, and fractions

8. Use **figures** for money amounts and percentages. Spell out *cents* and *percent* except in statistical copy.

   The 16 percent discount saved me $145; Bill, 95 cents.

9. Use **words** for fractions unless the fractions appear in combination with whole numbers.

   one-half of her lesson 5 1/2 18 3/4

Addresses

10. Use **words** for street names First through Tenth and **figures** or ordinals for streets above Tenth. Use **figures** for house numbers other than number **one**. (If street name is a number, separate it from house number with a dash.)

    One Lytle Place Second Avenue
    142—53rd Street

Spelling Rules

1. To make most nouns plural, add *s*.

boy	*boys*
chair	*chairs*
parent	*parents*

2. Add *es* to nouns ending in *s, x, z, ch,* or *sh*.

Jones	*Jones*
tax	*taxes*
buzz	*buzzes*
church	*churches*
wish	*wishes*

3. If a noun ends in a consonant plus *y*, change the *y* to *i* and add *es*.

puppy	*puppies*
fly	*flies*

4. Add *es* to some nouns ending in a consonant plus *o*.

potato	potatoes
BUT not pianos	

5. For some nouns ending in *f* or *fe*, change the *f* or *fe* to *ves*.

half	*halves*
wolf	*wolves*

6. Memorize or look up irregular nouns.

child	children
woman	women

7. Keep a silent e before a suffix that begins with a consonant. Drop it before a suffix that begins with a vowel.

excite	excitement
excite	exciting

8. When adding a suffix that begins with a vowel to a word that ends with a vowel and consonant, double the consonant.

commit	commitment
shop	shopping

9. When you add a prefix, the spelling does not change.

wash	prewash
view	preview

10. Put *i* before e except after c or when the letters sound like *a*, as in *neighbor* and *weigh*.

receive	*believe*
neighbor	*weigh*

Composition

Most careers require good writing skills. You can learn to be an effective writer with practice. Writing at the keyboard facilitates editing and is easier and more effective than handwriting documents. Editing requires complete focus on each of the following areas:

Content accuracy—Determine what needs to be included in a message and then check to see that necessary information is included and that all information is accurate.

Organization—Check sentence structure to see that ideas are presented logically and flow smoothly.

Writing style—Ensure that the message is clear, crisp, concise, and written at an appropriate level.

Mechanical correctness—Check for errors in grammar, spelling, punctuation, capitalization, number usage, and word usage.

Composition Guides

1. Begin with short, easy sentences and paragraphs on topics in which you have knowledge. Then work on putting the sentences and paragraphs together for complete messages.
2. Key your thoughts first and then edit them carefully. It is very difficult to write perfect copy when you begin keying.
3. Use familiar words and a simple, straightforward writing style.
4. Edit to ensure that sentences are carefully arranged, clear, and grammatically correct.
5. Structure paragraphs carefully, making sure that all sentences in the paragraphs relate to the same topic and that they flow logically.
6. Edit and proofread carefully.

Editing and proofreading usually make the difference between high-quality and mediocre writing.

Proofreading

Often the difference between high-quality and mediocre documents is in how carefully they are proofread. Careful proofreading ensures the accuracy of the final document.

Proofreading requires complete focus on each of the following areas:

Overall appearance of a document—check for appropriate stationery, attractive placement, and correct and consistent format.

Content accuracy—check for accuracy and completeness, such as making sure dates are correct and times are not left off.

Mechanical correctness—check for keying errors, as well as mistakes in spelling, grammar, punctuation, capitalization, word usage, and number usage. Review basic guides if you are not comfortable with your knowledge level in each of the areas listed.

Proofreading Guides

1. Check the document using the Spelling and Grammar commands.
2. Proofread the document on the screen slowly, on a word-by-word basis. Focus on words that may be spelled correctly but are misused, such as *you/your, is/in, if/it, there/their, two/to/too, then/than*, and *principle/principal*.
3. Check specifically for capitalization, punctuation, and number usage.
4. Check to see that the document is complete, ensuring that enclosure or copy notations are not left off.
5. Verify that each number is correct. The only way to ensure that a number is correct is to check it against the source from which it was keyed.
6. Preview the document on screen to ensure that placement is appropriate.
7. Print the document and proofread it again. It is helpful to use a guide (ruler, large envelope, or folded sheet of paper). Move it down line by line as you read. Mark the corrections using proofreaders' marks. Refer to a list of common proofreaders' marks found in the right column of this page.

Learn to proofread on the screen first and then, as a last check, proofread the printed document again.

Proofreading Statistical Copy

Statistical copy requires special attention. It is very easy to make errors in keying numbers, and it is very difficult to determine if a number keyed is correct.

The same thing is true for a date or time.

1. Verify numbers against the original source, verify dates against the calendar, and check computations with a calculator.
2. Read numbers in groups. For example, the telephone number 618.555.0123 can be read in three parts: *six-one-eight, five-five-five, zero-one-two-three*.
3. Read numbers aloud and preferably with a partner checking against the original copy.

An error in a number could have significant negative consequences; for example, keying $300,000 rather than $400,000 in quoting a price or authorizing a loan at 7% when the correct percentage is 8% could prove to be very costly.

Proofreaders' Marks

#	Add horizontal space
‖	Align
(wavy underline)	Bold
Cap or ≡	Capitalize
[ ]	Center
(close-up curves)	Close up
(delete mark)	Delete
^	Insert
“ ” (inverted carets)	Insert quotation marks
. . . or stet	Let it stand; ignore correction
/ or lc	Lowercase
(bracket)	Move left
(bracket)	Move right
(bracket)	Move up
(bracket)	Move down
¶	Paragraph
sp (circled)	Spell out
(transpose mark) or tr	Transpose
(underline)	italic or (ital)
wf	Wrong font

Formatting Decisions

Decisions regarding document formats require consideration of four elements: (1) attractiveness of the format, (2) readability of the format, (3) effective use of space on the page, and (4) efficiency in producing the format. Please note several formatting decisions made in this text regarding defaults in *Word 2016*.

Styles

Word 2016 offers a quick gallery of styles on the Home tab. Using these styles results in efficient production of attractive report headings, page number, and table styles.

Default Line Spacing

The default line spacing of 1.08 in *Word 2016* provides readers with an open and readable copy.

Space after the Paragraph

The default space after a paragraph in *Word 2016* is 8 point after the paragraph. This automatic spacing saves time and creates an attractive document.

Remove Space after the Paragraph

While enjoying the benefits of efficiency, it is also necessary to consider the amount of space that is being consumed. For example, extra spacing between the lines of the letter address requires too much space and is not an attractive layout. Other examples include removing the extra space between the writer's name and title in the closing lines of a letter. To remove the extra spacing, tap SHIFT+ENTER after those short lines.

Margins

The default margins for *Word 2016* are 1" top, bottom, left side, and right side. With the side margin default of 1", additional space is needed for the binding of leftbound reports.

Fonts and Document Themes

Microsoft provides true type fonts in *Office 2016* and a number of new document themes that incorporate color and a variety of fonts depending on the theme selected. Many documents presented in the text are based on the default document theme *Office*, and use the default heading font, Calibri Light, and the default body text font, Calibri 11 point. For the initial reports module, the *Word 2016* style set is applied to the document theme. See the illustration below of the default headings and fonts, using the Office theme and *Word 2016* style set.

Title (28 pt. Calibri Light, Automatic—Black)

Subtitle (11 pt. Calibri, Black, Text 1, Lighter 35%)

Heading 1 (16 pt. Calibri Light, Blue, Accent 1, Darker 25%)

Heading 2 (13 pt. Calibri Light, Blue, Accent 1, Darker 25%)

Heading 3 (12 pt. Calibri Light, Blue, Accent 1, Darker 50%)

Heading 4 (11 pt. Calibri Light, Italic, Blue, Accent 1, Darker 25%)

The default body text is Calibri, 11 pt. Color Automatic (Black).

Default Document Theme: Office

Letter Parts

Letterhead. Company name and address. May include other data.

Date. Date letter is mailed. Usually in month, day, year order. Military style is an option (day/month/year).

Letter address. Address of the person who will receive the letter. Include personal title (*Mr., Ms., Dr.*), name, professional title, company, and address. Remove the extra spacing in the letter address.

Salutation. Greeting. Corresponds to the first line of the letter address. Usually includes name and courtesy title; use *Ladies and Gentlemen* if letter is addressed to a company name.

Body. Message. Key in default line spacing; tap ENTER once between paragraphs.

Complimentary close. Farewell, such as *Sincerely.*

Writer. Name and professional title. If the name and title are keyed on two lines, remove the extra spacing between the lines.

Initials. Identifies person who keyed the document (for example, *tr*). May include identification of writer (*ARB:tri*).

Enclosure. Copy is enclosed with the document. May specify contents. If more than one line is used, align at 1" and remove the extra spacing between the lines.

Copy notation. Indicates that a copy of the letter is being sent to person named. If more than one line is used, align at 0.5" and remove the extra spacing between the lines.

Note: To remove extra spacing between lines, press SHIFT + ENTER.

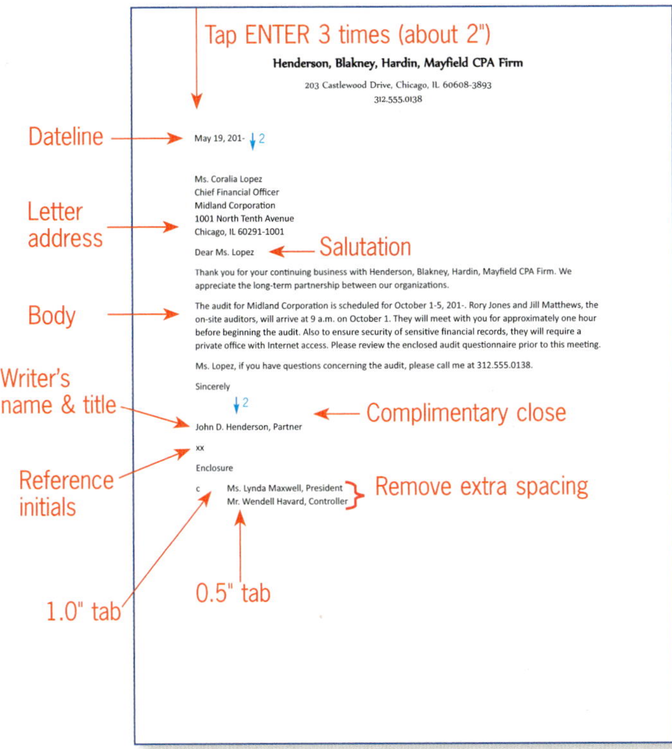

Henderson, Blakney, Hardin, Mayfield CPA Firm
203 Castlewood Drive, Chicago, IL 60608-3893
312.555.0138

May 19, 201-

Ms. Coralia Lopez
Chief Financial Officer
Midland Corporation
1001 North Tenth Avenue
Chicago, IL 60291-1001

Dear Ms. Lopez

Thank you for your continuing business with Henderson, Blakney, Hardin, Mayfield CPA Firm. We appreciate the long-term partnership between our organizations.

The audit for Midland Corporation is scheduled for October 1-5, 201-. Rory Jones and Jill Matthews, the on-site auditors, will arrive at 9 a.m. on October 1. They will meet with you for approximately one hour before beginning the audit. Also to ensure security of sensitive financial records, they will require a private office with Internet access. Please review the enclosed audit questionnaire prior to this meeting.

Ms. Lopez, if you have questions concerning the audit, please call me at 312.555.0138.

Sincerely

John D. Henderson, Partner

xx

Enclosure

c Ms. Lynda Maxwell, President
Mr. Wendell Havard, Controller

Block Letter (Open Punctuation)

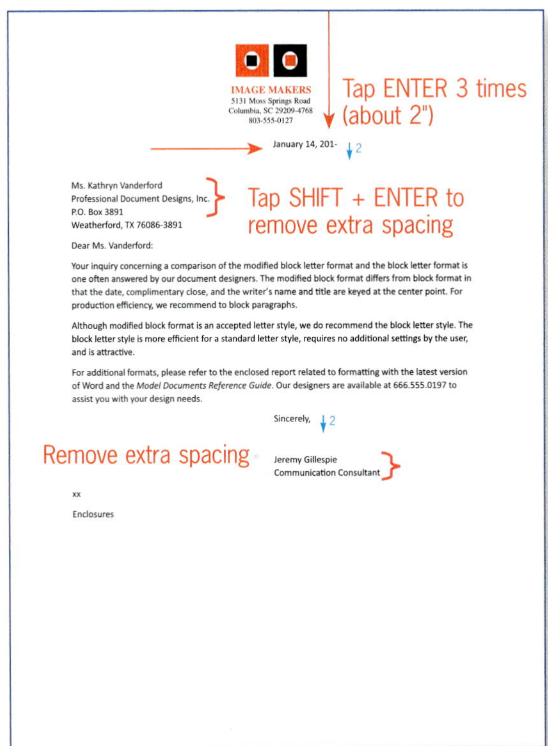

IMAGE MAKERS
5131 Moss Springs Road
Columbia, SC 29209-4768
803-555-0127

January 14, 201-

Ms. Kathryn Vanderford
Professional Document Designs, Inc.
P.O. Box 3891
Weatherford, TX 76086-3891

Dear Ms. Vanderford:

Your inquiry concerning a comparison of the modified block letter format and the block letter format is one often answered by our document designers. The modified block format differs from block format in that the date, complimentary close, and the writer's name and title are keyed at the center point. For production efficiency, we recommend to block paragraphs.

Although modified block format is an accepted letter style, we do recommend the block letter style. The block letter style is more efficient for a standard letter style, requires no additional settings by the user, and is attractive.

For additional formats, please refer to the enclosed report related to formatting with the latest version of Word and the *Model Documents Reference Guide*. Our designers are available at 666.555.0197 to assist you with your design needs.

Sincerely,

Jeremy Gillespie
Communication Consultant

xx

Enclosures

Modified Block Letter (Mixed Punctuation)

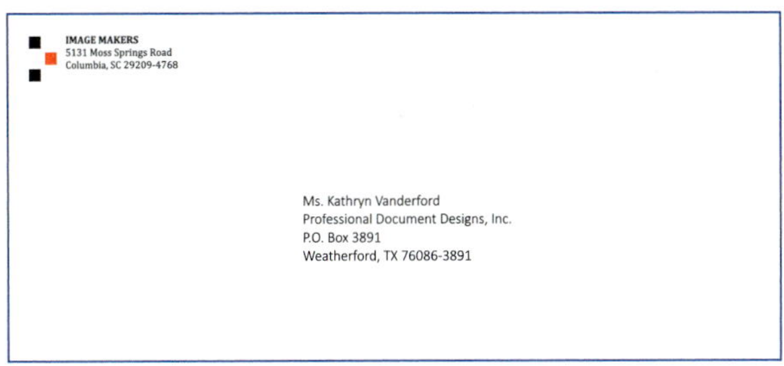

IMAGE MAKERS
5131 Moss Springs Road
Columbia, SC 29209-4768

Ms. Kathryn Vanderford
Professional Document Designs, Inc.
P.O. Box 3891
Weatherford, TX 76086-3891

Envelope

Academic Reports in MLA Style

Font: 12-point Times New Roman.

Margins: Side margins 1".

Report heading: Key at 1". Include writer's name, instructor's name, assignment name, and date in DDMMYY order (Ex. 10 April 2018).

Spacing: DS paragraphs and indent 0.5".

Report title: Center one line after the report heading; capitalize all main words.

Headings: Key Level 1 headings in this report at the left margin.

Numbers: Number pages at top right; include the writer's last name and the page number (LName 1).

Internal citations: References cited are indicated within the text in parenthesis. Indent quotes of 40 or more words 1" from left margin.

Works cited: Lists all references in alphabetical order by authors' last names. Format as hanging indent.

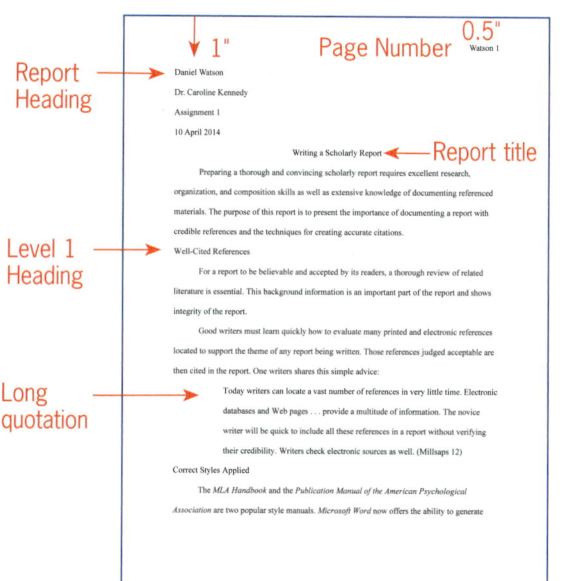

Watson 1

Daniel Watson

Dr. Caroline Kennedy

Assignment 1

10 April 2014

Writing a Scholarly Report

Preparing a thorough and convincing scholarly report requires excellent research, organization, and composition skills as well as extensive knowledge of documenting referenced materials. The purpose of this report is to present the importance of documenting a report with credible references and the techniques for creating accurate citations.

Well-Cited References

For a report to be believable and accepted by its readers, a thorough review of related literature is essential. This background information is an important part of the report and shows integrity of the report.

Good writers must learn quickly how to evaluate many printed and electronic references located to support the theme of any report being written. Those references judged acceptable are then cited in the report. One writers shares this simple advice:

> Today writers can locate a vast number of references in very little time. Electronic databases and Web pages . . . provide a multitude of information. The novice writer will be quick to include all these references in a report without verifying their credibility. Writers check electronic sources as well. (Millsaps 12)

Correct Styles Applied

The *MLA Handbook* and the *Publication Manual of the American Psychological Association* are two popular style manuals. *Microsoft Word* now offers the ability to generate

MLA Report, Page 1

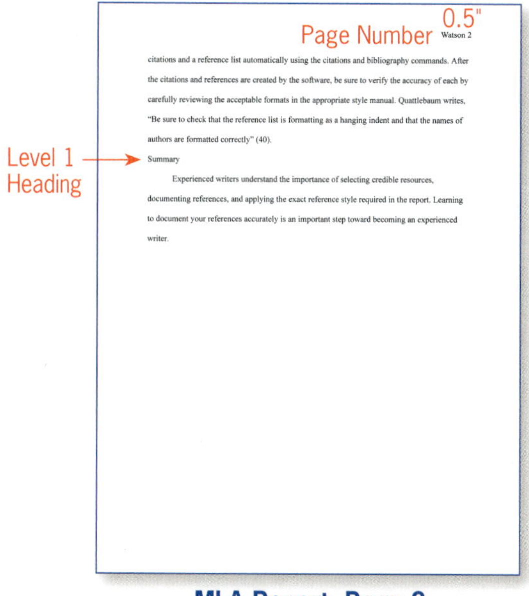

Watson 2

citations and a reference list automatically using the citations and bibliography commands. After the citations and references are created by the software, be sure to verify the accuracy of each by carefully reviewing the acceptable formats in the appropriate style manual. Quattlebaum writes, "Be sure to check that the reference list is formatting as a hanging indent and that the names of authors are formatted correctly" (40).

Summary

Experienced writers understand the importance of selecting credible resources, documenting references, and applying the exact reference style required in the report. Learning to document your references accurately is an important step toward becoming an experienced writer.

MLA Report, Page 2

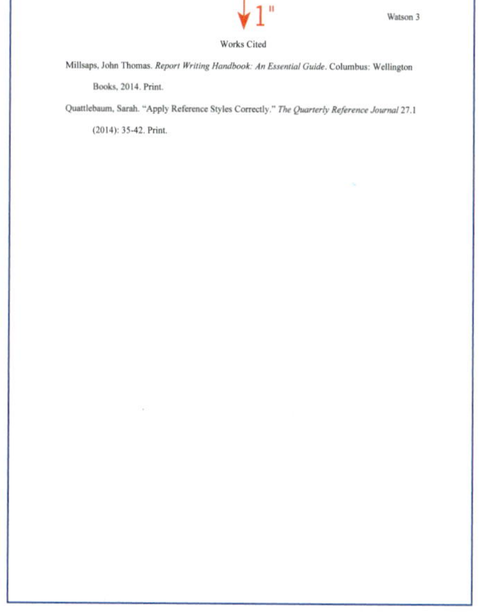

Watson 3

Works Cited

Millsaps, John Thomas. *Report Writing Handbook: An Essential Guide*. Columbus: Wellington Books, 2014. Print.

Quattlebaum, Sarah. "Apply Reference Styles Correctly." *The Quarterly Reference Journal* 27.1 (2014): 35-42. Print.

MLA Works Cited Page

Academic Reports in APA Style

Font: 12-point Times New Roman.

Margins: Side margins 1".

Spacing: DS paragraphs and indent 0.5".

Report title: Center one line after the report heading; capitalize all main words.

Headings: Key Level 1 headings in this report at the left margin.

Page numbers: Key a running head that includes the title of the paper (limited to 50 characters) at the left margin and the page number aligned at the right.

Internal citations: References cited are indicated within the text in parenthesis. Indent quotes of 40 or more words 0.5" from left margin.

Bibliography: Lists all references in alphabetical order by authors' last names. Format as hanging indent.

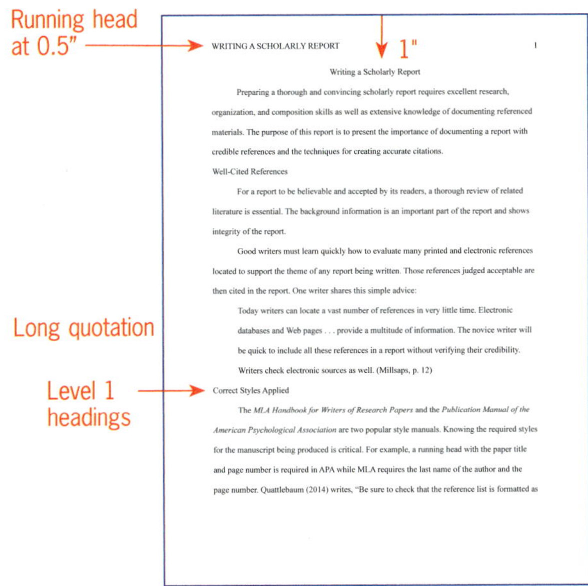

WRITING A SCHOLARLY REPORT 1

Writing a Scholarly Report

Preparing a thorough and convincing scholarly report requires excellent research, organization, and composition skills as well as extensive knowledge of documenting referenced materials. The purpose of this report is to present the importance of documenting a report with credible references and the techniques for creating accurate citations.

Well-Cited References

For a report to be believable and accepted by its readers, a thorough review of related literature is essential. The background information is an important part of the report and shows integrity of the report.

Good writers must learn quickly how to evaluate many printed and electronic references located to support the theme of any report being written. Those references judged acceptable are then cited in the report. One writer shares this simple advice:

> Today writers can locate a vast number of references in very little time. Electronic databases and Web pages . . . provide a multitude of information. The novice writer will be quick to include all these references in a report without verifying their credibility. Writers check electronic sources as well. (Millsaps, p. 12)

Correct Styles Applied

The *MLA Handbook for Writers of Research Papers* and the *Publication Manual of the American Psychological Association* are two popular style manuals. Knowing the required styles for the manuscript being produced is critical. For example, a running head with the paper title and page number is required in APA while MLA requires the last name of the author and the page number. Quattlebaum (2014) writes, "Be sure to check that the reference list is formatted as

APA Report, Page 1

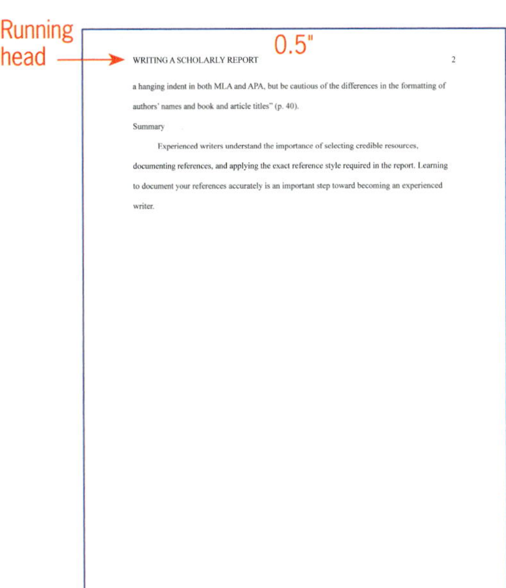

WRITING A SCHOLARLY REPORT 2

a hanging indent in both MLA and APA, but be cautious of the differences in the formatting of authors' names and book and article titles" (p. 40).

Summary

Experienced writers understand the importance of selecting credible resources, documenting references, and applying the exact reference style required in the report. Learning to document your references accurately is an important step toward becoming an experienced writer.

APA Report, Page 2

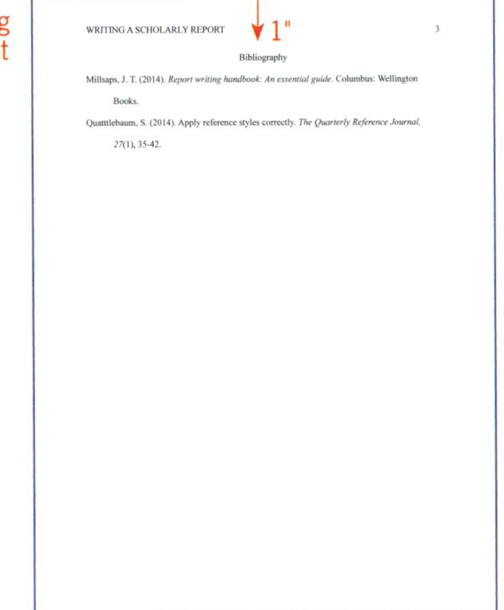

WRITING A SCHOLARLY REPORT 3

Bibliography

Millsaps, J. T. (2014). *Report writing handbook: An essential guide*. Columbus: Wellington Books.

Quatttlebaum, S. (2014). Apply reference styles correctly. *The Quarterly Reference Journal, 27*(1), 35-42.

APA Bibliography Page

Business Reports

Margins: Tap ENTER three times to begin first page of report at 2"; default 1" top margin for succeeding pages; default 1" for bottom margin.

Unbound report: Side margins 1"

Leftbound report: Side margins 1.5"

Titles: Title style. Main words capitalized.

Spacing: Default line spacing; paragraphs blocked. Tap ENTER once between paragraphs.

Page numbers: Second and subsequent pages are numbered at top right of the page. One blank line follows the page number.

Side headings: Heading 1 style. Main words capitalized.

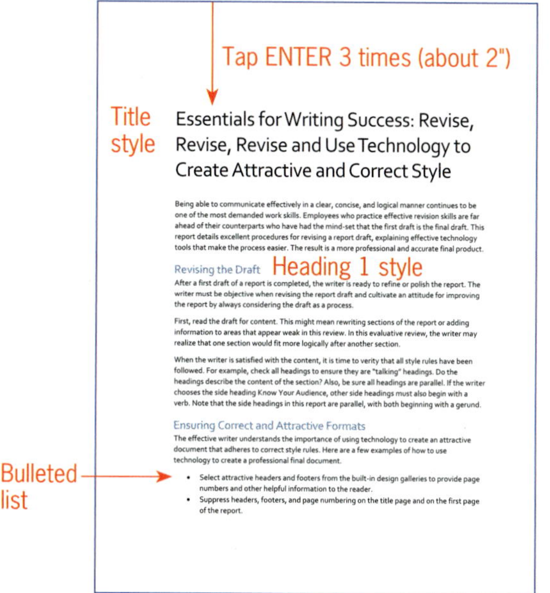

Essentials for Writing Success: Revise, Revise, Revise and Use Technology to Create Attractive and Correct Style

Being able to communicate effectively in a clear, concise, and logical manner continues to be one of the most demanded work skills. Employees who practice effective revision skills are far ahead of their counterparts who have had the mind-set that the first draft is the final draft. This report details excellent procedures for revising a report draft, explaining effective technology tools that make the process easier. The result is a more professional and accurate final product.

Revising the Draft

After a first draft of a report is completed, the writer is ready to refine or polish the report. The writer must be objective when revising the report draft and cultivate an attitude for improving the report by always considering the draft as a process.

First, read the draft for content. This might mean rewriting sections of the report or adding information to areas that appear weak in this review. In this evaluative review, the writer may realize that one section would fit more logically after another section.

When the writer is satisfied with the content, it is time to verity that all style rules have been followed. For example, check all headings to ensure they are "talking" headings. Do the headings describe the content of the section? Also, be sure all headings are parallel. If the writer chooses the side heading Know Your Audience, other side headings must also begin with a verb. Note that the side headings in this report are parallel, with both beginning with a gerund.

Ensuring Correct and Attractive Formats

The effective writer understands the importance of using technology to create an attractive document that adheres to correct style rules. Here are a few examples of how to use technology to create a professional final document.

- Select attractive headers and footers from the built-in design galleries to provide page numbers and other helpful information to the reader.
- Suppress headers, footers, and page numbering on the title page and on the first page of the report.

Unbound Report, Page 1

Page Number 0.5"

2

- Invoke the Widow/Orphan control feature to ensure that no lines display alone at the bottom or top of a page. Use the Keep with next command to keep side headings from appearing alone at the bottom of the page.
- Take advantage of automatic features, such as a table of contents and citations.
- Use styles to format tables and charts.
- Be sure to use the online thesaurus, spelling, and grammar features of the word processing software.
- Bookmark widely accepted online desk references and style manuals for easy use.
- Use the Show/Hide command to show the ¶ marks and other hidden formatting symbols.

These simple steps will assist you in your goal to create well-written and attractive reports. The next step is to practice, practice, and practice.

Unbound Report, Page 2 (Plain Number 3 Style)

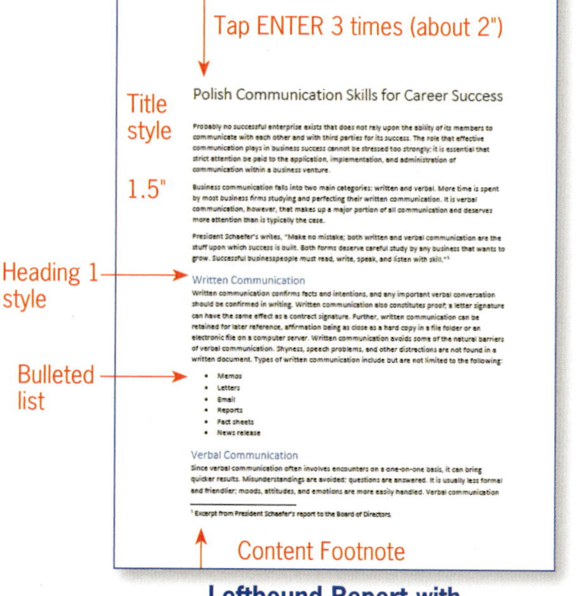

Polish Communication Skills for Career Success

Probably no successful enterprise exists that does not rely upon the ability of its members to communicate with each other and with third parties for its success. The role that effective communication plays in business success cannot be stressed too strongly; it is essential that strict attention be paid to the application, implementation, and administration of communication within a business venture.

Business communication falls into two main categories: written and verbal. More time is spent by most business firms studying and perfecting their written communication. It is verbal communication, however, that makes up a major portion of all communication and deserves more attention than is typically the case.

President Schaefer's writes, "Make no mistake; both written and verbal communication are the stuff upon which success is built. Both forms deserve careful study by any business that wants to grow. Successful businesspeople must read, write, speak, and listen with skill."[1]

Written Communication

Written communication confirms facts and intentions, and any important verbal conversation should be confirmed in writing. Written communication also constitutes proof; a letter signature can have the same effect as a contract signature. Further, written communication can be retained for later reference, affirmation being as close as a hard copy in a file folder or an electronic file on a computer server. Written communication avoids some of the natural barriers of verbal communication. Shyness, speech problems, and other distractions are not found in a written document. Types of written communication include but are not limited to the following:

- Memos
- Letters
- Email
- Reports
- Fact sheets
- News release

Verbal Communication

Since verbal communication often involves encounters on a one-on-one basis, it can bring quicker results. Misunderstandings are avoided; questions are answered. It is usually less formal and friendlier; moods, attitudes, and emotions are more easily handled. Verbal communication

[1] Excerpt from President Schaefer's report to the Board of Directors.

Leftbound Report with Footnote, Page 1

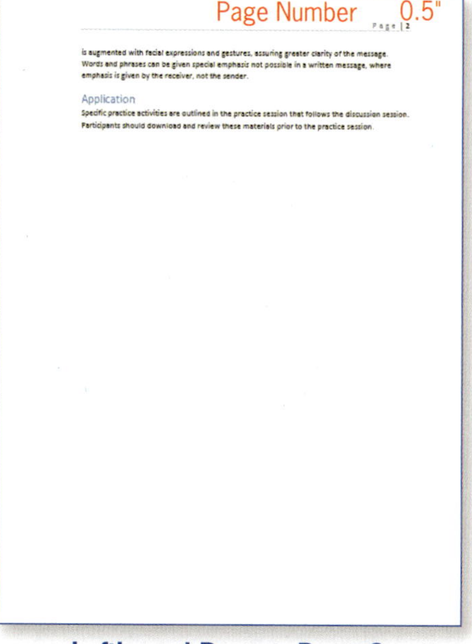

Page | 2

is augmented with facial expressions and gestures, assuring greater clarity of the message. Words and phrases can be given special emphasis not possible in a written message, where emphasis is given by the receiver, not the sender.

Application

Specific practice activities are outlined in the practice session that follows the discussion session. Participants should download and review these materials prior to the practice session.

Leftbound Report, Page 2 (Page Number Style)

Tap ENTER 3 times (about 2")

Tab (1" from left margin)

TO: Emily Welch, Brian McKenzie, Olivia von Staden

FROM: Michael Holcomb

DATE: July 18, 2018

SUBJECT: Video Conference Call Scheduled Friday, July 26

The final video conference call to select the contractor for the Keystone Community Project will be held on Friday, July 26, from 3:30 to 5:00 p.m. EST. To join the video conference, follow these steps:

1. Call 601.555.0168 and enter the passcode 8103622 when prompted.
2. Go to www.conferences.com/holcomb/PDS/ and join the meeting.

Please review the proposals carefully and be prepared to make a recommendation at the meeting. If you have questions about the proposals, please call me at 601.555.0193 or email me at mholcomb@svdco.com.

xx

Memo

REGENTS MEMORIAL MEDICAL CENTER February Seminars		
Seminar Title	**Description**	**Registration**
Surgical Weight Loss	Methods of losing weight, including healthy diet, exercise and medication, will be discussed in detail. Surgical weight loss is an option for those who are motivated and willing to commit to lifestyle changes.	Classes will be held at the Outpatient Surgery Center 75 Pacific Crest Laguna Niguel, CA 92677-5773. Call 949.555.0111 to register.
Life in Motion with Osteoarthritis	Osteoarthritis no longer means that you need to live with a painful disability. Modern medicine, diet, exercise, and surgery can help you enjoy life more fully. Intricate surgical procedures including joint replacement and spinal fusion will be covered.	Register online at www.regents.org/calendar. Materials fee $10.00.
Experts' Cancer Updates	The cancer experts of Regents Medical Center will unveil the results of the latest cancer studies. New breakthrough treatments will be discussed. They will explain what you should know about cancer screenings. Tips on preventing various types of cancers will be provided.	Call 949.555.0100 or register online at www.regents.org/calendar.

Table (formatted with Table Style)

Maria J. Rex
2104 Adger Road, Columbia, SC 29204-3253
803.555.0194 | Maria.Rex@wcc.edu | http://www.linkedin.com/in/rex

Current date

Mr. Eric Todd, President and CEO
CunCo Consulting Alliance
416 West Bay Street
Savannah, GA 31401-1115

Dear Mr. Todd

Ben Sullivan, your manager of Business Development, sent me a copy of the job description posted for the office manager position open at CunCo and suggested that I contact you. My qualifications match the requirements for the office manager you are seeking. Please consider me as an applicant for that position.

My education and my two years of experience managing the four-hour evening shift of two teams of trainers and one of nutrition counselors enabled me to develop the team management and the operational management skills that you require. Our teamwork resulted in a significant revenue increase and expense reduction.

My internship in the President's Office of Wexford Community College enabled me to refine my organizational, problem-solving, and soft skills. Both my experience at Pat's Fitness and Wellness Center and in the President's office required extensive Word, Excel, and PowerPoint use and excellent communication skills. I delivered high-quality products and met very tight deadlines consistently. I understand how those skills can be of value to CunCo.

After you have had an opportunity to review the enclosed resume as well as my LinkedIn Profile, I look forward to meeting with you to discuss how my qualifications and my office management career aspirations can be applied to your position at CunCo Consulting Alliance.

Sincerely

Maria J. Rex

Enclosure

Personal Business Letter

Maria J. Rex
2104 Adger Road, Columbia, SC 29204-3253
803.555.0194 | Maria.Rex@wcc.edu | http://www.linkedin.com/in/rex

Qualifications Profile for Office Manager

Highly effective, results-oriented, administrative office professional with AS degree and two years of relevant part-time work experience, including demonstrated effective supervisory, customer service, records management, time management, and project management skills. Create professional documents that enhance company image and productivity using Word, Excel, and PowerPoint. Strong written, oral, and electronic communication skills. Excellent interpersonal skills. Honest, ethical, and possess strong work ethic.

Education

AS degree in Business Administration with majors in Office Administration and Office Management from Wexford Community College, Columbia, SC, May 2016, 3.65 GPA.

High school diploma with career emphasis in English and Business, Maxwell High School, Charleston, SC, August, 2014, 3.85 GPA.

Experience

Wexford Community College, President's Office, Columbia, SC, internship, summer 2016.

- Prepared correspondence, reports, and presentations for senior administrators.
- Scheduled and coordinated special events with high-level constituents.
- Received outstanding evaluation, commending my professionalism, social skills, creativity, reliability, problem-solving skills, and the excellent quality of all work.

Pat's Fitness and Wellness Center, supervisor and promoted to office manager for the 3:30 to 7:30 shift (20-25 hours per week) from June 2014 through May 2016.

- Managed two teams of trainers and one team of nutrition counselors; resolved conflicts for clients. Responsible for correspondence with referring physicians, vendors, and clients.
- Managed facility, records, billing, equipment, and supplies; developed procedures.
- Increased client participation and revenue from my shift over 20 percent while reducing expenses by 12 percent.

Honors and Activities

Named a Dean's Scholar; received the Outstanding Business Student Award. Member of Student Advisory Council, president of the Wexford Honor Society, and president of the Office Management Club.

Resume

Appendix D Command Summary

Align Text	Home/Paragraph/Click desired alignment (Align Text Left, Center, Align Text Right, or Justify)	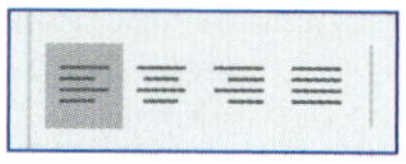
Bullets and Numbering	Home/Paragraph/Bullets or Numbering	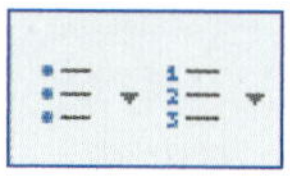
Center Page	Layout/Page Setup/ Dialog Box Launcher/Layout tab/Vertical alignment/Center	
Close Document	File/Close or Close button at upper right of screen	 Close
Columns—Create	Layout/Page Setup/Columns	 Columns
Cut, Copy, and Paste	Home/Clipboard/Cut, Copy, or Paste	 Cut Copy Paste Format Painter
Date and Time—Insert	Insert/Text/Date & Time	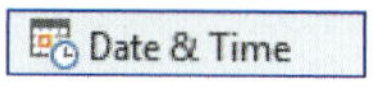 Date & Time
Document Themes	Design/Document Formatting/Themes	 Themes
Envelopes	Mailings/Create/Envelopes	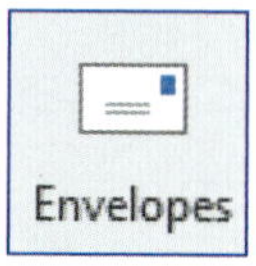 Envelopes
Find and Replace	Home/Editing/Find or Replace	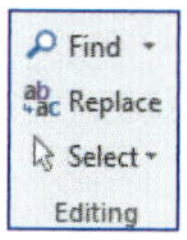 Find Replace Select Editing
Font Commands—Bold, Italic, Underline, Font Color, Font, Font Size, etc.	Home/Font/Command	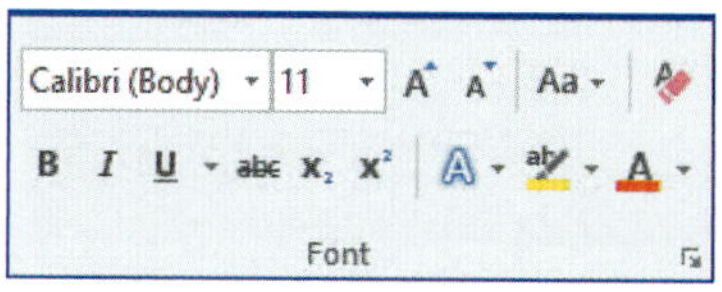 Calibri (Body) 11 Font

Footnotes	References/Footnotes/ Insert Footnote	AB[1] Insert Footnote
Format Painter	Home/Clipboard/Format Painter	
Graphics: Layout Options	Select graphic/Layout options displays	
Hanging indent	Ruler/Indent Markers	
Header	Insert/Header & Footer/ Header	Header
Increase/ Decrease Indent	Home/Paragraph/Increase Indent or Decrease Indent	
Indent Marker	Ruler/Indent Markers	
Insert File	Insert/Text/Object/ Text from File	Object Object... Text from File...
Line and Page Breaks	Home/Paragraph/Dialog Box Launcher/Line and Page Breaks tab	Indents and Spacing | Line and Page Breaks
Line Spacing	Home/Paragraph/Line and Paragraph Spacing	
Margins	Layout/Page Setup/Margins	Margins
Mini toolbar	Appears when text is selected	Calibri Light (11 A A B I U A Styles
New Document	File/New	New
Online Pictures	Insert/Illustrations/Online Pictures	Online Pictures

Online Video	Insert/Media/Online Video	Online Video Media
Open Existing Document	File/Open	Open
Orientation	Layout/Page Setup/Orientation	Orientation
Page Borders	Design/Page Background/ Page Borders	Page Borders
Page Break	Insert/Pages/Page Break	Page Break
Page Numbers—Insert	Insert/Header & Footer/ Page Number	Page Number
Paste Options	Home/Clipboard/Paste/ Click a Paste Option	Paste Options: Paste Special... Set Default Paste...
Pictures—Crop	Picture Tools Format/ Size/Crop	Crop
Picture—Format	Picture Tools Format	Picture Tools Format
Picture—Insert	Insert/Illustrations/Pictures/Locate and select picture/Insert	Pictures
Pictures—Size	Picture Tools Format/Size/Height or Width Arrows	Height: 4.88" Width: 6.5" Size

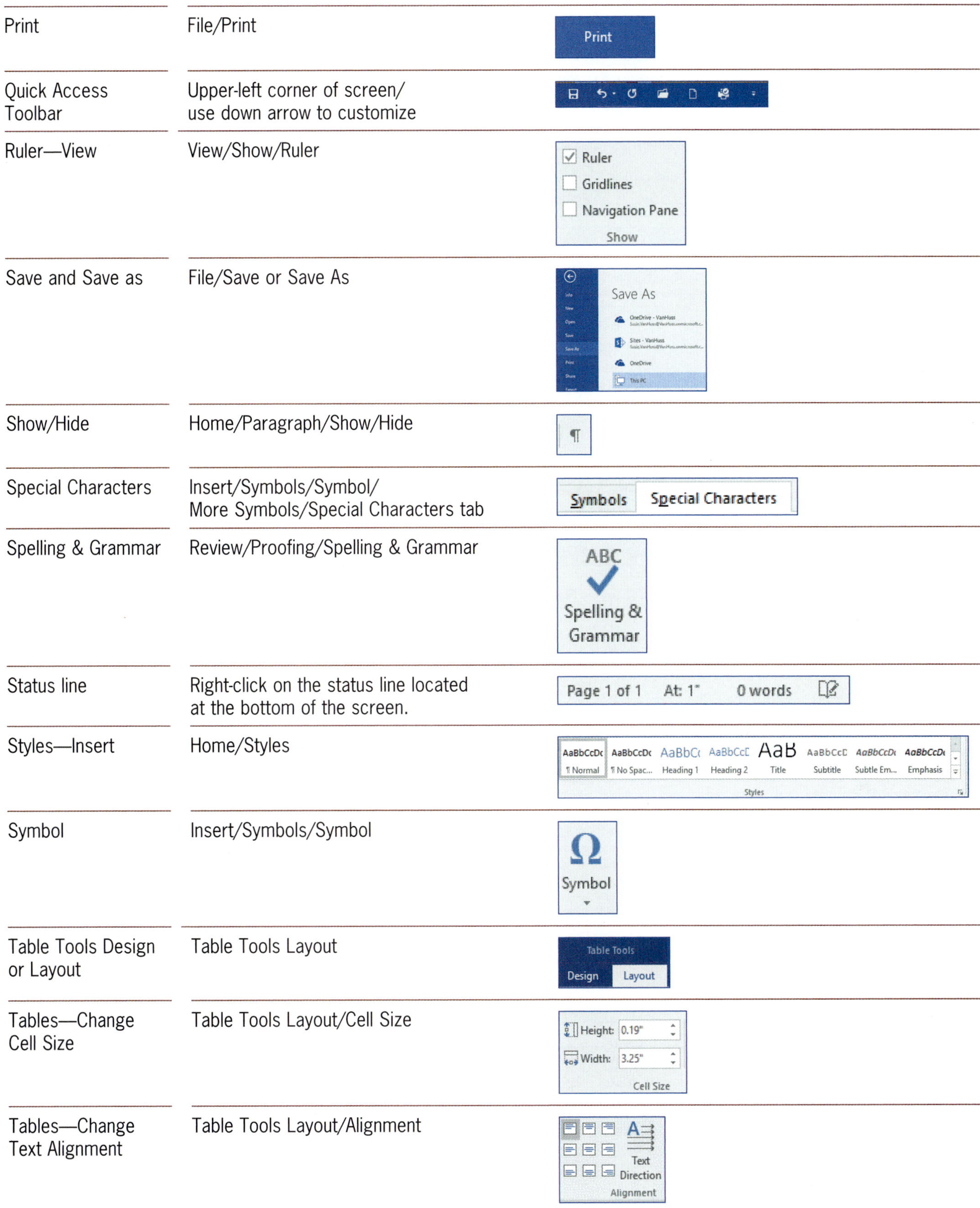

Print	File/Print
Quick Access Toolbar	Upper-left corner of screen/ use down arrow to customize
Ruler—View	View/Show/Ruler
Save and Save as	File/Save or Save As
Show/Hide	Home/Paragraph/Show/Hide
Special Characters	Insert/Symbols/Symbol/ More Symbols/Special Characters tab
Spelling & Grammar	Review/Proofing/Spelling & Grammar
Status line	Right-click on the status line located at the bottom of the screen.
Styles—Insert	Home/Styles
Symbol	Insert/Symbols/Symbol
Table Tools Design or Layout	Table Tools Layout
Tables—Change Cell Size	Table Tools Layout/Cell Size
Tables—Change Text Alignment	Table Tools Layout/Alignment

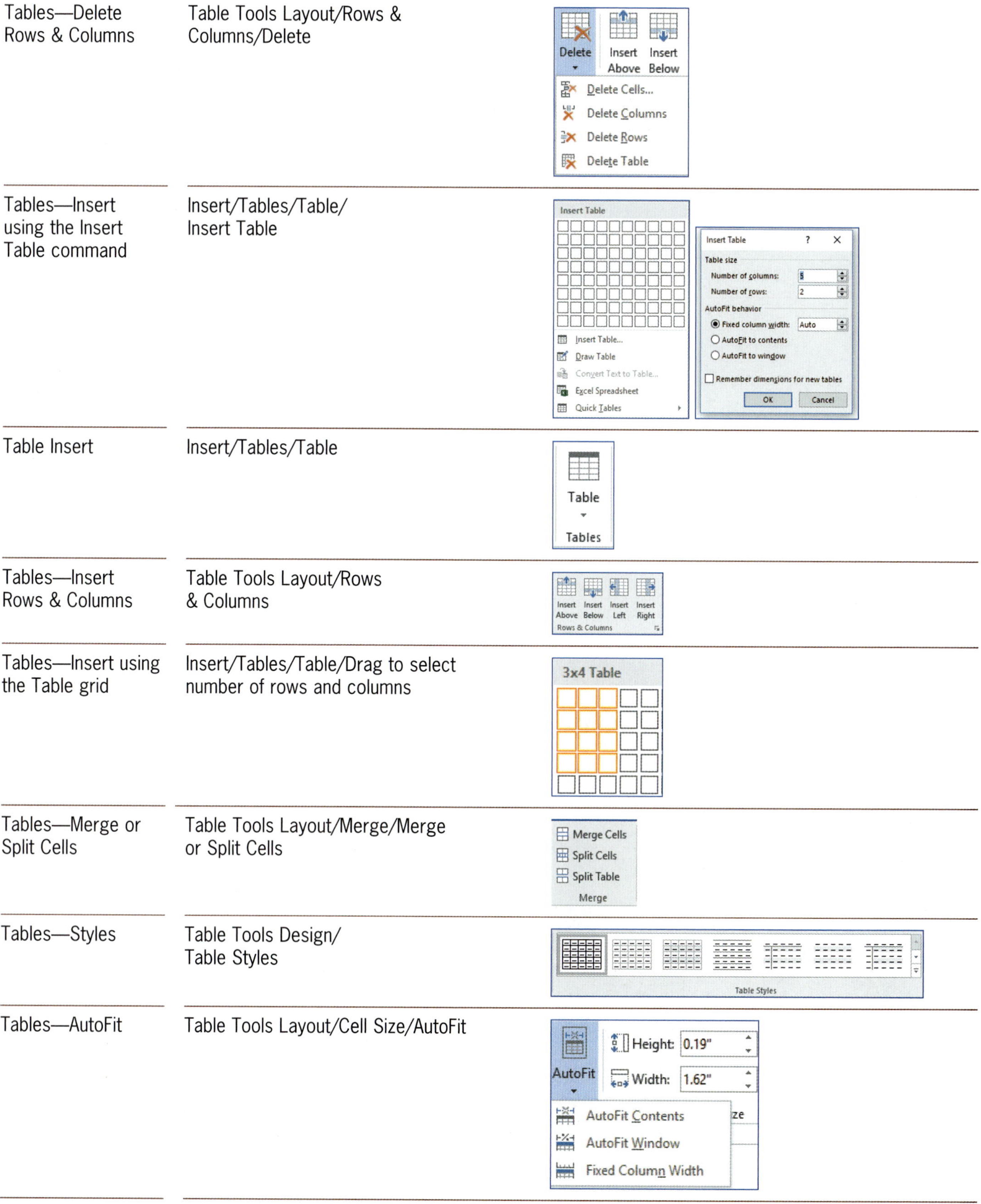

Tables—Delete Rows & Columns	Table Tools Layout/Rows & Columns/Delete	Delete, Insert Above, Insert Below; Delete Cells..., Delete Columns, Delete Rows, Delete Table
Tables—Insert using the Insert Table command	Insert/Tables/Table/ Insert Table	Insert Table; Insert Table..., Draw Table, Convert Text to Table..., Excel Spreadsheet, Quick Tables; Insert Table dialog: Table size, Number of columns: 5, Number of rows: 2, AutoFit behavior, Fixed column width: Auto, AutoFit to contents, AutoFit to window, Remember dimensions for new tables, OK, Cancel
Table Insert	Insert/Tables/Table	Table, Tables
Tables—Insert Rows & Columns	Table Tools Layout/Rows & Columns	Insert Above, Insert Below, Insert Left, Insert Right, Rows & Columns
Tables—Insert using the Table grid	Insert/Tables/Table/Drag to select number of rows and columns	3x4 Table
Tables—Merge or Split Cells	Table Tools Layout/Merge/Merge or Split Cells	Merge Cells, Split Cells, Split Table, Merge
Tables—Styles	Table Tools Design/ Table Styles	Table Styles
Tables—AutoFit	Table Tools Layout/Cell Size/AutoFit	AutoFit, Height: 0.19", Width: 1.62"; AutoFit Contents, AutoFit Window, Fixed Column Width

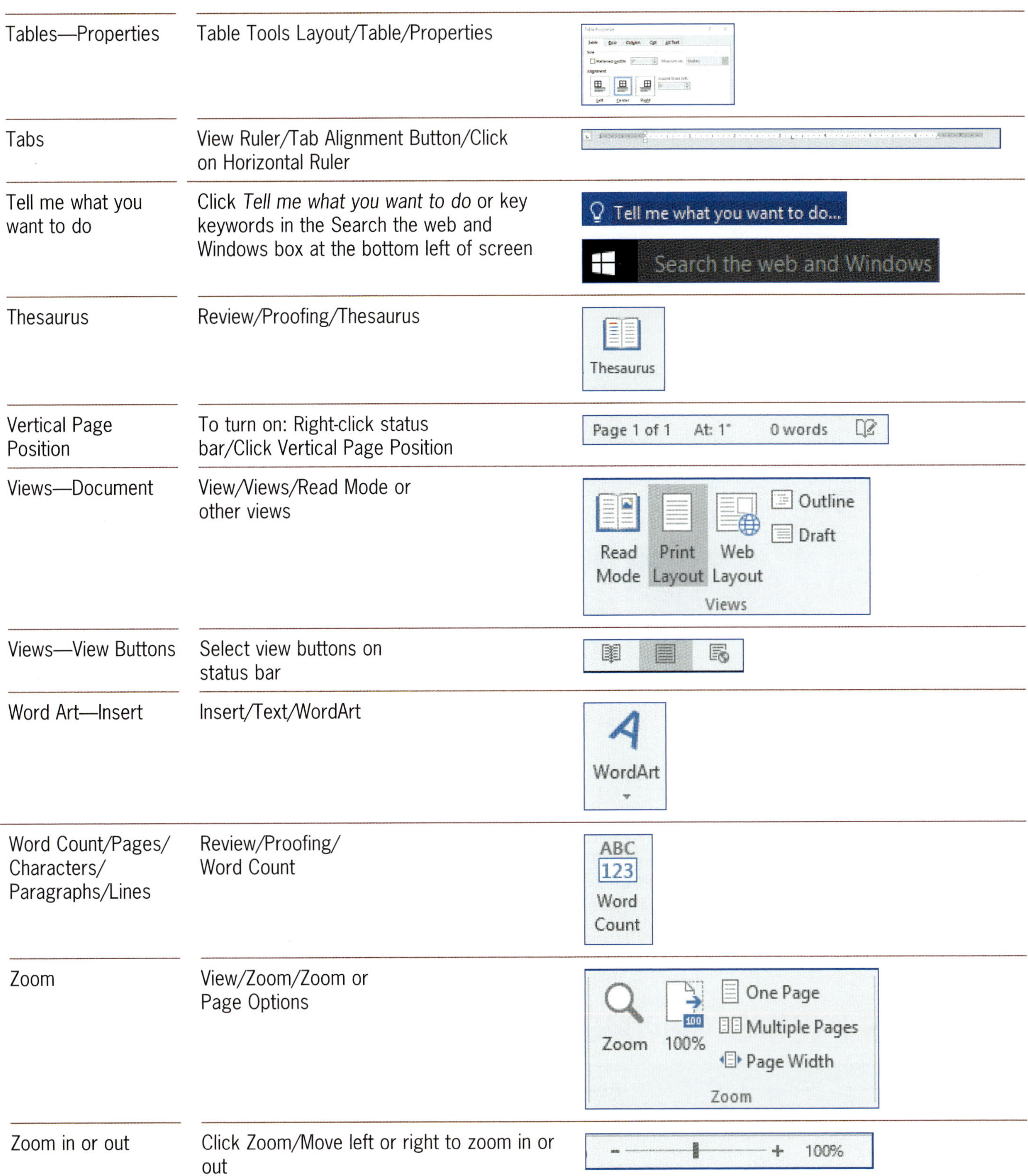

Tables—Properties	Table Tools Layout/Table/Properties
Tabs	View Ruler/Tab Alignment Button/Click on Horizontal Ruler
Tell me what you want to do	Click *Tell me what you want to do* or key keywords in the Search the web and Windows box at the bottom left of screen
Thesaurus	Review/Proofing/Thesaurus
Vertical Page Position	To turn on: Right-click status bar/Click Vertical Page Position
Views—Document	View/Views/Read Mode or other views
Views—View Buttons	Select view buttons on status bar
Word Art—Insert	Insert/Text/WordArt
Word Count/Pages/ Characters/ Paragraphs/Lines	Review/Proofing/ Word Count
Zoom	View/Zoom/Zoom or Page Options
Zoom in or out	Click Zoom/Move left or right to zoom in or out

Appendix E Prepare for Your Future

Path to Workplace Success...Develop Critical Skills

SKILLS REQUIRED FOR CAREER SUCCESS

The earlier you start planning and preparing for your career, the more likely you are to be successful.

The skills required for specific jobs vary significantly depending on your field of interest, the organization that hires you, the type of job, and the level of the job. Regardless of these factors, a common base of knowledge and a common set of skills are required for virtually every job. These skills can be grouped into three categories:

- Technical skills
- Soft skills
- Conceptual skills

Technical Skills

Technical skills are especially important for entry-level positions. You will develop technical skills in the courses you take.

These skills include:

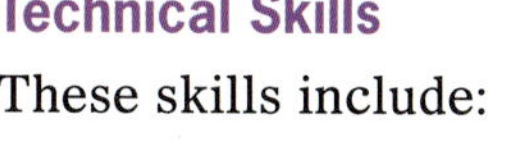
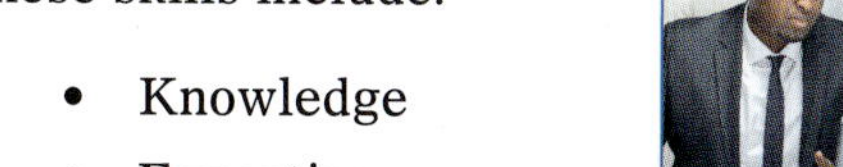

- Knowledge
- Expertise
- Ability to do the job

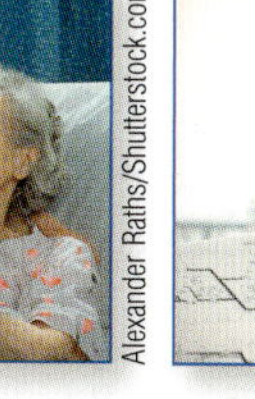
VGstockstudio/Shutterstock.com

Alexander Raths/Shutterstock.com

goodluz/Shutterstock.com

Examples of universal technical skills would be keyboarding skill and the ability to use applications such as *Word*, *Excel*, *Outlook*, and *PowerPoint*. The specific knowledge varies depending on the field, such as manager, medical professional, or architect.

Soft Skills

Softs skills are critical at every level. The remainder of this section focuses on soft skills.

Soft skills are personal attributes, interpersonal skills, and emotional intelligence. Soft skills relate to the way you interact with other employees. Examples of soft skills that are required in most jobs include:

- Communication skills
- Creativity
- Critical thinking and decision making
- Ethics, honesty, and integrity
- Accountability and responsibility
- Teamwork and collaboration
- Time management and productivity
- Work ethic

Conceptual Skills

You will learn conceptual skills in advanced courses and on the job. Conceptual skills are required for advancement in your position.

Conceptual skills are the ability to see the big picture and how things fit together. Conceptual skills enable you to understand how your job fits into the overall business strategy of your organization.

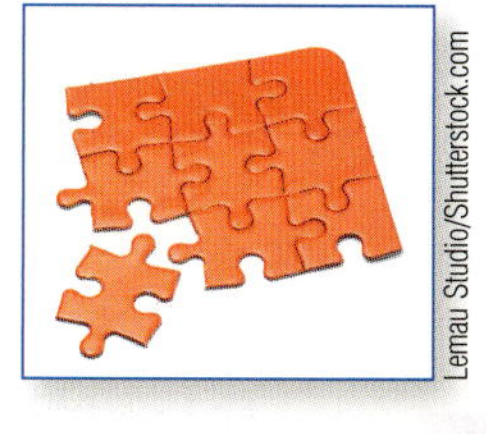
Lemau Studio/Shutterstock.com

Path to Workplace Success...Develop Soft Skills

CRITICAL THINKING AND DECISION MAKING

The ability to think critically helps you to make wise decisions that impact your work and your everyday life. Follow these five basic steps to make effective decisions.

1. **Identify the decision and collect facts**. Analyze objectively the situation requiring the decision. Get all the facts. Avoid making assumptions colored by stereotypes and preconceptions.
2. **Determine the options available**. Be creative in generating as many options as possible. In some cases options are predetermined.
3. **Analyze options carefully**. Try to view the situation from the perspective of everybody involved and that of the organization. Examine consequences for each person and for the organization.
4. **Select the best option and implement it**. Evaluate all of the options and get more facts if needed. Also consider what is necessary for the option to be successful. The way a decision is implemented often determines its success.
5. **Evaluate the effectiveness of the decision implemented**. Did it produce the desired results? Can it be improved?

For each of the scenarios below, key the following information in a *Word* document.

1. List the decision that must be made and the key facts to be considered. Add other things you think should be considered.
2. List the options available and the pros and cons of each.
3. Select the option and explain why it is best.

Scenario 1

Situation: Assume you live at home free and have saved enough money that you could (1) buy a small car so that you will have your own transportation, (2) use it to pay your tuition and other costs and avoid having to take out another substantial student loan, or (3) live in an apartment next year.

Facts: Family members lend you a car frequently when you need it. Most days you ride to classes with family or friends, but you would prefer to have your own car. Public transportation to your college is available and inexpensive. Your family provides free living and tries to help you, but they are not in a position to pay your tuition. You already have heavy student debt that you will have to begin paying as soon as you complete your program.

Decision: What decision is in your best interest? Why?

Scenario 2

Situation: You have been looking for a part-time job, and you have two opportunities: One is for the Foundation, which raises money for and supports your college. The other is a night job (6:00–11:00 p.m., four or five rotating nights a week) as the desk clerk at a local inn that is relatively inexpensive. With both jobs, you could work 20 to 30 hours per week. With the Foundation, you could work around your class schedule.

Facts: The Foundation duties include many that you are or will be studying—marketing, finance, accounting, management, and office technology. You would be able to interact with donors and board members who generally are business executives. The inn job duties include customer service skills, telephone skills, and basic office skills. The inn job pays $1 more per hour than the Foundation job. Before you make your decision, search for information about desk clerk jobs in hotels and inns and about jobs in educational-type foundations.

Decision: Which job would be in your best interest? Why? What other information do you need to make a good decision?

Path to Workplace Success...Develop Soft Skills

COMMUNICATION—MAKING A FIRST IMPRESSION

Building a strong network of professionals is essential on the path to success. Presenting yourself in a confident and energetic manner forms a positive first impression that opens the door to professional friendships. These five tips are highly recommended by communication experts.

1. **Initiate a conversation**. It's hard to build a network without starting a conversation, and often you are the one who must initiate the conversation. It's okay if you are shy—get over it.
2. **Give a firm handshake.** Show your interest and enthusiasm by giving a firm handshake—touching web to web. Please look at the person while shaking hands, and do smile.
3. **Maintain direct eye contact.** Look at the person while talking and avoid the nervous tendency to look away. You do not want to give the impression you are nervous or bored.
4. **Present good posture.** Stand tall and do not slouch. Lean forward as you are talking to indicate interest in the other person.
5. **Dress appropriately**. Attention to one's dress conveys interest in the person you are meeting for perhaps the first time. This first impression can determine the potential impact you may have on that person.

For each of the scenarios below, you will practice one of these essential communication skills. In a *Word* document, key a short explanation of what you learned in the practice activity.

Scenario 1

Situation: You have just been hired in an entry-level position, and you begin work in one week. You understand how important making a positive impression is—especially on the first day on the job. A proper handshake is the first skill you have decided to practice.

Think/Discuss/Research: What are the characteristics of a proper handshake for making a positive and powerful first impression? What are some poor techniques?

Apply: Pair with someone and practice shaking hands. For comparison, discuss and practice both effective and ineffective techniques.

Write: Describe the characteristics of a powerful handshake that you have learned are important for the first day on the job and every day.

Scenario 2

Situation: You are doing well in your position, but you know today will be important as you are sharing an idea at a team meeting. You know you must project confidence and have effective eye contact while in conversation with the team members.

Think/Discuss/Research: Why is eye contact important when sharing your ideas with your team or supervisor? What impression are you making?

Apply: With a group of at least three people, share an idea that you have. Topics might include (1) a suggestion you have for an improvement in your community or school, (2) how a person's dress has impacted your first impression of that person, or (3) time management strategies that have helped you in the past. Or you can choose a topic with which you are comfortable. Your goal is to have eye contact with each person in the group by the conclusion of the conversation.

Write: Describe your experience. Did the topic make a difference in the quality of eye contact? Did you feel uncomfortable looking at your team while you talked? Did you receive any feedback from your team by looking at them? Did you feel nervous and feel the need to look away from your team? How can you improve your next conversation?

Path to Workplace Success...Develop Soft Skills

ACCOUNTABILITY

Accepting a position in the workplace indicates agreement and commitment to fulfilling the duties and responsibilities of the position and the expectations of the manager. The organization prospers when each team member consistently meets and exceeds the position's requirements and the expected goals. A few fundamental accountability practices are essential to be successful.

1. **Arrive on time.** Punctuality is an outward sign that the job is important to the employee, and arriving early to be ready to begin work at the starting time shows commitment to excellence.
2. **Stay on task.** With today's social media and cell phones, an employee is easily tempted to lose focus on tasks at hand to quickly check for messages or play a game. The expectation is for employees to complete work tasks on company time.
3. **Commit to quality work.** An excellent employee sets high standards beyond the minimum requirements and commits to excellence in all areas. Doing mediocre work is not an option.
4. **Hone organizational skills.** Prioritizing projects and meeting deadlines are critical to fulfilling job responsibilities. Acquiring organizational skills is essential.
5. **Devote time to professional development.** Growing in the job is also an outward sign of accountability. During performance review meetings, the employee and manager agree on areas of development that will assist the employee and the company.

For each of the scenarios below, you will complete an activity related to accountability. In a *Word* document, key a short explanation of what you have learned.

Scenario 1

Situation: You have a major report due in two weeks. Your team depends on your leadership and organizational skills to produce a quality product and to meet the deadline. You have a tendency to procrastinate.

Research: Locate at least four time management suggestions recommended by time management experts.

Apply: Select at least two strategies you will use to ensure this deadline is met with a quality product. What technology will you choose to assist you?

Write: Describe the two strategies you will use and identify the selected technology tool. Explain how these strategies will assist you in avoiding procrastination and meeting your deadline.

Scenario 2

Situation: Your manager is completing a task analysis for each employee to determine the needs of the organization. If you are a full-time student and not employed, keep the log for all your activities.

Research: Keep a log for one day (if you are a part-time employee, use the hours you work) and list all activities completed. Start at 8 a.m. and list every activity for each 30-minute increment until 5 p.m.

Apply: Analyze the log. Did you use time wisely? If not, how was time wasted? Could you rearrange work activities to achieve better results? Did you arrive on time? Did you begin work promptly?

Write: Describe at least two areas that you think were effective in your daily log. Explain at least two things you could have done differently that would have allowed you to be more productive.

Path to Workplace Success...Capstone Project

SOFT SKILLS INTERVIEW WITH FOLLOW-UP ACTIVITIES

This project can be completed by a team or by each student individually. The team approach is recommended.

1. Your instructor will determine whether this is a team (three or four members) or an individual activity and will provide a timeline for you to complete the activities.
2. Obtain contact information for team members if appropriate.

Part I – 15-Minute Face-to-Face Interview (Required of Each Student)

1. Each student must select an individual who hires, supervises, or manages employees in a career area of interest. The person may be in a company in which you or a family member is employed or someone from your neighborhood, your church, or another group with which you are affiliated.
2. Contact the individual and request an appointment for a face-to-face 15-minute interview. Explain that you are studying the importance of developing soft skills as part of your career preparation. Describe one or two soft skills you explored in this activity.
3. In a *Word* document, key the five questions in item 4 below, leaving space after each question to take brief notes on the answers.
4. Conduct the interview and take brief hand-written notes.
   a. What soft skills are your strengths that helped you most to get your job and progress in your career?
   b. What soft skills do the people you manage need most?
   c. When you are hiring, how do you determine if a candidate has the required soft skills?
   d. How do you help your employees improve their soft skills?
   e. What advice would you give me about developing good soft skills?

Part II – Edit and Share Notes (Required for Both Teams and Individuals)

1. Edit and key your notes using complete sentences.
2. Share your notes with each team member **or**, if you are working individually, share your notes with your instructor.

Part III – Selection of Five Most Important Soft Skills

Part III contains two options for students to determine what they believe are the five most important soft skills for workplace success based on interview data and their joint views or their individual views plus research data.

Option 1 is to be completed by students who are working in teams to make the decision.

Option 2 is to be completed by students who are working individually to make the decision.

If you have a work schedule conflict, ask your instructor to approve your participation by telephone. All members must participate in the discussion.

Part III, Option 1 – Team Meeting and Discussion (Team Option)

1. Meet with your team and discuss the answers each of you obtained. If you are in the same location, use a face-to-face team meeting. If you are distance education students meeting in different locations, use a chat or discussion option.
2. List all soft skills recommended by the individuals interviewed.
3. Reach a consensus on what the team thinks are the five most important soft skills recommended by the individuals interviewed. (Do not vote—discuss until you agree on the important soft skills.)

Part III, Option 2 – Research Soft Skills (Individual Option)

1. Locate and find three current articles on soft skills needed most by employees. Make sure they come from reliable sources. Key the names and source information for the articles. Write a sentence or two on why you believe each source is reliable.
2. Compare the soft skills from your interview notes to those recommended in the three articles.
3. Prepare a list of at least ten important soft skills from your interview and the articles.
4. Review them carefully and list the five soft skills that you think are most important for your career.

Part IV – Soft Skills Assessment (Required for Both Teams and Individuals)

1. Use a 1 to 5 scale with 5 being the highest (your strengths) and 1 being the lowest (your weaknesses) to evaluate yourself honestly on the five most important soft skills listed in Part III, Option 1 or 2.
2. List things that you can do to improve on the two skills that were rated lowest in item 1 above. Use the Internet to research this topic if necessary.

Part V – Team Assessment (Team Requirement)

1. Rate each member of your team and yourself on the following points using the same 1 to 5 scale that you used in Part IV. Key the team member's name and the rating on each of the five following evaluation questions:
   a. Did the team member share good interview notes from his or her interview?
   b. Did the team member meet the timeline provided by your instructor?
   c. Did the team member participate effectively in the discussion?
   d. Did the team member respect the opinions of others and encourage all to share their thoughts?
   e. Did the team member do his or her fair share of the work?
2. For each team member, list the soft skills that were used most effectively during this activity.
3. In industry, leaders usually assess the results or outcomes produced by the whole team—not what each team member did. Would you be comfortable if the same standard were applied to your team— that is, the same grade would be given to all team members? Why or why not?

Index

S

T

U

V

W

X

Y

Z